HONG KONG: 160 YEARS' DEVELOPMENT IN MAPS

薛鳳旋 編著　By Victor F. S. Sit
（第二版 SECOND EDITION）

香港發展地圖集

香港發展地圖集（第二版）

責任編輯	楊　帆
書籍設計	吳冠曼
排　　版	林敏霞

編　　著	薛鳳旋
出　　版	三聯書店（香港）有限公司
	香港鰂魚涌英皇道 1065 號 1304 室
	Joint Publishing (H.K.) Co., Ltd.
	Rm. 1304, 1065 King's Road, Quarry Bay, Hong Kong
香港發行	香港聯合書刊物流有限公司
	香港新界大埔汀麗路 36 號 3 字樓
印　　刷	中華商務彩色印刷有限公司
	香港新界大埔汀麗路 36 號 14 字樓
版　　次	2010 年 6 月香港第一版第一次印刷
規　　格	8 開（257×355 mm）204 面
國際書號	ISBN 978-962-04-2994-1

© 2010 Joint Publishing (H.K.) Co., Ltd.
Published in Hong Kong

HONG KONG: 160 YEARS' DEVELOPMENT IN MAPS (SECOND EDITION)
By Victor F. S. Sit

Editor	Yang Fan
Art design	Wu Guan Man
Typeset	Lin Min Xia

Published by
Joint Publishing (H.K.) Co., Ltd.
Rm. 1304, 1065 King's Road, Quarry Bay, Hong Kong

Distributed in Hong Kong by
SUP Publishing Logistics (HK) Ltd.
3/F., 36 Ting Lai Road, Tai Po, N.T., Hong Kong

First published June 2010
Copyright ©2010 Joint Publishing (H.K.) Co., Ltd.

鳴謝陳瑞球博士的慷慨捐助和香港大學亞洲研究中心及香港浸會大學當代中國研究所的鼎力支持。

An acknowledgement on Dr. Chan Sui Kau's generous donation and support from Centre of Asian Studies, The University of Hong Kong and Advanced Institute for Contemporary China Studies, Hong Kong Baptist University.

目錄 Table of Contents

III. 城市　Urban Growth

第二版自序

《香港發展地圖集》是在1990年構思的，本來希望能在1997年中出版以慶祝香港回歸祖國，但回歸前因參與回歸的籌備工作及全國人大工作，而《地圖集》資料繁浩，我雖有近30年積累的資料並熟悉香港的各方面發展，仍然不能如願地使它在1997年面世。

2001年初出版的《地圖集》亦因而只是中文版。按當時計劃，應在不久後便出版英文版，但回歸後的香港紛紛亂亂，在各種干擾下，我歷數年仍未能拿出英文版的出版方案。可幸前輩兼好友陳瑞球先生鼓勵我，而且還出資捐助出版費，使我作進一步研究以包括回歸後十年的新發展，使我如願以償。在研究進行期間，我發現中文版中仍有重要缺遺，因此作出出版中英文雙語新版的決定，而不單是出版一本英文版。

在這中英文雙語版中，雖然文字篇幅加長了一倍，我仍盡量將文字所佔每一頁的版面控制在1/4以下。當然，文字的作用是十分重要的，一些重大的歷史事實，並非地圖或數字所能表達。

在新版中，補缺遺、更改錯誤和加入新的發展資料等使地圖數目在前版之上增加了一半左右。然而因為原則上希望能保持舊版的頁數，使《地圖集》不致過份笨重，可以便於使用和翻閱，版面上難免在個別地方出現“擁擠”，我因而極力要求出版社，寧犧牲部份版面的美感，也要以資料性和功能性的考慮為先。

《香港發展地圖集》作為一個城市連續160年的發展記錄，亦可說是一個先例。在這基礎上，我在過去兩年，還對澳門資料進行搜集整理，希望明年澳門發展地圖集能面世。

新版的研究和編排得到香港大學徐立之校長和亞洲研究中心黃紹倫教授暨中心同事的襄助，謹此致以萬分謝意。

新版的攻關工作，主要是近一年半時間進行的。這些有幸得到香港浸會大學高層的重視和支持，及研究所同仁的鼎力襄助。同時也感謝我的兩位研究助理蔡華思小姐和歐陽佩雯小姐的辛勤工作和耐心。

最後，謹以此書獻給香港——祖國的瑰寶、東方的明珠以及關心它的人士。

謹序！

薛鳳旋

香港浸會大學
當代中國研究所
2010年2月10日

Preface to the Sino-English Edition

The publication of *Hong Kong : 160 Years' Development in Maps* was conceptualized in 1990 and planned to be published in mid-1997 as one of the events to celebrate Hong Kong's return to the motherland. Yet the workload involved as a member of the Preparatory Committee for the Hong Kong Special Administrative Region, and a deputy of the National People's Congress of the PRC made it impossible for me to meet the target date. The large amount of materials included in the volume also forced me to accept its publication in Chinese with a separated volume in English to come out later.

Post-1997 Hong Kong, however, was characterized by economic, social and political turmoil, and I was distracted and unable to start preparation for the English volume for some years. Fortunately, with the encouragement of my respectful senior and good friend Mr. Chan Sui Kau and his generous donation, I started work to extend the coverage of the Atlas to 2007-2008 and fill up gaps that exist in the first publication. Besides, I decided that the new volume would be a bilingual edition.

In the new volume, I keep to the rule that the writing part should not exceed a quarter of the page space, with the understanding that critical historical events in history can never be fully expressed in maps and figures. It is also embellished by many new maps. In spite of new additions and the bilingual treatment, I have retained the physical size of the Atlas, i.e. keeping the number of pages of the old volume unchanged, such that it will not be too bulky. In doing so, a few pages may look a bit cramped.

As a continuous record of a city's many-faceted development over a period of 160 years, *Hong Kong : 160 Years' Development in Maps* is unique. Based on such an experience, I have also launched a similar project on the study of Macau and its publication. Macau development atlas will be out sometime in 2011.

In the course of the project, I have the facilitation and support from Professor Tsui Lap Chee, Vice-Chancellor of the University of Hong Kong and Professor Wong Siu Lun, Director of the Centre of Asian Studies, as well as help from the staff of the Centre.

The most critical part of the volume, however, was done in the past one and a half years after I have joined HKBU. The support of HKBU's senior management and staff of my Institute is gratefully acknowledged. Besides, Miss Cavis Choy and Miss Ada Au Yeung, my project research assistants, need to be specially mentioned and thanked for their hard work and patience.

Finally, I dedicate this Atlas to Hong Kong-the motherland's precious gem and the Pearl of the Orient, as well as to all who care for this piece of land.

Victor F. S. Sit
Advanced Institute for
Contemporary China Studies,
Hong Kong Baptist University
10 February, 2010

第二版序

　　我是個傳統的香港工業家，從事紡織和成衣製造業已有60多年，對香港的人、事及地貌在過去大半個世紀的變化頗有感觸！

　　十年人事幾番新，我在香港人身上深深體會到這道理，無論在民生、教養和財富方面，香港人均翻了百番；人口增長之快，更是舉世無雙！

　　香港人處事的靈活和適應力之強在香港百年的改變中可見一斑：小小漁港蛻變成國際大都會；工業隨着內地開放，工廠北移而式微，可幸金融及旅遊業能持續發展蓬勃，填補不少經濟轉移的空間。香港紡織和成衣製造業由五六十年代的山寨廠，發展到七八十年代的大型企業，全盛時期聘用四成全港就業人士，佔全港總出口金額40%，但隨着工廠北移而被評為"夕陽工業"，我活在其中又怎不唏噓！我的生產線亦隨大隊北移了！

　　每看到薛鳳旋教授年前送給我的一幅複印香港開埠初期的手繪地圖，我都會感慨良多！古今地貌相差之大，以我80多高齡也覺得不可思議，後一輩又如何能想像呢？幸虧當年有心人作圖為證，供後輩發思古之幽情。今有薛鳳旋教授不惜花十年時間搜集資料、校對編訂，以我們做廠的術語是慢工出細貨，出版了這本中英文雙語版的《香港發展地圖集》。閱讀這本地圖集，地道的香港人可以溫故而知新，初來香港或是在外地的人可以更了解香港的歷史和地貌。香港是怎樣在160年間蛻變？箇中答案留待大家（當然包括我在內）從薛教授的《香港發展地圖集》中尋找吧！

陳瑞球

長江製衣集團主席

2010年3月13日

Preface by Chan Sui Kau

As a traditional local industrialist engaged in textiles and garment manufacturing for over 60 years, I have witnessed tremendous changes in Hong Kong and in its appearance over the last half-century.

'Every decade has a major change' is a statement best used for describing Hong Kong's community and people; and its population increase rate is even more astonishing!

Hong Kong's century-long historical evolution from a small fishing village to a global metropolis has been living proof of the flexibility and adaptability of the local population. The opening of mainland China in the 1980s had led to a northward shift of local industries. Fortunately, the economy maintained its growth through the expansion of its finance and tourism sectors. The trajectory of textiles and garments are of special interest to me. They were pioneered by small-scale factories in the 1950s and 60s to become, in the 1980s, the mainstay of the economy and were then dominated by large enterprises. At its peak, they employed 40% of the local labour and contributed to an equal amount of local exports. After the 1980s, however, they became 'sunset industries'. As a member of the sector, my firm participated in the 'northern shift' with great regret.

Whenever I look at the panoramic drawing of old Hong Kong presented to me by Professor Sit, I cannot help feeling the greatness of the force of change. This would be difficult for young people to appreciate. Unlike an elderly person like me, they lack the chance to see much of it. It is good that most of these changes have now been documented in this Atlas. With it, our future generations can better understand how our present prosperity has come about. This piece of work represents Professor Sit's dedication and meticulous effort in collecting and collating relevant data for putting in place a useful reference for Hong Kong's 160 years of evolution. As the Atlas is bilingual, it also provides people of other countries a convenient source for knowing Hong Kong.

Chan Sui Kau
Chairman
YGM Group
13 March, 2010

序言

香港經過了156年的漫長歲月，在1997年7月1日回到祖國懷抱。

我們重新掌握自己的命運，邁進"一個國家、兩種制度"的歷史新紀元。

回顧過去，香港人經歷政治、經濟和社會的演變，面對種種挑戰，仍能堅毅不拔，把握機遇，推動香港蓬勃發展。《香港發展地圖集》總結了香港150多年來不同領域的發展經驗，給讀者提供指引，讓讀者尋源探本，追溯香港的發展軌跡，認識香港的變革過程，既能啟迪心靈，又可鼓舞鬥志。深盼讀者開卷之餘，更能同心同德，協力為香港繪出更美好的明天。

中華人民共和國
香港特別行政區行政長官
2000年6月5日

Preface by Tung Chee Hwa

Hong Kong has returned to the motherland after a long period of 156 years.

The people of Hong Kong have opened a new epoch by moving into 'One Country, Two Systems' in shaping their own destiny.

Looking back, the people of Hong Kong have persisted in vibrant development despite challenges posted by the changes in politics, the economy and society. *Hong Kong : 150 Years' Development in Maps* is a summary of Hong Kong's 150-year experience in different fields. It provides readers with an easy trail to the origin and historical path in Hong Kong's development. Besides being informative, it is enlightening and enhances our confidence in moving forward.

I wish that readers can take lesson from reading the Atlas in proactively striving for building a better Hong Kong.

Tung Chee Hwa
Chief Executive
Hong Kong SAR, PRC
5 June, 2000

序言

　　隨着香港回歸祖國，香港歷史地理的教學與研究成為教育界近年來的一個熱門課。過去有關這方面的書籍不多，尤其是適合青少年閱讀的更少。薛鳳旋教授花了六年心血，集20多年長期從事地理學研究之成果，編撰成《香港發展地圖集》，集中收集了香港150多年來在自然、經濟、城市、社會、環境等眾多方面的大量資料，是一部較詳細地反映香港近代發展與變化的綜合地圖集。該書內容翔實，圖文並茂，清楚明確，趣味性強。相信本書的出版為人們進一步了解香港的過去，特別是對廣大青少年認識香港的發展歷史，會起到很好的作用。值此書出版之際，特向作者薛鳳旋教授和香港三聯書店表示祝賀。

　　香港是國際金融、貿易和航運中心。香港回歸祖國近三年來，在"一國兩制"、"港人治港"、高度自治的方針指引下，香港同胞以自己的勤勞和智慧，戰勝了亞洲金融危機的衝擊，保持了香港的繁榮穩定。展望未來，香港的明天會更加美好，香港的前程會更加輝煌。

姜恩柱

中華人民共和國中央人民政府
駐香港特別行政區聯絡辦公室主任
2000年6月5日

Preface by Jiang En Zhu

Teaching and research on local history and geography have assumed increasing significance after Hong Kong's return to the motherland. Past reference materials about Hong Kong in published forms, especially those suitable for the young, are scarce. Professor Sit has devoted 6 years to collate his research results of the past 20 years in the present volume. It covers data on Hong Kong's 150 years' development and change in its natural environment, economy, urban growth and society. It is a comprehensive documentation of Hong Kong's historical trajectory. The information its texts and maps contain is clear and graphically presented to make reading easy. I believe that the volume will help people, especially our young people, to understand Hong Kong's past. I congratulate Professor Sit and Joint Publishing (H.K.) for their achievement.

Hong Kong is an international financial, trade and logistics centre. In the past 3 years, local residents have overcome shockwaves of the Asian Financial Crisis and maintained a stable and prosperous Hong Kong under the guidelines of 'One Country, Two Systems' and 'Hong Kong People Administering Hong Kong'. I foresee a better Hong Kong in the horizon.

Jiang En Zhu
Director
Liason Office of the Central
People's Government in
the Hong Kong SAR
5 June, 2000

序言

　　地圖不單是研究自然科學的工具，更是研究人文社會科學必不可缺的媒介。因為從各類地圖中，可以尋找出政治、社會、經濟、文化變遷的痕跡。因此，以地圖作為教材是符合現代教育理念，具啟發性和創意效能的。

　　薛鳳旋教授的《香港發展地圖集》以各類地圖為主要形式，全面地、深入地將香港的百年歷程記錄下來，並加上有關的坐標和文字說明。不論讀者是否對地理或地圖有興趣，閱讀這部地圖集，對香港的發展過程，必有深刻和獨到的認識和領悟。

　　地圖集資料翔實，覆蓋面廣，選材嚴謹，不單反映出香港的滄桑歷程，其內涵動力和特點，更顯示了香港和內地血脈相連的事實。

　　香港各界慶祝香港回歸委員會樂意資助此地圖集的出版，以慶賀中華人民共和國香港特別行政區成立三周年。一部份地圖集將以慶委會名義送贈本港及內地的大中小學及圖書館。

香港各界慶祝香港回歸委員會主席

2000年6月15日

Preface by Wu Wai Yung

Maps are not only important tools for research in natural sciences, they are also study aids for social sciences and humanities. Traces of change and development in politics, society, the economy and culture can be evidenced in maps. Thus, maps are indispensible tools in modern education with innovating visual effects.

Professor Sit's *Hong Kong : 150 Years' Development in Maps* uses maps as the medium to record major events and development of Hong Kong's century-long history, supplemented by text and figure annotations. Whether one is interested in maps or geography, he or she is sure to enjoy the benefit of a deeper understanding of Hong Kong's development path after reading this volume.

The volume is comprehensive in its coverage. The data has been logically organised to reflect Hong Kong's uniqueness in its growth history, major development drivers, as well as its close link with the mainland.

The Committee of Hong Kong People to Celebrate Hong Kong's Return to the Motherland is honoured to be the sponsor of the publication of the volume. It is a present to the local community on the third anniversary of the founding of the Hong Kong Special Administrative Region. Copies of the volume will be distributed to local and mainland schools and libraries in the name of the Committee.

Wu Wai Yung
Chairman
Committee of Hong Kong People to
Celebrate Hong Kong's Return to
the Motherland
15 June, 2000

自序

我從事地理研究已經有25年，接觸過很多中西方的地圖集，還擔任過科林斯─朗文（Collins-Longman）的中學教學地圖集的顧問，因此對地圖集在教學和科研上的重要性有切身的了解。

地圖集的種類很多。綜合性的地圖，有以一個地區為範圍的，也有以洲或國家為範圍的。專門性的地圖集包括更多種類，如以地質、城市、人口、文化、民族、語言、經濟、地貌及歷史等為主題的。使用地圖集時，我們往往要參閱幾種不同類型的地圖集，才能融匯貫通，透徹理解某一問題。反過來說，為了理解一個問題，只參閱一種地圖集，往往會感到資料不足。這是因為，一個問題，很多時候是自然環境、人文條件及歷史事實諸多因素交互作用所使然。因此，實有必要從地圖集使用者的角度來設計地圖集的內容。實際上不少專業地圖集及綜合性地圖集，都是以使用者為對象的。

清末以來，中國國勢積弱，加以外國強權的壓迫，香港因而淪為英佔區。但第二次世界大戰後，香港的經濟和社會發展成就也是有目共睹的。二者似乎是個矛盾體的兩面。我認為，自然地理條件及配套的政治經濟和地緣因素，是香港得以成為世界公認的經濟發展奇蹟的主要原因。本圖集希望能在這方面提供一些數據和事實。編製這本地圖集的另一目的是作為我數十年來愛港建港的一個小結，同時也作為對香港回歸祖國，成為特別行政區這一重大歷史事件的一份獻禮。

作為香港特區第一本綜合性的發展地圖集，本地圖集的編製是以發展過程作為中軸來安排的。因此，對於自然環境方面的主題，本書只收入了一些基本的自然地理地圖，並沒有包括諸如地質構造、地貌、土壤及植被等地圖。所幸這些地圖，已經廣泛流傳，讀者容易翻查得到。相反，本地圖集集中而系統地反映了香港自1841年以來的與本地居民較為密切的各方面變化及其空間分佈形態，包括基本設施的發展，經濟活動的轉變，城市化及人口遷移，人口素質的變化，財政、福利、環境的變更等等。香港和中國內地的關係及對外貿易的關係，也是香港發展過程中的主要內容，在本地圖集中亦有反映。此外，本地圖集也盡可能搜集了不同時期的規劃圖，和一些以地圖及坐標表示的重要的學術界意見，反映出香港在發展過程中不同的意見和各種可能的空間分佈形態。總之，發展的過程特徵和空間形態，是我們考慮的重點。

因此，和一般的綜合性地圖集有別，本地圖集不但包括了很多歷史上不同時期的發展事實，也包括了一些當時的意見，而其中一些意見是以往未曾公開出版過的。

明顯地，在內容的取捨上，編者的研究專長及愛好往往限制了他所編的地圖集的涵蓋寬度。同時，編繪發展地圖集通常是政府行為，因為要動用龐大資源。如今個人勉為其難，遺漏自多，雖然想盡量涵蓋更廣，也終因時間、資源、資料、能力的局限，而未能盡如人意。再者，不同的題材，其遺留下來的歷史記錄和資料的詳細程度也不一致，為了版面編排上的均衡，一些資料及圖表最後只能割愛。雖然如此，在很多角度上，本地圖集對於記錄香港的發展歷程，展示將來發展的可能方向，仍是個重要的參考。我希望本書能起拋磚引玉的作用，日後會有更好的這類地圖集編製問世。

在編製過程中，我發現有必要在每張圖或同一主題的數張圖上附上說明文字，以交代圖的背景和主要內容，以及有關的發展特點和動力。這樣，可以使讀者對有關地圖及其內容的理解更為透徹。在不少地圖上，加插不同的坐標及線圖能把主題作更詳盡的表達。同時，我也嘗試用一些歷史航空照片及採用一些古老的素描，以表達香港150年來地形、地貌和城鄉景觀的變化。

現代地理訊息系統（Geographical Information System）近年來已在香港應用。1961、1971、1981及1991年的人口普查及1976、1986、1996年的抽樣人口統計的部份資料，政府有關部門已經可以用GIS方式向公眾提供。其中1981年以後的資料微細至統計小區，但較早的資料仍比較粗略。以後，以人口普查數據為基礎的那些地圖的製作，必定會更為方便，而且可以全以用戶需求為主導。我希望將來也可以將GIS方法應用至本地圖集中那些非人口統計的圖上。

編製這地圖集共花了六年時間，其間香港大學地理及地質系的地圖繪製室成員關慶楷先生和黃廷波先生花了大量的心血，沒有他們的辛勞是絕對產生不了這本地圖集的。香港大學地理及地質系辦公室成員凌志瑩小姐、黃玉娟小姐、朱惠霞小姐及袁笑鄉小姐也在文字的打印上予以很大幫助。

多個政府部門為圖集提供了不少資料，從多位本地研究人員的研究成果中，我也採納了很多的資料、意見及圖像，我向他們致以萬分感謝。

更要感謝香港大學地理系的陳曾郭如女士，她在資料收集及整理上負統籌責任，為地圖集的成功編製做出了很大的貢獻。

香港各界慶祝香港回歸委員會資助本地圖集的出版以慶祝香港特別行政區成立三周年。香港大學研究與會議撥款委員會，以及劉皇發城市化研究基金和許愛周信託基金資助研究與資料搜集，我謹此向他們致以謝意。

最後，中華人民共和國香港特別行政區行政長官董建華先生、中華人民共和國中央人民政府駐香港特別行政區聯絡辦公室主任姜恩柱先生、香港各界慶祝香港回歸委員會主席鄔維庸先生為地圖集作序，本人深感榮幸並致以衷心感謝。

本地圖集仍會有不少錯漏，這純是我個人的責任，歡迎讀者指正、賜教。

2000年6月

Author/ Editor's Preface

In my 25-year indulgence in geography research, I have come across many atlases published in Asia and in the West. I have also served as editorial adviser to Collins-Longman for their school atlases. Therefore I am deeply aware of the significance of atlases in teaching and research.

There are many types of atlases. A comprehensive atlas provides a wide coverage of many topics for a region, country or even a continent. A special atlas may be devoted to a particular theme, e.g. geology, city, population, culture, races, language, economy, geomorphology and history. Sometimes one has to consult a number of atlases for more thorough understanding of an issue, as it is often the result of the interplay of forces of the natural environment, man and history. Atlases need to be designed with such user needs as their basic consideration.

In the mid-19th century, China had become a weak nation and the prey of greedy foreign powers. One such outcome was Britain's occupation of Hong Kong. However, since WWII, Hong Kong's economic growth has astounded the world; a fact seemingly conflicting with its colonial status. I believe that behind Hong Kong's success are the effects of its geography, a suitable political economy and its geopolitical situation. It is hoped that this Atlas will provide support to such a thesis. Another yet supplementary aim of the Atlas is to serve as a concluding note to my decades' devotion to Hong Kong and the motherland, and use this Atlas as a present to commemorate Hong Kong's historical return to the mainland.

As the first comprehensive atlas for the Hong Kong Special Administrative Region, Hong Kong's development in the past 150 years is the axis of its organization of data and main topics. Thus, it has not included some conventional topics in physical geography as they are easily available elsewhere. The focus of the atlas is on issues that reflect Hong Kong's change and evolution which affect its people and its spatial patterns since 1841. These include basic infrastructure, economic activities, urbanization, population movement, population quality, welfare and the environment, etc. Hong Kong's relations with the mainland and its foreign trade are also covered. Besides, the volume has collated local plans, figures and academic views of different times to reflect the spatial process of growth and change from different perspectives. Our purpose is to bring out the characteristics and spatial outcome of Hong Kong's development.

The volume therefore differs from conventional atlases by incorporating facts of different historical periods and important opinions, some of which are published for the first time.

In configuring the volume, the editor's specialization and interests may have restricted a broader coverage of topics. Besides, the production of such an atlas is usually the effort of a government, or a large team of researchers, as it involves huge resource support. As a single-researcher project, the volume may be lax in detail and comprehensiveness. In addition, historical data for different topics vary greatly in their continuity, comprehensiveness and details. While some useful materials of selected issues have been dropped to avoid too much details, data for some topics are deficient. Despite these, we have attempted to track Hong Kong's development through as many perspectives as possible and throw light on its possible future path, and I look forward to an improved version by other people in future.

In the course of the editing, it is felt that texts are required to explain or highlight one or several important issues or facts in the maps, such as laying out its background, or pointing out the drivers and characteristics they involve, as an aid to better appreciation of the maps by the reader. Line drawings and data charts are also used for similar purposes. In addition, air photographs and panoramic drawings have been adopted for illustrating Hong Kong's changes in landscape and geomorphology in the past 150 years.

GIS techniques have been increasingly used in Hong Kong in the past decade. Most census data (from 1961 to the recent ones of 2001 and 2006) have now been digitized for public consumption. Those after 1981 are even down to small sub-district level. I hope that in future GIS will also be applied to maps in this volume that are not based on census data.

The drawing of maps in the volume has taken six years. My sincere thanks to Mr. Kwan Hing Kai and Mr. Wang Ting Bor of the Cartographic Unit of the Department of Geography and Geology. Thanks also go to Ms Wing Chi Ying, Wong Yuk Guun, Chu Wei Hai and Yuan Siu Hang who helped in typing the text.

A number of government departments provided maps and other data. I have also adopted the data, opinions and drawings of some local researchers. I owe them heartful thanks.

The last individual I need to mention specifically is Mrs Chan Tsang Kwok Yu who provided useful assistance in data collection and collating–a great contribution to the successful production of the volume.

Financial support from the Committee of Hong Kong People to Celebrate Hong Kong's Return to the Motherland, the Research Committee, and Lau Wong Fat Urbanization Research Fund, Hui Oi Chow Trust Fund of HKU are equally gratefully acknowledged.

Lastly, I thank Mr. Tung Chee Hwa, Chief Executive of the HKSAR government, Mr. Jiang En Zhu, Director of the Liason Office of the Central People's Government in the HKSAR, and Mr. Wu Wai Yung, Chairman of the Committee of Hong Kong People to Celebrate Hong Kong's Return to the Motherland for writing the Prefaces.

There should be mistakes and faults in the volume. I look forward to feedbacks and comments from readers.

Victor F. S. Sit
June, 2000

資料與圖例說明

1. 本地圖集主要的資料採自香港政府地圖，部份來自學術界的研究成果，但大部份經簡化與整理以適合大眾閱讀。

2. 本地圖集資料以2001年版為基礎，盡量搜求至2008年。在有關的文字說明及評論中，我們力求對回歸前後作出比較。這些文字以中文為本，英文並非直譯。

3. 有關資料偏重於1961年後，這是由於在這之前的政府統計及其他統計不夠詳細和完整。

4. 一些統計資料的分區在歷史上經歷了多次變化，如人口普查的分區（特別是新界地區、石硤尾、半山等）就是如此。我們盡量作出調整以提供不同時期的比較。如果無法作出調整，我們便會留空或作出重估。

5. 一張圖或一個說明可能採用了多於一個出處的資料。為了使地圖集可讀性提高，所有資料的出處不在圖、表或文字標示，有需要深究的讀者可在"參考文獻"中尋找。

6. 除了有特別說明外，本書資料所採用的幣值皆為港元。沒有方向標的地圖以書的上方為北向，部份圖亦不加比例尺，以求精簡。一些有方向標及比例尺者多沿用原圖的風格，不強求統一。

7. 用以顯示經濟和社會活動分佈的地圖並不尋求統一的海岸線，以便保留不同時期的岸線。

8. 本圖以中文為主體，一些圖中不重要的中文地名並沒有譯成英文，以保持簡潔和可讀性。

9. 一些舊地圖為保持原有風格，並不加插或少加插翻譯文字。

Notes on Maps and Data

1. Most of the maps are sourced from the government, supplemented by some research findings from researchers, and all have been simplified and some redrawn for easy reading.

2. Most of the data have been updated to 2007 (some 2008) based on the first edition (published in 2001). In the text, we attempt to point out the change before and after 1997 wherever relevant and possible. Chinese is the main language used and the English version is not a direct translation.

3. The focus of maps and data err on 1961 and after, as earlier details are inadequate for a more balanced approach for the different time periods.

4. Boundaries of local districts have changed in history, especially census districts and sub-districts. We have attempted to get around this for historical spatial comparisons. Whenever it is impossible to do so, we have left the relevant space blank.

5. Both maps, figures and the text are often derived from different and numerous sources. To maintain readability, we have not denoted sources in the main body of the volume. Readers can consult the bibliography to identify these sources.

6. Except specifically mentioned, the currency used is the Hong Kong dollar. For maps and drawings without a directional sign, the upper edge of the volume denotes north. For the purpose of simplicity, some maps do not have a scale. Most directional signs and scales use the styles of the original maps.

7. Maps that show distribution of economic activities and social phenomena have not adopted the same coastline to reflect the coastlines of different time periods.

8. The volume uses Chinese as the main language. In some maps, Chinese names have not been translated into English to make the maps less crowded.

9. To preserve the style and look of old maps, we have not translated or limited the translation to a few terms to the other language, while names of places that differ from present ones or with different spellings in the past have been retained.

Geography, History and Administrative Divisions

I. 自然、歷史和政區

01 1845年的香港 Hong Kong in 1845

　　英國人於1842年從清王朝手中強取了香港島。兩幅在三年後（即1845年）由英國人哥連臣手繪的廣角素描，清楚地展示了當年香港島北岸及九龍半島的景象。雖然香港當時的發展和今天相比有如滄海桑田，但當年的香港也絕對不是當時英國首相所說的"一個荒蕪的小島，連馬也沒有一匹"。

　　按1841年5月15日港英政府的粗略人口統計：港島共有本土人口7,450人。最大聚落是赤柱，人口2,000，被稱為"首都，大城"。第二是筲箕灣，人口1,200。香港被稱為"大漁村"，人口200。 黃泥涌（跑

Britain snatched Hong Kong from the Qing Empire in 1842. Collinson produced two panoramic drawings in 1845 which highlighted details of the landscape. Though Hong Kong was then not a high-density urbanscape, it is not a barren small island as described by the British Prime Minister.

According to the first official census taken on 15 May 1841, there were 7,450 local people on the Island. The largest settlement was Chek-Chu (Stanley), labelled as 'The Capital, a large town' with 2,000 people. Soo-ke-wan was second with 1,200. Hong Kong was labelled as 'a large fishing village' with 200. Wong Nai Chung was 'an agricultural village' with 300. The site of Central District was called Kwan Tai-

● 1845 年的香港　Hong Kong in 1845

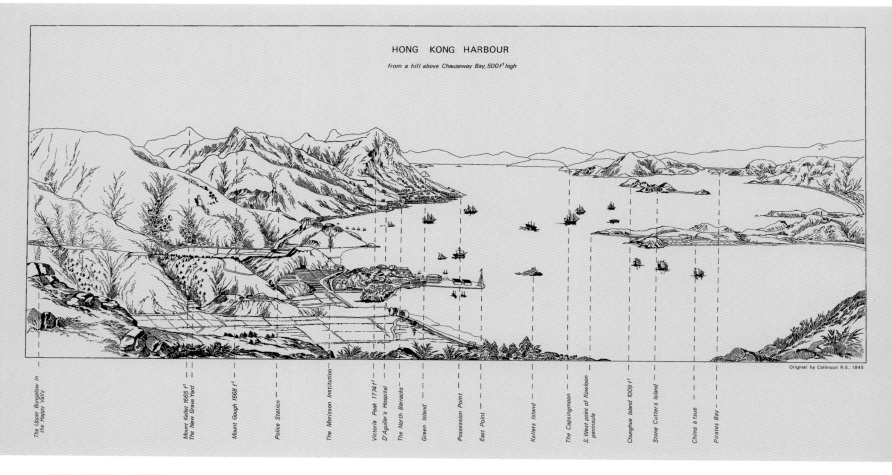

HONG KONG HARBOUR
from a hill above Chauseway Bay, 500 f¹ high

Original by Collinson R.E. 1845

　　本圖主要顯示由銅鑼灣至中環的山脈以及其間的發展情況，也包括了九龍半島及其西面的昂船洲、青衣島等。該圖是由銅鑼灣500英尺高的山上向中環西望。香港島山上仍沒有任何建築，但灣仔山坡上的"姻緣石"清晰可見。1841年義律是在佔領角（今天的水坑口）登陸的。該地已經為1843年填海掩蓋。由中環至金鐘兵房間，幾年之內已經蓋起不少兵房、官署和貨倉。灣仔沿岸至銅鑼灣，不少小丘也已鏟平，並蓋了房子。奇力島（今遊艇會會址）對岸也建了不少房屋和倉庫。跑馬地已全部闢為農田。1841年時香港島北岸唯一的農業區是黃泥涌。繪製此畫時，全香港島人口約5,000人，其中約2,000人是住在艇上的疍家人。圖中也顯示出寬闊的維多利亞港以及泊碇中的遠洋風帆。

This drawing illustrates coastal development from Causeway Bay to Central District against a background of hills. It also includes Kowloon Peninsula and Stonecutters Island, Tsing Yi Island and the distant Lantau Island. The perspective was taken from a hill in Causeway Bay looking towards Central District. There were no buildings on the slopes of the Island, yet the 'fertility' rock in Wan Chai is clearly visible. Captain Elliot landed on the Island at Possession Point (Shui Hang Kou) in 1841. The site had been submerged by reclamation in 1843. Barracks, government offices and go-downs had been erected between Central and Admiralty. From Wan Chai to Causeway Bay, many small knolls had been levelled for buildings such as those opposite Kellelt Island (present day Yacht Club). Happy Valley was filled with paddy fields, a new development, as in 1841 the only agricultural area on the northern part of Hong Kong Island was Wong Nai Chung. In 1845, Hong Kong had a population of about

● 1845 年英國海軍軍醫繪畫的維港水彩畫　A painting of Victoria Habour by a British naval surgeon in 1845

馬地）是個人口300的 "農村" ，而中環所在，被稱為 "群大路" ，人口50。群大路亦是統計報告唯一註上中文名字的地方。

廣角素描是一種傳統的地理學方法。這兩幅圖比較準確、形象而又詳細地保存了150年前九龍和香港島的自然地理、人文地理狀況。

與廣角素描差不多同時和同地描製的水彩畫及油畫，更形象地顯示出一些景物及建築，但缺乏前者較詳細的地貌形態和較準確的方位及面積比例。

loo with 50. It is also the only place with a Chinese name in Chinese characters on the Census report.

Panoramic drawing is a traditional field technique in geography. The drawings here preserved details of the physical and human landscape elements of Hong Kong of the time.

The two paintings drawn almost from the same vantage point and around the same time portray more vividly the scenery and antefacts of the place. Yet they do not show details of the geomophology, nor directions and proportions as accurately as panoramic drawings.

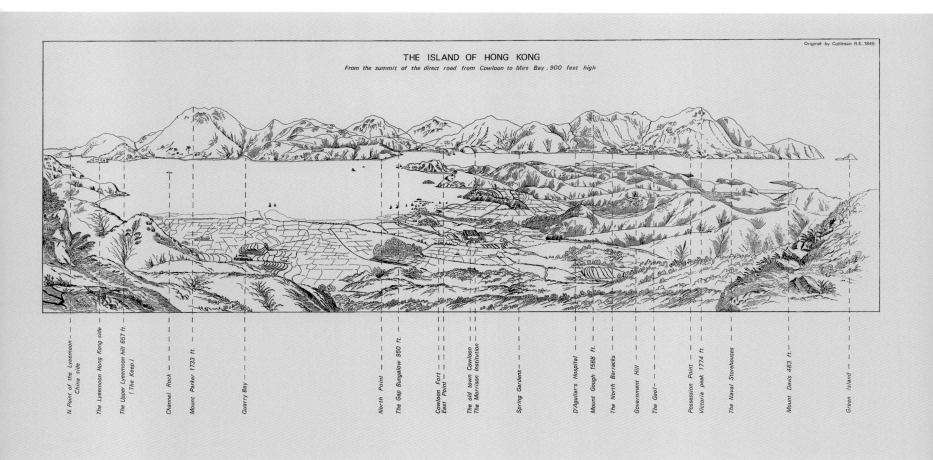

THE ISLAND OF HONG KONG
From the summit of the direct road from Cowloon to Mirs Bay . 900 feet high

Original by Collinson R.E.,1845

N Point of the Lyeemoon China side — The Lyeemoon Hong Kong side — The Upper Lyeemoon hill 657 ft. (The Keep) — Channel Rock — Mount Parker 1733 ft. — Quarry Bay — North Point — The Gap Bungalow 950 ft. — Cowloon Fort East Point — The old town Cowloon The Morrison Institution — Spring Gardens — D'Aguilars Hospital — Mount Gough 1588 ft. — The North Barracks — Government Hill — The Gaol — Possession Point — Victoria peak 1774 ft. — The Naval Storehouses — Mount Davis 483 ft. — Green Island

本圖顯示從今天的龍翔道位置，南望九龍及香港島。當時，九龍仍在清王朝治下。圖的前景盡現九龍半島的微細地貌以及發展狀況。圖中央的九龍寨城的方正城牆及城內屋宇十分清晰。城寨至九龍灣兩旁也有帶狀的連串屋宇，綿延至灣邊，灣內有大量船隻，可見九龍已是重要口岸。城寨周邊田疇起伏，農業興旺。九龍半島西南面，在一片沙灘兩邊有兩條沙咀向海中伸延，這是大角咀的前身。其北方（圖的下部）有一塘清水，150年前的九龍塘是個岸邊瀉湖。

5,000, 2,000 of which were Tanka (or boat people). The Victoria Harbour was dotted with large ocean-going sailing boats and small local crafts.

The panoramic view was taken from present day Lung Cheung Road, looking south at Kowloon and Hong Kong Island. Kowloon was then still under Qing rule. Micro-geomorphology details and features of development are shown in the foreground. Kowloon City, with its square wall, lies at the centre. Inside it, rows of houses are clearly shown. A linear pattern of settlement stretches from the city to Kowloon Bay where many boats anchored. Kowloon remained an important port in southern China. On the two sides of the city were paddy fields, underlining a prosperous local agriculture. Southwest of Kowloon Peninsula was a sand spit, the forerunner of Tai Kok Tsui. To its north was a small coastal lagoon–present day Kowloon Tong.

● 一位不知名人士的1858年的香港島及維港油畫　An oil painting of the Island and Victoria Habour by an unknown artist in 1858

02 今日香港鳥瞰 Hong Kong Today: a Bird's-eye View

今天的香港，約有一半的人口及八成的商業和服務業集中在香港島北岸及九龍半島。這裡以一般的地圖和航空照片拼圖來顯示這個地區的主要市街。

地圖與航空照片各有優點。二者配合使用，可以更好地了解急劇轉變的香港。

地圖有固定的比例，能準確地表達距離、大小及面積，也能以文字及符號表達一些不能用影像表達的事物，如地名及重要設施，像三條海底隧道及水深線、等高線等，提供了航空照片沒有的資訊。地圖上的資

Today, about half of the population and 80% of commercial and service activities are concentrated on the northern coast of Hong Kong Island and Kowloon. This section uses conventional maps and air photos to illustrate the cityscape of these main urban areas. The map and the air photo each has its useful features. When used together, they provide better understanding of Hong Kong's rapid urban growth and change.

A map has a fixed scale for accurately measuring distance, size and area. It also uses words and symbols to represent features that cannot be shown by imagery, e.g. place names, and important infrastructure such as the three cross-harbour tunnels,

● 香港地圖（1994） Map of Hong Kong, 1994

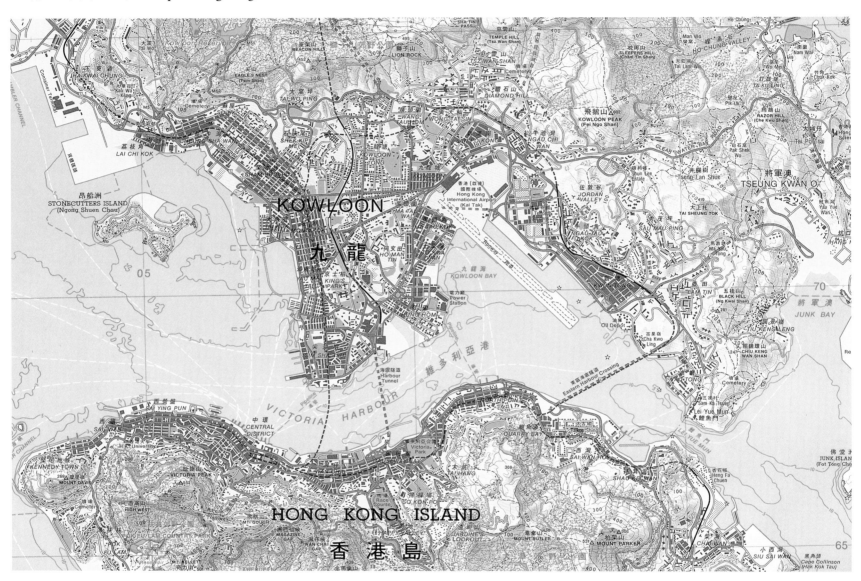

● 香港地圖（2008） Map of Hong Kong, 2008

● 香港 2008 年的航空照片 Air photo of Hong Kong, 2008

料一般比較滯後。由於測繪需時，地圖要很長時間才出新的版本。航空照片則可以在短時間內重拍。1994年圖顯示的資料應該是1980年代末期的狀況，因為九龍西及灣仔、中環的填海仍未表示出來。

isohyets, contour lines. The latter two respectively show depth of water and height of the land, which an air photo is unable to provide. However, due to the labourious work in surveying and map drawing, information provided by a map suffers serious time-lag. An air photo can be updated in a much shorter time period. The present map was published in 1994, and the information it contains may be of the late 1980s, as the reclaimed land in Kowloon West, Wan Chai and Central have not been shown.

● 香港 1994 年的航空照片　Air photo of Hong Kong, 1994

　　1994年的航空照片拼圖已經清楚顯示：九龍西和中環、灣仔這兩個區域的填海已進入最後階段，香港島及九龍半島的新岸線（至2008年）已經形成。

　　航空照片上顯示出不同的樓宇大小、建築密度及形態、分佈規律以及周圍的環境。我們可以分辨出貨櫃碼頭及機場的功能及其細節，同時也可以比較中環高級商務中心的樓宇與尖沙咀東部商業區樓宇的不同、西環與半山薄扶林的住宅區的不同。通過色澤的不同，也可以了解香港島山上植被的狀況、正在移山闢地的工地、維多利亞港的水深等。但這些需要一定的訓練才能判讀。同時，因為飛行高度及拍攝角度不同，拼圖不能完美吻合，物像的大小及位置也會有一定的誤差。

　　The 1994 air photo shows clearly new reclamations and the new coastline on the Island and Kowloon. It also clearly shows varying sizes of buildings, building densities and styles in different parts of the city, against different environment backgrounds. For example, we can differentiate the function and layout of the Container Terminal and the Airport, and differences between buildings in the CBD (Central) and the secondary commercial district of Tsim Sha Tsui East. Through differences in tone, variations in vegetation cover on slopes of the Island, worksite of reclamation, and depth of water in different parts of Victoria Harbour, etc. can be understood. Yet this requires training in air photo interpretation. Due to different flying heights and focal lengths, air photos are not of the same precision and visual quality and therefore distortion in size and location of selected features exists.

03 地理位置　Geographic Location

鑒定地理位置，最通用的辦法是地理坐標，也即是用地球表面上假想出來的經線和緯線來定位。香港位於東經114.10°和北緯22.20°。

經緯線是抽象的，不容易表示香港的地理位置如何優良。我們可以從地圖上詳細分析：（一）香港在北回歸線附近，因而處於亞熱帶地區，日照充足，四季暖和；又處於太平洋沿岸，雨量充沛，海運便利。（二）在時區上，香港處於倫敦和紐約中間，可和這兩個世界上最大的金融中心互補，聯成每天24小時不停的交易，成為跨國公司在世界版圖上重要的辦公中心之一。（三）香港處於經濟前景最好，人口和市場潛力最大的亞太地區的地理中心。在日本和東南亞、中國和東南亞的相對位置中，香港都是運輸的中樞點。（四）在國際海空運輸中，香港是美洲與東南亞及中國的橋樑，歐洲溝通東亞、東南亞和澳洲的孔道。

就中國而言，香港是珠江（南中國）的門戶，也是中國沿海最優良的港灣。

Geographic location may best be represented by longitudes and latitudes, a system of imaginary lattice on the surface of the Earth. Hong Kong's longitude and latitude is 114°10' E/22°20'N.

Yet longitudes and latitudes may not convey Hong Kong's advantageous geographic location. From the map, we may derive more detailed information and easily understand the status of Hong Kong's location: (1) Hong Kong is within the Tropic of Capricorn and thus within the subtropical zone, with plenty of sunshine and a warm temperature. It is on the coast of the Pacific, blessed with abundant rainfall and convenience in ocean shipping. (2) In terms of the time zone, Hong Kong is mid-way between London and New York. In global finance, it complements these two financial centers to provide round-the-clock global trading. As such, Hong Kong is attractive as a regional headquarters for global businesses. (3) Hong Kong is at the core of Asia Pacific, the world's largest region in population and potential market, and the fastest growing economic region. It is the nodal point between Japan, China and Southeast Asia in international maritime and air transport, and serves as the bridge between the Americas, China and Southeast Asia, and a conduit between Europe, East Asia, Australasia and Asia Pacific.

Within China, Hong Kong is the gateway of the Pearl River Delta and possesses the best harbour along the China coast.

● 地理位置　Geographic location

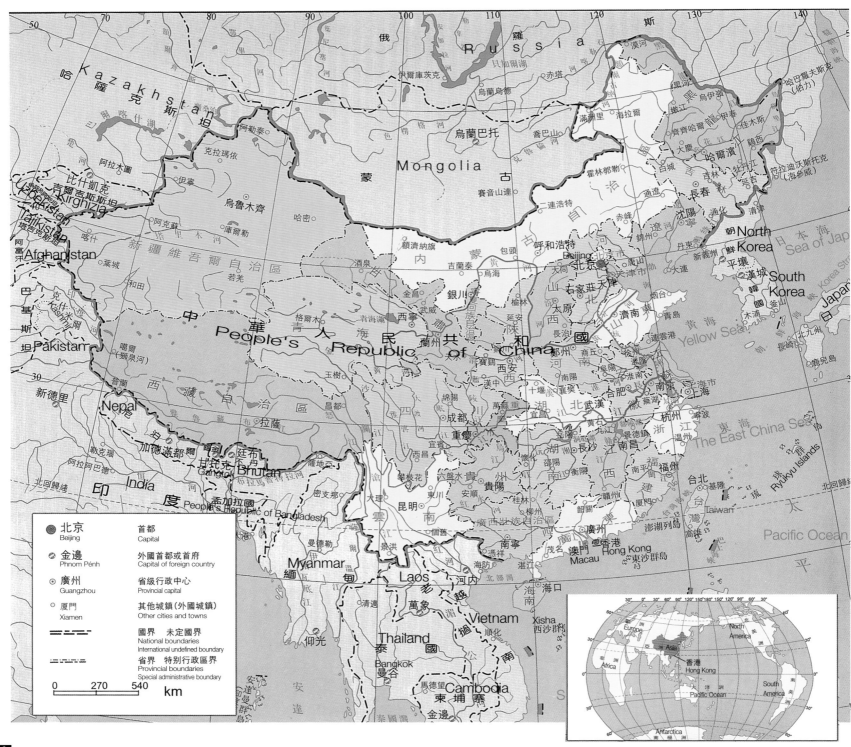

香港面積細小。包括填海所得只有1,090平方公里，和上海、北京的規劃市區面積差不多，但只是它們的全部管轄區（包括郊區和市轄縣）的1/6和1/16，約等於新加坡的1.5倍。跟北京、上海的城區以及新加坡不同，在香港的總面積中，坡地佔了七成。由於坡度較大（通常在1：5和1：2之間），香港的山坡多為不可建地區。

坡地構成了香港主要的高地和山地，其中部份曾受到海水和河流的淹沒和切割。從地質而言，主要的岩石為火成岩，中以火山岩及花崗岩佔多。前者抗風化力較強，構成香港的主要高峰。山多東北—西南走向，最高峰是大帽山主峰，高957米。陡峭的地形，構成香港島、大嶼山和西貢、荃灣、大埔、屯門、沙田等地的主要地貌。

低地及平原地區狹小。最大的是元朗—錦田平原、上水—粉嶺平原和九龍半島。這些平地中不少已經發展為商業、工業和住宅用地。城市化和工業化使平原上原有的大量耕地轉為城市用途，現在耕地只佔總面積的6%。

因為地質史上的陸升、陸沉，近岸形成了235個島嶼。這些島嶼，加上海浪的作用，營造了眾多的優良海灣和沙灘。

Hong Kong has only a territory of 1,090 sq km (including reclaimed land)–about the area of the planned urban area (or the core) of both Shanghai and Beijing, or about 1/6 of Shanghai and 1/16 of Beijing based on total municipality territory, and is about 1.5 times of Singapore. Yet, quite different from Shanghai, Beijing and Singapore, over 70% of Hong Kong's territory are steep slopes unsuitable for urban development. Most of the territory (with a gradient of 1:2-1:5) is highland and hilly.

Igneous rocks are the major rock type, with predominance of volcanic rock and granite. The former, being more resistant to weather and erosion, form major peaks and ridges that run generally NE-SW. Tai Mo Shan is the highest mountain. Steep slopes constitute the main geomorphologic characteristic.

Plains and lowlands are few and small. The largest are Yuen Long-Kam Tin, Sheung Shui-Fanling and Kowloon Peninsula. Most have been developed as industrial, residential and commercial areas. Urbanization and industrialization have led to the decline in agricultural land. At present, agricultural land (including fish ponds) only accounted for 6% of the territory in area.

Repeated submergence and emergence in geological times led to the formation of 235 islands, some of which yield excellent fishing shelters and bathing beaches.

● 1960 年地勢圖 　*Geomorphology (1960)*

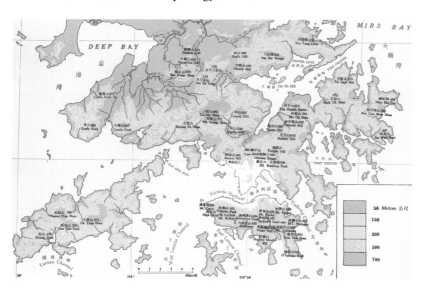

● 2007 年地勢圖 　*Geomorphology (2007)*

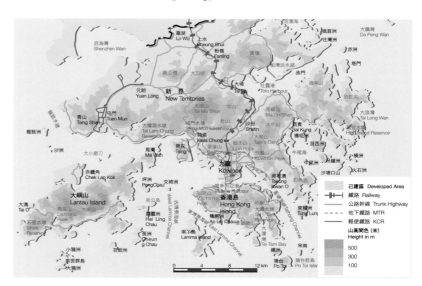

● 2007 年地質圖 　*Geology (2007)*

05 氣候 Climate and Weather

香港處於亞熱帶季候風地區，天氣受到中國內地及太平洋氣團的影響，全年溫度偏高，平均攝氏22.8度。夏季可長達八個月，最高月平均氣溫28.6度，最高溫度達37度。冬季最低月平均氣溫15.6度，最低可在0度。1998年錄得攝氏達37度，是100年來最熱的，該年還是1884年有記錄以來最和暖的一年。

香港四季分明。3月、4月是潮濕多霧的春天；5月至9月是多風多雨的炎夏；10月至11月初為短暫涼爽的秋天；11月初至次年的2月是冬季，一般乾燥晴朗，但間歇性的冷鋒會帶來冬寒及陣雨。

香港氣溫高，雨量充沛。全年雨量集中在5月至9月間（佔全年降雨量的3/4）。降雨多是由夏季東南風送來。年平均雨量2,224毫米。歷史上

Hong Kong is located within the subtropical Monsoon Belt and is affected by air masses of the mainland and the Pacific. It has a high annual average temperature of 22.8°C. Summer lasts for 8 months, with the highest mean monthly temperature of 28.6°C. On some days, it may reach 37°C. The lowest mean monthly temperature in winter is 15.6°C. Yet 0°C may be registered. In 1998, over 33°C was recorded consecutively for 4 days. In one day, it even reached 37°C–the hottest year in over a 100 year period and the hottest year since the first year (1884) of meteorological record.

Hong Kong has four distinct seasons. Spring is foggy and moist and falls in March and April. May to September is summer. It is rainy, hot and frequented by typhoons. Autumn is October to November, a short season of cool weather. December to February brings in sunny weather of winter. Then, frontal activities

● 1951-1980年月平均氣溫及相對濕度 Average monthly temperature and relative humidity, 1951-1980

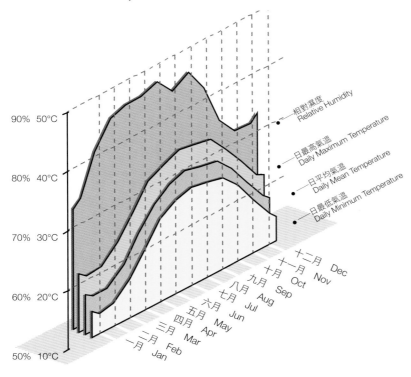

● 1997及2007年月平均氣溫及相對濕度 Average monthly temperature and relative humidity in 1997 and 2007

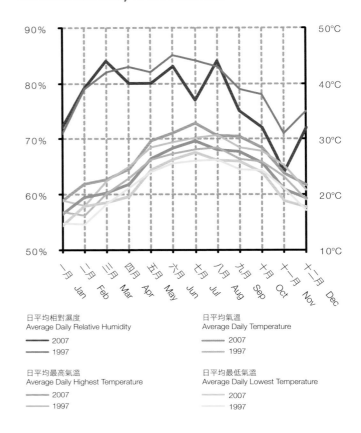

日平均相對濕度
Average Daily Relative Humidity
— 2007
— 1997

日平均氣溫
Average Daily Temperature
— 2007
— 1997

日平均最高氣溫
Average Daily Highest Temperature
— 2007
— 1997

日平均最低氣溫
Average Daily Lowest Temperature
— 2007
— 1997

● 風向及風速頻率 Wind directions and speed

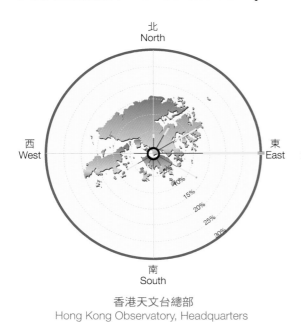

香港天文台總部
Hong Kong Observatory, Headquarters

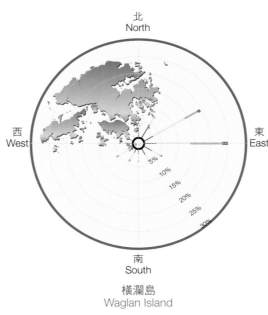

橫瀾島
Waglan Island

蒲福風級及相等之風速 Beaufort Wind Scale and the equivalent wind speed		
形容詞 Adjective		持續風速以海里／時計 Sustained wind(knots/h)	蒲福風級 Beaufort scale
無風	Calm	<1	0
微風	Gentle	1-6	1-2
和緩風	Moderate	7-16	3-4
清勁風	Fresh	17-21	5
強風	Strong	22-33	6-7
烈風	Strong Gale	34-47	8-9
暴風	Violent Storm	48-63	10-11
颶風	Hurricane	>63	12

風速 Wind speed
蒲福風級 Beaufort force
■ 1-2 ■ 3-4 ■ 5-6 ■ >6

最少的年份只有900毫米。1982年是歷史上雨量次高年，達3,247毫米。1997年是雨量最多的一年，降雨3,343毫米，比正常超出51%。而8月22日這一天，在兩個小時內降雨超過了200毫米，是有記錄以來最多的。

雨量的多寡和年內低壓槽和颱風侵襲次數有關。降雨受地形及方向影響很大：東面及南面高地降雨量最高，西北元 朗屯門地區最低。

根據香港天文台分析，香港氣候受到全球變暖及本地城市化的協同影響，走向暖化。

may bring occasional chill and rain.

Hong Kong is characterized by high temperature and heavy rainfall. 3/4 of its annual rainfall falls between May and September, brought mainly by the southerly monsoon. The mean annual rainfall is 2,224 mm. The driest year in record had about 900 mm. 1982 and 1997 are the wettest, with 3,247 and 3,343 mm respectively. On 22 August, 1997, over 200 mm was registered in a two-hour period–the highest record in Hong Kong's history.

The direction of on-shore monsoon and local relief account for heavier rain in Hong Kong's eastern and southern hilly areas.

According to a study by the Hong Kong Observatory, Hong Kong is affected by global warming and increasing urbanization. The weather is trending towards further warming.

● 1953-1982年平均雨量地區分佈
Average rainfall between 1953-1982

● 1982年歷史上雨量次高年份的雨量地區分佈
The second wettest year in Hong Kong history, 1982

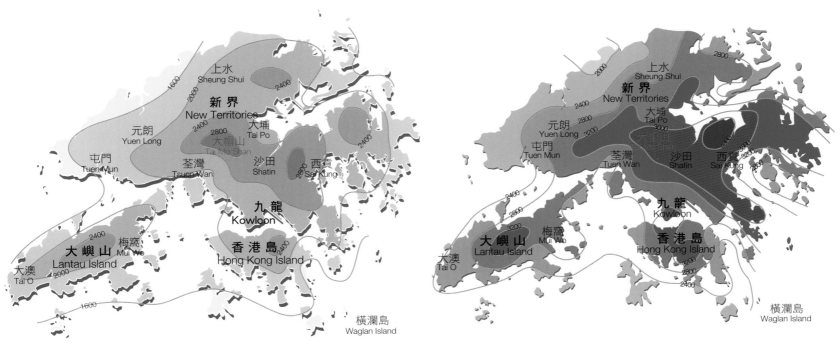

——— 等雨量線 (毫米)　Isohyet (mm)

● 1887-1990年各月雨量分佈　Rainfall distribution, 1887-1990

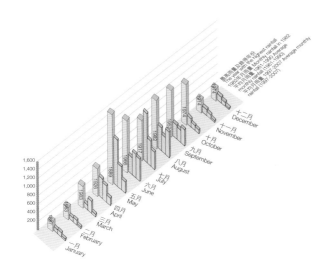

● 香港氣候變化趨勢　Weather trend in Hong Kong

參數 Elements	趨勢 Trend	
氣溫 Temperature	↑	上升 Increase
雨量 Rainfall	↑	上升 Increase
海平面 Mean sea level	↑	上升 Increase
雲量 Cloud amount	↑	上升 Increase
太陽輻射量 Solar radiation	↓	下降 Decrease
出現低能見度時數* Hours with reduced visibility*	↑	上升 Increase

* 能見度低於8公里的時數（雨、薄霧、霧及相對濕度在95%或以上不計）
* Number of hours with visibility below 8 km（relative humidity below 95 % and not counting rain, mist or fog）

● 1885-2005年香港天文台總部錄得的年平均氣溫　Annual mean temperature recorded at Hong Kong Observatory Headquarters, 1885-2005

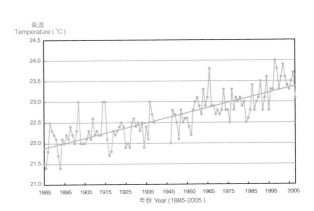

06 歷史地圖及地名 Historical Maps and Local Names

香港秦時屬南海郡番禺縣。東晉至中唐，番禺縣改為寶安縣。唐中葉至明，又改為東莞縣。明神宗時，劃東莞南部為新安縣，縣治在南頭。至1841年，香港仍屬新安縣。1866年的新安縣圖顯示，其西路延至沙井，東路包括大鵬半島的大部份。

香港一些地名在明代已出現，但亦有不少地名在歷史上和今天的不同。新地名也因應人口與各種活動和建設需要而訂立。例如新界、青山和屯門在1866年仍稱清山和團門。香港島上主要山峰的名字在1866年後也有變更。"群帶路"一名，只在1866年圖中出現。東印度公司在1810年偷繪的地圖內的中英文地名，部份和今天常用的很不同。南丫島和交椅洲的舊名是薄寮和高洲。

Hong Kong lay within Punyu County of Nanhai Prefecture in Qin Dynasty. From Eastern Jin to mid-Tang Dynasty, Hong Kong was part of Xinan County, whose seat was at Nantau. It remained part of Xinan until 1841. Xinan at 1866 extended westward to Shajing while its eastern territory included most of Dapang (Mirs) Bay.

Some local names date back to Ming Dynasty. Yet, some are different from their present-day names, reflecting changes through time. New names have also since been created and incorporated, which are bi-products of population growth and development. For example, the Chinese characters of Tsing Shan and Tuen Mun in 1866 are different from present-day characters. The peaks on Hong Kong Island at present bear different names from those appearing in 1866 too. Quan Dai Lu, an old name on Hong Kong Island, only appeared in the map of 1866. Lamma Island and Kauyi Island were then known as Pok-liu and Kozhou.

On the map produced from the East Indian Company's illegal surveys, many names are different from the present ones.

● 新安縣全圖（1866） Map of Xinan (San-On) County (1866)

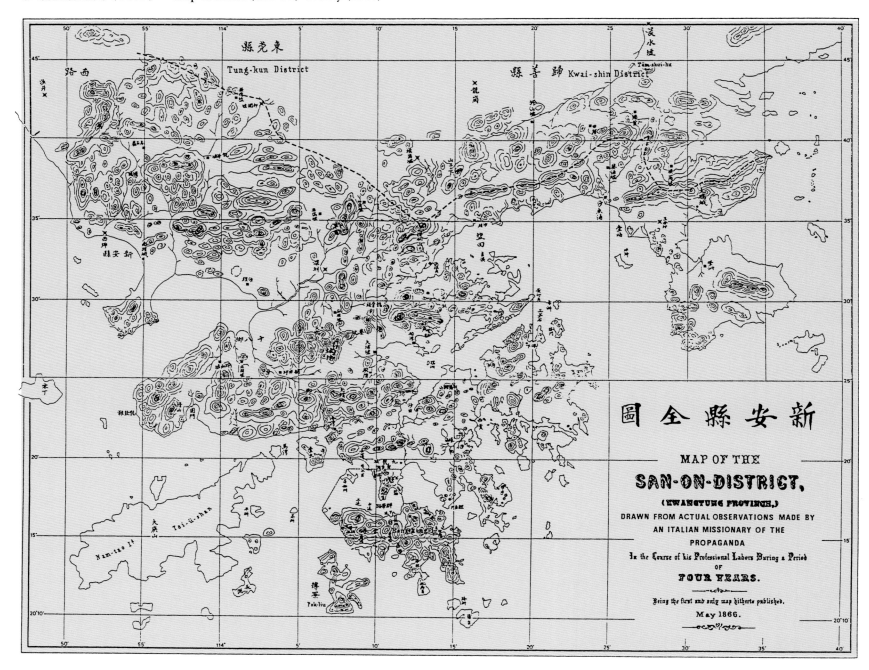

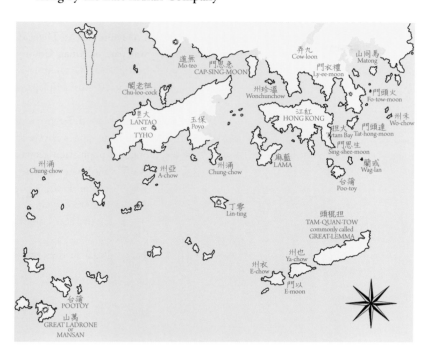

● 16世紀末廣東沿海圖　Coastal map of Guangdong in late 16th century

● 1553年全廣海圖　Coastal map of Guangdong by Ying Ka (1553)

1	Shek Pik	11	Kwai Chung	21	Nantou Military Division	f	Entrance for ships from the North-west
2	Tai O	12	Tsim Sha Tsui	22	Nantou (Shekou)	g	Old Man Shan
3	Ngoi Ling Ding	13	Kowloon Hill	23	Mo To Chau (The Brothers)	h	Ships of Nantou mooring
4	Cheung Chau	14	Coast Guards of Kun Fu	24	Kap Shui Mun	i	Fat Tong Mun
5	Pok Liu	15	Tseung Kwan O (Junk Bay)	25	Tam Kon Chau (Lema Islands)	j	One 'shao shui' to Tai Tam and half 'shao shui' to Fat Tong Mun
6	Chek Lap Chau (Chek Lap Kok)	16	Lei Yue Mun	a	Foreign (Barbarian) ships mooring	k	Shek Wan
7	Tuen Mun	17	Noi Ling Ding	b	Heung Shan Au (Macau)	l	Da Peng
8	Shing Shan	18	Xinan County (Shenzhen)	c	Place inhabited by barbarians	m	Da Peng City
9	So Kwun Wat	19	Nam Shan	d	Coast Guards of Heung Shan City		
10	Chien Wan (Tuen Wan)	20	Xixiang Village	e	Canton		

07 考古及文物重點 Archaeological Sites

　　香港近年的考古成果證明，本地區在4,000年前，即新石器時代中後期，已經有人在今離島馬灣聚居（稱馬灣人）。不但如此，1955年在李鄭屋村發現的東漢墓更顯示，最遲在東漢，即約1,700年前，香港已和中原文化打成一片，屬於中原文化的一部份。下圖顯示，考古遺址多在沿岸地方，可能與當時先民多從水路來香港定居，以及過着半漁半農的生活有關。

Archaeological finds support the belief that Ma Wan Man started to populate the territory on Ma Wan Island about 4,000 years ago (in the middle or latter part of the Neolithic Age). The discovery of a major tomb of Eastern Han with lavish burial goods in 1955 proves that the territory was closely linked to the predominant Han civilization on the mainland at least 1,700 years ago. Most important archaeological finds are sited along the coast. The early settlers might thus possibly have arrived by water and led a semi-fishery and semi-arable life.

● 香港考古及文物重點 Hong Kong's archaeological sites

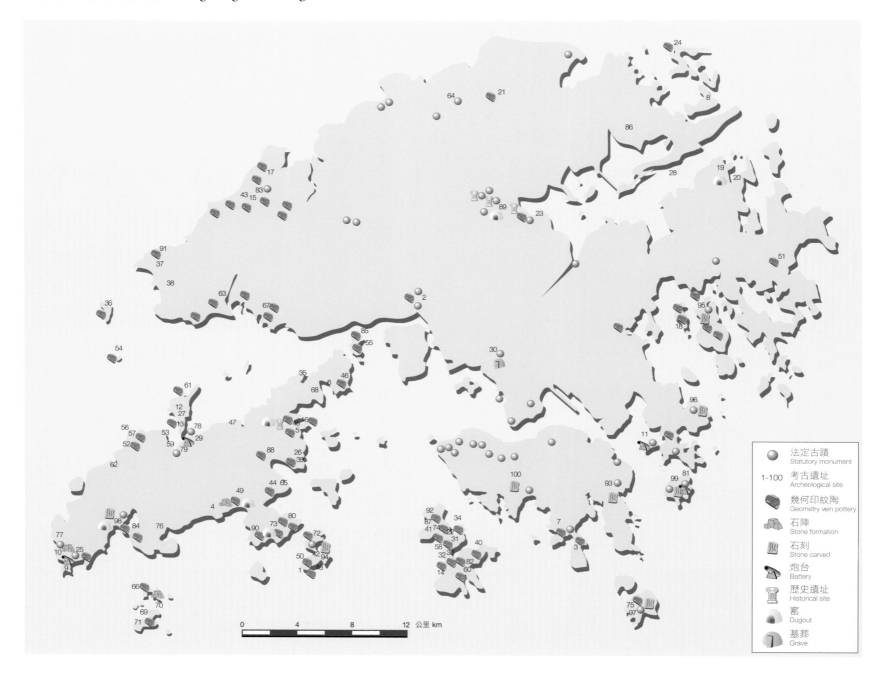

位於南丫島深灣的地層縱切圖
Archaeological soil profile of Sum Wan at Lamma Island

地面
Surface

信史時期 Historical Period	公元前220—現代 220 B.C. - Present
青銅時期 Bronze Age	公元前1200—前220年 1200 B.C. - 220 B.C.
新石器時代 New Stone Age	後期公元前2200—前1200年 前期公元前4000—前2200年 Later stage 2200 B.C. - 1200 B.C. Earlier Stage 4000 B.C. - 2200 B.C.
未有人類居住 No Human Existence	

發現馬灣人地層
Stratum with Ma Wan Man discovery

考古遺址 Archaeological sites	石器時代 Stone Age	青銅器時期 Bronze Age	信史時期 Historical Period
1. 美經援村　Care Village	*	*	
2. 柴灣角　Chai Wan Kok	*	*	
3. 赤柱灣　Chek Chue Wan	*	*	
4. 長沙　Cheung Sha	*	*	
5. 長沙欄　Cheung Sha Lan	*	*	
6. 竹篙灣　Chok Ko Wan			*
7. 春坎灣　Chung Hom Wan	*	*	
8. 往灣洲　Wong Wan Chau	*	*	
9. 分流炮台　Fan Lau Fort			*
10. 分流西灣　Fan Lau Sai Wan	*	*	
11. 佛頭洲稅關遺址　Fort ruins at Fat Tong Mun			*
12. 虎地灣　Fu Tei Wan	*	*	
13. 蝦螺灣　Ha Lo Wan			*
14. 下尾灣　Ha Mei Wan	*	*	
15. 廈村　Ha Tsuen	*	*	
16. 蟹地灣　Hai Tei Wan	*	*	
17. 坑口村　Hang Hau Tsuen	*	*	*
18. 廈門灣　Hap Mun Bay	*	*	
19. 海下　Hoi Ha	*	*	
20. 海下窰　Hoi Ha Yiu			*
21. 孔嶺　Hung Leng	*	*	
22. 洪聖爺　Hung Shing Ye	*	*	
23. 元洲仔　Yuen Chau Tsai	*	*	
24. 吉澳洲北　Kat O Chau (N)	*	*	
25. 狗嶺涌　Kau Ling Chung	*	*	*
26. 狗虱灣　Kau Shat Wan	*	*	
27. 過路灣　Kwo Lo Wan	*	*	
28. 荔枝莊（北）　Lai Chi Chong (N)			*
29. 流浮沙　Lau Fau Sha	*	*	
30. 李鄭屋古墓　Lei Cheng Uk Tomb			*
31. 蘆鬚城（北）　Lo So Shing(N)	*	*	
32. 蘆鬚城（西）　Lo So Shing(W)	*	*	
33. 蘆鬚城　Lo So Shing	*	*	
34. 鹿洲　Luk Chau	*	*	
35. 鹿頸　Luk Keng			*
36. 龍鼓洲　Lung Kwu Chau	*	*	
37. 龍鼓上灘　Lung Kwu Sheung Tan		*	
38. 龍鼓灘　Lung Kwu Tan	*	*	
39. 萬角咀　Man Kok Tsui	*	*	
40. 模達灣　Mo Tat Wan	*	*	
41. 南丫北段公立小學　Northern Lamma School	*	*	
42. 南灣　Nam Wan		*	
43. 鰲磡石（丁）　Ngau Hom Shek (D)		*	
44. 牛牯灣　Ngau Muk Wan	*	*	*
45. 稔樹灣　Nim Shue Wan	*	*	
46. 扒頭鼓　Pa Tau Kwu	*	*	
47. 白芒　Pak Mong	*	*	*
48. 鮋魚灣　Po Yue Wan	*	*	
49. 貝澳　Pui O	*	*	
50. 西灣（長洲）　Sai Wan (Cheung Chau)	*	*	
51. 西灣（西貢）　Sai Wan (Sai Kung)	*		

考古遺址 Archaeological sites	石器時代 Stone Age	青銅器時期 Bronze Age	信史時期 Historical Period
52. 磡石灣　San Shek Wan			*
53. 磡頭　San Tau	*	*	*
54. 沙洲　Sha Chau	*	*	*
55. 沙柳塘灣　Sha Lau Tong Wan	*	*	
56. 沙螺灣(西)　Sha Lo Wan (W)	*	*	
57. 沙螺灣　Sha Lo Wan	*	*	
58. 砂塱灣　Sha Long Wan	*	*	*
59. 沙嘴頭　Sha Tsui Tau			*
60. 深灣　Sham Wan	*	*	*
61. 深灣村　Sham Wan Tsuen	*	*	*
62. 深屈　Sham Wat			*
63. 石角咀　Shek Kok Tsui	*	*	
64. 上水華山　Sheung Shui Wa Shan	*	*	
65. 水井灣　Shui Tseng Wan	*	*	
66. 小鴉洲　Siu A Chau	*	*	
67. 掃管笏　So Kwun Wat	*	*	
68. 四白　Sze Pak	*	*	
69. 大鴉洲（乙）　Tai A Chau (B)	*	*	
70. 大鴉洲（丙）　Tai A Chau (C)	*	*	
71. 大鴉洲　Tai A Chau	*	*	
72. 大鬼灣　Tai Kwai Wan	*	*	
73. 大浪　Tai Long	*	*	
74. 大灣（南丫島）　Tai Wan (Lamma Island)	*	*	
75. 大灣（蒲台）　Tai Wan (Po Toi)	*	*	*
76. 塘福　Tong Fuk	*	*	
77. 煎魚灣　Tsin Yue Wan	*		*
78. 東涌小炮台　Tung Chung Battery			*
79. 東涌炮台　Tung Chung Fort			*
80. 東角　Tung Kok	*	*	
81. 東龍炮台　Tung Lung Fort			*
82. 東澳　Tung O	*	*	
83. 東頭村　Tung Tau Tsuen	*	*	*
84. 東灣（石壁）　Tung Wan (Shek Pik)	*	*	*
85. 東灣仔　Tung Wan Tsai	*	*	
86. 橫嶺頭　Wang Leng Tau			*
87. 橫塱　Wang Long	*	*	
88. 橫塘　Wang Tong	*	*	
89. 碗窰　Wun Yiu			*
90. 二浪　Yi Long			*
91. 湧浪　Yung Long	*	*	*
92. 榕樹灣　Yung Shue Wan	*	*	*

考古遺址　Archaeological sites

93.	大浪灣石刻	Big Wave Bay Rock Carving
94.	長洲石刻	Cheung Chau Rock Carving
95.	滘西洲石刻	Kau Sai Rock Carving
96.	龍蝦灣石刻	Lung Ha Wan Rock Carving
97.	蒲台島石刻	Po Toi Rock Carving
98.	石壁石刻	Shek Pik Rock Carving
99.	東龍洲石刻	Tung Lung Rock Carving
100.	黃竹坑石刻	Wong Chuk Hang Rock Carving

08 關於香港的不平等條約　Hong Kong-related 'Unequal Treaties'

這裡展示割佔或租借香港地區的不平等條約的附圖。

1841年圖是英國海軍繪製的。原圖的水文資料已被省略。此圖是早期最精確的九龍及香港島地圖，但一些山名已經用上英國人的名字，而交椅洲及南丫島也不用中國的舊名字高洲和博寮。

1860年圖是《北京條約》的附圖，顯示英國割佔前的九龍半島。當時九龍塘在海岸邊，深水埗是個深凹的海灣，而土瓜灣名為土家灣，昂船洲寫作盎船州。尖沙咀、油麻地及旺角一帶多是農田。

1898年圖附於《展拓香港界址專條》內。圖中新界北面的邊界在海上均達深圳灣及大鵬灣，香港海域包括了這兩個海灣，而不是至海灣的中線。陸上邊界由附圖顯示，主要沿深圳河北岸。香港北面邊界的這種畫法之後常出現爭議。

1898年條約訂明九龍城寨的治權仍屬清廷，但一年後，英國找借口驅逐城寨官員出境。雖中國多次反映，英國一直不理，使城寨成為「城中之城」式的「三不管」地帶。至1980年代才在中英協議下清拆，改為公園。

Here are shown the territory maps attached to the three unequal treaties whereby Britain obtained Hong Kong and Kowloon, and leased the New Territories.

The 1841 map was drawn by the British navy with detailed navigation information omitted in the present reproduction. It is the most accurate map of Hong Kong at the time. On it, former Chinese names for some peaks and islands have been replaced, some with English names.

The 1860 map shows the situation of Kowloon before being ceded to Britain. Kowloon Tong was then a coastal lagoon. Sham Shui Po was a bay. The Chinese name for To Ka Wan was different. Then it means the Bay of the To Family. Stonecutters Island, then had a different Chinese name. Tsim Sha Tsui, Yau Ma Tei and Mongkok were then largely agricultural.

The 1898 map indicates that the leased territory included the entire Deep Bay and Mirs Bay, rather than the mid-line of these bays. The land border also lies along the northern bank of Shenzhen River.

The 1898 Treaty provided that Kowloon Walled City should be retained under Qing rule. However, the British ousted the Qing officers stationed there a year later. It remained 'a city within a city' until 1980s when the Chinese and British governments agreed to replace it by a park.

● 1841年條約附圖（由英國海軍卑路乍勘繪）　Treaty map 1841 (surveyed by Captain Sir Edward Belcher)

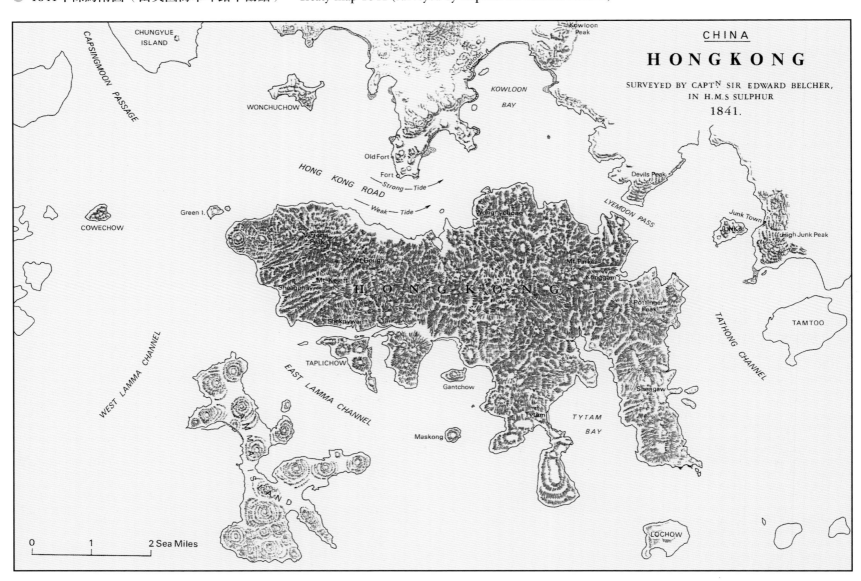

● 1860年《北京條約》附圖
Treaty map, Beijing Treaty 1860

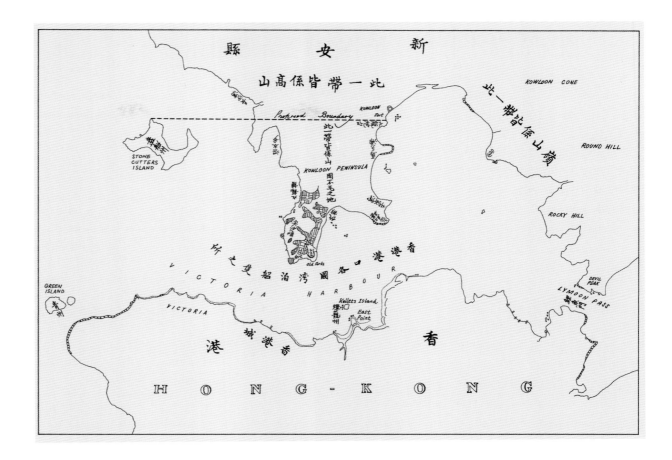

● 1898年《展拓香港界址專條》附圖　Map attached to The Convention for the Extension of Hong Kong Territory, 1898

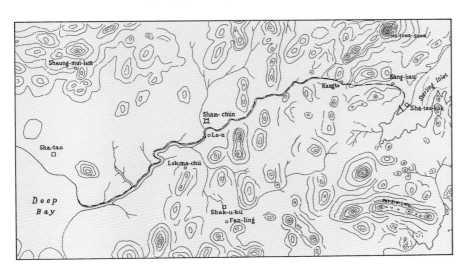

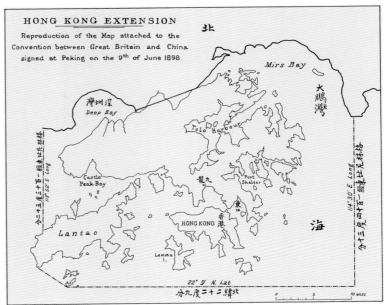

● 九龍城寨　Kowloon Walled City

▼ 1980年代清拆分期
Clearance programme,
1988-1990

▶ 位置及原官署
Location and Qing
Government Office

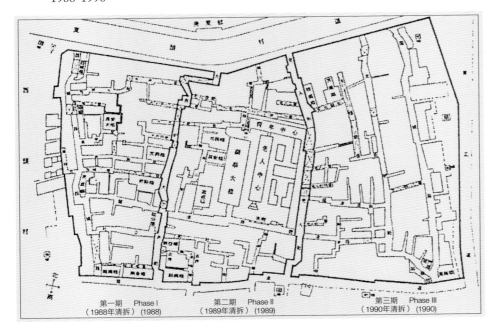

第一期　Phase I
(1988年清拆) (1988)

第二期　Phase II
(1989年清拆) (1989)

第三期　Phase III
(1990年清拆) (1990)

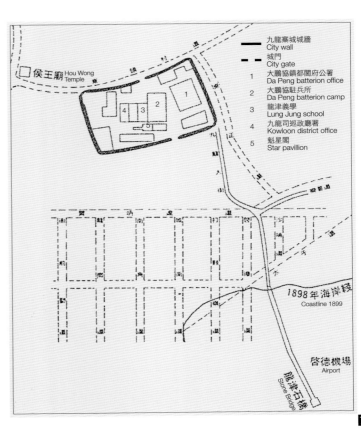

九龍寨城城牆
City wall

城門
City gate

1 大鵬協鎮都閫府公署
Da Peng batterion office

2 大鵬協駐兵所
Da Peng batterion camp

3 龍津義學
Lung Jung school

4 九龍司巡政廳署
Kowloon district office

5 魁星閣
Star pavillion

09 北部邊界 Northern Border

香港繪製的三幅不同時期的邊界圖，體現出香港與深圳的邊界隨着政治現實的不同而變遷，同時也展現了因填海造田而導致的海岸線變化。

上節1898年圖顯示深圳三角洲較為細小，邊界在深圳河北高潮抵達的地方。在東面，邊界由鏡渡北經鏡口南走向沙頭角。沙頭角北岸邊界線不明確。但條約規定：「所租與英國之地，內有大鵬灣、深圳灣水面，惟議定該兩灣中國兵船無論在局內局外，仍可享用。」

1905年的邊界仍以高潮達至的地方為準，現在的深圳大學及深圳灣整個紅樹林區，包括深圳河的三角洲，都在香港境內。

1946年地圖沒有劃出兩個海灣北部的界線，但深圳河三角洲仍在香港境內。深圳河及元朗河出口的沼澤區已填成陸地，包括現在的米埔。

1951年，港英政府以保安理由，將邊境約寬500米的土地，共2,800公頃，劃為禁區，除了本地居民，其他人士要申請特殊通行證進出，不但凍結了地區發展，也使香港和內地明顯分隔開來。內地改革開放後，深圳河的深圳一邊已發展為繁華市區，而香港一邊仍是荒蕪一片。2006年特區政府將其中2,400公頃解禁，但同時又將絕大部份面積建議劃為綠色生態區，以為深圳過渡的「緩衝」。這計劃在2009年提出並進行諮詢。

1991年的邊界再有新的變化。沿深圳河分界已採用中流線，深圳河三角洲納入深圳內。米埔外圍形成的人工堤清楚展示為兩條筆直的岸線。

The three maps of Hong Kong drawn by the local authority at different times indicate the changing border with Shenzhen due to varying political realities of the time. They also illustrate how reclamation has modified the coastline of northeastern New Territories.

In the previous map of 1898, Shenzhen River entered Deep Bay in a small delta. The border ran along the northern bank of the river reached by high tide. In the east, the border ran overland from Kangto to Kanghou. Yet the border between Sha Tau Kok and the eastern coast was not clear. The Treaty provides that: "the British leased territory includes the waters of Deep Bay and Mirs Bay. It is also agreed that Chinese Warships can use these bays as usual."

In the 1905 map, Hong Kong's northern border in Deep Bay and Mirs Bay were marked by high tide. Hong Kong then included present-day Shenzhen University campus, the mangrove area and the whole of the Delta.

In the 1946 map, the border in Deep Bay and Mirs Bay were not shown, reflecting the sensitive situation of the time, though the whole Delta was still included into Hong Kong. The map indicates that the marshy lands at the mouths of Shenzhen River and Yuen Long River had already been reclaimed, including the present day Mai Po Nature Reserve.

In 1951, the government used security as a reason to zone off 2,800 ha of border area as 'restricted area' that required a special permit for entrance. It froze the development potential of the area and created a physical division between Hong

● 1905、1946年和1991年香港深圳邊界圖　Boundaries between Hong Kong and Shenzhen in 1905, 1946 and 1991

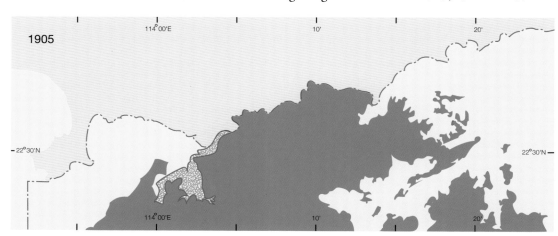

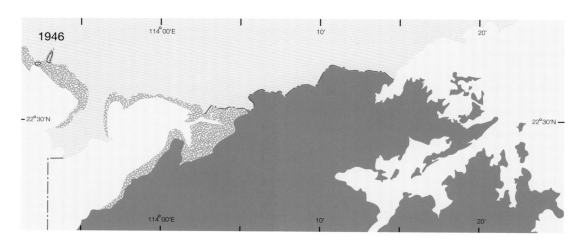

1997年1月，廣東、香港兩地政府經過九年商討，簽訂了邊境管理線諒解備忘錄。香港新增96公頃土地（主要是因為拉直深圳河得來），在海域上增減了一部份領域。這是自1900年以後，兩地第一次就界線達成協議，為香港回歸作準備。

Kong and the mainland. After the Opening and Reform of 1978, the Shenzhen side of the border has developed into a bustling commercial and residental area while the Hong Kong side remained an area of wilderness. In 2006, the Hong Kong SAR released 2,400 ha of the 'restricted area'. Yet a government proposal in 2009 suggested that this land should be rezoned as a green ecoregion acting as a buffer between Hong Kong and Shenzhen.

Further change of the border was obvious in 1991. The border along Shenzhen River for the first time ran along mid-stream, and the delta fell outside of Hong Kong.

In January 1997, after a 9-year negotiation, the government of Guangdong signed a memorandum with Hong Kong on an agreed boundary line. Hong Kong gained 96 ha of land due to the straightening of a bend of Shenzhen River, with some increases and decreases of marine territories. The agreement paved the way for Hong Kong's return to the mainland in mid-1997.

● 1900年香港的邊界　Boundary of Hong Kong, 1900

● 一張1998年圖仍沿用舊有的香港邊界　A map of 1998 still showing the old boundary

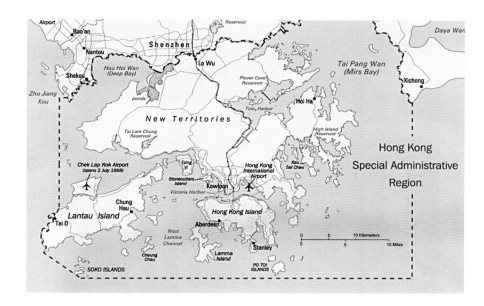

● 1997年香港特別行政區的邊界　Boundary of the Hong Kong Special Administrative Region, 1997

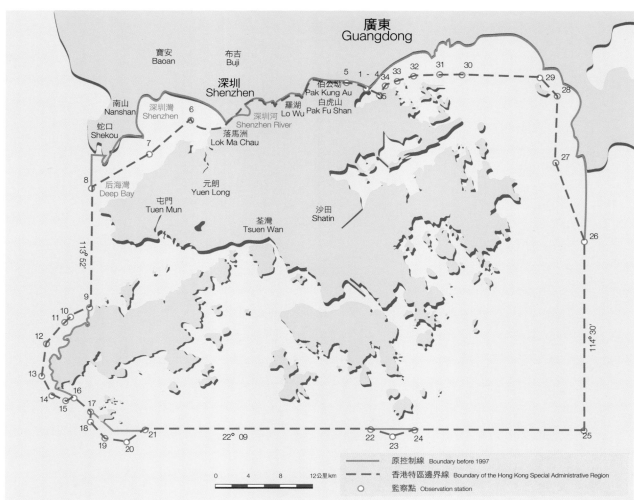

原控制線　Boundary before 1997

香港特區邊界線　Boundary of the Hong Kong Special Administrative Region

監察點　Observation station

10 日軍攻佔及東江游擊隊抗日 Japanese Occupation and Anti-Japanese Activities by East River Brigade

1941年12月8日上午7時日軍空襲啟德機場，對香港不宣而戰。香港政府立即徵召所有小輪及汽車，港九兩地交通近乎癱瘓，但直到晚上才向市民公佈戰爭爆發。當日早上六七時英軍已將新界邊境及沿鐵路的橋樑破壞，並向南撤退。英印兵約10,000人依靠由醉酒灣、城門水塘至牛尾海的一條17公里長的主防線，以抵禦日軍。這條防線經營數年，英軍曾揚言可以抵禦日軍半年之久，但防線在開戰後兩天便被攻破。

12日，英軍全部撤回港島。25日晚，英軍向日軍無條件投降。

日軍襲港前，在港英軍請求中方火速兵援，包括要求東江和瓊崖游擊隊合作保衛香港。12月下旬，中國軍隊主力進至惠州，前鋒已達樟木

Japan air-raided Kai Tak Airport at 7 am on 8 December 1941, starting the unannounced war on Hong Kong. The colonial government enlisted all ferries, and motor vehicles for military deployment. Transport between Hong Kong Island and Kowloon came to a standstill. Yet the public only heard the related broadcast in the evening. By then, Japanese soldiers had debouched onto the New Territories and destroyed bridges along the railway. The British main defence, the 'Gin Drinkers' Line' with 10,000 strong Indian soldiers, running along a 17 km line of crests of Kowloon peaks, fell in two days, despite the British claim that it could hold Japanese offence for up to 6 months.

By 12 December, all British forces withdrew to Hong Kong Island and by 25 December, they surrendered unconditionally.

Shortly before the Japanese invasion, Chinese military aid was requested,

● 1941年日軍進攻路線圖 Routes of Japanese invasion, 1941

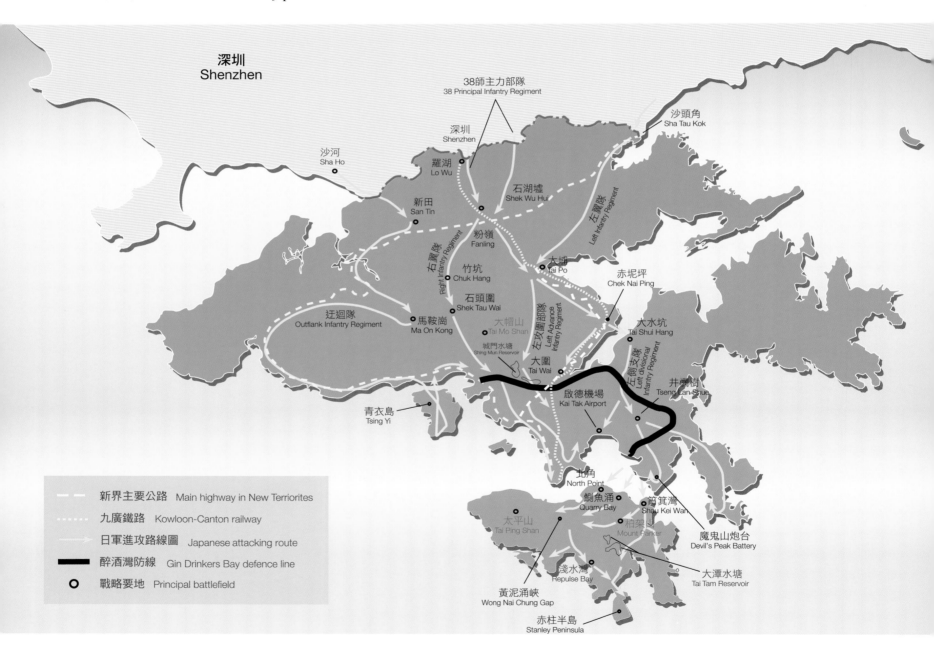

頭，可惜港英政府卻迅速投降。據各方透露，英軍迅速投降是受英相丘吉爾指令，理由乃新界租約未滿，勝利後可向日本索還，但若落入中國軍隊之手，問題便會變得複雜。

日軍統治下，中國東江縱隊港九獨立大隊救護盟邦及知名中國人士，破壞敵偽設施，保衛人民利益，又在和平來臨後立即將武裝人員撤回。但他們三年多的抗日護港業績和因此犧牲的烈士，到1997年回歸後才由特區政府予以承認。

which included co-defence of Hong Kong by the East River and Qinya Brigades. In mid-December, Chinese forces reached Huizhou and its vanguard advanced to Zhangmutou. According to some reports, Winston Churchill ordered Hong Kong troops to surrender. His reason was that as the New Territories' lease had not yet expired, Britain could reclaim the whole of Hong Kong after the war from Japan; but if it fell into Chinese hands, this would be impossible.

During Japanese occupation, the East River Brigade attacked Japanese institutions and rapidly helped famous Chinese personalities and officials of the Allied Nations to exit Hong Kong safely. When peace returned, they pulled out from Hong Kong. Their deeds and fallen men were acknowledged, given recognition and honoured only after 1997.

● 東江縱隊港九獨立大隊活動圖　Activity space of Hong Kong Independent Battalion, Dongjiang Column

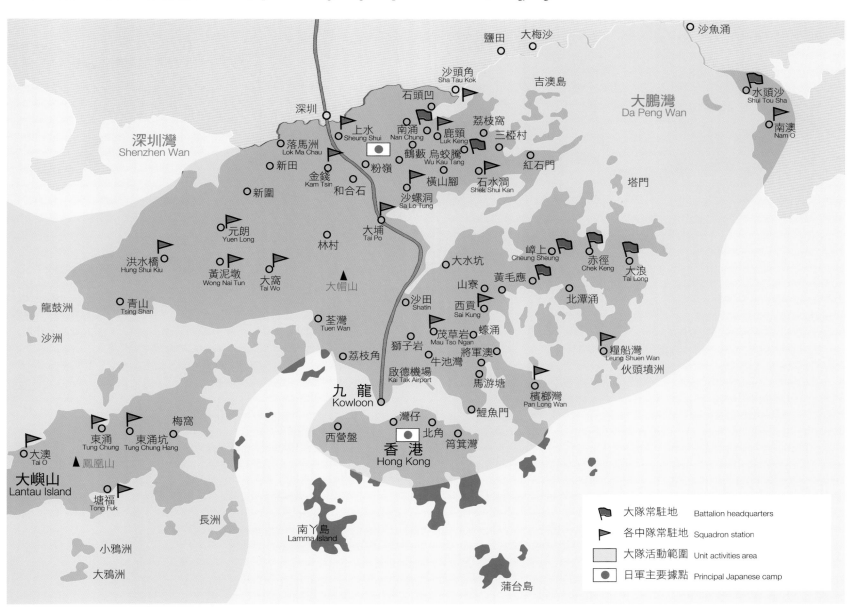

11 填海及海岸線變化 Reclamation and the Changing Coastline

香港的自然條件和城市發展格局有利於大規模填海：海岸線曲折而多淺灘，潮差不大，水流不急，而陸地上及海床的充填物豐富。同時，維多利亞港兩岸平地不足。在中心城區填海加地便成為最有效的城市擴展方式。

填海始於1843年。至1851年止，都是規模較小的私人填海。以後填海成為政府工程。第二次世界大戰前，填海只局限於香港島及九龍半島。戰後才開始在新界填海。1990年後因為新機場及貨櫃碼頭的興建，填海擴大，不單在維多利亞港兩岸，更擴展至大嶼山東岸和北岸。

The physical geography and pattern of urban growth in Hong Kong favour large-scale reclamation. The winding coastline, its numerous shallow bays and inlets, small amplitude, slow water currents, and plentiful fill are ideal for reclamation. The city thus expands on the shores of Victoria Habour through reclamation.

The earliest reclamation was in 1843. Up to 1851, these had been small-scale private efforts. From then on, reclamation was confined to the Island and Kowloon and done by the government. It extended to the New Territories as a result of new towns development since the late 1960s. Mega urban infrastructure projects after 1990, including the new airport and container port development, led to more

● 1887-2011年的填海區及海岸線變化　Reclamation and change of coastline in 1887-2011

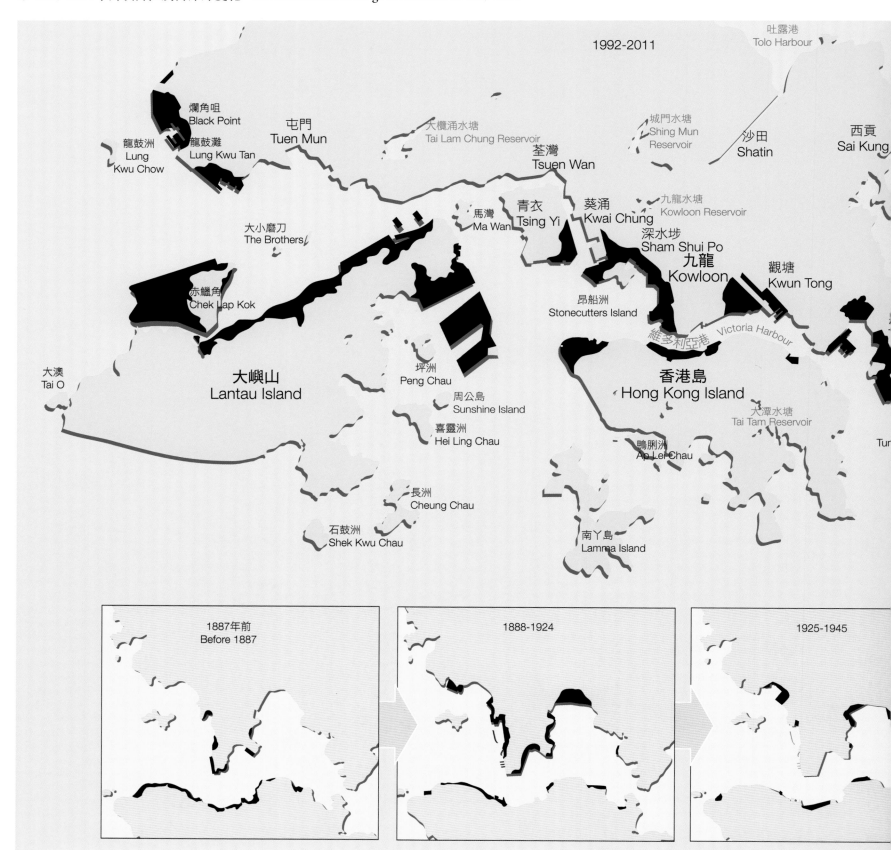

已進行的和計劃進行的1992–2011年填海量，預計可得土地比半個香港島還大。

填海利弊互見。填海改變了海岸線的走勢，對水流及水中生態產生影響，也改變了城市景觀。最近一次對維多利亞港的填海建議，被指破壞市中心的景觀。大嶼山東大量的填海，也因需求的原因而受質疑，兩個計劃都被迫縮小。

reclamation. The amount reclaimed in 1992-2011 is about half of the area of Hong Kong Island.

Reclamation changes the coastline, with impacts on water currents and shoreline ecology, besides changing the cityscape. The latest proposal was opposed by the public. The proposal on eastern Lantau was also queried on the basis of demand. Both projects have since been substantially modified.

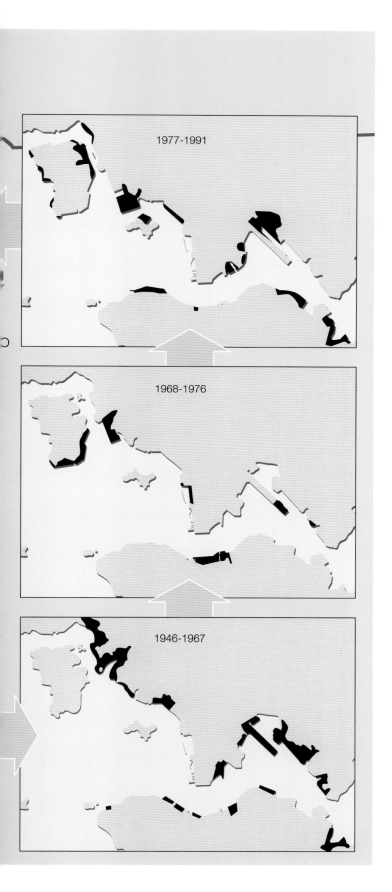

● 填海得地量　Amount of reclaimed land

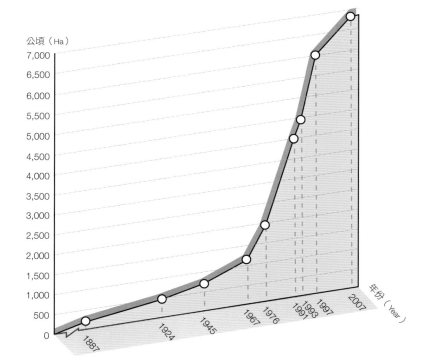

公頃（Ha）

年份（Year）

12 統計區及政區　Administrative and Electoral Divisions

政區界定隨人口、城市和經濟的發展而變化。為了使統計資料更詳盡，對規劃更具指導性，人口普查的分區也越分越細。1961年和1991年的人口普查區域，在數目與形狀上變化都很大。小區及街區兩個更低層的分區，並未在圖中顯示出來。

人口普查區分成五大規劃區。

1981年起立法局、市政局、區域市政局和區議會逐步進行分區直選。每一次選舉，選區區界和數目都有一些變動。1998年1月舉行的特區首屆立法會的選區只有五個，是多議席選區，每個選區有三個至五個議席。

政府的行政管治，也以人口普查區及選區為基礎釐訂出不同的行政管治區域。這些區域的劃分因管理部門而異。

Administrative divisions of a city have to be redrawn frequently in response to spatial variations in population, economic activities and pattern of growth. Census districts are also increasingly small for more detailed information to aid planning. The census sub-districts of 1961 and 1991 differ notably in shape and total number. Below are small census tracks and street blocks which have not been shown.

The five planning districts are derived from census sub-districts.

Since 1981, Hong Kong started district-based direct election for a number of seats in the Legislative Council, Urban Council and District Council. Redrawing of electoral divisions forms a continual exercise. In the first post-1997 Legislative Council election of 1998, there were only 5 divisions, each had 3-5 seats.

The administrative districts of the government are based on both census sub-districts and electoral districts, and vary in size and number for different departments.

● 1961年及1991年香港人口普查分區圖 **Census districts in 1961 and 1991**

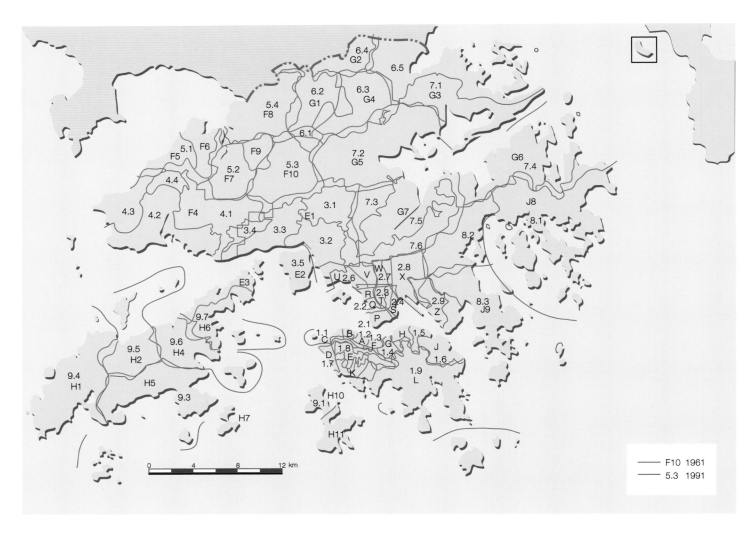

● 2001年香港人口普查分區圖　Census districts in 2001

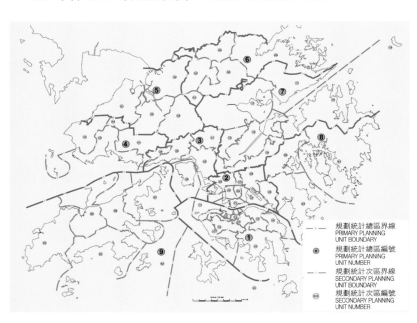

● 香港城市規劃分區　Town planning districts

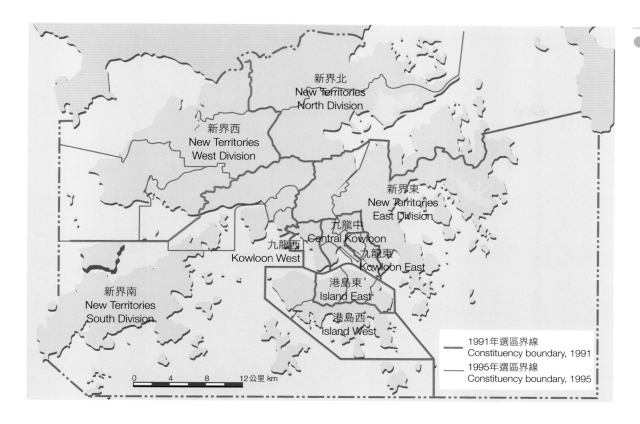

新界北
New Territories
North Division

新界西
New Territories
West Division

新界東
New Territories
East Division

九龍中
Central Kowloon

九龍西
Kowloon West

九龍東
Kowloon East

港島東
Island East

新界南
New Territories
South Division

港島西
Island West

1991年選區界線
Constituency boundary, 1991
1995年選區界線
Constituency boundary, 1995

0   4   8   12公里 km

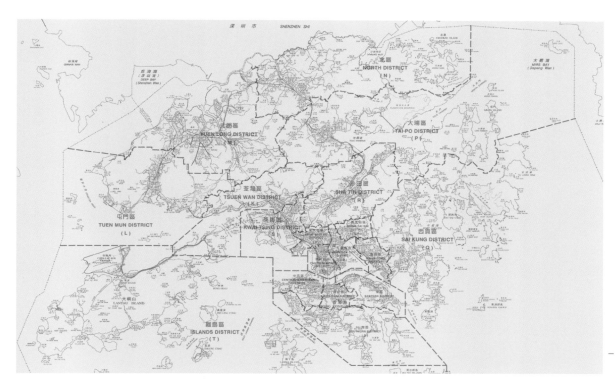

2007年區議會選區分界
District Council electoral boundaries,
2007

區界線
District boundary

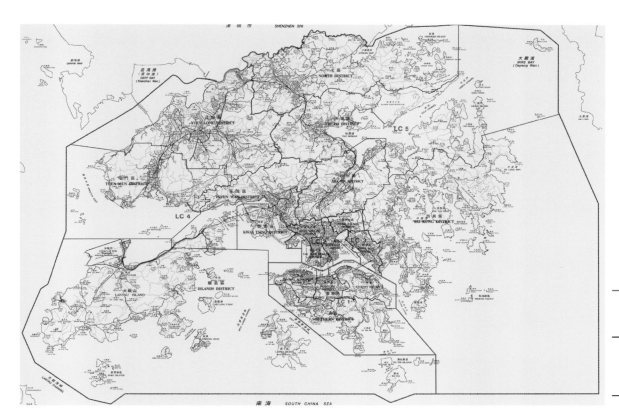

2008年立法會選區分界
Legislative Council electoral boundaries,
2008

2008年立法會地方選區界線
(與區界線重疊)
2008 Legislative Council
Geographical constituency area boundary
(coincides with district boundary)

區界線
District boundary

LC 1   2008年立法會地方選區代號
2008 Legislative Council
Geographical constituency area code

特別行政區界
Boundary of Special Administrative Region

Economic
Development

II. 經濟

01 對外貿易：1841-1949　External Trade: 1841-1949

貿易是香港開埠的基礎。在香港160年的歷史裡，前半是基於以鴉片為主的"三角貿易"。

1841-1910年：以鴉片為主的三角貿易

這一時期，香港是三角貿易（即中國、英國和印度）的中樞港。在這個體系中，中國向印度和英國輸出茶、絲、瓷器和白銀，印度向中國輸出鴉片和棉花，英國向中國及印度輸出百貨，印度向英國輸出棉花。1841年前相當一段時間，英國向中國平均每年輸出3萬箱鴉片（每箱約120磅）。香港開埠之後，每年從印度平均進口4.5萬箱。1850年代增至6.2萬箱。自1856年起鴉片貿易合法化後，年均更高達約9萬箱。1900年代，因為內地自己生產等原因，香港進口鴉片減為每年平均3萬箱。1910年鴉片貿易列為非法，進口鴉片進一步下降。1920年代每年只有約1,000箱。香港進口的鴉片約3/4是轉口至中國內地的，因此在150年的英殖民地統治中，大約一半時間，鴉片成為主要的商品，也是政府在土地之後的第二大財政收入。但實際上，土地收入也只是鴉片貿易利潤的部份轉移，三角貿易基本上是鴉片貿易。

1910-1950年：食物和布匹

自鴉片被列為非法後，香港的轉口貿易轉趨正常。以1932年為例，食物和布匹佔全部輸入的一半，也是全部轉口的2/3。貿易夥伴仍以中國內地及英國為主，其次是日本和東南亞地區。以1932年為例，中國內地來源佔全部輸入的35%，英國及海外屬地佔15%。轉口貨則48%輸往中國內地，15%輸往英國及其屬地。

香港：中國勞工的出口港

在150年的香港與世界經濟關係中，還有一件不光彩的事。在1849年至1930年間，香港是中國勞工出口的主要港口。從1849年的323人起，發展至1880年代的每年平均約20萬人。1910-1923年，年平均仍在10萬人以上。這些"豬仔"被運送至北美洲、中南美洲、澳洲和東南亞地區，做種植園、礦山及鐵路公路工程的勞工。香港的"豬仔館"及輪船公司賺了不少。這些勞工在異地勞役致死，及在長途海運中死亡的比率很高。如在1848-1857年，運往古巴的23,928人中，途中死亡的達25%。

Trade was the raison d'etre of Hong Kong's founding. The first half of its 160 years of history was based on opium.

1841-1910: Trianglar Trade based on opium

Hong Kong was then an entrepôt in the trianglar trade between China, UK and India. For a considerable period of time before 1841, UK exported annually about 30,000 chests (1 chest=120 lbs.) of opium to China. Hong Kong served as its trans-shipment hub since 1841, importing about 45,000 chests annually from India. In the 1850s, it rose to 62,000 chests. Since the import of opium was legalised by China in 1856, Hong Kong's annual in-take jumped to 90,000 chests. Around 3/4 of the opium were re-exported into China. However since the beginning of the 20th century, Chinese production and the international ban on opium trade depressed import demand. The annual import of Hong Kong dropped to 30,000 chests in 1900-1910. It was only around 1,000 chests a year in the 1910s. The money derived from opium trade formed the second largest source of government revenue after proceeds from land sales.

1910-1950: Food and Textiles

Since opium trade was made illegal, Hong Kong's re-export trade changed to focus on normal conmodities. In 1932, food and textiles formed about half of the imports, and 2/3 of the re-exports. Mainland and UK remained as Hong Kong's major trade partners, followed by Japan and Southeast Asia. In 1932, 35% of the imports came from the mainland; UK and British dependent territories accounted for 15%; 48% of re-exports went into the mainland, and 15% to UK and its dependents.

Hong Kong as a labour export port

From 1849 to 1930, Hong Kong served as mainland's largest port for the export of cheap labourers. In 1849, only 323 were shipped to the New World. The yearly average rose to 200,000 in the 1880s. Over 100,000 annually were shipped in 1910-1923 to the Americas, Australasia and Southeast Asia to work in plantations, mines and railway construction projects. Hong Kong's 'labour agents' and shipping companies profited much from such indecent trade. Inhumane situation prevailed in the drafting, shipping and deployment of such labour. Of those that were shipped to Cuba in 1848-1857 (23,928), around 25% died on their way.

● 1841 - 1910 年進出口商品構成圖　Composition of import and export, 1841-1910

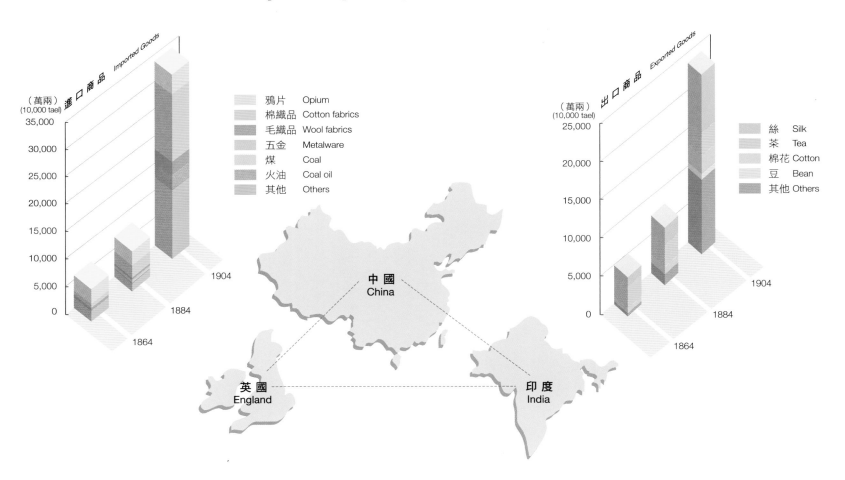

1884-1930 年中國的外貿夥伴　China's trading partners, 1884-1930

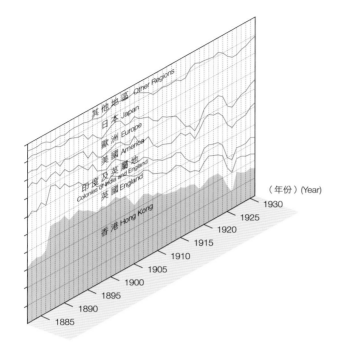

香港經濟發展的歷史軌跡　History of Hong Kong's economic development

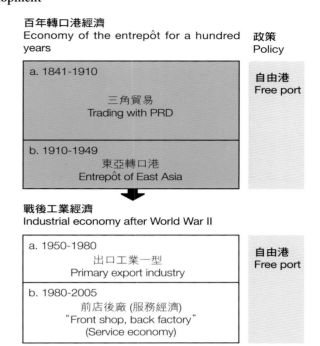

百年轉口港經濟
Economy of the entrepôt for a hundred years

政策
Policy

| a. 1841-1910 三角貿易 Trading with PRD | 自由港 Free port |
| b. 1910-1949 東亞轉口港 Entrepôt of East Asia | |

戰後工業經濟
Industrial economy after World War II

| a. 1950-1980 出口工業一型 Primary export industry | 自由港 Free port |
| b. 1980-2005 前店後廠 (服務經濟) "Front shop, back factory" (Service economy) | |

1910-1950年進出口商品構成圖　Composition of import and export, 1910-1950

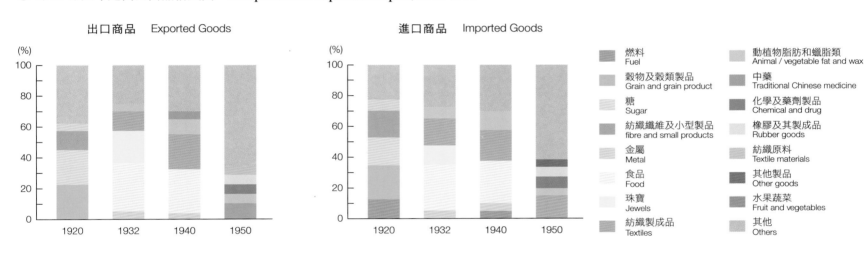

出口商品　Exported Goods

進口商品　Imported Goods

燃料　Fuel
穀物及穀類製品　Grain and grain product
糖　Sugar
紡織纖維及小型製品　fibre and small products
金屬　Metal
食品　Food
珠寶　Jewels
紡織製成品　Textiles

動植物脂肪和蠟脂類　Animal / vegetable fat and wax
中藥　Traditional Chinese medicine
化學及藥劑製品　Chemical and drug
橡膠及其製成品　Rubber goods
紡織原料　Textile materials
其他製品　Other goods
水果蔬菜　Fruit and vegetables
其他　Others

1920-1950 年進出口夥伴構成圖　Composition of import and export partners

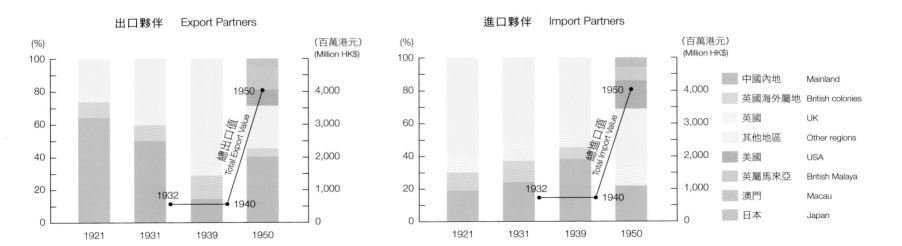

出口夥伴　Export Partners

進口夥伴　Import Partners

中國內地　Mainland
英國海外屬地　British colonies
英國　UK
其他地區　Other regions
美國　USA
英屬馬來亞　British Malaya
澳門　Macau
日本　Japan

02 對外貿易：1951-2007 External Trade: 1951-2007

1951-1980年：工業出口帶動的貿易

　　香港經濟由戰前的轉口經濟轉為出口導向型工業經濟，貿易夥伴和貨品構成也起了變化。貿易夥伴主要是以美國為首的工業國。本地製造的工業品成為主要的出口品。進口除了食物、燃料外，還包括機器、工業原料及半製成品。

1951-1980: Led by export-oriented industrialization

After WWII, the former entrepôt economy was replaced by a new export-led industrial economy with accompanying changes in the composition of trade. The US and other industrialized countries became Hong Kong's major trading partners as local manufactured products figured as major exports. Besides food and fuel, machinery, industrial raw materials and parts and components dominated the imports.

● 1994年貿易進口分佈　Distribution of import, 1994

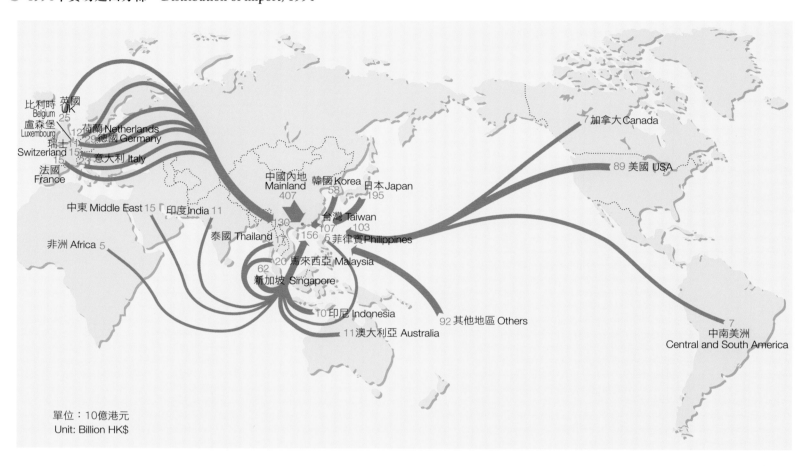

單位：10億港元
Unit: Billion HK$

● 2007年貿易進口分佈　Distribution of import, 2007

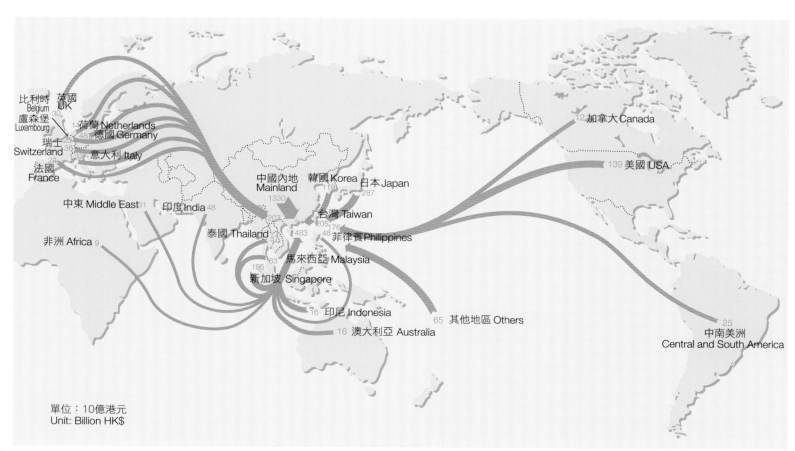

單位：10億港元
Unit: Billion HK$

1980-2007年：內地成為最大貿易夥伴

由於中國內地改革開放，香港工業北移，中國內地在出口、進口及轉口方面都成為香港的最大夥伴。轉口更迅速復蘇為主流，本地製品因而在出口構成中大幅度下降。

1980-2007: The mainland became the largest trade partner

China's economic reform since 1978 and Hong Kong's increased factor costs induced a large-scale northern shift of local industries into the Pearl River Delta. The mainland became Hong Kong's major partner in export, import and re-export. Resurgence of re-export was concurrent with the rapid decline of local manufacturing. Since 2000, this hollowing out of local industries and rapid expansion of export industries on the mainland fuelled Hong Kong's export of services and third-party trade.

● 1951-2007年進口商品與地區構成　Commodity and regional composition-imports, 1951-2007

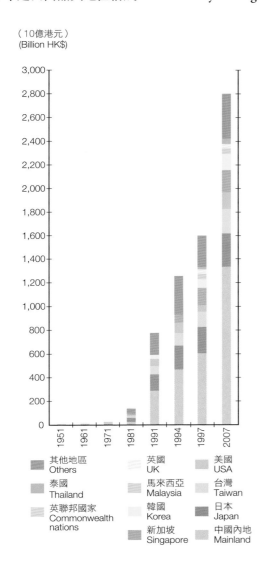

（10億港元）
(Billion HK$)

其他地區 Others
泰國 Thailand
英聯邦國家 Commonwealth nations
新加坡 Singapore
英國 UK
馬來西亞 Malaysia
韓國 Korea
美國 USA
台灣 Taiwan
日本 Japan
中國內地 Mainland

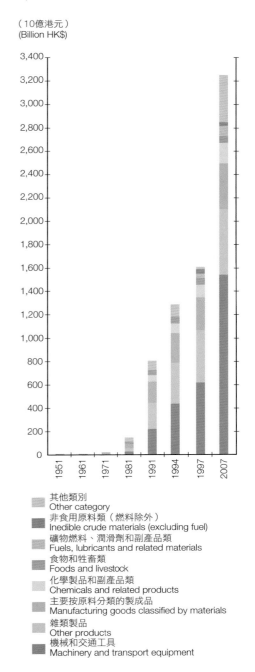

（10億港元）
(Billion HK$)

其他類別 Other category
非食用原料類（燃料除外）Inedible crude materials (excluding fuel)
礦物燃料、潤滑劑和副產品類 Fuels, lubricants and related materials
食物和牲畜類 Foods and livestock
化學製品和副產品類 Chemicals and related products
主要按原料分類的製成品 Manufacturing goods classified by materials
雜類製品 Other products
機械和交通工具 Machinery and transport equipment

● 1983-2007年貿易趨勢：入口，本地產品出口和轉口　Trading trend 1983 - 2007: import, domestic export and re-export

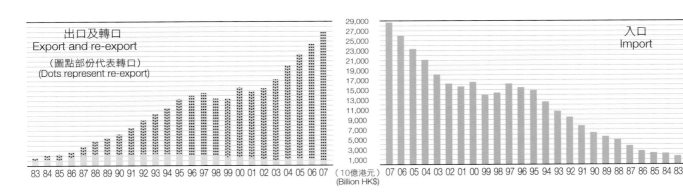

出口及轉口 Export and re-export
（圖點部份代表轉口）
(Dots represent re-export)

入口 Import

（10億港元）
(Billion HK$)

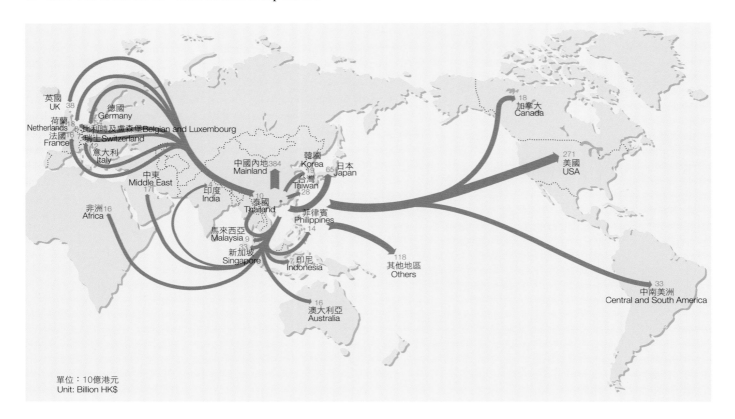

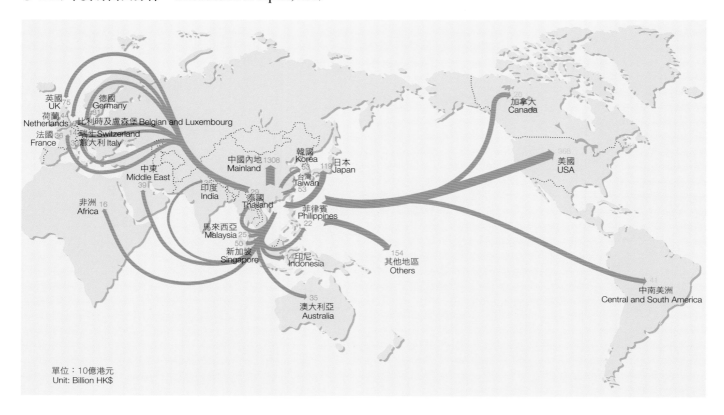

● 1951-2007年出口（包括轉口）商品與地區構成　Commodity and regional composition of export (including re-export), 1951-2007

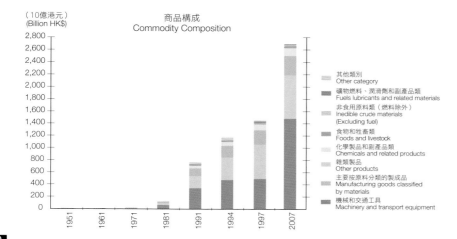

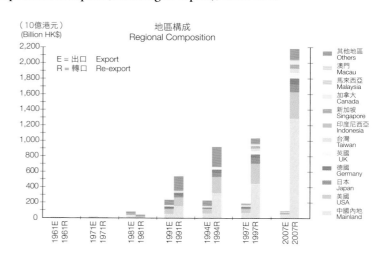

03 海港 The Seaport

戰後香港經濟轉型為以出口型工業為主，但仍極依賴貿易。因此，香港的海港一直是她的重要生存因素之一。

港區的發展，不但因應貿易量的增加，也因應海運技術和城市發展而演變。香港在1990年代已成為世界上最大的貨櫃碼頭港，但不少船隻仍在海中的浮標上碇泊和裝卸貨物，成為海運特色和高效率的原因之一。隨着貨櫃船對深水和陸域空間的新要求，港區已由維多利亞港中部及兩旁，移至北九龍半島的西邊和大嶼山之間的寬闊海面。

Before WWII, trade was Hong Kong's economic mainstay. The post-war economy that relied on export-oriented industries was equally trade-creative. Thus, the seaport remained an important factor in Hong Kong's economic growth.

Increasing volume of freight, new maritime technology and physical growth of the city led to new developments of the port, as reflected in the location, design and facilities of the terminals. Hong Kong has been the world's largest container port since early 1990s (with the exception of a few years). Yet, mid-stream operation remains a local character that underlies the port's high efficiency and its lack of quay-side space. Demands for deep water and land-side space by container operation accounted for the shift of the port from Victoria Harbour to its western margin and the eastern shore of Lantau, as well as its leapfrogging to Shenzhen.

● 1920 年的香港海港　Port of Hong Kong, 1920

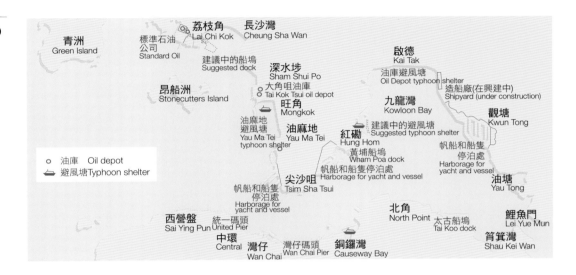

● 1960年的香港海港　Port of Hong Kong, 1960

燈塔 LIGHTHOUSE
燈標 LIGHT BEACON
航道燈光浮標 FAIRWAY LIGHT BUOY
港內日夜風訊處 LOCAL STORM SIGNALS DAY & NIGHT
港內日間風訊處 LOCAL STORM SIGNALS DAY ONLY
港內夜間風訊處 LOCAL STORM SIGNALS NIGHT ONLY
海港檢疫碇泊處 QUARANTINE & IMMIGRATION ANCHORAGE
港口衛生浮筒 PORT HEALTH BUOY
渡海航線 FERRY LINE
帆船航道禁止碇泊區 JUNKWAY PROHIBITED ANCHORAGE
浮筒 MOORING BUOY

香港貨櫃碼頭概況 Overview of Hong Kong container terminal

貨櫃碼頭（編號）Container terminal (No.)	完成年份 Year completed	泊位 Berth	面積（公頃）Terminal area (ha)	岸線長度（米）Quay length (m)	吞吐量（百萬/標準箱）Throughput (million teus)		所轄公司 Operators
					1995	2007	
CT-1	1972	1			* (2)	# (1)	現代貨箱碼頭有限公司 Modern Terminals Limited
CT-2	1973	1			* (2)	# (1)	現代貨箱碼頭有限公司 Modern Terminals Limited
CT-3	1973	1			0.5	>1.2	杜拜環球港務 Dubai Ports World
CT-4	1976	3	152.31	4,484	* (3)	# (5)	香港國際貨櫃碼頭有限公司 Hong Kong International Terminals Limited
CT-5	1975	1			* (2)	# (1)	現代貨箱碼頭有限公司 Modern Terminals Limited
CT-6	1988	3			* (3)	# (5)	香港國際貨櫃碼頭有限公司 Hong Kong International Terminals Limited
CT-7	1990	4			* (3)	# (5)	香港國際貨櫃碼頭有限公司 Hong Kong International Terminals Limited
CT-8	1993	4	58.54	1,380	1.8	# (5)+>2	中遠—國際及亞洲貨櫃碼頭有限公司 COSCO-HIT Terminals(Hong Kong) Limited and Asia Container Terminals Limited
CT-9	2003	6	68.00	1,940	1.8	# (1)+# (5)	現代貨箱碼頭有限公司及香港國際貨櫃碼頭有限公司 Modern Terminals Limited and Hong Kong International Terminals Limited
總數 Total		24	278.85	7,804	7.2	17.3	

* (2)：1, 2, 5 號吞吐量共1.6百萬標準箱。
*(2): Total throughput of CT 1, 2, 5 were 1.6 million teus.

* (3)：4, 6, 7 號吞吐量共3.3百萬標準箱。
*(3): Total throughput of CT 4, 6, 7 were 3.3 million teus.

(1)：1, 2, 5, 9 號吞吐量共5.7百萬標準箱。
#(1): Total throughput of CT 1, 2, 5, 9 were 5.7 million teus.

(5)：4, 6, 7, 9 號吞吐量共9.0百萬標準箱。
#(5): Total throughput of CT 4, 6, 7, 9 were 9.0 million teus.

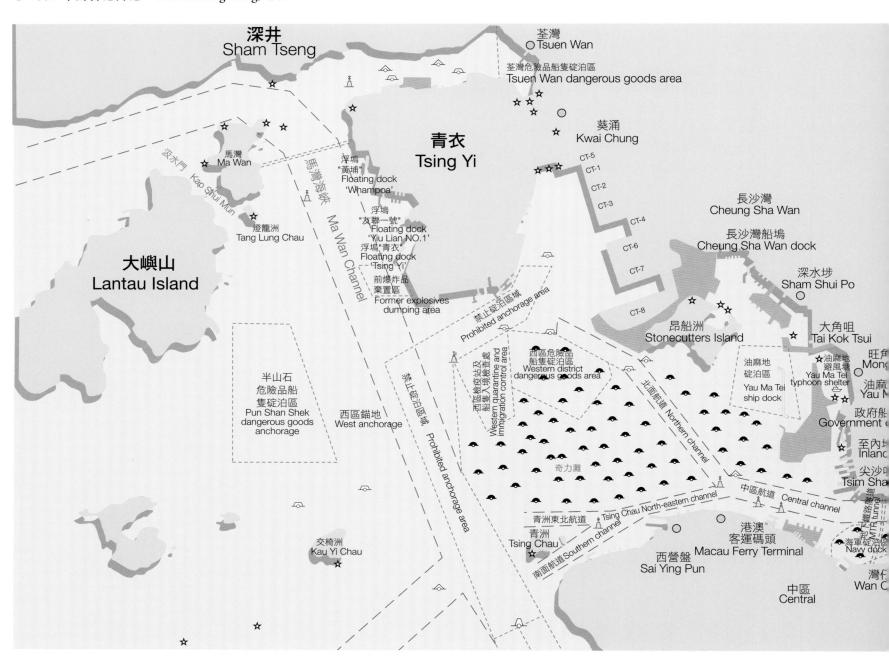

深井
Sham Tseng

荃灣
Tsuen Wan

荃灣危險品船隻碇泊區
Tsuen Wan dangerous goods area

青衣
Tsing Yi

葵涌
Kwai Chung

馬灣
Ma Wan

長沙灣
Cheung Sha Wan

浮塢
"黃埔"
Floating dock
'Whampoa'

長沙灣船塢
Cheung Sha Wan dock

燈籠洲
Tang Lung Chau

浮塢
"友聯一號"
Floating dock
'Yiu Lian NO.1'

深水埗
Sham Shui Po

浮塢"青衣"
Floating dock
'Tsing Yi'

大嶼山
Lantau Island

前爆炸品
棄置區
Former explosives
dumping area

禁止碇泊區域
Prohibited anchorage area

昂船洲
Stonecutters Island

大角咀
Tai Kok Tsui

半山石
危險品船
隻碇泊區
Pun Shan Shek
dangerous goods
anchorage

西區檢疫站及
船隻入境檢查處
Western quarantine and
immigration control area

西區危險品
船隻碇泊區
Western district
dangerous goods area

油麻地
碇泊區
Yau Ma Tei
ship dock

油麻地
避風塘
Yau Ma Tei
typhoon shelter

旺角
Mong

西區錨地
West anchorage

禁止碇泊區域
Prohibited anchorage area

北面航道 Northern channel

油麻
Yau M

政府船
Government

至內地
Inland

奇力灘

交椅洲
Kau Yi Chau

青洲東北航道
Tsing Chau North-eastern channel

中區航道 Central channel

尖沙咀
Tsim Sha

青洲
Tsing Chau

港澳
客運碼頭
Macau Ferry Terminal

西營盤
Sai Ying Pun

海軍碇泊區
Navy dock

南面航道Southern channel

中區
Central

灣仔
Wan C

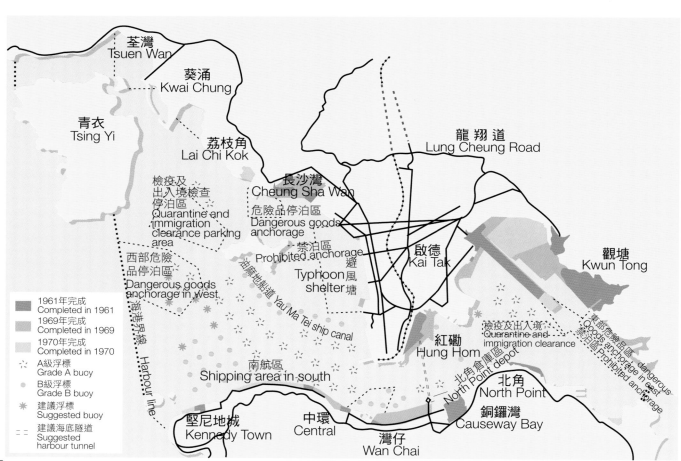

荃灣
Tsuen Wan

葵涌
Kwai Chung

龍翔道
Lung Cheung Road

青衣
Tsing Yi

荔枝角
Lai Chi Kok

長沙灣
Cheung Sha Wan

檢疫及
出入境檢查
停泊區
Quarantine and
immigration
clearance parking
area

危險品停泊區
Dangerous goods
anchorage

啟德
Kai Tak

觀塘
Kwun Tong

西部危險
品停泊區
Dangerous goods
anchorage in west

禁泊區
Prohibited anchorage

避
風
塘

油麻地船塢 Yau Ma Tei ship canal

Typhoon
shelter

檢疫及出入境
Quarantine and
immigration clearance

東部危險品停泊區
Goods anchorage in east
禁泊區 Prohibited anchorage

香港界線 Harbour line

紅磡
Hung Hom

北角倉庫碼頭
North Point depot

南航區
Shipping area in south

1961年完成
Completed in 1961

1969年完成
Completed in 1969

1970年完成
Completed in 1970

北角
North Point

北角
North Point

A級浮標
Grade A buoy

B級浮標
Grade B buoy

建議浮標
Suggested buoy

建議海底隧道
Suggested
harbour tunnel

堅尼地城
Kennedy Town

中環
Central

灣仔
Wan Chai

銅鑼灣
Causeway Bay

香港(啟德)
國際機場
Hong Kong (Kai Tak)
International Airport

九龍
Kowloon

牛頭角
Ngau Tau Kok

觀塘
Kwun Tong

調景嶺
Tiu Keng Leng

將軍澳
Tseung Kwan O

土瓜灣
...wa Wan

紅磡
...ung Hom

東區檢疫站及
船隻入境檢查處
Eastern quarantine and
immigration control area

Hung Hom tunnel

...eastern corridor

東面航道 Eastern channel

東區海底隧道
Eastern harbour tunnel

禁止停泊區
Prohibited anchorage area

油塘
Yau Tong

北角
North Point

鰂魚涌
Quarry Bay

將軍澳
危險品
船隻碇泊區
Tseung Kwan O
dangerous goods area

銅鑼灣
...useway Bay

鯉魚門 Lei Yue Mun

佛堂洲
Fat Tong Chau

筲箕灣
Shau Kei Wan

香港島
...ong Kong Island

柴灣
Chai Wan

公共貨物裝卸區
Public cargo
working area (PCWA)

助航燈標
Navigational buoy

燈標
Light beacon

繫泊浮泡
Mooring buoy

有燈繫泊浮泡
Mooring buoy with light

避風塘
Typhoon shelter

填海區
Reclamation area

● 1983-2008年進出遠洋輪船的數量與裝卸貨量　Number of ocean vessel arrivals and departures, and amount of cargo handled

年份 Year	船隻總數 Total vessels	總註冊噸位（萬噸） Total registered tonnage (10,000 tons)	貨物（千噸）Cargo (1,000 tons)		
			卸Discharged	裝Loaded	總數Total
1983	22,959	13,578	24,138	7,430	31,568
1984	23,783	13,692	26,451	8,842	35,293
1985	26,747	15,158	29,657	10,032	39,689
1986	28,326	16,002	35,101	12,367	47,468
1987	30,481	17,261	38,942	14,615	53,557
1988	34,244	18,980	44,258	17,063	61,321
1989	38,141	20,679	45,792	18,863	64,655
1990	40,865	22,059	46,242	19,766	66,008
1991	45,348	23,390	52,899	23,546	76,445
1992	57,417	26,108	58,882	24,500	83,382
1993	66,153	29,855	68,226	27,873	96,199
1994	73,749	32,430	76,672	34,274	110,946
1995	82,759	34,595	87,048	40,127	127,175
1996	82,132	36,444	86,094	39,145	125,338
1997	86,591	39,756	91,950	41,351	133,301
1998	81,780	41,622	90,104	37,378	127,482
1999	74,480	43,063	88,621	39,601	128,222
2000	74,051	48,468	88,003	42,934	130,937
2001	73,770	54,968	88,506	42,170	130,676
2002	70,530	58,362	93,444	44,857	138,301
2003	70,910	59,119	99,363	49,255	148,618
2004	71,370	61,263	104,612	54,006	158,617
2005	78,380	649,891	106,695	54,772	161,467
2006	78,460	694,658	106,579	59,629	166,208
2007	74,420	742,955	109,435	67,912	177,347
2008	71,820	76,795	110,220	69,755	179,974

● 香港、新加坡、上海、深圳的貨櫃吞吐量比較　Comparison of freight handling capacity between Hong Kong, Singapore, Shanghai and Shenzhen

單位：千個20呎貨櫃
Unit: 1,000 containers
(With length of 1/3 m per container)

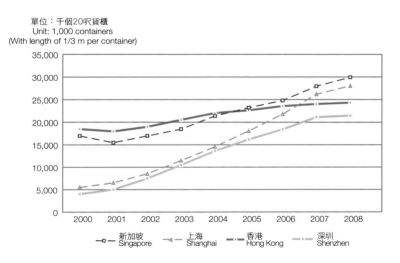

─□─ 新加坡
Singapore　─△─ 上海
Shanghai　─── 香港
Hong Kong　─·─ 深圳
Shenzhen

04　倉庫與海港遠景　Warehouses and the Port's Future

倉庫

倉庫用地是港口及貿易發展的伴隨產物。

早期的倉庫集中在維多利亞港兩翼的尖沙咀、紅磡，以及香港島的中環、上環和北角等地區。

貨櫃海運技術的出現，使舊市區的倉庫變得不適合。一些主要的舊倉庫公司，如九龍倉、會德豐及和記，在1970年代逐步發展成為包括地產的多元功能公司。原來的倉庫用地也多數發展為住宅及商業用地。

主要港區倉庫已轉移至葵涌貨櫃碼頭附近，因此荃灣是目前倉庫用地及倉庫行業最集中的地區，其次是觀塘。這兩個地區也是1970-1990年間的大工業區，是進出口服務需求比較集中的地區。空運量的增加，也使啟德機場附近成為新的倉庫區。

1980年代末起，市區的擠迫使部份倉庫遷往沙田新市鎮，形成了第三個主要倉庫區。

Warehouses

Warehousing accompanies port and trade development.

In the early days, warehouses were concentrated in Tsim Sha Tsui, Hung Hom, Central, Sheung Wan and North Point.

Container technology changed the space requirement. Urban growth added further pressure. Since 1970, Hong Kong's main port zone had been relocated to Kwai Chung and Kwun Tong, Hong Kong's largest industrial areas. The proximity of Kwun Tong's location to the airport accounted for its significance as air freight increased. Major warehousing operators had also changed into multi-functional corporations and redeveloped old urban warehouses into residential and commercial uses.

In the late 1980s, urban congestion had led to leapfrogging of warehousing to Shatin New Town—the third largest warehousing location.

● 1970年工業及倉庫分佈圖　Industrial and allied uses, 1970

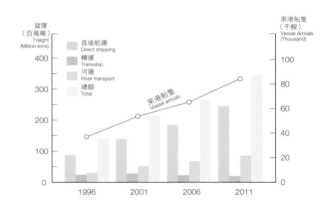

● 港口貨運現狀及預測　Port cargo

● 1994年倉庫分佈　Distribution of warehouses, 1994

● 1975-2007年倉庫面積及行業就業人數　Area of warehouses and number of employed persons in the industry, 1975-2007

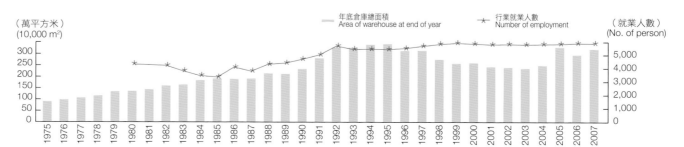

海港遠景

香港在1996年作出港區規劃，並批准九號(CT9)貨櫃碼頭的興建。另外，為了配合深圳大港的建設，在大嶼山以西準備挖築一條新的深水航道，這將會使南中國的國際海運設施分佈比現在更為分散。

深圳的鹽田、媽灣和珠海的高欄近年已崛起成為大型海港，並分流了不少珠三角進出口貨櫃業務。由於它們仍然是由香港公司合資，實際上成為香港港區和海運跨界發展的重要方向。這將會形成一個新的海港系統。但香港在1996年規劃的10號至16號碼頭(CT10-CT16)是否有需要建設已成疑問。

The Port's Future

In 1996, the last colonial government announced a future plan for the port and sanctioned the construction of Container Terminal 9 (CT 9). Besides, it proposed to dredge a deep fair-way west of Lantau.

Since the late 1990s, Yantian and Ma Wan in Shenzhen and Golan in Zhuhai have emerged as major nearby ports. They have diverted substantial imports and exports of the Pearl River Delta from Hong Kong. As Hong Kong terminal operators have substantial stacks in them, they in fact form a port cluster with the Hong Kong port. CT 10-CT 16, as planned in 1996, may never be realized, as Hong Kong lacks cost advantage and cargo source.

● 1996年港區遠景規劃　Port planning vision, 1996

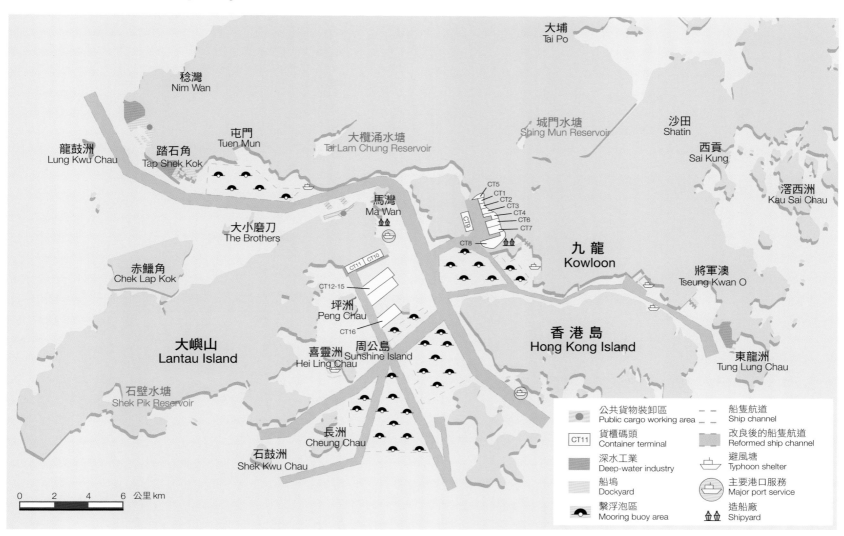

● 2007年港區遠景規劃　Port planning vision, 2007

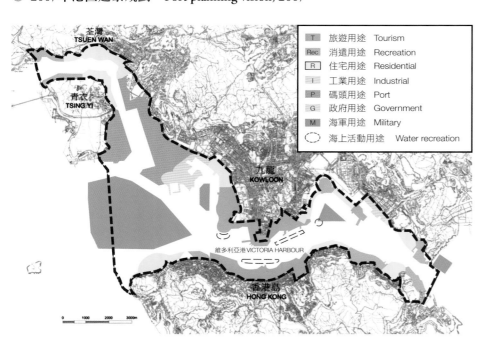

港口設施用地需求預測
Estimates on demand for port facilities

港口設施 Port facilities	1996	2001	2006	2011
		累積總數 Cumulative total		
貨櫃碼頭 Container terminals				
泊位數目 Number of berths	15	29	39	42
用地面積（公頃） Area (ha)	323	533	653	789
貨櫃碼頭後勤用地 Container terminal back-up area	162	258	319	395
中流貨物處理區 Mid-stream cargo handling				
濱水區長度（米） Length of the waterfront area (m)		6,777	6,927	7,202
用地面積（公頃） Area (ha)		114	116	122
內河貿易碼頭 River trade terminal				
濱水區長度（米） Length of the waterfront area (m)	2,732	6,051	4,390	4,665
用地面積（公頃） Area (ha)	50	109	157	231
公眾貨物裝卸區 Public Cargo Working Area (PCWA)	20	20	20	20
總用地面積（公頃） Total area (ha)	555	1,034	1,265	1,557

05 機場 Airport

啟德機場（1924-1998）

啟德機場始建於1924年。它在1957年時曾有兩條1,663米和1,447米的跑道，年客量13萬人，貨量42萬噸，當時已成為大型國際機場。1962年擴充時改為單跑道。1996年總客流量為2,960萬人次，貨運量156萬噸，飛機升降架次158,797架。貨運量是世界第二大，而客運則排名第四。

啟德機場始建時，離當時的九龍市區較遠。第二次世界大戰後，城市的急速發展將它團團包圍，使它和稠密的住宅區相接。由於啟德機場達致飽和，港英政府在1989年單方面提出建新機場。新機場選點並不理想，成為中英政府在有關過渡安排上的最重大爭議。中英政府在1991年底達成"諒解備忘錄"，協議香港加快新替代性機場的建設。赤鱲角機場啟用後，碩大的飛機掠過九龍市區街道上空的圖景已成為歷史。

機場對香港的貢獻很大，除了外國旅客主要由航機抵港外，香港進出口和轉口貨物以價值計有相當部份是空運的。1996年共有66家航空公司擁有往返香港的定期航線，它們每周有1,500次不同的往返航班，將香港和世界上約100個城市連接。在2000年，香港共有三家本地航空公司：國泰航空公司擁有至77個城市的航班，港龍航空公司擁有至79個城市(主要是中國內地城市)的航班，而香港航空擁有35個城市的航班。

Kai Tak International Airport (1924-1998)

Kai Tak was constructed in 1924. In 1957, it developed into a two-runway system and registered a passenger and cargo volume of 130,000 persons and 420,000 tonnes, ranking as a major international airport. In 1962, it reverted back to a single runway. In 1996, it handled 29 million passengers and 1.56 million tonnes of cargo, ranking second in passenger and fourth in cargo volume in the world.

In 1924, the airport was situated far from the urban district in Kowloon. After WWII, it was soon engulfed by urban development, yielding spectacular views of aircrafts almost touching high-rise buildings prior to landing. In 1989, the last colonial government unilaterally announced the construction of a replacement airport at Chek Lap Kok. The new site is other than ideal. The proposal became a 1997 transitional issue between the British and Chinese governments. An agreement was reached in late 1991 and the Chinese government guaranteed its rapid construction.

The airport served the local economy by bringing in tourists. It also shipped fair proportions of Hong Kong's imports, exports and re-exports. In 1996, there were 66 airlines serving the airport, linking Hong Kong with over 100 cities by about 1,500 scheduled flights per week. In 2000, of the three local airlines, Cathay Pacific operated flights to 77 cities, Dragon Air to 79 cities, and Hong Kong Air to 35 cities.

● 啟德機場航空攝影圖　Kai Tak Airport: air photograph

● 香港舊啟德機場擴建過程　Expansion process of Kai Tak Airport

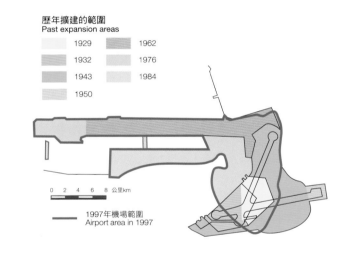

歷年擴建的範圍
Past expansion areas
1929 1962
1932 1976
1943 1984
1950

1997年機場範圍
Airport area in 1997

● 啟德初步發展大綱圖　Preliminary outline development plan for Kai Tak

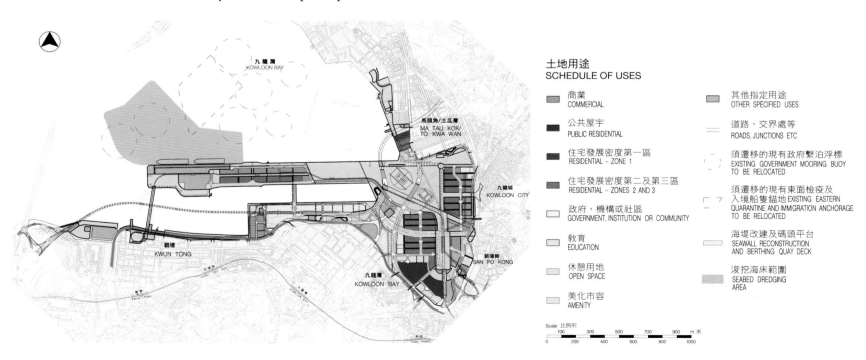

土地用途
SCHEDULE OF USES

商業 COMMERCIAL
公共屋宇 PUBLIC RESIDENTIAL
住宅發展密度第一區 RESIDENTIAL - ZONE 1
住宅發展密度第二及第三區 RESIDENTIAL - ZONES 2 AND 3
政府、機構或社區 GOVERNMENT, INSTITUTION OR COMMUNITY
教育 EDUCATION
休憩用地 OPEN SPACE
美化市容 AMENITY

其他指定用途 OTHER SPECIFIED USES
道路、交界處等 ROADS, JUNCTIONS ETC
須遷移的現有政府繫泊浮標 EXISTING GOVERNMENT MOORING BUOY TO BE RELOCATED
須遷移的現有東面檢疫及入境船隻錨地 EXISTING EASTERN QUARANTINE AND IMMIGRATION ANCHORAGE TO BE RELOCATED
海堤改建及碼頭平台 SEAWALL RECONSTRUCTION AND BERTHING QUAY DECK
浚挖海床範圍 SEABED DREDGING AREA

赤鱲角國際機場（1998年啟用）

新的機場位於大嶼山北的赤鱲角。面積1,255公頃，建築成本為707億元，加上配套的各項核心工程，總成本為1,564億元，是世界上最昂貴的單項工程。它的總面積和預計總客運量均比啟德機場大三倍左右。1998年啟用的是3,800米長的單跑道及Y字形的客運大樓的一部份，估計可處理年客流量約3,500萬人次。第二條跑道在1999年完成。

2008年，機場已有兩條跑道和兩個客運大樓，客運量達4,860萬人，貨量360萬噸，每小時最高升降56架次。但由於自1990年代中起，珠三角分別建成澳門、珠海、深圳和廣州新機場，香港機場的客貨運年增長率不斷下降，目前務求與深圳機場加強合作，以保持中國南方門戶的地位。

Chek Lap Kok International Airport (opened in 1998)

Located on North Lantau with a 1,255-ha site, its construction cost was HK$ 70.7 billion. With the addition of supplementary road and rail projects etc., the total cost was HK$ 156.4 billion, making it the world's most expensive single construction project. Its passenger capacity and site area are about 3 times of that of Kai Tak. At the 1998 opening, it had 1 runway and 1 terminal with an annual passenger capacity of 35 million. The second runway was completed in 1999. In 2008, it operated two runways and 2 terminals, and handled 48.6 million passengers and 3.6 million tonnes of cargo. The hourly peak craft movements was 56.

Due to the opening of new airports in Macau, Zhuhai, Shenzhen and Guangzhou, growth in Hong Kong's airport slackened in recent years. Hong Kong currently seeks cooperation with Shenzhen Airport to maintain its gateway position in South China.

● 香港赤鱲角新機場規劃圖（1997） Plan of the new Hong Kong International Airport at Chek Lap Kok (1997)

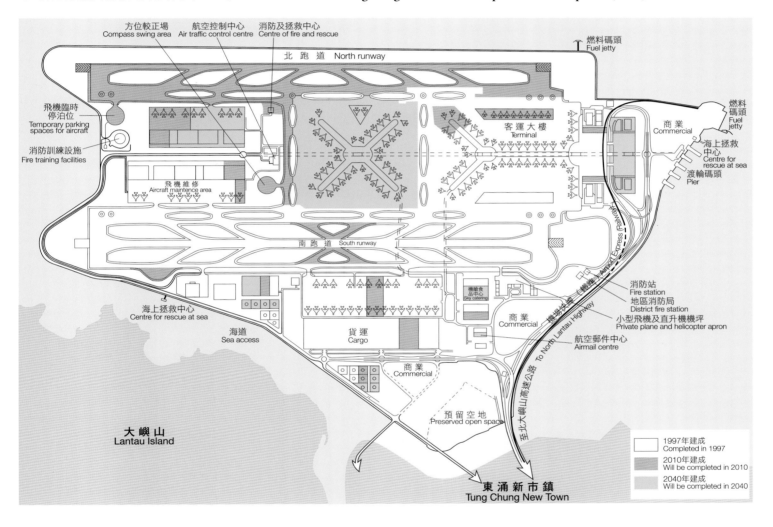

空運記錄及預測
Record and forecast of air traffic

新舊機場的容量比較
Comparison of capacity between the old and new Hong Kong Airport

設施 Facilities	啟德機場 Kai Tak Airport	赤鱲角新機場 Chek Lap Kok Airport	
		初期 Phase I	現況 Present
機場總面積（公頃） Total airport site area (ha)	333.8	1,248	1,255
每年客運量（萬人次） Annual Passenger throughput (10,000)	2,950（1996實際數字） (Actual count in 1996)	3,500（計劃容量） (Planning capacity)	4778.3
每年貨運量（萬噸） Annual Air cargo throughput (10,000 tons)	156（1996實際數字） (Actual count in 1996)	300（計劃容量） (Planning capacity)	374.2
跑道 Runways	1	1	2
跑道長度（米） Runway length (m)	3,393	3,800	3,800／每條 each
滑行道長度（米） Taxiway length (m)	7,100	26,000	N/A
停機坪佔地（平方千米） Apron area (km²)	1.03	1.25	N/A
客運大樓總面積（平方千米） Total passenger terminal floor area (km²)	0.066	0.515	0.71
零售面積（平方米） Retail areas (m²)	13,600	30,000	N/A
店舖數目 Retail outlets	40	120	320
停機位 Aircraft Parking Bays	69	78	125
自動行人道 People movers	0	48	N/A
候機大堂座位 Lounge seating	3,812	12,530	16,500
航班資料顯示板 Flight information display boards	283	2,000	N/A

06 旅遊業　Tourism

　　香港戰後旅遊業的發展約始於1960年，該年到香港的外國旅客只有約18萬人。當時中國內地來港的旅客並不多。在1960年代和1970年代，香港的旅客資料甚至不將內地及台灣旅客作為一個外來旅客的統計項目。

　　香港旅遊的起飛和中國內地的改革開放有關。自1980年起，到港旅客的數字大幅度上升，13年內的增幅有三倍。中國內地的旅客增長更快，1984-1993年間，由32萬人升至173萬人，即約5.5倍。1996年到港旅客1,170萬人，比上年增長14.7%。旅遊業是主要經濟行業，它在1996年對GDP的貢獻約8%。1996年中國內地旅客佔總旅客量1/4。1997年總旅客量受回歸年限制來港旅客量影響，下降至1,040萬人。亞洲金融風暴因素使1998年來港旅客下降至只有960萬人。

　　從來源看，香港的旅客的確來自世界各大洲，這使香港成為一個真正東西方交匯的國際城市。

Post-WWII tourism began in 1960. In that year, 180,000 tourists arrived, few of whom were from the mainland. In the 1960s and 1970s, the industry did not even count visitors from the mainland and Taiwan as tourists.

The take-off of tourism has been related to the mainland's opening up. In 1980-1993, tourist arrivals escalated by 3-fold with increased mainland tourists. In 1996, tourist arrivals reached 11.7 million, and tourism contributed to 8% of the GDP–its fastest growing sector. In that year, mainland tourists accounted for 1/4 of total arrivals. The drop in 1997 and 1998 was linked to effects of the 'hand-over' ceremony and the Asian Financial Crisis (AFC).

Hong Kong's tourists are from all parts of the world, reflecting its transport hub and international city status and being a confluence between the East and the West.

● 1993年到港旅客來源與人次　Number of visitor arrivals by source 1993

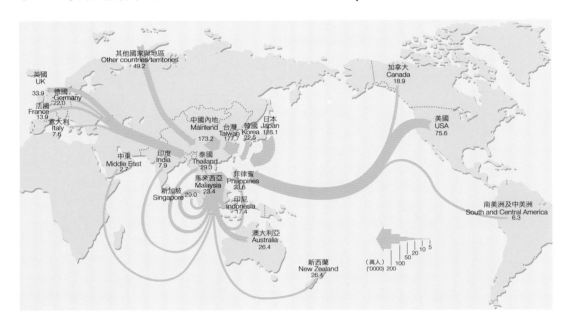

● 1967-1993年到港旅客構成
Composition of passenger arrivals in 1967-1993

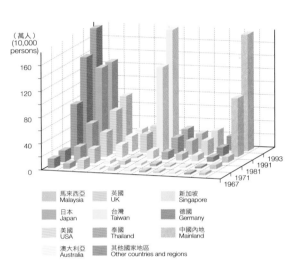

● 2007年到港旅客來源與人次　Number of visitor arrivals by source 2007

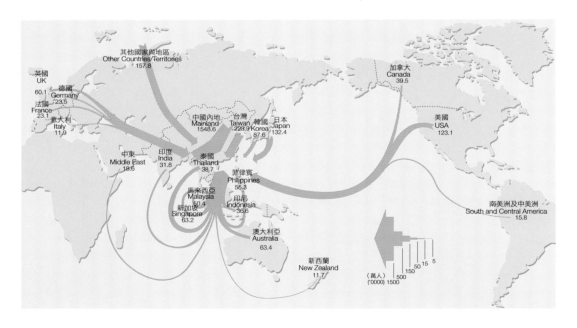

● 旅遊從業員人數　Number of workers in tourism industry

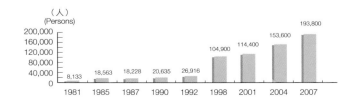

● 旅遊消費額　Tourist spending

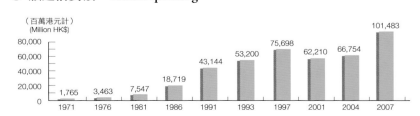

香港的高級酒店集中在中環、灣仔及尖沙咀區，餘下的大多數分佈在九龍半島和香港島北岸其他地區。

香港的旅遊熱點不多，主要是維多利亞港及太平山的景色、淺水灣海濱浴場和香港仔漁村，人工旅遊點如海洋公園（排名世界第四）、大嶼山天壇大佛（世界最大）和2005年在大嶼山建成的迪士尼主題公園。

1998年的亞洲金融風暴和2003年的"沙士"，使香港經濟和旅遊業滑坡。在香港的請求下，中央政府推行了內地部份省市公民來港旅遊"自由行"的新措施，使內地旅客大增，達至總來港旅客人數一半左右，使香港旅遊業產生量與質的變化。

Its star-grade hotels are concentrated in Central, Wan Chai, and Tsim Sha Tsui, reflecting the shopping and convention purposes of most tourists. Recreational attractions include Victoria Harbour, the Peak, Repulse Bay and the Aberdeen fishing port. Since 1980s, man-made attractions have been constructed to boost tourism, such as the Ocean Park (world's number 4), the largest sitting bronze Buddha in Lantau, and the Disney Theme Park.

In 1998-2003, Hong Kong was plagued by AFC and SARS. At the request of the Hong Kong government, Beijing initiated an 'Individual Tourist programme' to relax measures for citizens in selected mainland provinces and cities to visit Hong Kong. It jetted up mainland tourist arrivals which at present accounted for about half of Hong Kong's total tourists.

● **1997年的旅遊點及酒店分佈　Tourist spots and hotel distribution, 1997**

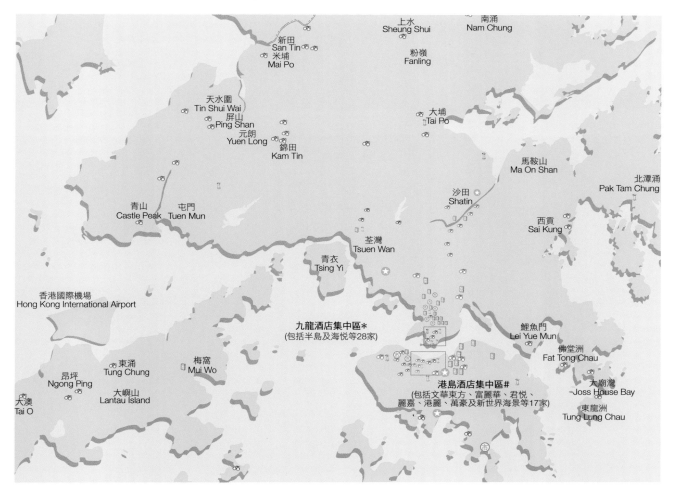

● **2006年海港遠景旅遊規劃　Harbour vision for tourism planning, 2006**

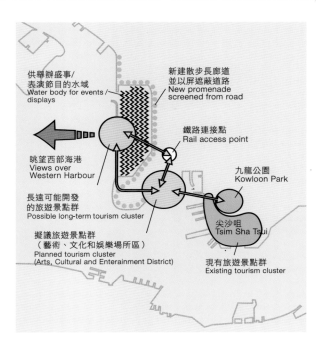

● **酒店房間數目　Number of hotel rooms**

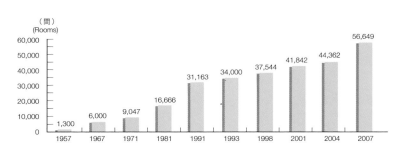

● **酒店從業員人數　Number of hotel workers**

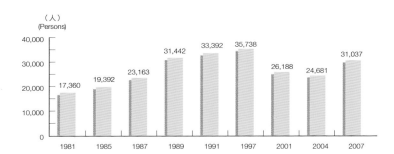

07 公共交通網 Web of Public Transport

香港島首條公路是皇后大道，由上環通至銅鑼灣，於1842年建成。當時皇后大道的主要路段都在維多利亞港岸邊。香港島其他一些主要道路的建成順序是：般含道、堅道（1851），正街、第二街、第三街、東邊街、西邊街、太平街（1860），羅便臣道（1861），寶寧頓道、堅拿道（1864），堅尼地道、寶雲道（1889），麥當奴道（1892），白加道、吉列道（1898），英皇道（1936）。

新界的道路建築，自1900年以來便在東西兩翼展開。舊大埔道1902年由深水埗通至沙田，1914年建至粉嶺。舊青山道屯門至屏山段1910年完成。由九龍至新田的舊青山公路全線在1918年完成。九龍鐵路在1911

Queen's Road, completed in 1842, was the first modern main road. It extended from Sheung Wan to Causeway Bay along the coast. Other roads on the Island were gradually added: Bonham Road and Caine Road (1851); Main Street, Second Street, Third Street, Eastern Street, Western Street, Taiping Street (1860); Robinson Road (1861); Bowrington Road, Canal Road (1864); Kennedy Road, Bowen Road (1889); MacDonnell Road (1892); Barker Road, Chamberlain Road (1898) and King's Road (1936).

Road building linking Kowloon and the New Territories started in 1900. Old Tai Po Road from Sham Shui Po to Shatin was completed in 1902, and extended in 1914 to Fanling. Old Castle Peak Road from Tuen Mun to Ping Shan was

● 1960年水陸交通圖　Marine and land communications in 1960

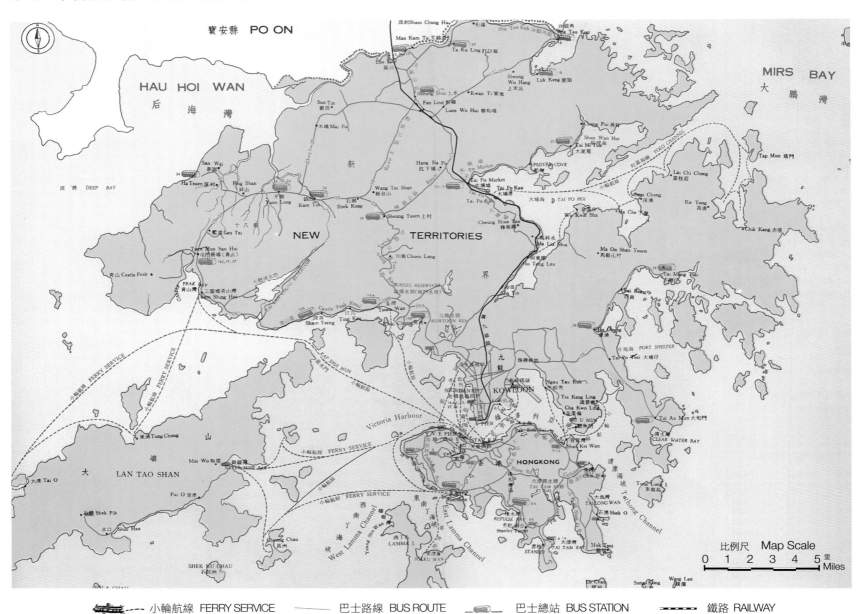

🚢----- 小輪航線 FERRY SERVICE　───── 巴士路線 BUS ROUTE　🚌 巴士總站 BUS STATION　-----・ 鐵路 RAILWAY

1960年新界的公路網　Highway network in the New Territories, 1960

1978年新界的公路網　Highway network in the New Territories, 1978

年完成。因此新界的主要陸上交通線在1920年前基本建成。上述兩條新界的主要大動脈，從1970年代後期起進行了分期改造。至1990年代，緊貼舊大埔道與舊青山道沿線建成了新界環迴公路。

1950年代後期曾有環新界鐵路、環港島九龍地鐵圈及維港大橋的規劃，但都沒有落實。

至1996年止，香港分別建成四條汽車穿山隧道、兩條汽車海底隧道、一條地鐵海底隧道。1997年，又新建成汽車及地鐵海底隧道各一條，跨海的交通網更為完善。以往聯繫九龍、港島及新界離島的渡輪，因而大受影響，航線不斷萎縮。

completed in 1910, and the run to San Tin was finished in 1918. Kowloon Railway was completed in 1911. The main roads had been upgraded in the 1970s, with a New Territories Circular Road added in the 1990s.

In the late 1950s, there were plans for a Circum New Territories Rail, a Hong Kong-Kowloon underground rail circuit, and a harbour bridge. They have not been pursued.

By 1996, 4 road tunnels, 2 vehicular and 1 submarine railway tunnels were in operation. One road, and another submarine rail tunnel were added in 1997. They led to the decline of the ferry in cross-harbour traffic.

● **1997年的公共交通網　Public transport network in 1997**

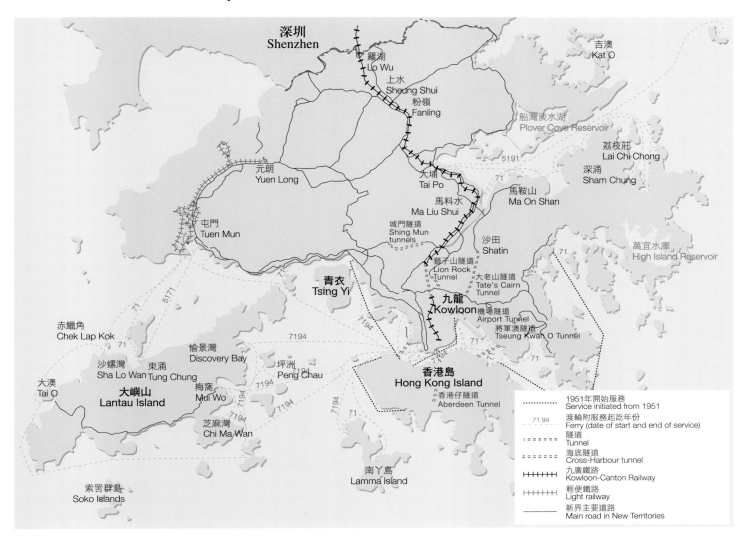

● **1960年市政建設藍圖　Future development plans of Hong Kong at 1960**

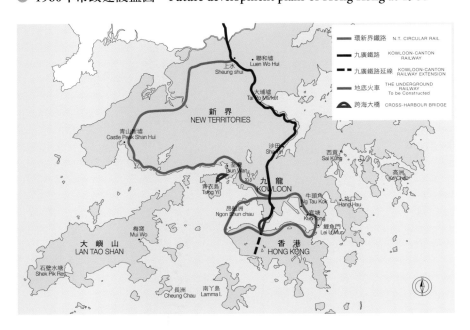

● **1994年市內交通狀況　Inner-city transport 1994**

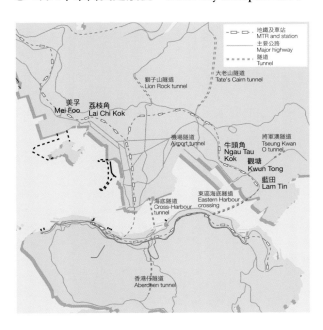

08 市內交通 Urban Transport

香港的市內交通，步行之外，一直以公共交通工具為主，佔總體載客量90%。1998年小汽車有318,137輛（2007年為40萬輛），摩托車23,345輛，總車輛也只有50萬輛，私人擁有率只有5.0%，若以全部車輛為基數，擁有率也只有7.3%。自行車一向都不是香港的常用代步工具，這跟中國內地的城市很不同。

市內交通主要是靠專利巴士，1992年在全香港的公共交通工具載客量中專利巴士共佔46%。它們包括了九龍巴士(營業範圍為九龍及新界)、中華巴士(營業範圍為香港島)。此外，香港島區和新界在1990年代初有新巴巴士公司投入競爭——城市巴士和大嶼山巴士。中華巴士在1998年停止服務，新世界第一巴士和龍運巴士分別在1998年和1997年投入營運。

1992年地鐵在市區內共有三線：荃灣—中環、柴灣—上環和太子—觀塘—鰂魚涌，由1979年逐步通車，總長43.2公里，佔了公共交通客量的28%，成為第二大交通工具。市內鐵路還包括港島北的電車(長26.4公里，始建於1904年)和太平山的登山纜車(始建於1888年)。此外，還有九

Public transport accounts for about 90% of total passenger trips. In 1998 there were 318,137 (400,000 in 2007) registered private cars included in the total of 500,000 registered motor vehicles. The private car owership ratio was only 5%. Bicycles are rarely used.

Franchised buses used to be the main mode of public transport. In 1992, they accounted for 46% of the ridership. Kowloon Motor Bus operated in Kowloon and the New Territories, while China Motor Bus on Hong Kong Island. Since 1990, two new companies appeared: City Bus and Lantau Bus. The later operated in Lantau. China Motor Bus ceased in 1998. New Bus and Dragon Bus began service in 1998 and 1997.

In 1992, there were 3 MTR lines with a total mileage of 43.2 km and accounted for 28% of the total trips. Rail services included the tramway on the Island (26.4 km, built in 1904), Peak Tram (built in 1888), and the Kowloon section of the Kowloon-Canton Railway. These rails accounted for 15% of the ridership.

Public light buses included the fixed route Green Minibus and the general service Red Minibus, took 9.3% of the ridership. The share of ferries dropped to 3%

● 1991年九龍市區有九巴行駛的街道 (圖中數字為使用此始發點或重要站的路線數目) KMB routes in urban Kowloon, 1991 (number showing no. of routes using the spot as terminal or major station)

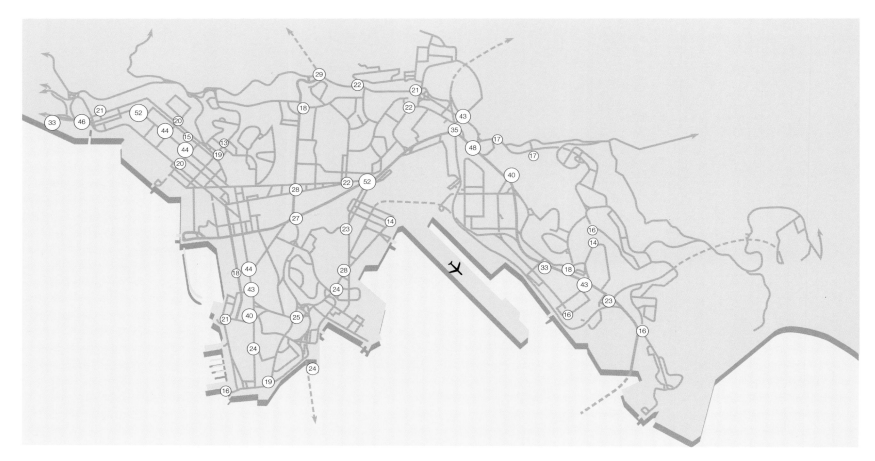

● 1949年九龍市區九巴路線 KMB routes in urban Kowloon, 1949

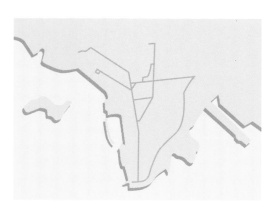

● 1979年九龍市區九巴路線 KMB routes in urban Kowloon, 1979

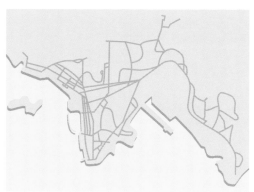

● 1964-2007年香港公共交通年載客量 Passenger load by public transport, 1964-2007

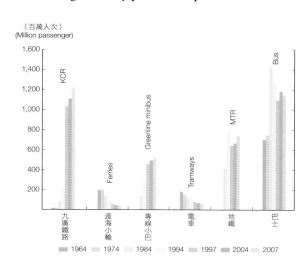

廣鐵路九龍段。1992年這些定軌交通的市場佔有率為15%。

另外的公共交通為專線小巴 (綠色) 和一般小巴 (紅色)，佔總客運量9.3%。小輪在市內的交通功能，因為兩條海底隧道和地鐵的建成而大減，只佔不到3%。在新界西的屯門和元朗區，公共交通還包括一條輕便鐵路。

2007年香港擁有道路1,936公里，12條行車隧道(三條海底)，以車輛計，每公里道路有275輛車。

2007年，地鐵擴大至總長54.5公里，共六條線。2008年地鐵和九鐵合併，總系統包括輕鐵共有十線，長175公里。

2007年公共交通載客量為每天1,152萬人次，專利巴士的比率減至34.4%，地鐵佔36.5%，小巴佔15.7%，而的士佔9.5%。的士的比率相當高。

人口和經濟活動集中在香港島北及九龍西。這裡的巴士路線幹道及鐵路路線也比較多。

when the tunnels and the MTR began to operate. The KCR operated a Light Rail in Tuen Mun and Yuen Long.

By 2007, Hong Kong possessed 1,936 km of motor roads and 12 road tunnels (3 submarine). It registered 275 cars per km road space. In that year, the MTR expanded to 6 lines with a mileage of 54.5 km. Since 2008, the MTR corporation took over KCR. Including the light rail, the new MTRC operated 175 km track with 10 lines.

In 2007, public transport trips numbered 11.52 million per day. The share of major modes are: franchised buses 34.4%, trains 36.5%, light buses 15.7%, taxi 9.5%.

As most economic activities and the population concentrate on the northern coast of the Island and Kowloon, so are the bus routes and rail lines.

● **2008年鐵路路線圖　MTRC system map, 2008**

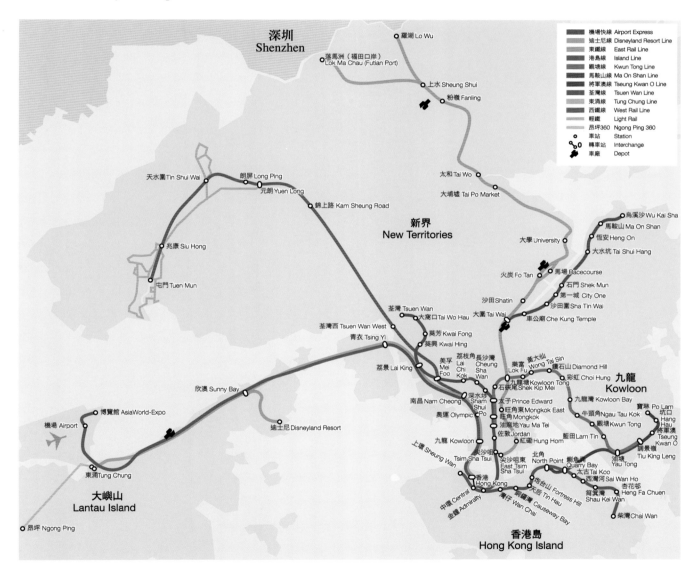

● **1951-2007年客量及機動車架數　Passenger journeys and motorised vehicles number, 1951-2007**

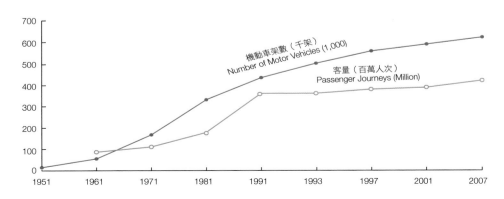

09 長遠交通發展 Long-term Transport Development

1997年決定興建新界西北客運鐵路，即"西部走廊"。這條新鐵路已於2003年通車，它連接九龍、新界西部至皇崗及羅湖邊界，成為新的過境鐵路。地鐵馬鞍山線由九龍的鑽石山站延至沙田的烏溪沙，亦於2004年通車，成為一條新的近郊客運線，緩和了九廣鐵路的緊張，促進了沙田新市鎮向西北方向的擴展。大嶼山至迪士尼專線也於2005年通車。2000年5月政府公佈在2008-2016年間計劃花800-1,200億元建造六條鐵路走廊。2000年全部鐵路系統每天載客300萬人次，佔全部公共交通客運量三成。六條新走廊建成後，估計可每天載客700萬人次，佔預計公共交通客量的45%。

我們可從當時的規劃中看到：

The West Rail linking Kowloon, Northwest New Territories and Shenzhen across the border was decided in 1997 and completed in 2003, making it the second cross-border rail. Ma On Shan Line opened in 2004. Linking Wu Kai Sha and Diamond Hill of Kowloon, it was the first suburban line of the MTR. Within Lantau, the special Disneyland Rail was completed in 2005. In 2000, the SAR announced a plan for constructing 6 lines in 2008-2016, costing HK$ 80-120 billion. In that year, the MTR and KCR networks had a daily ridership of 3 millions. The plan envisages a total of 7 million when the 6 lines begin operation, raising the share in total ridership of the rail mode from 30% in 2000 to 45% in 2016. The plan underlines:

1. the 'Rose garden' planning spirit that pervaded Hong Kong around 1997,

● 1996年規劃的市內交通遠景圖　Vision of inter-city transport planned at 1996

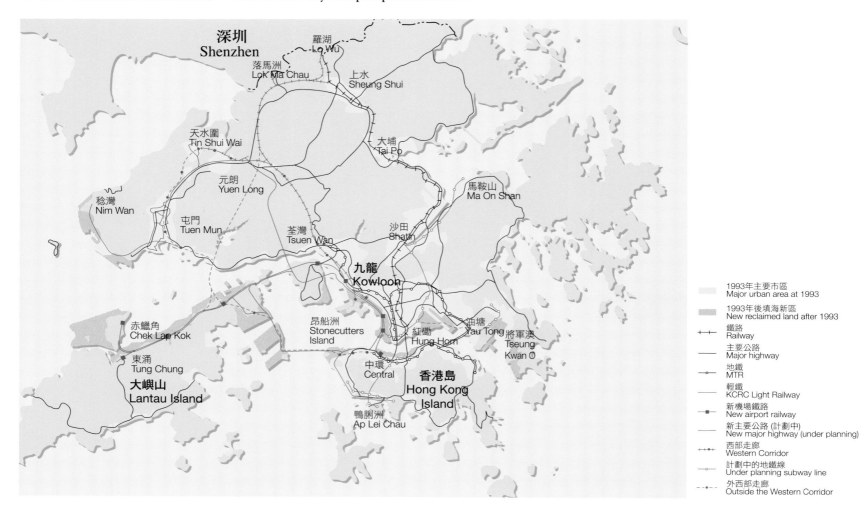

	1993年主要市區 Major urban area at 1993
	1993年後填海新區 New reclaimed land after 1993
	鐵路 Railway
	主要公路 Major highway
	地鐵 MTR
	輕鐵 KCRC Light Railway
	新機場鐵路 New airport railway
	新主要公路 (計劃中) New major highway (under planning)
	西部走廊 Western Corridor
	計劃中的地鐵線 Under planning subway line
	外西部走廊 Outside the Western Corridor

● 規劃中的港珠澳大橋　The planned Hong Kong-Zhuhai-Macau bridge

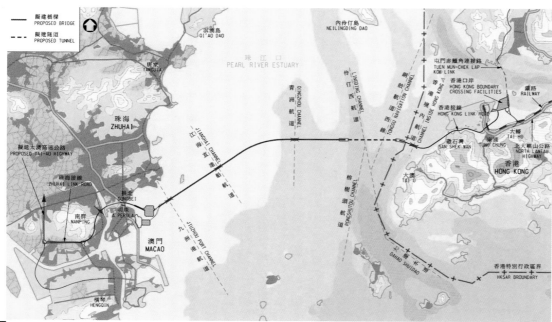

（一）1997年前後出現了大量規劃上的"玫瑰園"；

（二）和中國內地跨境連接的目的成為主要長遠交通規劃的方向；

（三）公共交通傾向大型集體運輸系統和環保型交通工具。

遠景規劃包括多條可能的過境客貨運輸線和市區地鐵延伸線。正在考慮中的赤鱲角機場和深圳機場的專線，及和廣州、北京連接的高速鐵路，將會加強香港和珠三角及內地的交通通達度，也和全國新高鐵網連接，以保持香港在全國的交通樞紐作用。

公路規劃也體現了過境的需求。跨越后海灣的西部通道已在2007年通車，連接香港、澳門和珠海的大橋，也在2010年動工。

2. cross-border link with mainland becomes a focus, and

3. bias towards fixed rail and environmental-friendly networks in public transport infrastructure.

The long-term plan includes a number of cross-border proposals for passengers and cargo. Since 2007, preliminary planning has been done on a special rail link between the Hong Kong and Shenzhen airports, and extension of the Guangdong-Beijing high-speed rail into West Kowloon.

In highway construction, the Western Crossing in Deep Bay opened in 2007. Besides, the Hong Kong-Macau-Zhuhai bridge began construction in 2010.

● 2000年公佈在2008-2016年間建設的新鐵路項目　New railway construction between 2008-2016 as announced in 2000

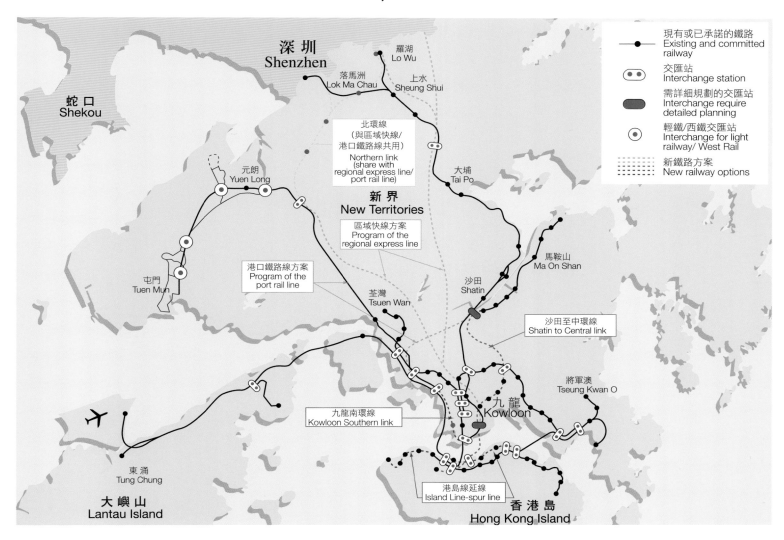

● 中國內地重點建設的鐵路客運專線　Plan for key passenger railway lines in China

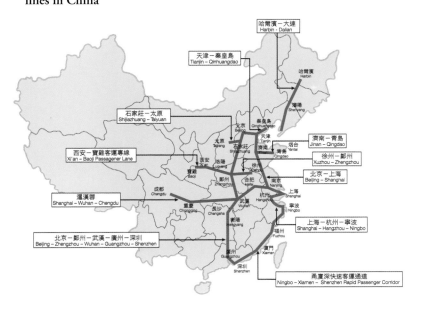

● 大珠三角地區已有和擬建的鐵路　Existing and proposed railways in the Pearl River Delta

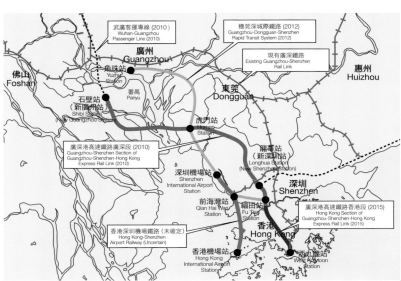

10 與珠三角的經貿基建和城市發展關係 Economic, Trade and Urban Links with the Pearl River Delta

第二次世界大戰前的香港和上海有些相似，都依賴中國內陸腹地並以溝通中外的貿易為生。因此，香港一直與珠江三角洲關係密切。但1949年後，兩地的關係基本上局限於後者對香港的水及食物的供應。1978年內地改革開放後，兩者聯繫開始越來越密切，人口流動也越趨頻繁。

自1980年起，香港出口型輕工業轉移到珠江三角洲發展，使香港經濟由製造業向服務業轉型，也使珠江三角洲的工業經濟高速發展。這個"前店後廠"港珠合作模式使香港與珠江三角洲在經濟中連為一體，形成一個都會經濟區（Extended Metropolitan Region）。

香港都會經濟區以香港為核心，還包括廣州、深圳、澳門和珠海四個副核。這個經濟區自1990年起，成為中國最重要的外向型經濟地區，成員之間的人、物及資金流頻密。

Before WWII, Hong Kong was similar to Shanghai, i.e. much dependent economically on its hinterland as its gateway for international trade and investments. Since 1949, Hong Kong's relationship with its hinterland, the Pearl River Delta (PRD), was restricted to the latter's supply of water and food. Since the mainland's economic reform in 1978, the relationship between Hong Kong and the PRD becomes very close.

From 1980 onward, Hong Kong's export-oriented light industries began to shift into the PRD, allowing Hong Kong's economy to restructure into a service economy to support the emerging industrial economy in the Delta. This 'front-shop, back-factory' cooperation model integrated the two into a new economic unit– the Extended Metropolitan Region (EMR). Hong Kong is the core of the EMR, while Guangzhou, Shenzhen, Macau and Zhuhai are the sub-cores. From 1990, the EMR has been China's most important export-oriented economic region, with an intensive flow of people, materials and capital among its component urban units.

● 香港都會經濟區結構圖 Structural drawing of the Hong Kong extended metropolitan region

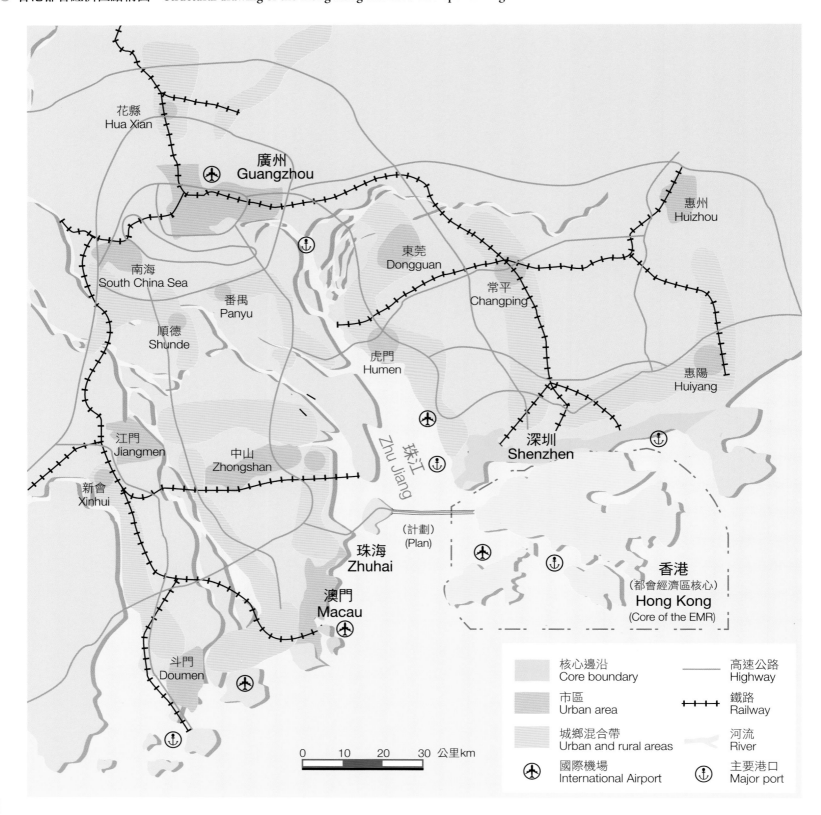

核心邊沿 Core boundary		高速公路 Highway	
市區 Urban area		鐵路 Railway	
城鄉混合帶 Urban and rural areas		河流 River	
國際機場 International Airport		主要港口 Major port	

0 10 20 30 公里km

大珠三角城市區域空間結構 　Spatial structure of cities in Greater Pearl River Delta

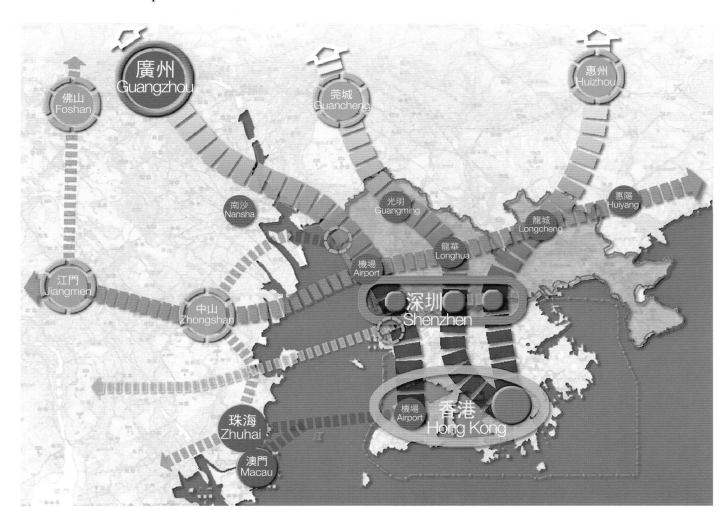

1982-1995年來往中國內地與香港旅客數量 (百萬人次) 　Visitors travelling between mainland and Hong Kong (million), 1982-1995

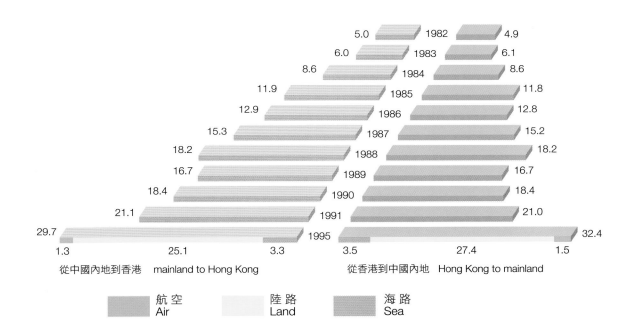

	mainland to Hong Kong 從中國內地到香港		年份	Hong Kong to mainland 從香港到中國內地	
		5.0	1982	4.9	
		6.0	1983	6.1	
		8.6	1984	8.6	
		11.9	1985	11.8	
		12.9	1986	12.8	
		15.3	1987	15.2	
		18.2	1988	18.2	
		16.7	1989	16.7	
		18.4	1990	18.4	
		21.1	1991	21.0	
29.7 / 1.3	25.1	3.3	1995	3.5	27.4 / 1.5 → 32.4

從中國內地到香港　mainland to Hong Kong　　從香港到中國內地　Hong Kong to mainland

航空 Air　　陸路 Land　　海路 Sea

大珠江三角洲主要機場　Major airports in the Greater Pearl River Delta

機場 Airport	名稱 Name	客流量(百萬人次) Passenger flow (million)	
		最大設計 Maximum capacity	2007
香港 Hong Kong	赤鱲角 Chek Lap Kok	87	47.8
廣州 Guangzhou	白雲/花都 Baiyun/Huadu	65	31.0
深圳 Shenzhen	福永 Fuyong	50	20.6
澳門 Macau	澳門 Macau	10	5.5
珠海 Zhuhai	九洲 Jiuzhou	24	1.0

大珠江三角洲主要海港　Major ports in the Greater Pearl River Delta

港口 Harbor	名稱 Name	貨物吞吐量(億噸/年) Cargo throughput (100 million tons / year)	
		最大設計 Maximum capacity	2007
香港 Hong Kong	葵涌 Kwai Chung	3.5	2.7
深圳 Shenzhen	媽灣 Mawan	0.5	2.0
	鹽田 Yantian	0.8	
珠海 Zhuhai	高欄 Gaolan	1.0	0.3
廣州 Guangzhou	黃埔 Huangpu	0.6	3.7

● 全國城鎮發展空間結構規劃圖（2006-2020年）中之珠三角位置　Pearl River Delta within the spatial structure plan of urban development in China, 2006-2020

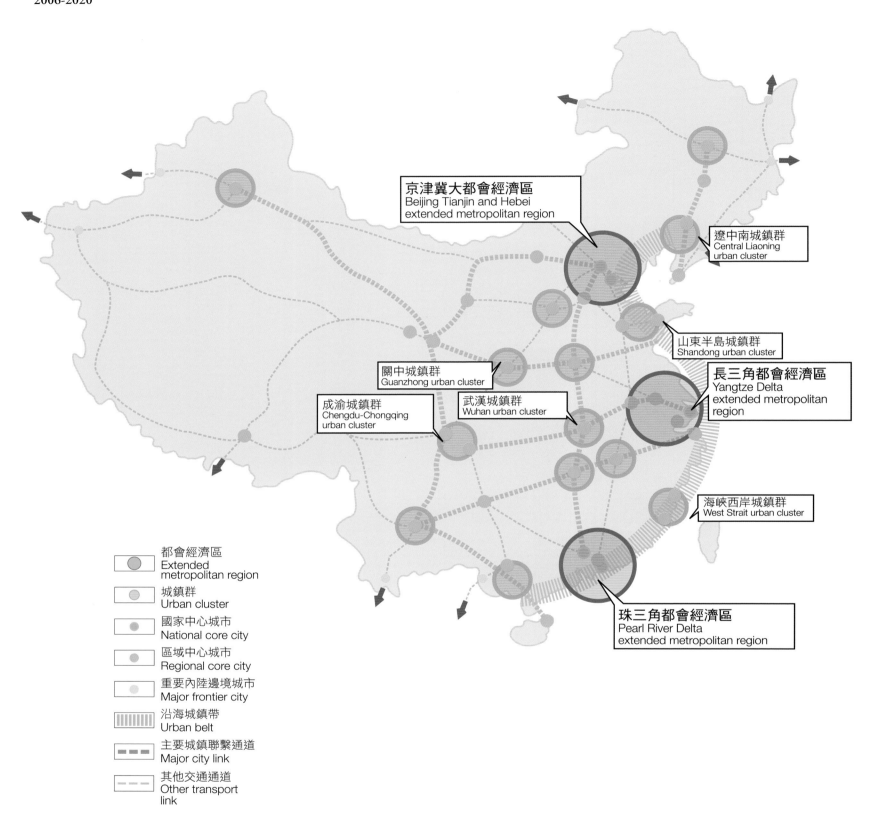

京津冀大都會經濟區
Beijing Tianjin and Hebei extended metropolitan region

遼中南城鎮群
Central Liaoning urban cluster

山東半島城鎮群
Shandong urban cluster

關中城鎮群
Guanzhong urban cluster

長三角都會經濟區
Yangtze Delta extended metropolitan region

成渝城鎮群
Chengdu-Chongqing urban cluster

武漢城鎮群
Wuhan urban cluster

海峽西岸城鎮群
West Strait urban cluster

珠三角都會經濟區
Pearl River Delta extended metropolitan region

都會經濟區
Extended metropolitan region

城鎮群
Urban cluster

國家中心城市
National core city

區域中心城市
Regional core city

重要內陸邊境城市
Major frontier city

沿海城鎮帶
Urban belt

主要城鎮聯繫通道
Major city link

其他交通通道
Other transport link

● 香港與珠三角及內地高速客運鐵路連絡圖　Hong Kong's high-speed rail link with the mainland through the Pearl River Delta

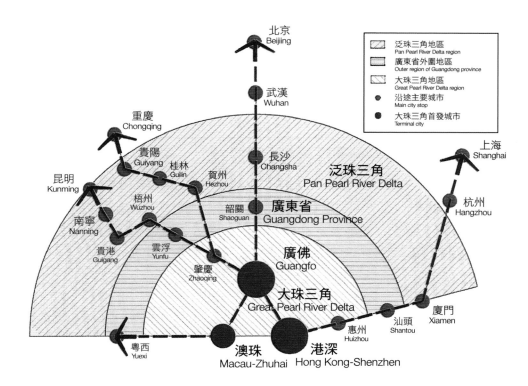

● 2007年按跨界旅客類型劃分的比例　Proportion share according to type of cross-border passengers, 2007

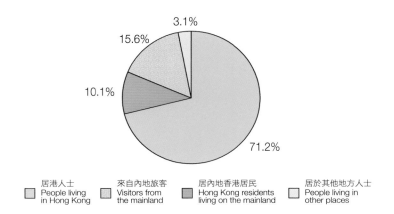

● 港深跨界車輛種類構成　Types of cross-border vehicular traffic between Hong Kong and Shenzhen

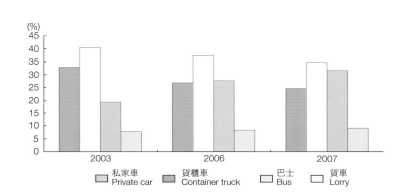

● 1998-2007年香港與內地跨界客運交通分擔比例　Hong Kong and mainland's share in cross-boundary passenger transport in 1998-2007

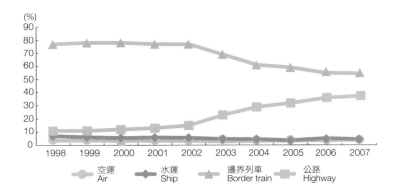

● 港深陸路跨界客流　Cross-border passenger traffic between Hong Kong-Shenzhen 1998-2007

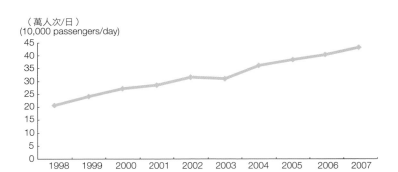

01　商務中心區(CBD)　Central Business District (CBD)

自1978年中國內地推行開放政策以來，香港工業大量北移，而香港對中國內地的轉口貿易亦大增。反映在香港的GDP構成中，工業的比例下降，第三產業不斷擴大。經濟轉型給第三產業為主的"曼哈頓化"增添了活力，使高檔第三產業的集中地——商務中心區更加蓬勃發展。

在市場經濟下，大城市核心地帶內位置最好、交通最便利的地方，通常形成商務中心區(CBD—Central Business District)。這裡有城市的主要官署、議會及法院。但一般而言，CBD主要由金融企業私人的高級寫字樓、酒店和高檔商場構成，行政功能一般位於邊沿。CBD除了是金融中心和各種專業性商業服務集中地，也是城市的最高級、最大的商業中心。

香港的CBD以中環為核心。中環是香港開埠初期的商貿中心和政府所在地，最初名為群帶路，1841年經《英皇制誥》改名為維多利亞城。九龍半島被割佔後，它是香港島最接近九龍的地方，地理中心地位明顯。以中環為核心的CBD不斷向東西伸延，部份躍過維多利亞港至尖沙

After the Open and Reform in 1978, many local factories shifted into the mainland, Hong Kong's re-exports upwards. Within the local GDP, the cortribution of manufacturing declined while that of the tertiary sector increased. Such economic restructuring intensified 'Manhattenizaion' and expansion of high-level services in the CBD.

The CBD is formed under market forces at the core of most big cities where accessibility is most convenient. Within it are major government offices, the parliament and law courts. More importantly, it is the city's concentration of financial enterprises, privately-owned offices, hotels and high-end department stores. Administrative functions are more at its periphery. The CBD is the city's financial centre, location of professional services and the highest-level commercial centre.

Central District is Hong Kong's CBD core. It has been the commercial and administrative centre since Hong Kong's founding in 1841. Its position as Hong Kong's geographical centre was reinforced after Kowloon was ceded.

● 商務中心與商業中心　The CBD and lesser business centres

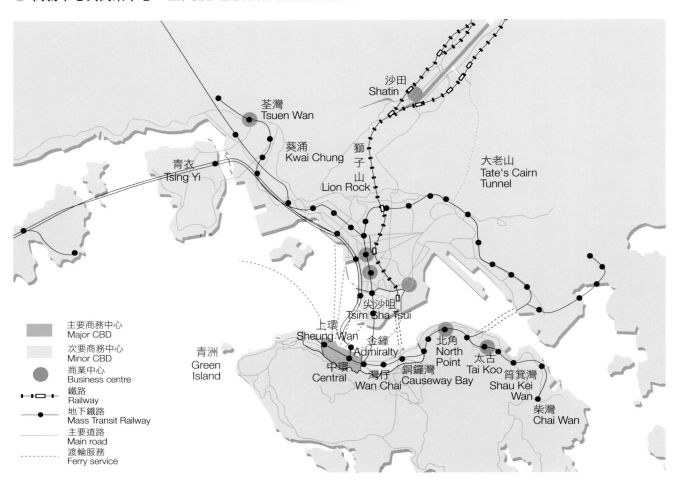

● 1996-2005年商務中心區不同界別就業情況　Employment in various sectors in the CBD, 1996-2005

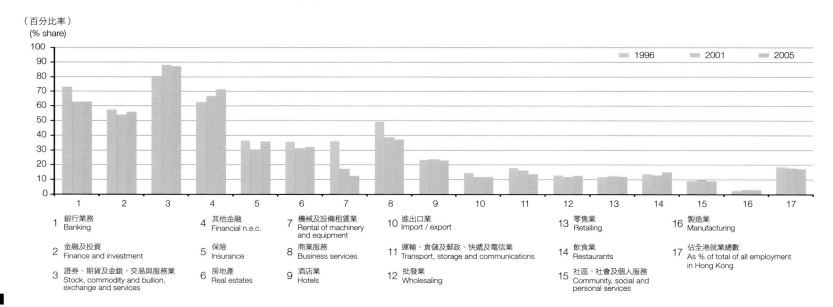

咀東部。其間不少舊大廈重建和改變用途，以容納更多的中心區功能。因此CBD內樓宇樓齡較小，樓層較高，設計新穎，形成現代化大城市中心區景觀。

香港的CBD只佔香港很小面積，但卻提供了近18%的就業。加上往返的客戶，使它成為香港每日人流的最集中地區。

其他的商業中心，以旺角—油麻地是CBD之外規模最大和歷史最長的。

地鐵的便利，也使商業向上述主要地區高度集中。其他地區的商業並不發達。

香港的CBD是個"行人城市"，整個地區有多條高架及穿過辦公樓的有蓋行人走廊連接。這個效率高的行人通道，使整個地區可在步行20分鐘之內到達。這是全球CBD的唯一例子。

The CBD later expanded westwards to Wan Chai and eastwards to Sheung Wan, and some functions leapfrogged to Tsim Sha Tsui, leading to replacement and redevelopment of old buildings to accommodate increased CBD functions.

Although the CBD is small in area, it has provided 18% of Hong Kong's total employment and forms the largest magnet for commuters.

Other than the above, Mongkok-Yau Ma Tei is the next largest commercial district and has the longest history.

Due to the convenience of the MTR, commercial uses are highly concentrated in these few districts.

Hong Kong's CBD is a true 'walking city'. A system of covered pedestrain walkways enable walking access to all parts of the CBD within 20 minutes. It is the only CBD in the world with such an efficient 'people-flow' system.

● 1968-1989年商務中心區範圍的變化　Extent of the CBD in 1968-1989

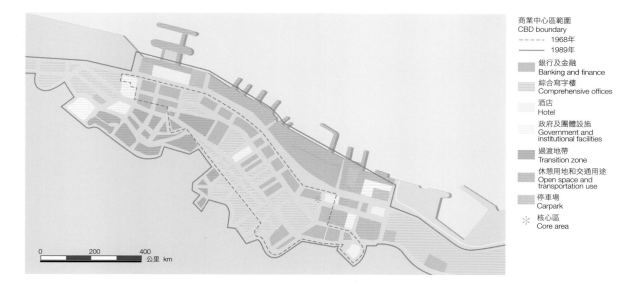

● 商務中心區的交通節點及行人天橋系統　Transport nodes and skywalk system in the CBD

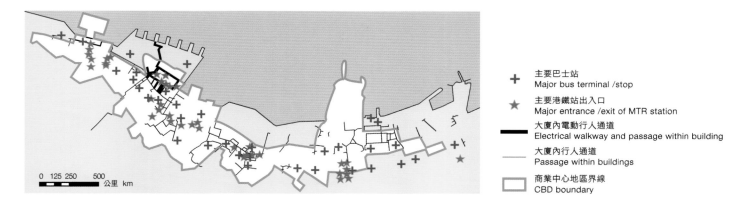

● 2005年商務中心區界線　CBD boundary, 2005

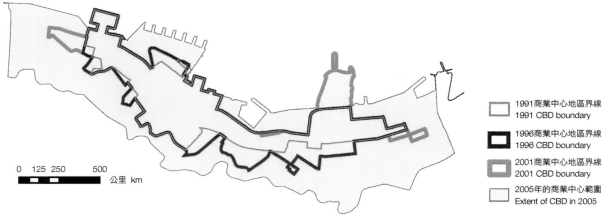

02 高級寫字樓與租金　Office Buildings and Their Rental

自1980年代製造業北移後，第三產業成為最主要的產業。高級寫字樓的分佈反映了這些活動的空間分佈。政府將寫字樓分為甲、乙、丙三類。甲類（最高檔）寫字樓，近九成集中在中環、尖沙咀和灣仔三區。新市鎮中這一類樓宇就寥寥可數了。

中環是傳統高級寫字樓的集中地，甲類寫字樓總量，是全香港總量的1/3。尖沙咀和灣仔的興起，是1980年後的事，顯示出高級商業活動仍是趨向於中環。

寫字樓的租金當然以中環最高，灣仔次之，上環及尖沙咀第三。在其他次中心，月租明顯較低。香港最昂貴的高級寫字樓，已經超過東京，成為世界上租金最高的。

Tertiary services is Hong Kong's economic mainstay. The distribution of office buildings, especially Grade A offices, reflects the spatial pattern of these activities. Grade A offices concentrate in Central District, Tsim Sha Tsui and Wan Chai. Very few are located in the new towns.

Central District accounts for 1/3 of all Grade A offices. The rise of Wan Chai and Tsim Sha Tsui began only after 1980, reflecting Central District's established nodal position. Office rentals are highest in Central District, followed by Wan Chai, Sheung Wan and Tsim Sha Tsui. Central District is already the world's most expensive office location in per-unit-floor-space rental.

● **1994年香港甲類寫字樓面積及1981-1994年月租金變化**
Area of Grade A offices in Hong Kong at 1994 and changes in monthly rents in 1981-1994

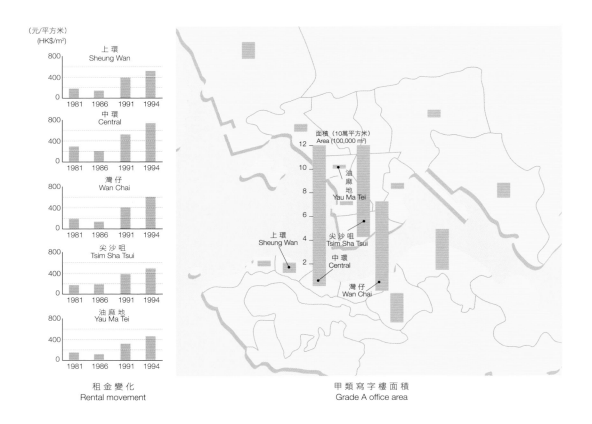

● **按主要區域分的甲類和非甲類寫字樓使用比率**　Usage ratio of grade A and non-grade A offices by broad area

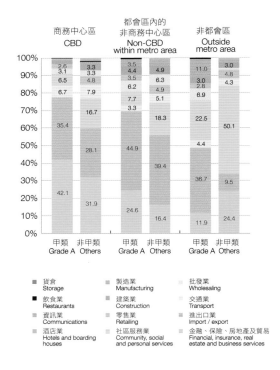

● **核心城市中甲類寫字樓的平均租金**
Average rent of Grade A private offices in core urban districts

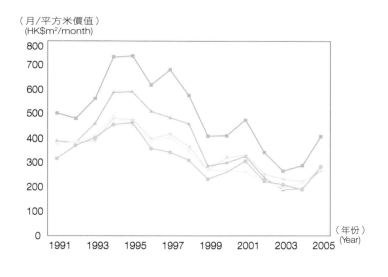

● **1991-2005年香港甲類寫字樓庫存**
Stock of Grade A private offices in Hong Kong, 1991-2005

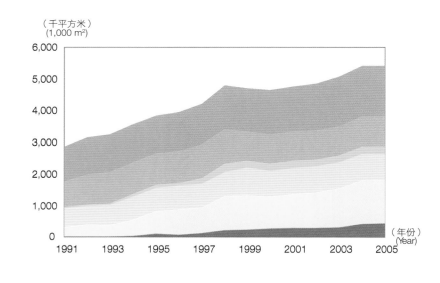

零售、飲食等商業樓宇租金 Rental of Retailing, Restaurants and Other Commercial Uses

零售商業樓宇（一般稱舖位）的租金，由該樓宇所在地的人口集中度、交通通達度以及消費力的相互作用決定。

香港舖位平均月租以九龍半島最高，香港島次之，新九龍再次之。新界最低。九龍的油麻地—尖沙咀地區是商業最繁盛地區。油麻地、尖沙咀和銅鑼灣也構成CBD之後的三大次商業中心。

近十年來新界的人口雖然增加迅速，但人口密度依然較低，並以中、低收入階層較多，舖位的平均租金只有全港平均數的六成左右。沙田鄰近市區，有方便的鐵路交通，公屋較少，是舊市區中產階級的新臥城，因而商舖需求大，月租達到全香港的平均值。

Rentals for shop space is determined by population density, accessibility, and spending power of residents. It is highest in Kowloon, followed by Hong Kong Island and New Kowloon. The New Territories is the lowest. Yau Ma Tei, Tsim Sha Tsui and Causeway Bay are also the three busiest commercial districts after the CBD.

Population growth in the New Territories has been rapid. Yet, density is relatively low and its population consists of mainly middle and low income groups. The average rental for a shop there is only about 60% of that of Hong Kong. Shatin is an exception. Being a dormitory town with more middle class, shop rental there is about Hong Kong's average.

● 1995年香港零售商業樓宇租金分佈圖　Rental of Hong Kong's retail and commercial buildings, 1995

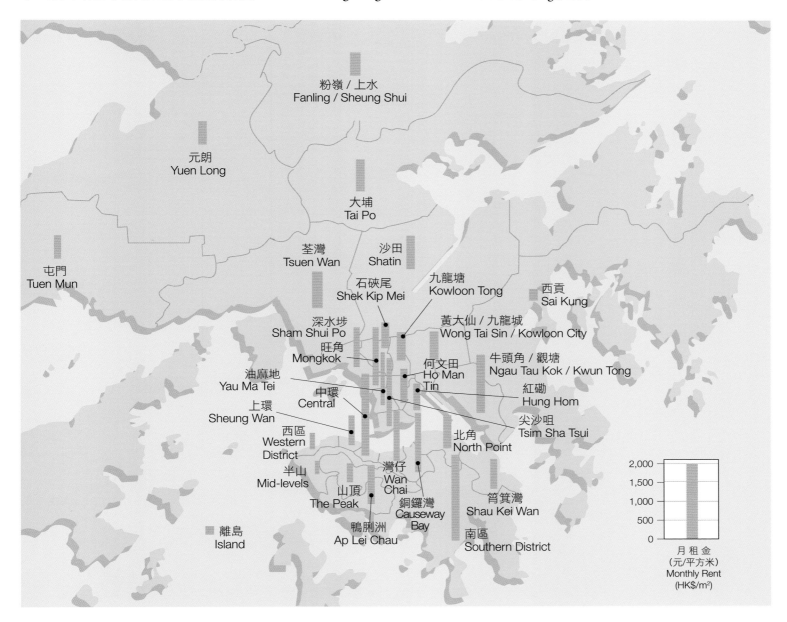

● 1980-2005年製造業及服務業對就業及本地生產總值的貢獻　Contribution of manufacturing and service sectors to employment and GDP, 1980-2005

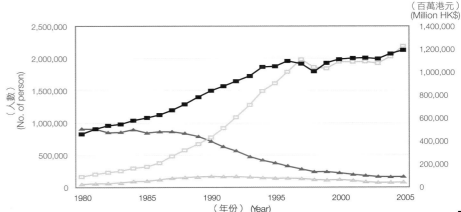

製造業所佔生產總值
GDP by manufacturing

服務業所佔生產總值
GDP by services

製造業就業人數
Employment in manufacturing

服務業就業人數
Employment in services

04 製造業 Manufacturing Industries

香港在二次大戰後的工業化是一種空間轉移式的工業化(Transferred Industrialization)，工廠主要由中國內地的上海搬遷而來。1949年不少上海工業家帶同他們的資金、設備、市場關係、技術和主要管理及工程人員南遷香港，成為荃灣及長沙灣自1950年起工業興起的根源。1951年香港有各類工廠1,702間，僱用9萬多人，1961年有工廠5,624間。至1961年，製造業過半數的就業仍集中在舊市區，新九龍也佔37%。但自1971年起，製造業主要轉移至九龍及荃灣。

香港製造業一直以紡織及成衣為主。早期佔第二位的是塑膠及五金製品，1981年起為電子產品。1998年製造業的最大行業仍為成衣及紡織。

Post-WWII industrialization in Hong Kong is a 'transferred industrialization', i.e. most of the factories had been relocated from Shanghai in 1949, together with know-how, capital, and market connections. The new industries first settled in Tsuen Wan and Cheung Sha Wan. In 1951, there were 1,702 factories with 90,000 workers. By 1961, factories increased to 5,624, with about half in the old urban area, while New Kowloon accounted for 37%. Since 1971, manufacturing has shifted mainly to Kowloon and Tsuen Wan.

Textile and garments were the main local manufacturing businesses, followed by plastics and fabricated metal products. Electronics emerged since 1980 as the second largest branch.

● 1973-2007年工業企業、僱用人數及產值分區佔全港比例變化 Changes in the proportion of industrial enterprises, employment and output value in major districts,1973-2007

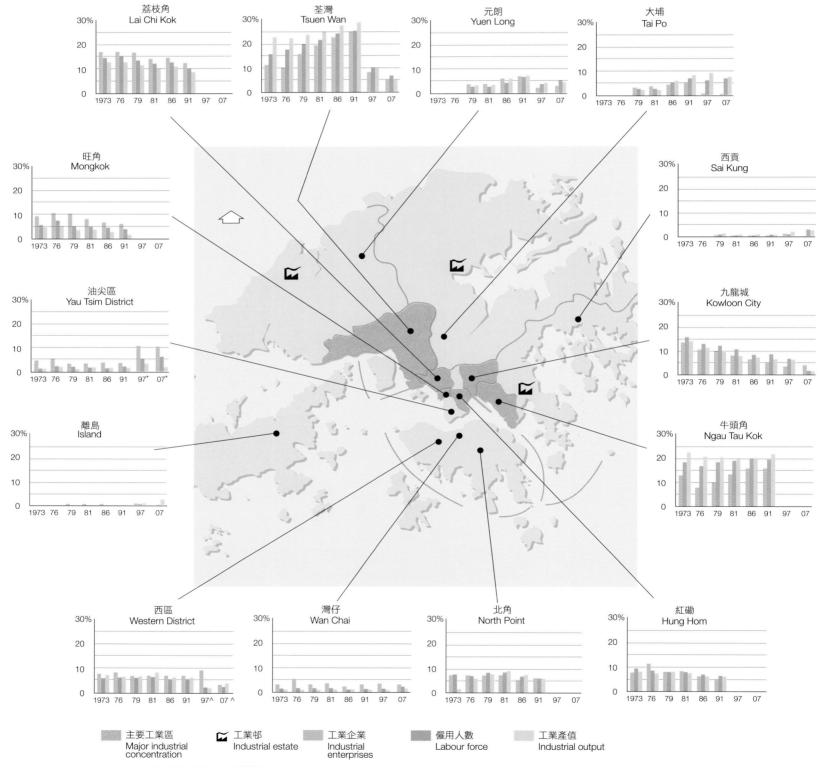

八成以上香港工業品是出口的，其中北美市場在1960-1980年代一直佔總出口的四成或以上，其次是日本及歐洲國家。自1980年代末起，中國內地成為香港工業品的最大市場。

香港的工廠主要是小型工廠。以1984年為例，僱用50人以下的小廠，佔了總廠數的92.6%，總僱用人數的42.4%；500人以上的大廠只有139間，在4萬多間廠中佔不到0.4‰；而工廠的平均僱用人數為18.5人。

在製造業發展的高峰期，製造業對本地生產總值的直接貢獻達30%，提供了全港近一半的就業。1998年製造業佔總就業人數只有11%。對GDP的貢獻降至6.2%。2008年，這些比率再降至5.2%及2.5%。

About 80% of local manufactured products were exported. In 1960-1980, North America accounted for 40% of the market. From the late 1980s on, the mainland has become the largest market.

Hong Kong factories are mostly small, e.g. in 1984, factories with less than 50 workers accounted for 92.6% of all factories, and 42.4% of the industrial employment. There were only 139 or 0.4‰ of factories that employed over 500 workers singly.

At its peak, manufacturing accounted for 30% of GDP and half of all employment. In 1998 these dropped to 6.2% and 11%. They fell to 2.5% and 5.2% in 2008.

● 2001年1月開始的工業用地用途變化
Rezoning of industrial land since January 2001

位置 Location	改劃為"其他指定用途 (乙類)"及其他用途（公頃） Rezoned to "OU(B)" and other uses (ha)	餘下的"I"區（公頃） Remaining "I" zone (ha)
都會區域 Metro area :		
堅尼地城 Kennedy Town	0.22	0.76
筲箕灣 Shau Kei Wan	1.79	—
香港仔 / 鴨脷洲 Aberdeen/Ap Lei Chau	8.30	10.29
柴灣 Chai Wan	10.38	14.54
鰂魚涌 Quarry Bay	0.75	—
大角咀 Tai Kok Tsui	5.31	—
長沙灣 Cheung Sha Wan	21.57	—
紅磡 Hung Hom	7.85	—
新蒲崗 San Po Kong	10.96	2.67
九龍灣 Kowloon Bay	22.06	—
觀塘 Kwun Tong	43.73	—
茶果嶺/油塘 Cha Kuo Ling/Yau Tong	1.49	—
西南九龍 Southwest Kowloon	—	2.11
啟德 Kai Tak	15.72	—
葵涌 Kwai Chung	40.54	49.08
青衣 Tsing Yi	5.62	—
荃灣 Tsuen Wan	14.59	28.75
昂船洲 Stonecutters Island	—	4.44
區域總計 Sub-total :	210.88	112.64
新界 New Territories :		
粉嶺/上水 Fanling/Sheung Shui	0.16	58.37
沙田 Sha Tin	21.76	52.06
大埔 Tai Po	2.24	—
屯門 Tuen Mun	—	57.16
元朗 Yuen Long	11.63	—
屏山 Ping Shan	—	9.86
唐人新村 Tong Yan San Tsuen	—	14.80
區域總計 Sub-total :	35.79	192.25
合計 Total :	246.67	304.89

● 工業樓宇建築面積需求
Demand and supply of industrial floor space

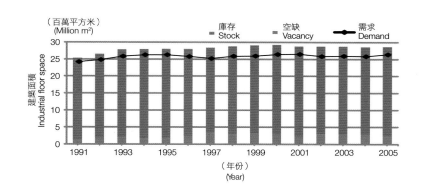

● 現存"工業"地帶（2005年12月）　Existing "industrial" land use (December 2005)

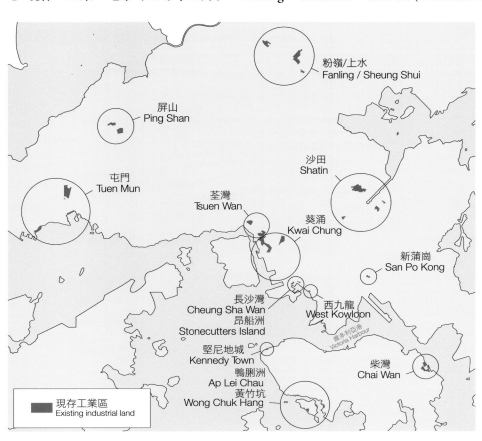

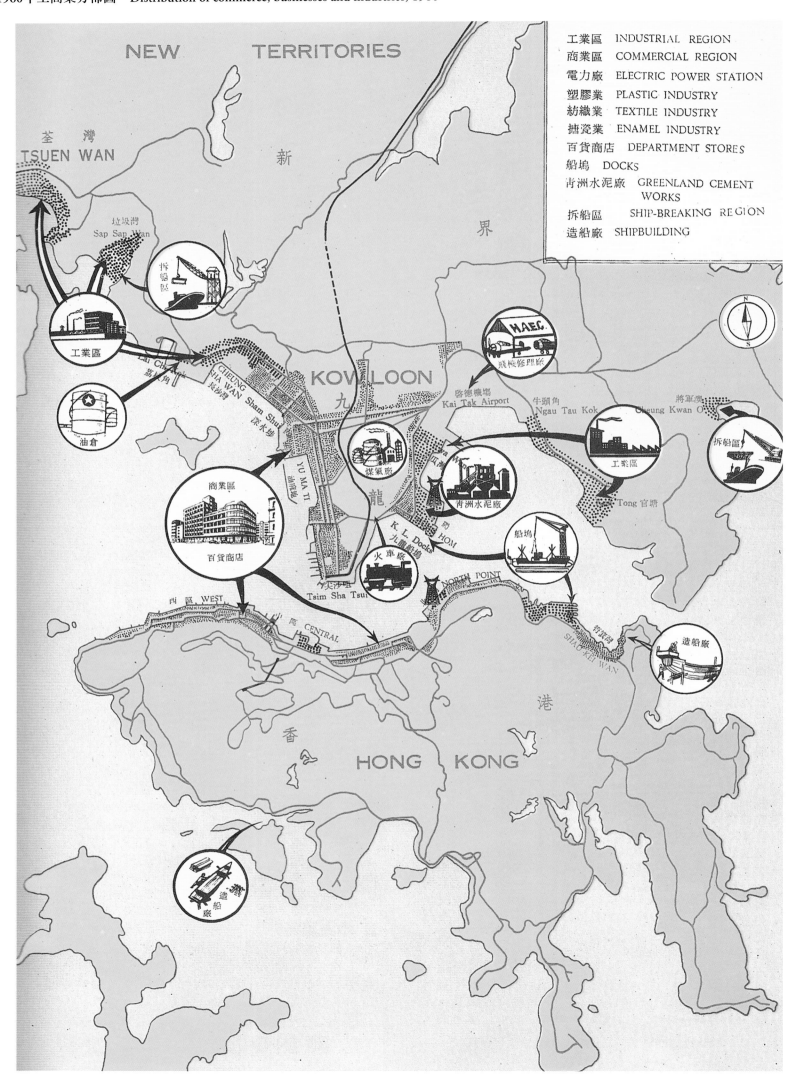

全港工廠總數
Number of factories in Hong Kong

（萬間）
(10 thousand rooms)

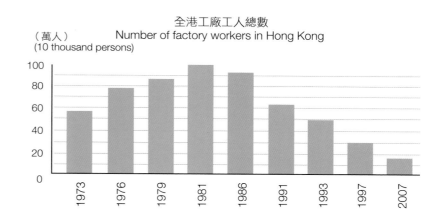

全港工廠工人總數
Number of factory workers in Hong Kong

（萬人）
(10 thousand persons)

全港工業生產總值
Gross industrial production in Hong Kong

（百萬港元）
(Million HK$)

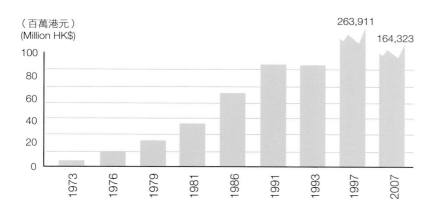

● 1961-1991年製造業的地理分佈　**Geographical distribution of manufacturing industry, 1961-1991**

地區 District	企業數 Number of enterprises			僱員數 Number of employees				產值（百萬港元） Output value (Million HK$)		
	1971	1981	1991	1961	1971	1981	1991	1971	1981	1991
香港島 Hong Kong Island	4,670	8,120	6,545	124,338	106,041	152,983	69,733	2,284	23,698	35,497
九龍 Kowloon	8,302	9,782	4,146	129,236	140,128	147,280	36,172	3,683	18,261	24,818
新九龍 New Kowloon	10,240	17,388	16,875	174,267	322,099	419,087	295,139	13,117	52,012	116,390
荃灣 Tsuen Wan	1,357	9,169	10,614	25,245	71,240	212,078	160,331	5,932	33,778	88,649
新界 New Territories	1,580	3,865	5,714	17,572	31,573	64,453	90,028	1,514	8,739	50,419
總數 Total	26,149	48,324	43,894	470,658	671,081	996,421	651,404	26,530	136,488	315,773

05 荃灣工業區 Tsuen Wan Industrial Zone

荃灣現代工業，以戰後由上海轉移而來的輕紡工業為主。自1950年代末的大規模規劃與建設後，1971年荃灣已成為最大的工業區，佔全港工業產值的二成，1991年更達37%。1961-1976年間，荃灣的就業人口有六成受僱於製造業，"藍領"程度是全港之冠，並形成了青衣島沿岸的重型和危險工業地帶。

荃灣工業用地較為混亂。工廠大廈與住宅大廈交錯，是佈局較不合理的舊工業區。區內專門設計的工廠和多層式的廠廈比較多，工廠規模一般比市區工廠大，但這裡也還有不少徙置工廠和臨時屋(木屋)工廠。

1980年代開始的工業北移，對荃灣影響很大。工廠與工人數目持續下降。不少廠廈已改建為住宅或其他用途。

Tsuen Wan's modern industries were first set up in the early 1950s as some textiles manufacturing were relocated from Shanghai. The district then underwent large-scale construction. It became the largest industrial zone, accounting for 20% of local industrial value added by 1971, and 37% in 1991. In 1961-1976, about 60% of the town's working population was in manufacturing. In Tsing Yi were also Hong Kong's heavy industries and dangerous goods depots.

Tsuen Wan's land use was highly mixed and poorly planned. Factory buildings mingled with residential blocks. There were multi-storey factories and many temporary 'squatter' factories and resettlement factories.

The industrial shift since the 1980s has led to the rapid decline of local manufacturing. Many factory buildings have been converted to residential and other uses.

● 1980年荃灣工業用地狀況 Industrial land use in Tsuen Wan, 1980

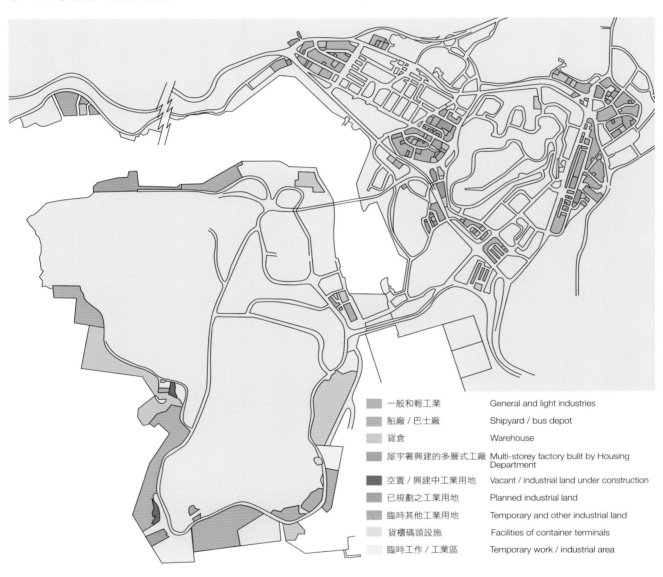

一般和輕工業	General and light industries
船廠 / 巴士廠	Shipyard / bus depot
貨倉	Warehouse
屋宇署興建的多層式工廠	Multi-storey factory bulit by Housing Department
空置 / 興建中工業用地	Vacant / industrial land under construction
已規劃之工業用地	Planned industrial land
臨時其他工業用地	Temporary and other industrial land
貨櫃碼頭設施	Facilities of container terminals
臨時工作 / 工業區	Temporary work / industrial area

● 荃灣歷年工業產值、工廠數目及僱用人數 Tsuen Wan's industrial output, number of factories and employment over the years

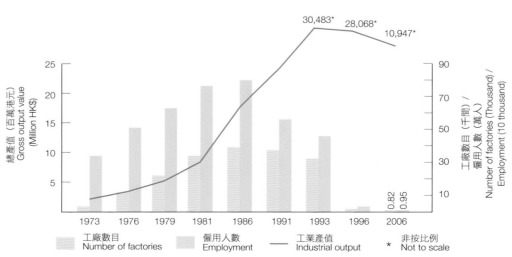

1996年荃灣市區土地利用　Urban land use of Tsuen Wan, 1996

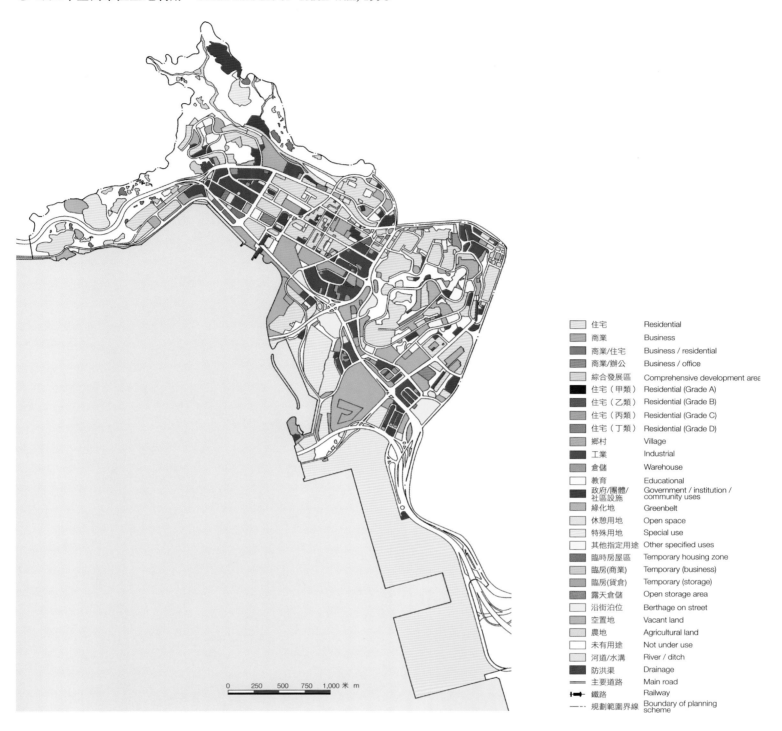

	住宅	Residential
	商業	Business
	商業/住宅	Business / residential
	商業/辦公	Business / office
	綜合發展區	Comprehensive development area
	住宅（甲類）	Residential (Grade A)
	住宅（乙類）	Residential (Grade B)
	住宅（丙類）	Residential (Grade C)
	住宅（丁類）	Residential (Grade D)
	鄉村	Village
	工業	Industrial
	倉儲	Warehouse
	教育	Educational
	政府/團體/社區設施	Government / institution / community uses
	綠化地	Greenbelt
	休憩用地	Open space
	特殊用地	Special use
	其他指定用途	Other specified uses
	臨時房屋區	Temporary housing zone
	臨房(商業)	Temporary (business)
	臨房(貨倉)	Temporary (storage)
	露天倉儲	Open storage area
	沿街泊位	Berthage on street
	空置地	Vacant land
	農地	Agricultural land
	未有用途	Not under use
	河道/水溝	River / ditch
	防洪渠	Drainage
	主要道路	Main road
	鐵路	Railway
	規劃範圍界線	Boundary of planning scheme

0　250　500　750　1,000 米 m

2007年荃灣分區計劃大綱圖　Outline Zoning Plan of Tsuen Wan in 2007

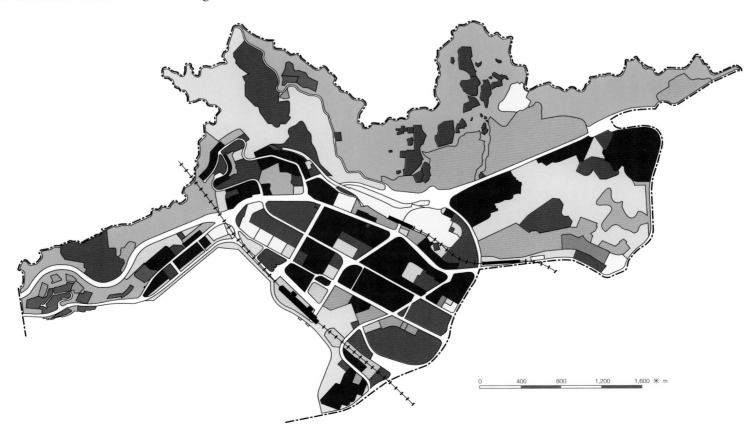

0　400　800　1,200　1,600 米 m

06 觀塘工業區　Kwun Tong Industrial Zone

觀塘工業區的建立、發展和衰微，印證了香港戰後工業化的歷程和特點。創建於1960年代初，它是香港第一個有規劃的工業區。首家工廠在1957年出現，頂峰時，區內有近8,000家，佔全香港工廠二成，僱用近18萬工人。自1980年起工業北移，觀塘工業區也空洞化，並在2000年納入市區重建計劃。

觀塘的工廠以紡織和成衣為主。1968年的用地及樓宇剖面用途圖，體現香港戰後的工業土地利用特色：不同工廠擠用同一多層廠廈，在同一樓層也有不同的工業企業。香港地少人多，工業也要向高空發展，形成一種特殊的城市生態群落。1995年的用地圖顯示不少原工廠大廈已經拆掉，成為空置土地，一些更變為商廈及住宅。

The establishment, growth and decline of Kwun Tong Industrial Zone (KTIZ) testify Hong Kong's post-war industrialization and its characteristics. Founded in the early 1960s, KTIZ was the first planned industrial zone. At its peak, it housed 8,000 factories (20% Hong Kong total) and 180,000 workers. From 1980, it suffered rapid decline and was destined as an urban redevelopment zone since 2000.

Manufacturing there was dominated by textiles and garments. The land use and urban transect maps testify Hong Kong's unique industrial land use: small-medium factories clustered within one floor of a building. Hong Kong's high-density environment had also led to 'vertical' development in manufacturing land use. The 1995 map shows that many factories were demolished. Their sites were vacant or redeveloped into commercial or residential uses.

● 1968年觀塘工業用地圖　Industrial land use of Kwun Tong, 1968

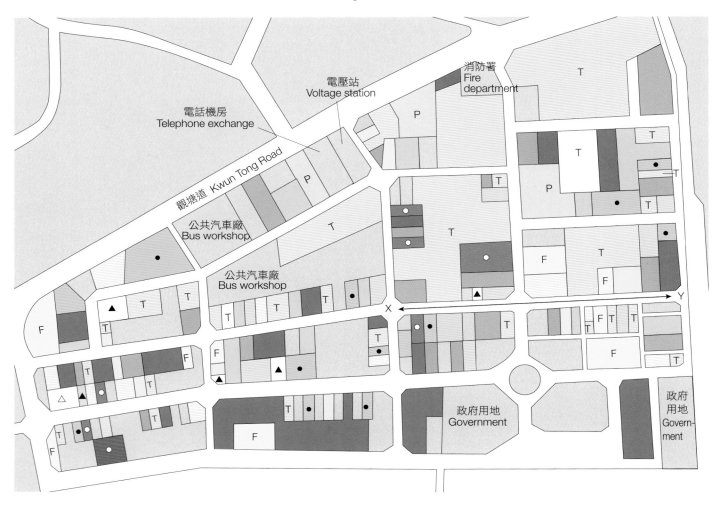

● 1968年觀塘鴻圖道工業大廈用途剖面　Transect of industrial buildings along Kwun Tong's Hung To Road, 1968

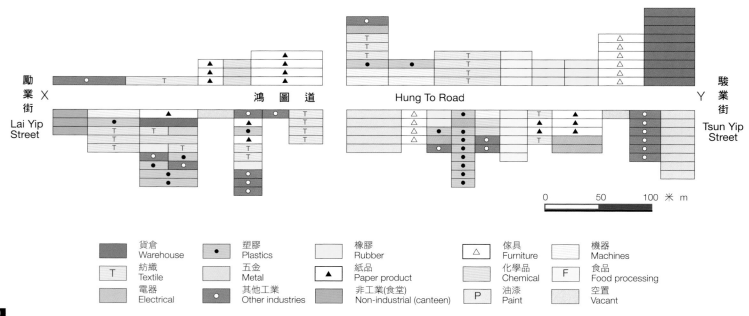

	貨倉 Warehouse		塑膠 Plastics		橡膠 Rubber		傢具 Furniture		機器 Machines
	紡織 Textile	T	五金 Metal		紙品 Paper product	▲	化學品 Chemical		食品 Food processing
	電器 Electrical		其他工業 Other industries		非工業(食堂) Non-industrial (canteen)		油漆 Paint	P	空置 Vacant

1995年觀塘工業用地圖　Industrial land use of Kwun Tong, 1995

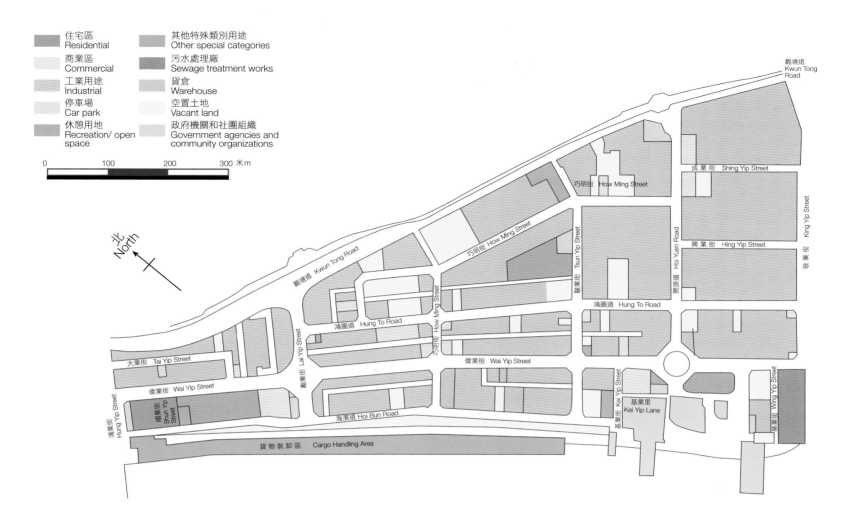

住宅區
Residential

商業區
Commercial

工業用途
Industrial

停車場
Car park

休憩用地
Recreation/ open space

其他特殊類別用途
Other special categories

污水處理廠
Sewage treatment works

貨倉
Warehouse

空置土地
Vacant land

政府機關和社團組織
Government agencies and community organizations

市建局重建觀塘市中心範圍——主地盤及月華街地盤
Urban Redevelopment Authority's Kwun Tong Town Centre (KTTC) redevelopment area-main site and Yuet Wah Street site

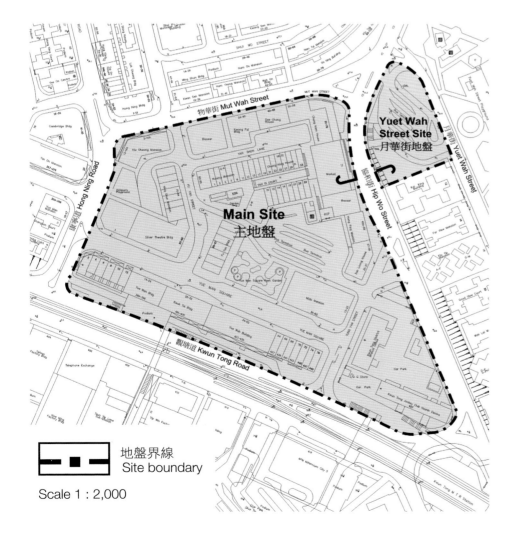

地盤界線
Site boundary

Scale 1 : 2,000

1957-2006年觀塘工業區工廠、工人和產值變化
Number of factories, workers and output value in Kwun Tong industrial area, 1957-2006

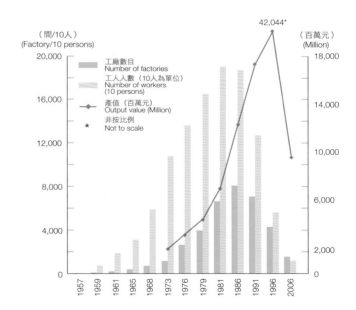

工廠數目
Number of factories

工人人數（10人為單位）
Number of workers (10 persons)

產值（百萬元）
Output value (Million)

非按比例
Not to scale

07 商業 Commercial Districts

商業包括了批發、零售、進出口、飲食和酒店業。它是香港最大的行業。

香港商業一直發展迅速，並且主要集中在九龍。但以營業額算，九龍並不比香港島高很多，反映香港島的消費力比九龍高。荃灣及新界地區的商業佔全香港的很小部份，顯示人口往這些地區遷移並沒有影響人們慣性地到舊市區進行商業活動。

各類商業中，酒店業明顯集中在中環、灣仔和尖沙咀開市。批發業一貫集中在上環、長沙灣和旺角，但近十年來在觀塘和荃灣有急速發展。進出口業集中在中上環以及尖沙咀，近年亦向灣仔、長沙灣、觀塘、荃灣分散，飲食業一直以灣仔為盛，但近年尖沙咀和香港島東區已成為新的中心，新界的飲食業也因應人口的增加而大幅增長。

The commercial sector includes wholesaling, retailing, import and export, restaurants and hotels. It is Hong Kong's largest economic pillar, and is largely concentrated in Kowloon. In sales volume, Hong Kong Island leads showing its stronger spending power, while Tsuen Wan and the New Territories contribute meagrely. The latter underlines the habit of shopping in the old urban districts despite the trend of population dispersal.

Hotels are clustered in Central, Wan Chai and Tsim Sha Tsui. Wholesaling concentrates in Sheung Wan, Cheung Sha Wan and Mongkok, with a recent rapid growth in Tsuen Wan and Kwun Tong. Import and export businesses follow a similar dispersal trend. Restaurants are mostly congregated in Wan Chai, though Tsim Sha Tsui and Hong Kong East are catching up. So is the rapid increase in the New Territories due to rapid population increase.

● 1977-2003年商業企業、產值及僱員人數分區分佈圖　Geographical distribution of commercial enterprises, their output value and employees, 1977-2003

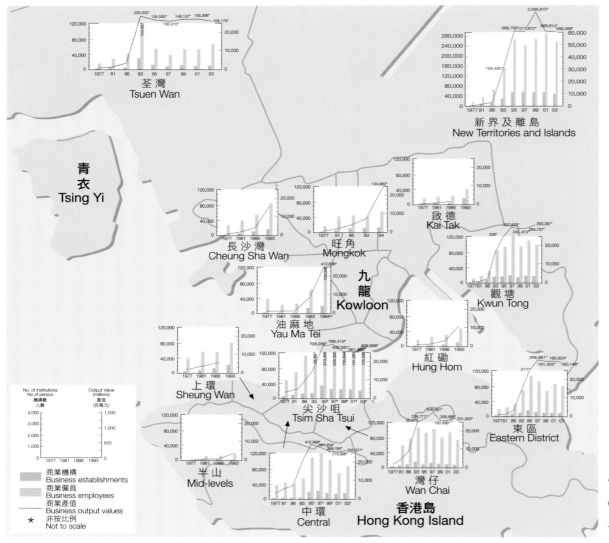

^ 1994年數字包括尖沙咀數據。
Figure in 1994 includes the data of Tsim Sha Tsui.

1995-2003年數字包括油麻地及旺角數據。
Figure in 1995-2003 includes the data of Yau Ma Tei and Mongkok.

+ 1995-2003年數字為中西區數據。
Figure in 1995-2003 showing data of Central and Western District.

● 1977-2003年商業企業數（單位：萬間）
Number of commercial enterprises, 1977-2003 (unit: 10 thousand)

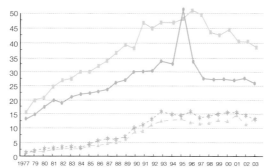

● 1977-2003年商業僱員人數（單位：萬人）
Number of commercial employees, 1977-2003 (unit: 10 thousand)

● 1977-2003年商業產值（單位：百億元）
Output value in commerce, 1977-2003 (unit: 10 billion)

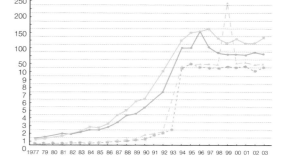

香港島 Hong Kong Island　九龍 Kowloon　荃灣、葵涌、青衣 Tsuen Wan, Kwai Chung and Tsing Yi　新界及其他 New Territories and others

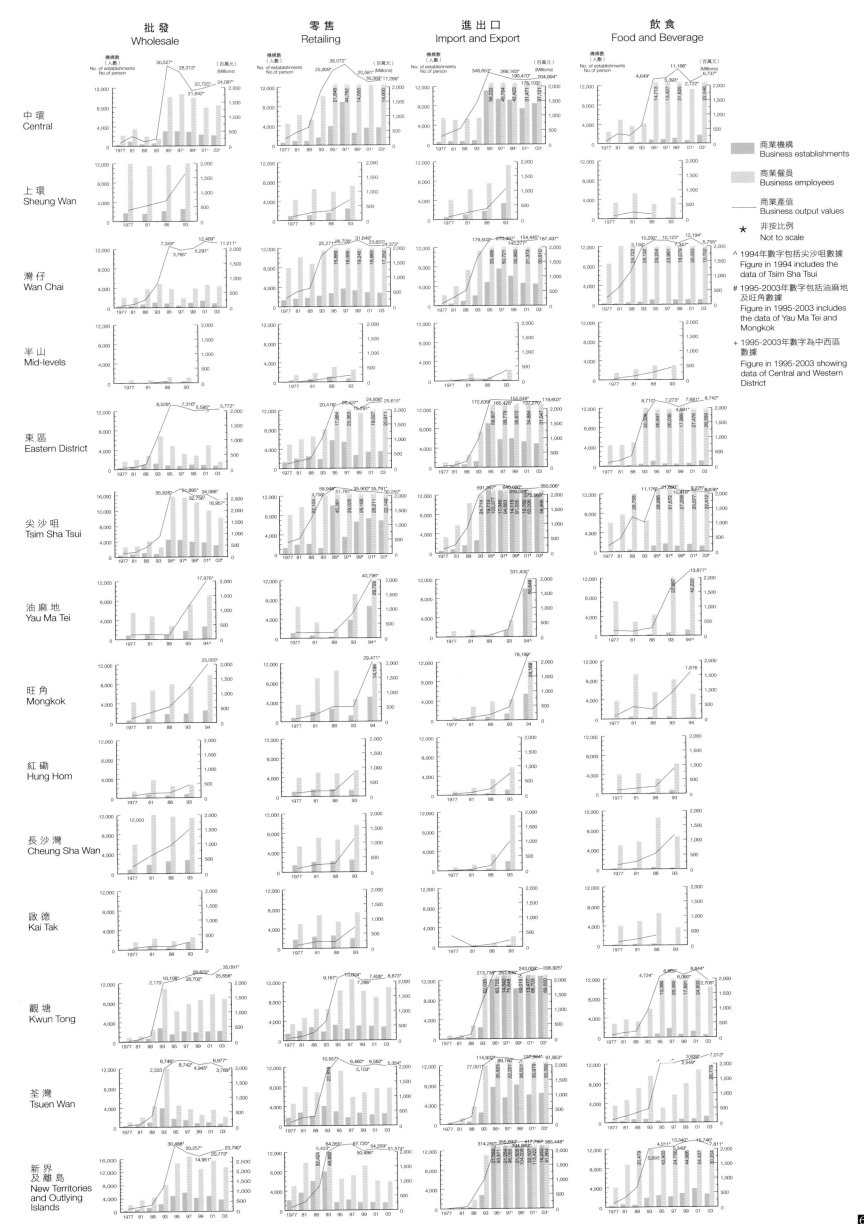

批發
Wholesale

零售
Retailing

進出口
Import and Export

飲食
Food and Beverage

中環
Central

上環
Sheung Wan

灣仔
Wan Chai

半山
Mid-levels

東區
Eastern District

尖沙咀
Tsim Sha Tsui

油麻地
Yau Ma Tei

旺角
Mongkok

紅磡
Hung Hom

長沙灣
Cheung Sha Wan

啟德
Kai Tak

觀塘
Kwun Tong

荃灣
Tsuen Wan

新界
及離島
New Territories
and Outlying
Islands

機構數
（人數）
No. of establishments
No.of person

（百萬元）
(Millions)

商業機構
Business establishments

商業僱員
Business employees

商業產值
Business output values

★ 非按比例
Not to scale

^ 1994年數字包括尖沙咀數據
Figure in 1994 includes the
data of Tsim Sha Tsui

1995-2003年數字包括油麻地
及旺角數據
Figure in 1995-2003 includes
the data of Yau Ma Tei and
Mongkok

+ 1995-2003年數字為中西區
數據
Figure in 1995-2003 showing
data of Central and Western
District

63

08 中環、灣仔高級商務區發展遠景 Development of Central Business in Central and Wan Chai

中環和灣仔已在1990年代前半期進行了填海，並打算於1990年代後半期起進行第二期填海。但這期填海因為反對意見太多而被延遲並作出大幅縮減。按原計劃，填海可為商務中心區增加20多公頃，及提供30多公頃公共綠地和54公頃路面面積。

2008年的填海區大為縮小，而且所得土地主要提供公共用地和綠地，亦是政府新總部所在，近似一個新的行政、文化中心。新設計原則上採納了數位知名人士（何顯毅、鄔維庸、劉迺強）的意見，商業用地稍有減少，整體上以香港特區新的行政和文化中心為設計目標。此外，政府接受了本港商人提議在香港島西北岸發展以資訊科技和電子電腦科技為主要活動的新高科技產業中心。這個名為"數碼港"的商務中心，是高級商業活動由中環、灣仔向西面沿岸的延伸。

Large-scale reclamation in Central and Wan Chai began in early 1990s, followed by a second-phase reclamation. The latter has been delayed until 2008 and is reduced in scope due to widespread objection. Originally, it was planned to provide 20 ha of office space, 30 ha of green area and 54 ha of roads. In the new plan, public green space is the major use, with a new government headquarters and the Legislative Council building, creating a new zone for government administration and cultural activities.

The government also partnered with the private sector to develop the Cyberport, an office area oriented towards high-tech and digital service enterprises in Hong Kong West, extending high level office activities from Central westwards along the harbour coast.

● 1988年已建渡輪航線與碼頭 Ferry services and terminals in 1988

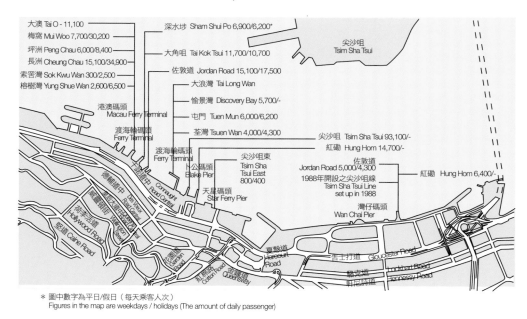

* 圖中數字為平日/假日（每天乘客人次）
Figures in the map are weekdays / holidays (The amount of daily passenger)

● 港島商務中心區土地用途及分區表（1993年建議）
CBD land use (proposed in 1993)

用途 Purpose	中區 Central 面積（平方米）Area (m²)	%	添馬艦區 Tamar area 面積（平方米）Area (m²)	%	會展區 Exhibition area 面積（平方米）Area (m²)	%	總數 Total 面積（萬平方米）Area (10,000 m²)	%
地區性公眾休憩用地 Regional public open space	88,126	18.4	97,219	22.6	60,817	19.1	24.6	20.0
本區公眾休憩用地 Public open space areas	2,588	0.5	32,793	7.6	8,594	2.7	4.4	3.6
美化市容地帶 Amenity area	1,813	0.4	—	—	—	—	0.2	0.2
港灣（灣仔內灣）Harbour (Inner Bay in Wan Chai)	—	—	17,218	4.0	—	—	1.7	1.4
其他指定用途 Other specified uses	15,754	3.3	12,362	2.9	3,313	1.0	3.1	2.5
團體及社區用途 Groups and community use	3,720	0.8	3,167	0.7	6,449	2.0	1.3	1.1
政府保留用地 Government reservation	26,264	5.5	6,043	1.4	13,500	4.2	4.6	3.7
綜合發展區 Comprehensive development area	42,100	8.8	—	—	—	—	4.2	3.4
商業 Commercial	65,806	13.8	87,309	20.3	33,620	10.5	18.7	15.2
酒店 Hotel	5,714	1.2	14,046	3.3	7,350	2.3	2.7	2.2
住宅 Residence	—	—	—	—	31,229	9.8	3.1	2.5
道路 Road	226,265	47.3	160,118	37.2	154,253	48.4	54.1	44.1
總數 Total	478,150	100.0	430,275	100.0	319,125	100.0	122.7	100.0

● 中環、灣仔高級商務區發展遠景 (1989-2006) Planned business uses in Central and Wan Chai, 1989-2006

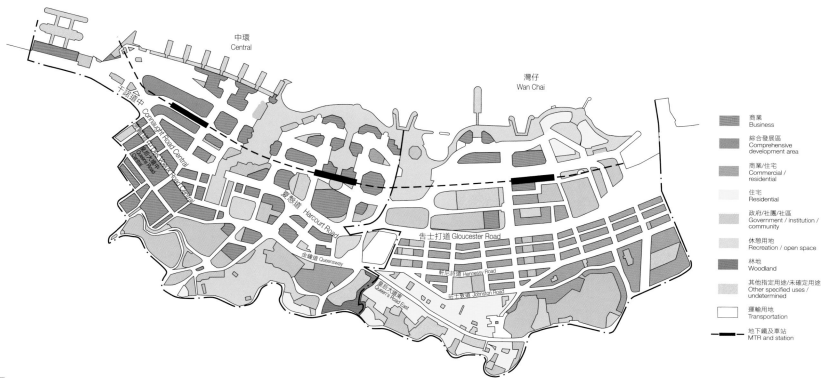

商業 Business

綜合發展區 Comprehensive development area

商業/住宅 Commercial / residential

住宅 Residential

政府/社團/社區 Government / institution / community

休憩用地 Recreation / open space

林地 Woodland

其他指定用途/未確定用途 Other specified uses / undetermined

運輸用地 Transportation

地下鐵及車站 MTR and station

● 中區分區計劃（擴展部份）大綱核准圖　Approved Central District (extension) outline zoning plan

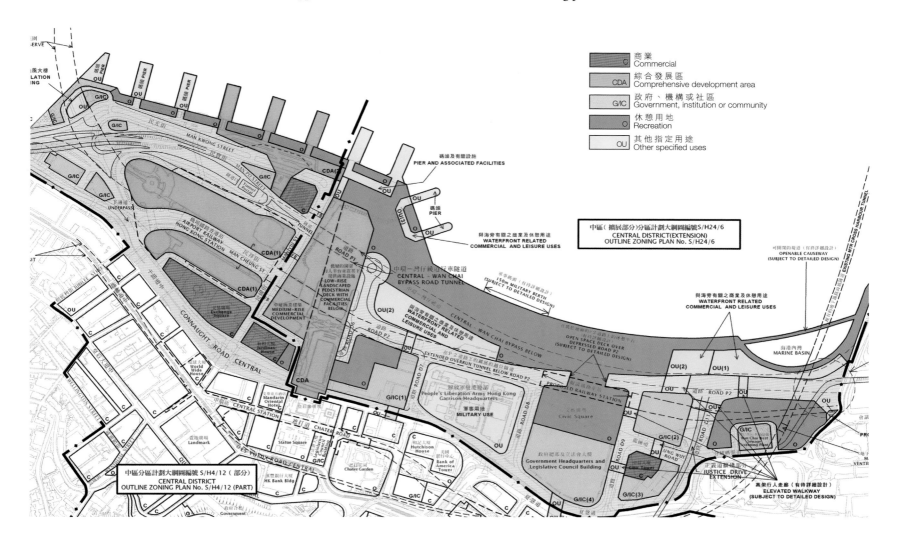

商業 Commercial
綜合發展區 Comprehensive development area
政府、機構或社區 Government, institution or community
休憩用地 Recreation
其他指定用途 Other specified uses

● 示意中區（擴展部份）總綱發展藍圖A示意圖　Illustrative master layout plan A of Central District (extension)

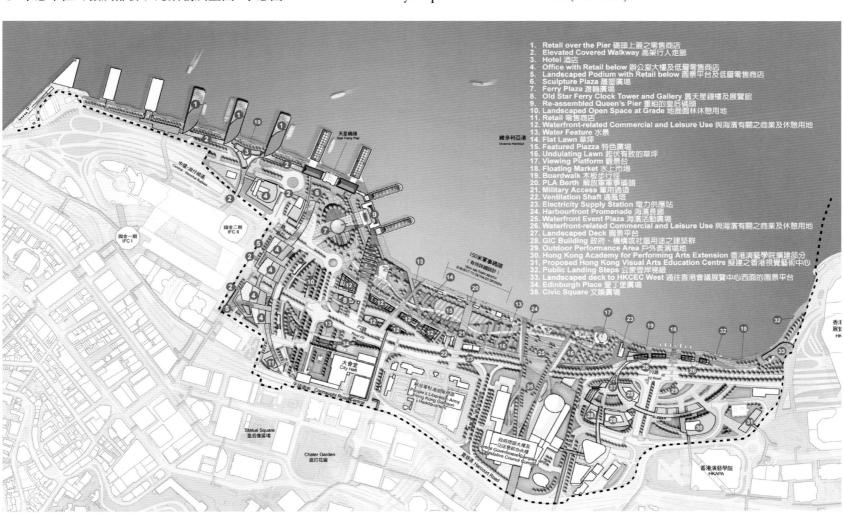

1. Retail over the Pier 碼頭上蓋之零售商店
2. Elevated Covered Walkway 高架行人走廊
3. Hotel 酒店
4. Office with Retail below 辦公室大樓及低層零售商店
5. Landscaped Podium with Retail below 園景平台及低層零售商店
6. Sculpture Plaza 雕塑廣場
7. Ferry Plaza 渡輪廣場
8. Old Star Ferry Clock Tower and Gallery 舊天星鐘樓及展覽館
9. Re-assembled Queen's Pier 重組的皇后碼頭
10. Landscaped Open Space at Grade 地面園林休憩用地
11. Retail 零售商店
12. Waterfront-related Commercial and Leisure Use 與海濱有關之商業及休憩用地
13. Water Feature 水景
14. Flat Lawn 草坪
15. Featured Piazza 特色廣場
16. Undulating Lawn 起伏有致的草坪
17. Viewing Platform 觀景台
18. Floating Market 水上市場
19. Boardwalk 木板步行徑
20. PLA Berth 解放軍軍事碼頭
21. Military Access 軍用通道
22. Ventilation Shaft 通風井
23. Electricity Supply Station 電力供應站
24. Harbourfront Promenade 海濱長廊
25. Waterfront Event Plaza 海濱活動廣場
26. Waterfront-related Commercial and Leisure Use 與海濱有關之商業及休憩用地
27. Landscaped Deck 園景平台
28. GIC Building 政府、機構或社區用途之建築群
29. Outdoor Performance Area 戶外表演場地
30. Hong Kong Academy for Performing Arts Extension 香港演藝學院擴建部分
31. Proposed Hong Kong Visual Arts Education Centre 擬建之香港視覺藝術中心
32. Public Landing Steps 公眾登岸梯級
33. Landscaped deck to HKCEC West 通往香港會議展覽中心西面的園景平台
34. Edinburgh Place 愛丁堡廣場
35. Civic Square 文娛廣場

01　農業　Agriculture

清初的海禁在1669年解除，經康熙、雍正二朝招墾，吸引了大量客家農民遷入包括了香港的南中國地區，農業成為香港的經濟支柱。1901年香港島有耕地406英畝，九龍404英畝，但仍未有新界地區數字，原因是土地註冊工作仍未完成。1904年成立土地法庭後審理的自稱擁有土地的提案就有35萬多宗，顯示了新界農業的發達。1911年香港島和九龍的耕地仍為810英畝，新界耕地為41,967英畝。

1911-1940年，農業增長不大。1940年耕地為50,252英畝，30年間只增加7,475英畝。1941-1951年是農業最大的增長期。其間，日本佔領軍刺激農業發展以解決戰爭用糧的短缺。這十年，耕地面積增加一倍。1951-1961年，耕地再增四成。1953-1954年圖代表了香港農業最盛期，稻米種植及飼養業皆盛。稻米和蔬菜是當時主要農產品。從1960年代末起耕地面積開始下降。

1951年起稻田面積下降，但菜地和魚塘明顯增加。1971年開始，荒置農地增加，不少成為露天倉庫及舊壞車的堆場和空貨櫃堆場，破壞了

In 1901, there were 406 ac of farm land on Hong Kong Island, 404 ac in Kowloon. In 1904, the Land Tribunal received a total of 350,000 cases of claim on farmland ownership in the New Territories. Indeed, agriculture was the New Territories' economic mainstay since the 17th century. In 1911, it had an acreage of 41,967 ac, whereas Hong Kong and Kowloon had only 810 ac By 1940, Hong Kong's overall total was 50,252 ac, having increased only 7,475 ac over a period of 30 years. During the Japanese occupation, local agriculture was boosted in an effort to supply the Japanese forces and farm acreage was doubled. In 1951, it remained at about 100,000 ac. It further increased by 40 % in the post-war years reaching the peak in local agriculture. Then, both paddy growing and animal husbandry were thriving. From 1951, there was a shift from paddy fields to fish ponds.

Since 1971, abandoned farmland increased. Many were turned into open storages, old car dumps and empty container yards. This fouled the countryside scenery and harmed neighbouring farms.

In 1954, Yuen Long and Tuen Mun was the largest agricultural area, with 14,892 ac fish ponds concentrated in Yuen Long. Until 1964, there were still plenty

---

● **1953-1954年耕地及農產品分佈圖　Distribution of agricultural land and agricultural products, 1953-1954**

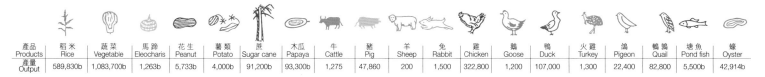

產品 Products	稻米 Rice	蔬菜 Vegetable	馬蹄 Eleocharis	花生 Peanut	薯類 Potato	蔗 Sugar cane	木瓜 Papaya	牛 Cattle	豬 Pig	羊 Sheep	兔 Rabbit	雞 Chicken	鵝 Goose	鴨 Duck	火雞 Turkey	鴿 Pigeon	鵪鶉 Quail	塘魚 Pond fish	蠔 Oyster
產量 Output	589,830b	1,083,700b	1,263b	5,733b	4,000b	91,200b	93,300b	1,275	47,860	200	1,500	322,800	1,200	107,000	1,300	22,400	82,800	5,500b	42,914b

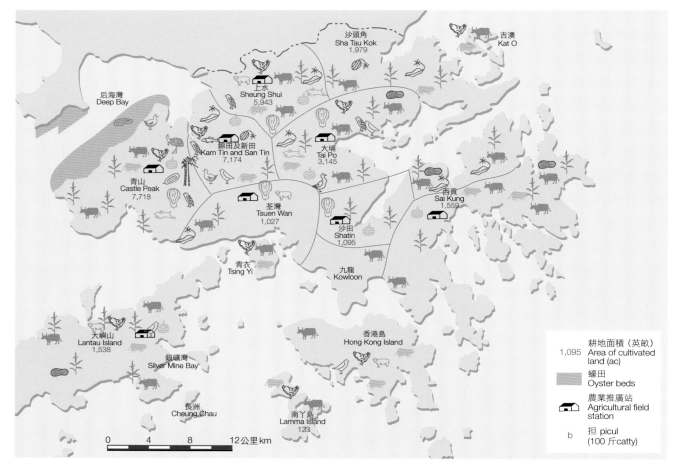

耕地面積（英畝）
1,095　Area of cultivated land (ac)

蠔田
Oyster beds

農業推廣站
Agricultural field station

擔　picul
b　(100 斤catty)

● **1951-2007年農業用地變化　Change in agricultural land use, 1951-2007**

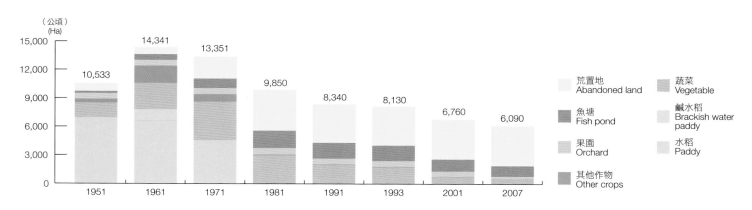

荒置地　Abandoned land　　蔬菜　Vegetable
魚塘　Fish pond　　鹹水稻　Brackish water paddy
果園　Orchard　　水稻　Paddy
其他作物　Other crops

郊野景色，也為害其他農地。

　　1954年圖顯示元朗和屯門是最大的農業區，共有14,892英畝。魚塘更大量集中在元朗。地理環境影響農業的分佈至為明顯。1964年時，除了九龍、港島和荃灣外，各區仍有少量稻田，1993年稻田差不多完全消失。這和集水區的擴大、新市鎮的建設以及農業經營成本高有關。

　　1995年，本地農產品的自給率為：蔬菜26%，活家禽23%，生豬7%，淡水魚11%，總產值為12億元。農業和漁業合計的產值為15.9億元，只佔香港GDP的0.2%。1998年耕地面積減為3.1%，自給率為：蔬菜14%，活家禽10%，生豬15%，淡水魚11%。2006年的在耕農地（包括魚塘）面積減至4,616英畝（1,909公頃），只有全港面積1.7%，上述的自給率在2008年分別為3%、46%、7%及5%。

of paddy fields except in Hong Kong Island, Kowloon and Tsuen Wan. By 1993, paddy fields have virtually disappeared.

　　The local self-sufficiency rate for a number of farm products in 1995 were: vegetables 26%, live poultry 23%, live pigs 7%, and fresh-water fish 11%, contributing only 0.2% of GDP.

　　In 1998, the agricultural area was reduced to 3.1% and the self-sufficiency rates were: vegetables 14%, live poultry 10%, live pig 15% and fresh-water fish 11%. In 2006 the cultivated farmland acreage (including fish ponds) declined to 4,616 ac (1,909 ha) or 1.7% of the total area while the above self-sufficiency rates in 2008 were 3%, 46%, 7% and 5% respectively.

● 1964 年耕地及農業活動分佈圖　Distribution of cultivated land and agricultural activities, 1964

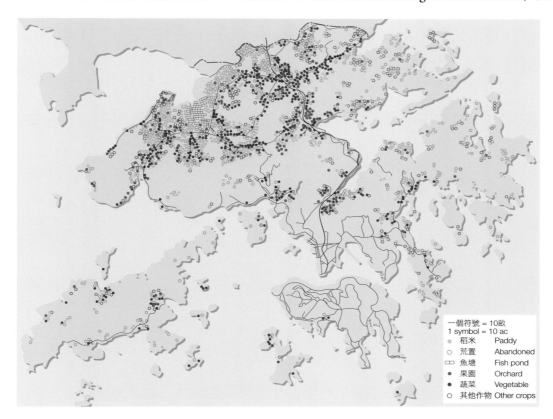

● 1993 年耕地及農業分佈圖　Distribution of cultivated land and agricultural activities, 1993

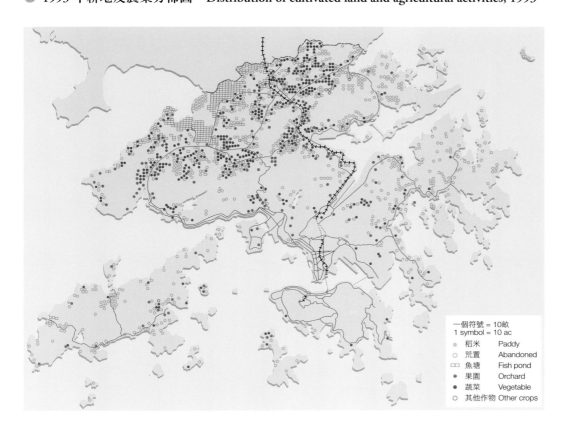

● 1993年農業產量和進口量　Agriculture output and imports, 1993

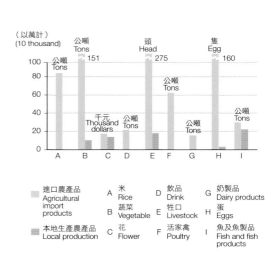

02 元朗區農業土地 Agriculture in Yuen Long

1950年的元朗海岸線和1900年時很不同。1900年時仍是漲潮時被淹沒的紅樹林沼澤，到了1950年已變成鹹水稻田和魚塘。青山公路元朗一段建於1930年，促進了元朗新墟的發展。1950年米埔已經圍起來了，但依然是紅樹林沼澤，並未建成蝦塘。元朗的平地在1900及1950年時，主要種植淡水稻。

在1960年的農業圖，青山公路穿過新墟，平原上大部份為淡水稻田，有三造的和兩造的。北面和東北角沿后海灣的沼澤上，仍有鹹水草的種植。一年一造的鹹水稻田在西北角也有發現。南面及元朗墟北的坡地上有果園及旱地作物。新墟的附近以及沿青山公路兩旁出現了不少菜

Yuen Long's coastline in 1950 has changed considerably from that in 1900 as most mangroves then were turned into fish ponds and brackish-water paddy fields. The shrimp ponds in the present-day Mai Po Nature Reserve were not yet constructed.

In the 1960 agricultural map, Castle Peak Road could be seen going through San Hui. On Yuen Long Plain, the main crop was paddy which yielded 2-3 crops a year. On the swampy coast of Deep Bay, straw weed was grown. On gentle slopes were fruits and field crops. Along Castle Peak Road and around San Hui were mainly vegetable fields, as improved transportation link with Kowloon encouraged vegetable growing.

● 1960年元朗區土地利用圖 Land use of Yuen Long in 1960

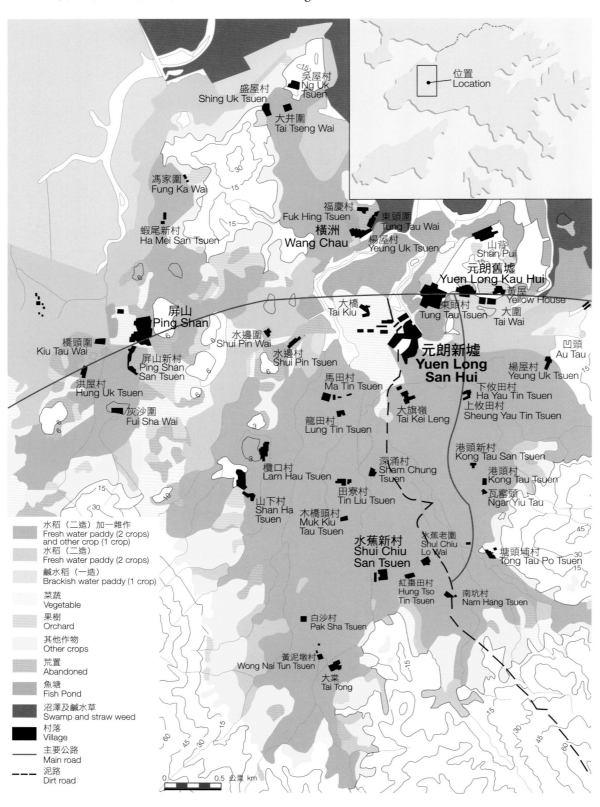

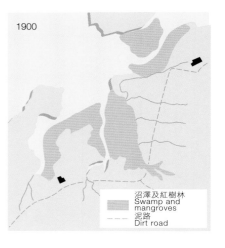

地。交通的改善，使新鮮蔬菜可以供應九龍市區。

圖中的農村聚落比前稠密多了。自1930年代以來，新墟更替代了舊墟，成為元朗平原的主要墟鎮。

1993年的元朗墟已是個人口近10萬的新市鎮。墟鎮南北以及沿公路的農業用地已經轉為城市用地。舊墟北的南生圍仍有大片魚塘。在其他平地上，只有分散零碎的菜地和果園，更多的農地被荒置，這個香港最大的農業區已經殘缺不全了。

San Hui replaced the Old Market in the 1930s. By 1993, it was a new town with about 100,000 people. Most of the former surrounding farmland has become urban land or abandoned and speculated for a change of land use, although there were still many fish ponds and vegetable farms. This former largest agricultural area has become fragmented and is in absolute decline.

1993年元朗區土地利用圖　Land use of Yuen Long in 1993

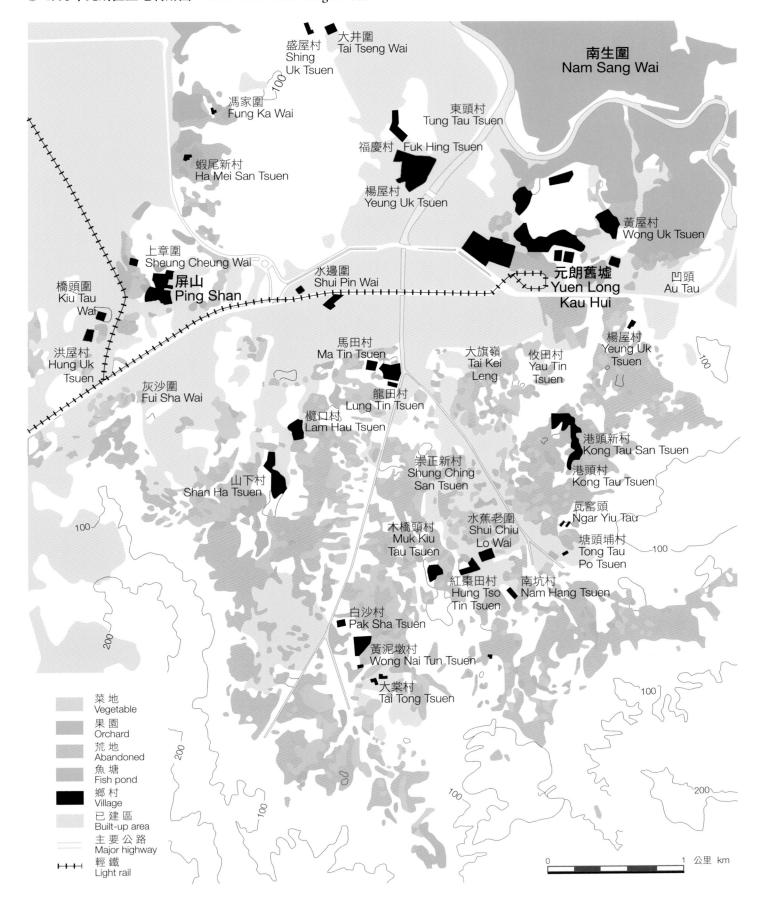

盛屋村 Shing Uk Tsuen
大井圍 Tai Tseng Wai
南生圍 Nam Sang Wai
馮家圍 Fung Ka Wai
東頭村 Tung Tau Tsuen
蝦尾新村 Ha Mei San Tsuen
福慶村 Fuk Hing Tsuen
楊屋村 Yeung Uk Tsuen
黃屋村 Wong Uk Tsuen
上章圍 Sheung Cheung Wai
屏山 Ping Shan
水邊圍 Shui Pin Wai
元朗舊墟 Yuen Long Kau Hui
凹頭 Au Tau
橋頭圍 Kiu Tau Wai
洪屋村 Hung Uk Tsuen
灰沙圍 Fui Sha Wai
馬田村 Ma Tin Tsuen
大旗嶺 Tai Kei Leng
攸田村 Yau Tin Tsuen
楊屋村 Yeung Uk Tsuen
龍田村 Lung Tin Tsuen
欖口村 Lam Hau Tsuen
港頭新村 Kong Tau San Tsuen
港頭村 Kong Tau Tsuen
山下村 Shan Ha Tsuen
崇正新村 Shung Ching San Tsuen
瓦窰頭 Ngar Yiu Tau
木橋頭村 Muk Kiu Tau Tsuen
水蕉老圍 Shui Chiu Lo Wai
塘頭埔村 Tong Tau Po Tsuen
紅棗田村 Hung Tso Tin Tsuen
南坑村 Nam Hang Tsuen
白沙村 Pak Sha Tsuen
黃泥墩村 Wong Nai Tun Tsuen
大棠村 Tai Tong Tsuen

菜地 Vegetable
果園 Orchard
荒地 Abandoned
魚塘 Fish pond
鄉村 Village
已建區 Built-up area
主要公路 Major highway
輕鐵 Light rail

0　　　1 公里 km

03 沙田區農業土地 Agriculture in Shatin

1902年，沙田谷地和沿海淺灘有大片的鹹水稻田和魚塘。在擔竿埔對開有一片紅樹林沼澤。當時聚落不多，最大的是大圍和曾大屋。當時的兩個小村——沙田及沙田頭，大概與這個地區的命名有關。溺谷口大片在退潮時現出的沙灘，也是"沙田"命名的另一來源。

In 1902, Shatin was a drowned valley rimmed by sandy beaches. Its main land uses were paddy and fish ponds. Mangroves were found at Tam Kon Po. Settlements were scarce, the largest being Tai Wai and Tsang Tai Uk. Shatin may get its name from two small villages–Shatin and Sha Tin Tau, or the large stretch of sandy beaches exposed in low tide at the mouth of the valley.

● 1902年沙田農業土地利用 Agricultural land use in Shatin, 1902

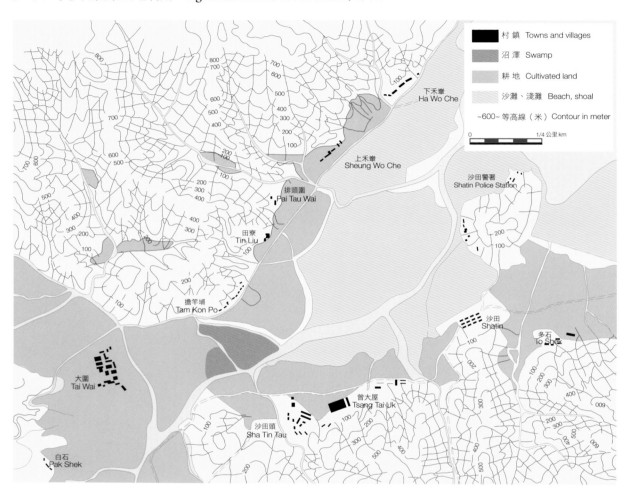

● 1960年沙田農業土地利用 Agricultural land use in Shatin, 1960

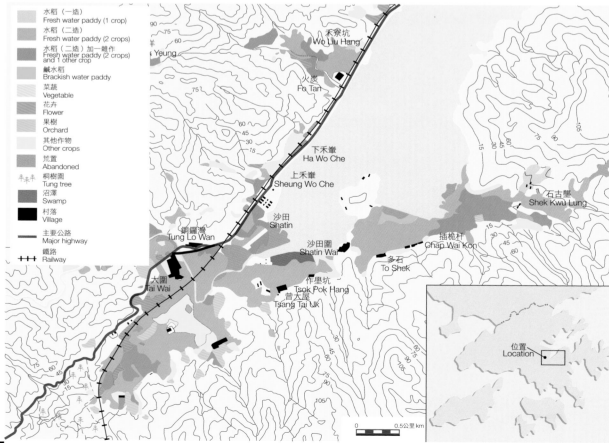

鹹水稻田在1960年已被淡水稻田和菜田所替代。早期的紅樹林沼澤，部份也變為淡水稻田。新出現了沙田墟、火炭、銅鑼灣等較大的聚落。坡地上有新墾的果園和其他旱地作物。

1990年的沙田已是城市景觀，總人口達54.5萬，73%住在公共房屋。大量填海將溺谷谷口的淺海轉為平地。傳統海岸線向北移2,000米，只留下人工做成的城門河道。曾大屋周圍的農田完全消失了，只餘山坡上零星的果園和荒置農地。整個谷地和沿海平地已變成城市用地，農業只餘下在新市鎮緣帶中的殘餘果園。自1981年起，沙田向馬鞍山和烏溪沙擴展，使新市鎮的規劃人口再增20萬。

1998年沙田新市鎮人口約60萬。住在公共房屋的人口比例為68%。新市鎮發展面積為2,000公頃。

Brackish water paddy was replaced by fresh water paddy and vegetables as the main crops by 1960. The mangroves were reclaimed to become paddy fields. Larger settlements (Shatin Market, Fo Tan and Tung Lo Wan) appeared. Horticulture and field crops took hold on gentle slopes.

Shatin in 1990 was a large city of 545,000 persons with 73% in public housing. Reclamation turned most of the shallow channel into flat land as the coastline retreated 2 km northwards, leaving only an artificial ditch. The only remains of agriculture were orchards on slopes and abandoned fields.

Since 1981, Shatin expanded towards Ma On Shan and Wu Kai Sha, with an additional target population of 200,000.

By 1998, Shatin New Town had 600,000 people.

● **1990 年沙田農業土地利用**　Agricultural land use in Shatin, 1990

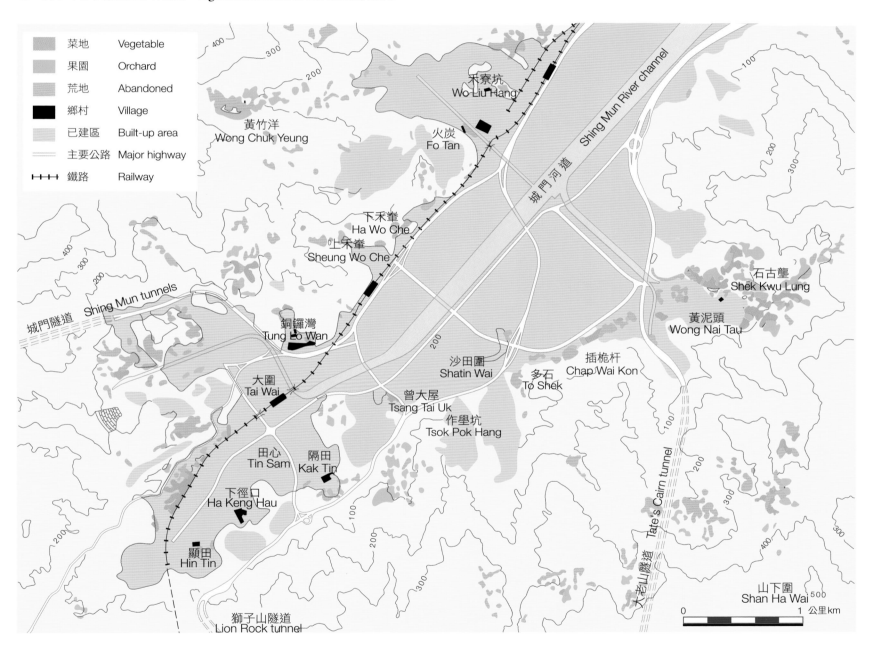

	菜地	Vegetable
	果園	Orchard
	荒地	Abandoned
	鄉村	Village
	已建區	Built-up area
	主要公路	Major highway
	鐵路	Railway

04 漁業 Fishing Industry

香港最早的經濟活動應該是漁業，因為香港有優良的港灣，鄰近南中國的近海(至200米深)魚場，有淡水供應等。在香港島1845年的人口中，有四成是蜑家或水上居民。1911年的人口普查，也報導了全新界地區有9,855名水上居民，其中長洲便有4,442人。

1953年圖記錄了香港漁業在高峰時期的狀況。它顯示出香港的近海魚場位置以及拖網、繩釣、刺網和圍網四種捕魚法。雖然漁船和器械大有改進，但所用的還是這些傳統方法。主要的魚種及魚產量也變化不大。當時最大的漁港香港仔有漁工16,722人，漁船1,602艘。其他漁港有長洲、大澳、青山、筲箕灣和大埔，各有3,000以上漁工。當年漁工總數達53,261人。1996年香港仍有漁船4,800艘，漁民21,600人。海魚產量，佔

The earliest economic activity in Hong Kong should be fishery as it has sheltered bays, fresh water supply and was close to South China's fishing grounds.

Among the 1845's population of the Island, 40% were Tanka, a fishing population living on boats. In the 1911 census, there were 9,855 such people in the New Territories, of which Cheung Chau accounted for almost half. The 1953 map registers the height of local fishery and its main operation data and locations. The four traditional fishing methods are still used today despite advancement in technology. Aberdeen, the largest fishing community at the time, employed 16,722 workers with 1,602 crafts. Sizeable fishing harbours with over 3,000 employees in the industry included Cheung Chau, Tai O, Castle Peak, Shau Kei Wan and Tai Po. The total workers employed at that time were 53,261 persons with a total catch of

● 1953年漁業實況 **Fishing industry in 1953**

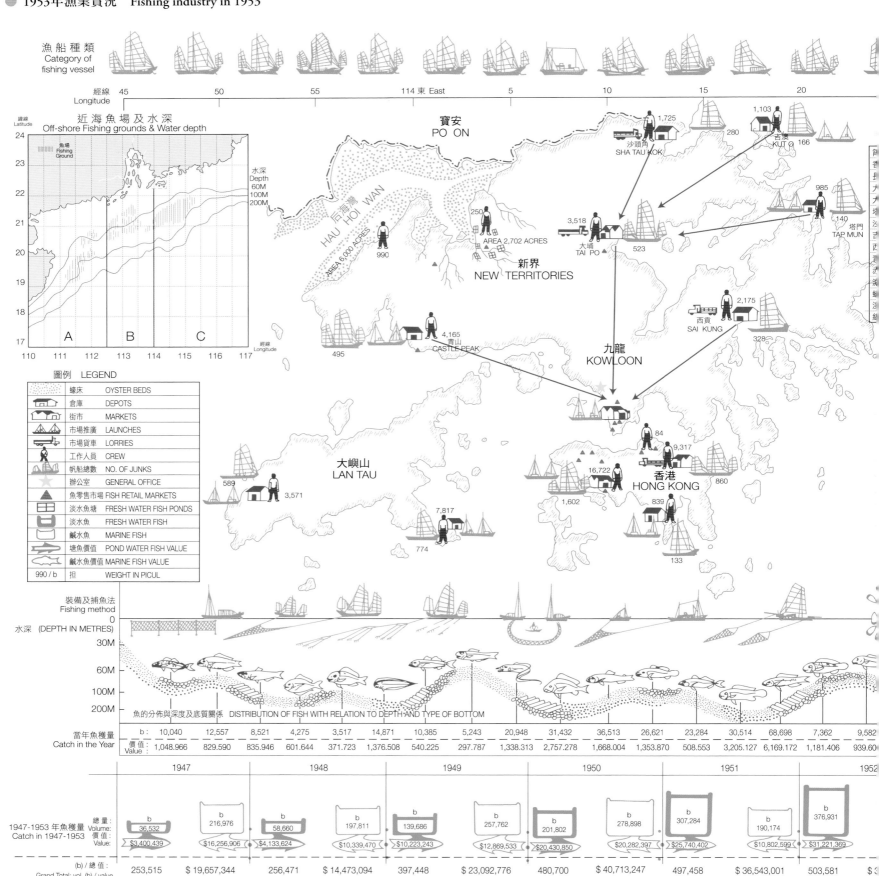

全香港消耗量53%。1998年漁船減至4,500艘,漁民19,200人,海魚產量18萬噸,批發總值23億元。此外活海鮮總產量為84,000噸。不少活海鮮由26個劃定養殖區供應。此外,淡水養殖的魚塘區主要集中在元朗,1998年共有1,100公頃,和1954年差不多;本地淡水魚只佔本地魚產的4%以及香港淡水魚消費的11%。2008年仍有魚塘約1,000公頃,但淡水魚產量只佔總供應量的7%。

漁業從業員數字在高峰1961年是8萬人,以後人數減少,但總產量因漁業效率的提高而沒有下降。

80,000 tonnes at its peak in 1961.

In 1998, there were 4,500 fishing boats, employing 192,000 persons, with 180,000 tonnes of catch. In addition, there were 26 marine fish farms along the coast that produced 84,000 tonnes of live fish. Fresh-water fish ponds totalling 1,100 ha mainly concentrated in Yuen Long. The industry produced about half of the marine fish and 11% of fresh-water fish consumed locally. In 2008, there were still about 1,000 ha of fish ponds, but local production of fresh-water fish accounted for only 7% of local demand.

The number of fishery workers declined from its peak of 80,000 in 1961, though the volume of catch has increased due to higher efficiency.

● 1994年漁業圖　Fishing industry in 1994

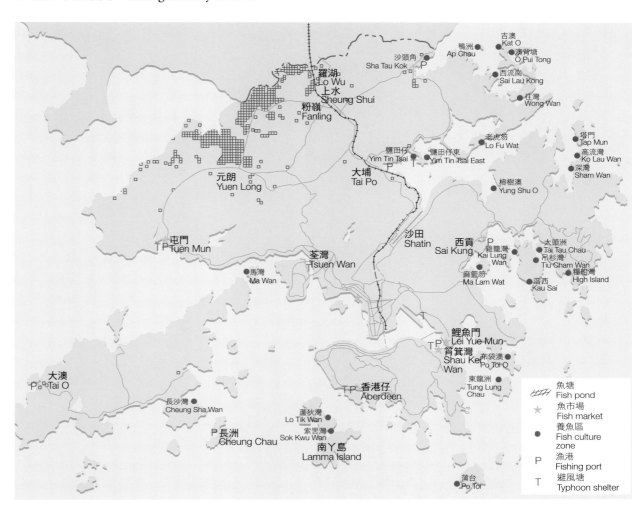

● 香港漁業　Fishing industry

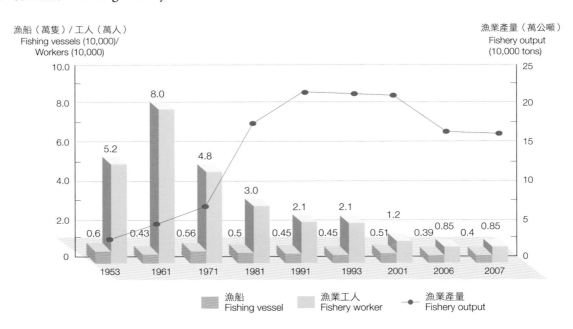

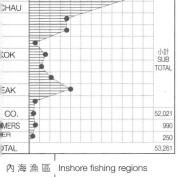

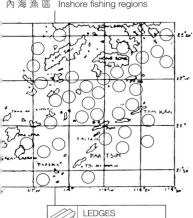

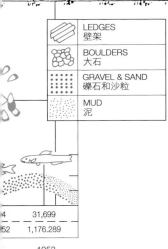

05 植林與郊野公園 Afforestation and Country Parks

香港陡峭的地形使大部份土地不能開發使用。同時，為了保護水庫集水區，很多坡地定為法定保護區。

香港有2,800種野生植物、300多種鳥類、200種蝴蝶和50種其他野生動物。保護坡地的自然環境，可以同時保護自然生態。

郊野公園除了可達致上述目的之外，還可以作康樂及教育之用。1977年立例成立郊野公園，由漁農處負責規劃和管理。目前共有21個郊野公園，佔地約4萬公頃，是香港總面積的四成。

The steep gradient renders most land areas in Hong Kong unsuitable for development. At the same time, to conserve water catchment areas, most such places were under legislative protection. These areas provide an environment of rich natural life in Hong Kong, which includes over 2,800 plants, 300 birds, 200 butterfly species and about 50 wild animals. Besides these goals, country parks are educational and recreational.

Legislation in 1977 led to the establishment of these parks under the management of the former Department of Agriculture and Fishery. There are now

● 1993年的郊野公園 Country parks, 1993

▨ 林地 Woodland

▨ 郊野公園 Country Parks

1	城門	Shing Mun	8	船灣	Plover Cove	15	馬鞍山	Ma On Shan
2	金山	Kam Shan	9	大嶼山南	Lantau South	16	橋咀	Kiu Tsui
3	獅子山	Lion Rock	10	大嶼山北	Lantau North	17	船灣(擴展區)	Plover Cove (extension)
4	香港仔	Aberdeen	11	八仙嶺	Pat Sin Leng	18	薄扶林	Pok Fu Lam
5	大潭	Tai Tam	12	大欖	Tai Lam	19	大潭(鰂魚涌擴展區)	Tai Tam (Quarry Bay extension)
6	西貢東	Sai Kung East	13	大帽山	Tai Mo Shan	20	清水灣	Clearwater Bay
7	西貢西	Sai Kung West	14	林村	Lam Tsuen	21	石澳	Shek O

☆ 現存特殊郊野公園及其他特殊區域 Designated special country parks and other special areas

▨ 計劃中的郊野公園 Country Parks under construction

A	大嶼山北	Lantau North	H	大帽山	Tai Mo Shan
B	南丫島南	South Lamma Island	I	林村	Lam Tsuen
C	馬鞍山	Ma On Shan	J	八仙嶺	Pat Sin Leng
D	東龍洲	Tung Lung Chau	K	紅花嶺	Robin's Nest
E	灣仔	Wan Tsai	L	大欖	Tai Lam
F	蒲台	Po Toi	M	薄扶林	Pok Fu Lam
G	沙田	Shatin	N	馬屎洲	Ma Shi Chau

▨ 計劃中的海岸公園與保護區 Marine Parks and Marine Reserves under construction

I	鶴咀	Cape D'Aguilar
II	海下灣	Hoi Ha Wan
III	印洲塘	Yan Chau Tong

1995年頒佈了海岸公園條例，以規劃和管理海岸公園和海岸保護，總面積2,160公頃。香港的近岸和海洋動物近200種，活躍於鹹淡水交界處的駝背豚（中華白海豚），是香港的代表性海洋生物。

21 country parks, covering 40,000 ha, or 40% of Hong Kong.

The Marine Country Park legislation was passed in 1995. Marine parks now cover 2,160 ha, protecting over 200 coastal marine species, which include the Hong Kong symbol: the Chinese White Dolphin.

● 2008年的郊野公園　Country parks, 2008

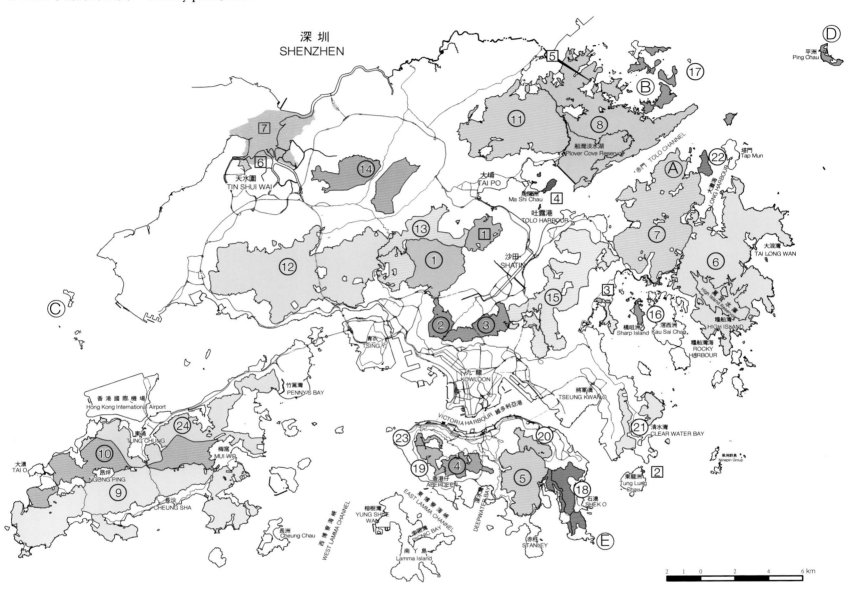

香港現已劃定的郊野公園
Designated country parks in Hong Kong

編號 No.	地點 Location		面積(公頃) Area (ha)	劃定日期 Date of designation
①	城門	Shing Mun	1,400	24/6/1977
②	金山	Kam Shan	337	24/6/1977
③	獅子山	Lion Rock	557	24/6/1977
④	香港仔	Aberdeen	423	28/10/1977
⑤	大潭	Tai Tam	1,315	28/10/1977
⑥	西貢東	Sai Kung east	4,477	3/2/1978
⑦	西貢西	Sai Kung west	3,000	3/2/1978
⑧	船灣	Plover Cove	4,594	7/4/1978
⑨	南大嶼	Lantau south	5,640	20/4/1978
⑩	北大嶼	Lantau north	2,200	18/8/1978
⑪	八仙嶺	Pat Sin Leng	3,125	18/8/1978
⑫	大欖	Tai Lam	5,370	23/2/1979
⑬	大帽山	Tai Mo Shan	1,440	23/2/1979
⑭	林村	Lam Tsuen	1,520	23/2/1979
⑮	馬鞍山	Ma On Shan	2,880	27/4/1979
⑯	橋咀	Kiu Tsui	100	1/6/1979
⑰	船灣（擴建部份）	Plover Cove (extension)	630	1/6/1979
⑱	石澳	Shek O	701	21/9/1979
⑲	薄扶林	Pok Fu Lam	270	21/9/1979
⑳	大潭（鰂魚涌擴建部份）	Tai Tam (Quarry Bay ext.)	270	21/9/1979
㉑	清水灣	Clear Water Bay	615	28/9/1979
㉒	西貢西（灣仔擴建部份）	Sai Kung west (Wan Tsai ext.)	123	14/6/1996
㉓	龍虎山	Lung Fu Shan	47	18/12/1998
㉔	北大嶼（擴建部份）	Lantau north (extension)	2,360	7/11/2008
	總面積 Total area		43,394	

香港現已劃定的特殊地區（位於郊野公園外）
Designated special areas in Hong Kong (outside country parks)

編號 No.	地點 Location		面積(公頃) Area (ha)	劃定日期 Date of designation
1	大埔滘自然護理區	Tai Po Kau Nature Reserve	460	13/5/1977
2	東龍洲	Tung Lung Fort	3	22/6/1979
3	蕉坑	Tsiu Hang	24	18/12/1987
4	馬屎洲	Ma Shi Chau	61	9/4/1999
5	荔枝窩	Lai Chi Wo	1	15/3/2005
6	香港濕地公園	Hong Kong wetland park	61	1/10/2005
	總面積 Total area		610	

其他香港特別地區（位於郊野公園外）
Other special areas in Hong Kong (outside country parks)

編號 No.	地點 Location		面積(公頃) Area (ha)	指定日期 Listed date
7	拉姆薩爾濕地	Ramsar Site	1,540	4/9/1995
	總面積 Total area		1,540	

指定的海岸公園及海岸保護區
Designated marine parks and marine reserves

編號 No.	地點 Location		面積(公頃) Area (ha)	劃定日期 Date of designation
Ⓐ	海下灣海岸公園	Hoi Ha Wan	260	5/7/1996
Ⓑ	印洲塘海岸公園	Yan Chau Tong	680	5/7/1996
Ⓒ	沙洲及龍鼓洲海岸公園	Sha Chau and Lung Kwu Chau	1,200	22/11/1996
Ⓓ	東平洲海岸公園	Tung Ping Chau	270	16/11/2001
Ⓔ	鶴咀海岸保護區	Cape D'Aguilar	20	5/7/1996
	總面積 Total area		2,430	

Urban Growth

III. 城市

Urban Growth

III. 城市

01 19世紀的香港與九龍 Hong Kong and Kowloon in the 19th Century

1843年新設總測量一職，工作是規劃香港核心地區——中上環。1845–1855年圖顯示當年法院及郵政總局位於現今的華人行，炮台徑及美利道的名稱源於美利炮台，海事署在今天的皇后大道中九號，對面就是雪廠街的製冰廠。皇后大道中北沿都是外商（特別是英商），只有兩家華人商號。

1860年英國接管了九龍半島，規劃亦擴至九龍。1861年的最早規劃圖顯示：（一）有大量的軍營和軍事設施；（二）基於軍事目的，它十分重視交通規劃。當時半島的平地主要仍是農田；九龍城寨是個較大的聚落；大角咀是個伸出海灣的沙咀；宋皇台就是海旁的一個石階；旺角還是個農業地區，地圖上寫成望崗（Mong Kong）。1861年規劃圖也顯

The position of Surveyor General was created in 1843 for the planning of Central and Sheung Wan. The resultant 1843-1855 map shows the General Post Office and Law Court on the present China Building's site, and the origins of Battery Path and Merril Street were traced to the Murray Battery. The Marine Department was situated on No. 9, Queen's Road Central of today, and the old Dairy Farm Ice House was on its opposite–origin of Ice House Street. North of Queen's Road were mainly western merchant houses, including Dent, the leading opium trader.

The earliest plan (1861) to develop Kowloon stressed (1) barracks and other military facilities, and (2) transport. The lowlands were largely farmed. The Walled City was the largest settlement. Tai Kok Tsui was a small promontory, and Song Emperor's Terrace was a small knoll at the seaside. Mongkok was then Mong

● 1861年九龍規劃圖 Plan for Kowloon in 1861

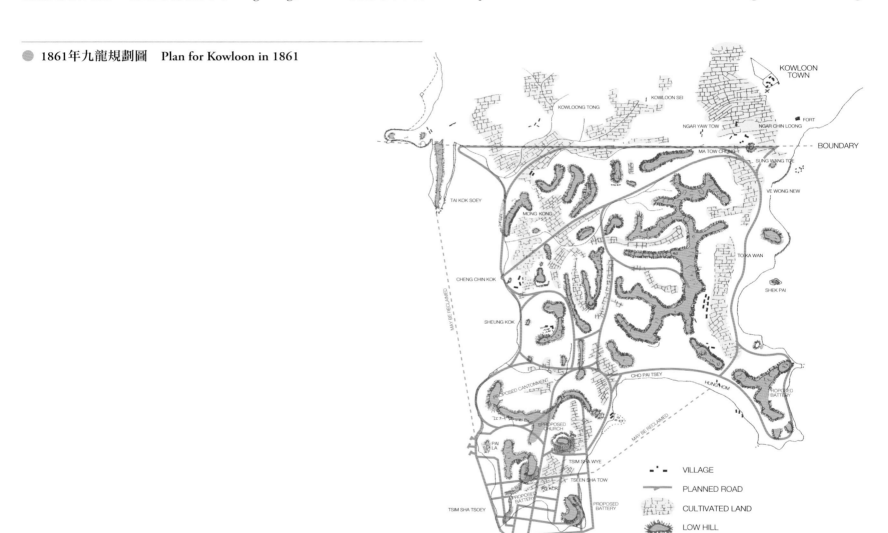

● 1843-1855年香港島規劃圖 Plan for Hong Kong Island in 1843-1855

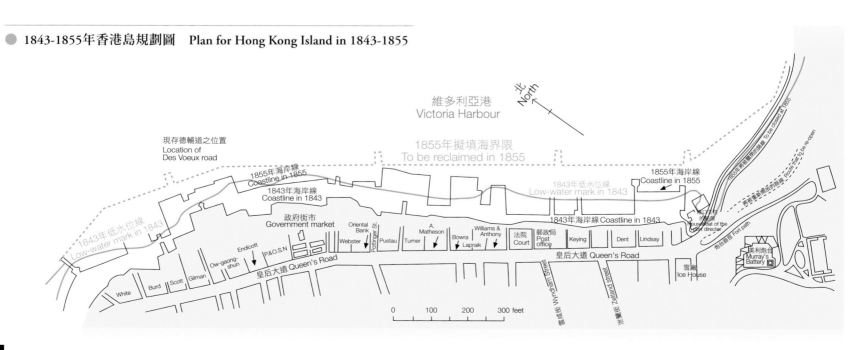

示了大規模填海的設想。

1888年的九龍雖被割讓30多年，仍然是軍事地區，只有尖沙咀、油麻地和觀塘有一點發展。香港的發展仍集中在北岸的維多利亞城，那裡已非常繁盛。地圖也顯示了在中環和灣仔填海的建議。由灣仔到銅鑼灣，只有斷續的沿岸帶狀發展。

在1900年圖中，九龍已有相當發展，包括了在規劃中的九廣鐵路。但九鐵的總站卻原本放在今天的海運大廈地點。城寨及其周邊仍是發展最稠密的地區。旺角仍是個農業地區。港島北岸的發展，似乎在1900-1920年間並不明顯。

圖中英文地名沿用舊圖拼法，不少與現今不同。

Kong, meaning a 'lookout' and was largely agricultural. The plan shows large-scale planned reclamations.

In 1888 Kowloon remained basically a military zone with limited urbanization in Tsim Sha Tsui, Yau Ma Tei and Kwun Tong. Hong Kong's main urban growth concentrated in Victoria City, where coastal linear urban growth was extended to Causeway Bay, with large planned reclamations.

More urban development in Kowloon was evident in 1900, with the Kowloon-Canton Railway being planned. Yet its terminal was originally planned at the present-day Ocean Terminal's site. The Walled City and its surrounding area was the largest cluster of settlement. Today's Mongkok remained an agricultural area. The pace of development of Island North seemed to have reached a peak in 1900, as there had not been much change in 1900-1920.

The spellings of many names of places differ from those of the present.

● 1888年香港島北岸與九龍半島南端　Hong Kong Island North and Kowloon Peninsula South in 1888

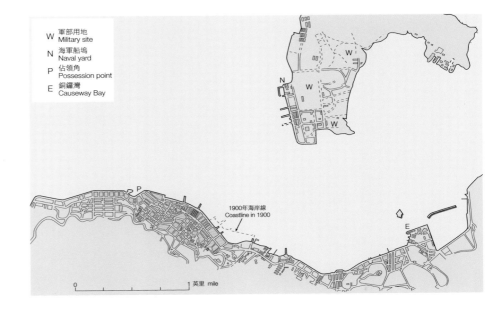

● 1900年的香港島及九龍　Hong Kong and Kowloon in 1900

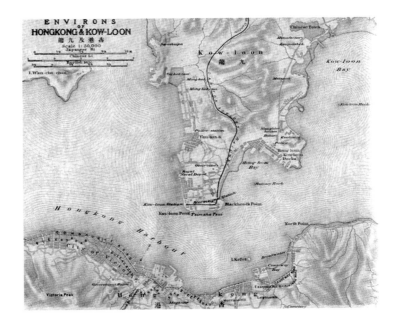

● 1920年香港島北岸　Northern coastline of Hong Kong Island in 1920

02　20世紀初的九龍　Kowloon in Early 20th Century

　　1904年九龍東及九龍西仍有大片農田。大角咀已填海發展，成為一個以沿海船塢為主體的新區。望角咀已有道路及樓房出現，但望角（即1861年圖中的望崗）仍是耕地。這是望角（譯自英文Mong Kok）這一名稱的首次出現，可能是從望崗（Mong Kong）訛轉而來。"旺角"，是後於此圖的再一次演化。望角咀、油麻地已成為華人商住的混雜區，紅磡成為船塢和倉庫區。彌敦道只建成尖沙咀一段，是個洋人地區，和華人商住區分隔。城寨外的九龍城，成為另一個華人商住區。

　　1904-1924年間，九龍的農田在減少。彌敦道及九廣鐵路已經建成。沿岸又加添了新填地，特別是在長沙灣、九龍城和紅磡。界限街已開始規劃了。深水埗、塘尾及土瓜（家）灣正形成新的市區。圖中九龍塘（Kau Lung Tong）應該是塘尾。

In 1904, farming persisted in northern Kowloon. Tai Kok Tsui was reclaimed into a new district of docklands. Mong Kok Tsui was quite urbanized, yet Mong Kong remained agricultural. 'Mong Kok Tsui' appeared for the first time, likely to evolve from 'Mong Kong'. Later 'Mong Kok' replaced Mong Kok Tsui. Then, Mong Kok Tsui and Yau Ma Tei constituted a district of Chinese residence and commercial activities. Hung Hom was a warehousing and dock area. The Tsim Sha Tsui section of Nathan Road was completed. Tsim Sha Tsui was a European quarter separated from Mong Kok Tsui and Yau Ma Tei. Kowloon City, next to the Walled City, was another major Chinese settlement.

By 1924, agricultural land area in Kowloon had declined substantially. Nathan Road and the Kowloon-Canton Railway's Kowloon section were completed. New reclaimed land appeared in Cheung Sha Wan, Kowloon City and Hung Hom.

● 1887-1904年的九龍　Kowloon between 1887 and 1904

● 1904-1924年的九龍　Kowloon betwee

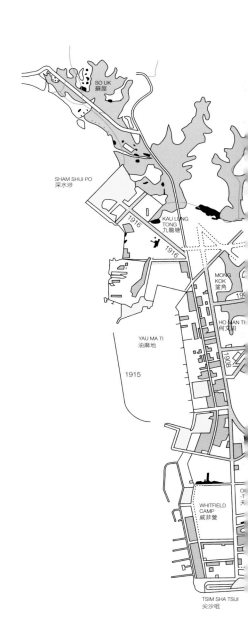

1887-1904 年後填海地
Land to be reclaimed after 1887-1904

1941年的九龍內的各個填海區和新區，已建成商住區。除了南部的軍用地和中部的山崗外，整個半島已成為一個稠密城市。界限街以北的城市發展已受到北面山崗的阻礙。城寨已成為一個被隔離的小聚落。

20世紀的上半段，九龍的發展速度明顯超越了港島。

Boundary Street was being planned while Sham Shui Po, Tong Mei and To Ka Wan became new urban areas. Kau Lung Tong in the map should be Tong Mei.

The various reclamations and new areas have been well built up by 1941. With the exception of the military land in the south and the hilly grounds in the middle, Kowloon has become an extensive city. However, its northern extension was already blocked by the hills north of Boundary Street. The Walled City lapsed into a small segregated settlement.

In the first half of the 20th century, the pace of development of Kowloon exceeded that of Hong Kong Island.

24

● 1941年九龍街道圖　Kowloon street map in 1941

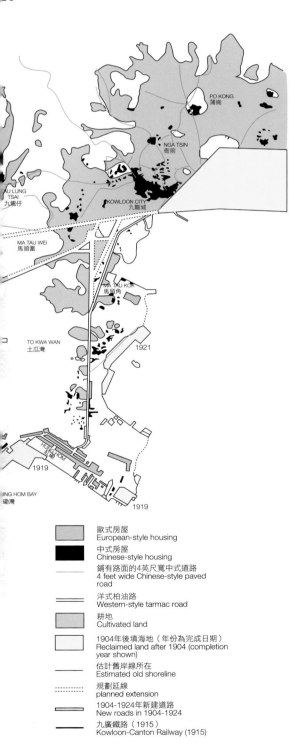

歐式房屋
European-style housing

中式房屋
Chinese-style housing

鋪有路面的4英尺寬中式道路
4 feet wide Chinese-style paved road

洋式柏油路
Western-style tarmac road

耕地
Cultivated land

1904年後填海地（年份為完成日期）
Reclaimed land after 1904 (completion year shown)

估計舊岸線所在
Estimated old shoreline

規劃延線
planned extension

1904-1924年新建道路
New roads in 1904-1924

九廣鐵路（1915）
Kowloon-Canton Railway (1915)

03 九龍舊市區的土地利用及遠景規劃 Land Use and Planning for Kowloon Peninsula

九龍半島是舊市區的主要部份。由於平坦，差不多全部是建成區。1993年圖中除了土地現狀外，也包括了建議中的填海，及啟德機場的搬遷。但九龍西填海以及舊區重建仍未顯示出來。圖中主要為住宅用途。香港市區的特色是高密度和向高空垂直發展，住宅區內普遍商住混合。

綠地不足以及舊區的落後道路網使九龍西、九龍中、紅磡、馬頭圍和九龍城等地區需要重建。經濟轉型也使舊市區的就業產生變化。預期它們的計劃人口會大幅度下降。西九龍填海和啟德機場的搬遷為這些地區的重新規劃和發展帶來了機會。

Kowloon Peninsula accounts for the major part of the old urban district. Due to its flat relief, most of it is built-up area. The 1993 map shows existing and planned land uses, reclamations, and the re-deployed Kai Tak Airport, though West Kowloon reclamation and major urban renewal projects are not shown. One characteristic in Hong Kong's urban areas is high-density and high-rise land use, and within residential districts, residential and commercial uses are generally blended.

Inadequate green open space and road networks necessitate urban redevelopment in Kowloon Peninsula. Economic restructuring in 1980-2000 has also changed its employment structure, leading to a decline in population. West

● **1993年九龍土地利用圖** **Land use of Kowloon in 1993**

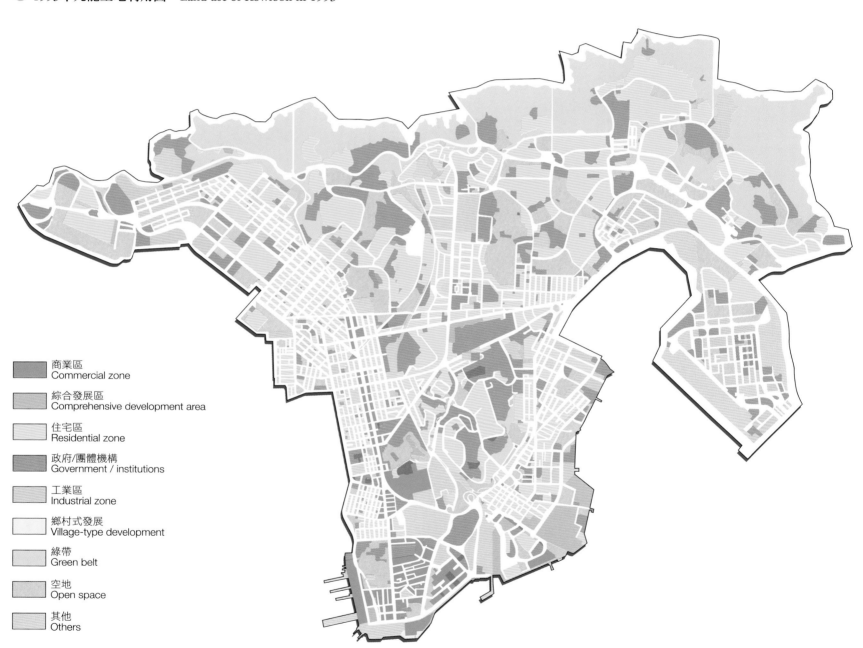

商業區
Commercial zone

綜合發展區
Comprehensive development area

住宅區
Residential zone

政府/團體機構
Government / institutions

工業區
Industrial zone

鄉村式發展
Village-type development

綠帶
Green belt

空地
Open space

其他
Others

這裡展示了不同時期的西九龍和東南九龍規劃圖,有關這些地區在2000年的發展,可以和本圖冊的相關部份互為參閱。

Kowloon reclamation and redeployment of the old airport site will bring new growth and opportunities.

Here are selected planning proposals for West Kowloon and Southeast Kowloon of different dates. They may be refered to in connection with relevant parts of this Atlas in order to understand the post-2000 development of these areas.

1994年提出的西九龍區重建計劃
Redevelopment plan for West Kowloon proposed in 1994

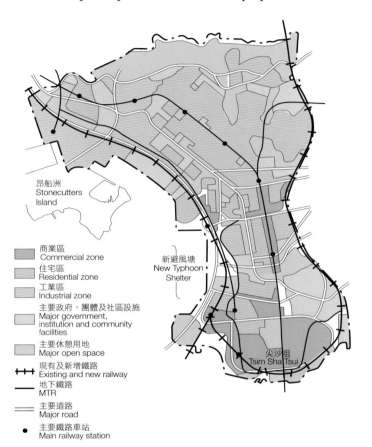

昂船洲
Stonecutters
Island

新避風塘
New Typhoon
Shelter

尖沙咀
Tsim Sha Tsui

- 商業區
  Commercial zone
- 住宅區
  Residential zone
- 工業區
  Industrial zone
- 主要政府、團體及社區設施
  Major government, institution and community facilities
- 主要休憩用地
  Major open space
- 現有及新增鐵路
  Existing and new railway
- 地下鐵路
  MTR
- 主要道路
  Major road
- 主要鐵路車站
  Main railway station

1994年提出的東南九龍區重建計劃
Redevelopment plan for Southeast Kowloon proposed in 1994

- 商業寫字樓／酒店
  Commercial office / hotel
- 住宅
  Residential
- 綜合性發展區
  Comprehensive development area
- 工業
  Industrial
- 政府／團體／社區
  Government / institution / community
- 其他用途
  Other uses
- 休憩用地
  Open space
- 地下鐵路
  MTR

啟德機場
Kai Tak
Airport

2009年西九龍分區計劃大綱圖
Outline Zoning Plans of West Kowloon in 2009

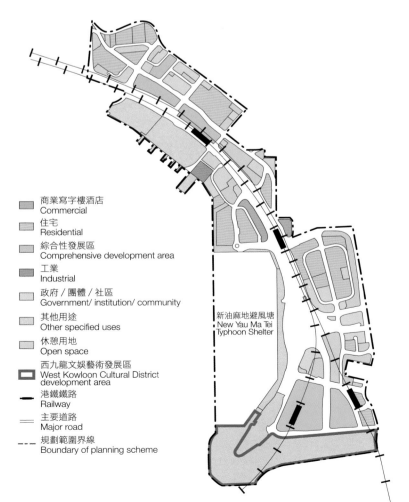

- 商業寫字樓酒店
  Commercial
- 住宅
  Residential
- 綜合性發展區
  Comprehensive development area
- 工業
  Industrial
- 政府／團體／社區
  Government/ institution/ community
- 其他用途
  Other specified uses
- 休憩用地
  Open space
- 西九龍文娛藝術發展區
  West Kowloon Cultural District development area
- 港鐵鐵路
  Railway
- 主要道路
  Major road
- 規劃範圍界線
  Boundary of planning scheme

新油麻地避風塘
New Yau Ma Tei
Typhoon Shelter

04 木屋區位置及人口　Squatter Camps

二次世界大戰後香港人口激增，加上戰爭的破壞，1950年代初出現了嚴重的房屋不足。當時的香港和第三世界的大城市的境況一樣，很多居民棲身在市區邊沿及港口的空置官地或非法佔用的私人地上搭建的木屋或寮屋裡。1950年代末，木屋居民佔全香港居民的25%。木屋居民在1960年更達60多萬人。

1953年石硤尾大火，導致香港政府展開木屋清拆和公共房屋計劃。早期的木屋集中在九龍的邊沿，如大角咀、石硤尾、九龍仔、李鄭屋一帶，對市區擴展造成障礙。加上出口工業發展對擴建工廠的土地需求，清拆木屋有明顯的市場價值。估計每清拆一地，只需1/3用以安置原木屋

Post-war population increase and wartime destruction led to serious housing shortage in the early 1950s. Like major Third World cities, squatter housing mushroomed in Hong Kong's urban fringe, and 25% of its population lived in temporary illegal wooden sheds. In 1960, about 600,000 squatter population was registered. A fire in 1953 in the largest squatter camp in Shek Kip Mei led to the launching of the resettlement programme. Hence, squatter camps were cleared gradually and their residents resettled in government constructed resettlement units–public housing estates. Then, large-scale squatters of low-income citizens in Shek Kip Mei, Kowloon Tsai, Li Cheng Uk, etc., formed a belt of non–conforming land use and strangled urban expansion in Kowloon. To create new land to support

● 1995年木屋區的分佈　*Distribution of squatter areas in 1995*

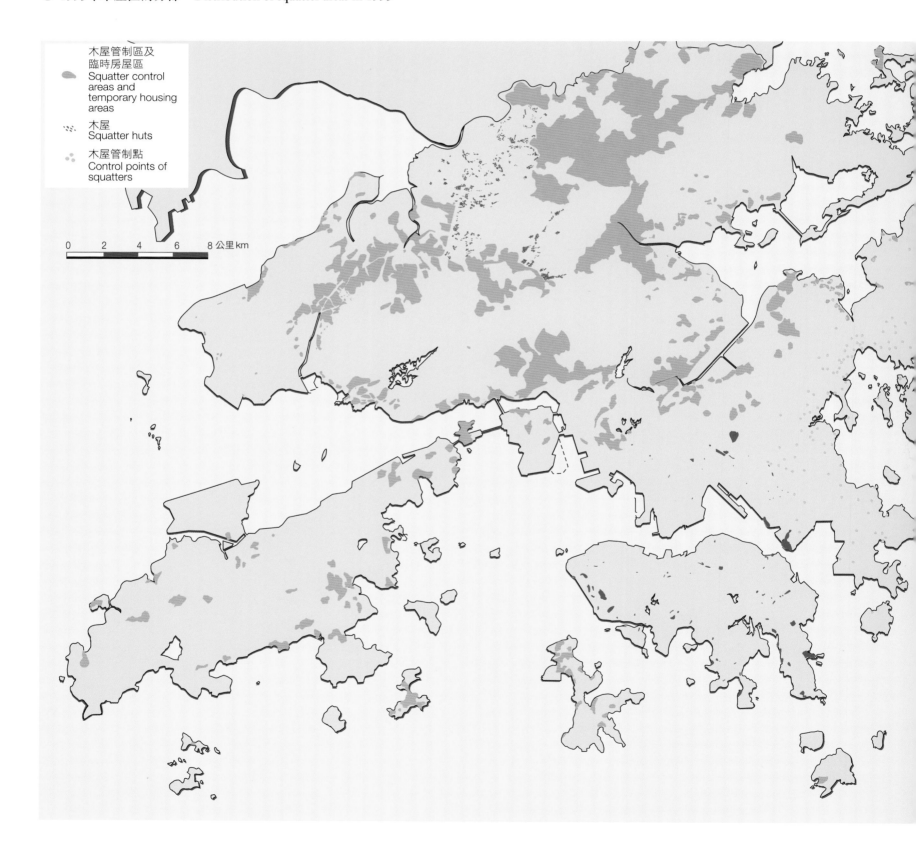

木屋管制區及臨時房屋區
Squatter control areas and temporary housing areas

木屋
Squatter huts

木屋管制點
Control points of squatters

0　2　4　6　8 公里 km

居民，1/3改善道路、社區及教育等設施，1/3可供私人發展。因此木屋清拆並不純出於福利考慮。

隨着城市發展，木屋區逐漸變成城建區的一部份。1980年代初，香港島最後的一片東區木屋也清拆了。現今木屋大部份位於新界的公路旁和新市鎮邊沿。臨時房屋成了受清拆木屋居民遷入公共房屋前的過渡居所。2000年全港仍有23萬多木屋居民，其中2萬人住在市區木屋。

industrialization, squatter clearance became imminent. Besides, it was economically sound to do so, as 1/3 of the site may be put for auction to private developers after meeting resettlement and infrastuctual improvement demands.

By early 1980s, major squatter camps on Hong Kong Island have disappeared. They were found only in the New Territories, especially on the fringes of new towns. The squatter population in 2000 was around 230,000, only 10% of which was in the urban areas.

● 1955年木屋區的分佈　Distribution of squatter areas in 1955

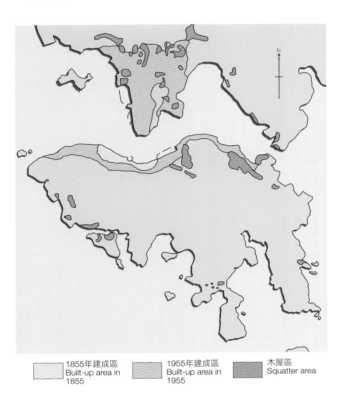

1855年建成區
Built-up area in 1855

1955年建成區
Built-up area in 1955

木屋區
Squatter area

● 1971年木屋區的分佈　Distribution of squatter areas in 1971

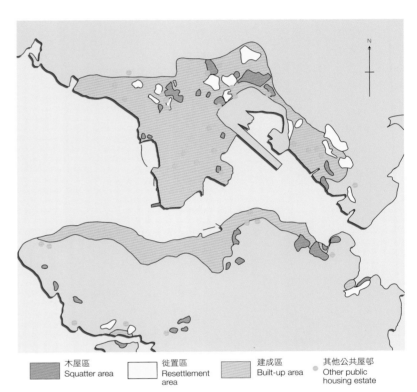

木屋區
Squatter area

徙置區
Resettlement area

建成區
Built-up area

其他公共屋邨
Other public housing estate

● 1982-1995年木屋數目及居住人數
Number of squatter huts and squatter population in 1982-1995

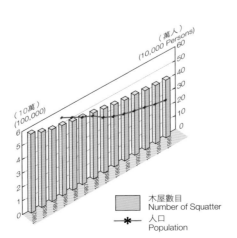

木屋數目
Number of Squatter

人口
Population

● 1961-2007年臨時屋居住人口　Temporary structure population in 1961-2007

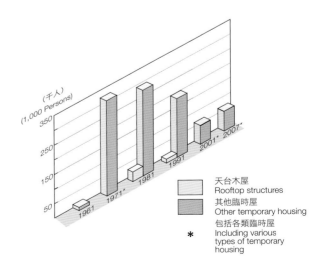

天台木屋
Rooftop structures

其他臨時屋
Other temporary housing

包括各類臨時屋
Including various types of temporary housing

05　公共房屋　Public Housing

　　戰後公共房屋的興起，是為了應付人口劇增和高速經濟發展的土地需求。租金低廉的公共房屋亦成為消除工資壓力和穩定社會的重要政策，以及新市鎮建設的重要手段。

　　1954年政府成立徙置事務署，以清拆木屋，並建設"徙置區"，即舊型公屋。1963年又成立房屋委員會，為低收入家庭提供廉租屋。這兩個機構在1973年合併為房屋委員會。早期政府以財政補貼及僅收地價1/3或1/2的辦法支持公共房屋的建設，目前仍以優惠價批地給房委會。1948年成立的房屋協會也提供低租住宅予低收入及"夾心人士"（中等收入）家庭。

　　1996年各類公營房屋共有約92萬個單位，佔全香港住宅總數46%，住了全香港人口的一半（318萬）。1998年政府推出輔助性出售出租公

Public housing was a post-war development due mainly to squatter clearance. Low rental in these high-density and small-unit-size housing was a social stabilizer and a means to maintain low labour costs and low inflation. Later, public housing was used as a means to attract population to boost the new towns.

The Resettlement Department was set up in 1954 after the Shek Kip Mei fire, for squatter clearance and public housing development. In 1963, the Housing Committee was founded to extend low-cost housing to non-squatter, low-income families. The two merged in 1973 to form the Housing Authority. Subsidies and concessionary land prices (1/2 -1/3 of market rate) were major forms of official support to public housing in early years. The Housing Society, a non-profit-making, semi-government organization, also offers low-rent housing to low and middle-income families.

By 1996, there were 920,000 public housing units, 46% of the total. They

● 公共房屋發展　Public housing development

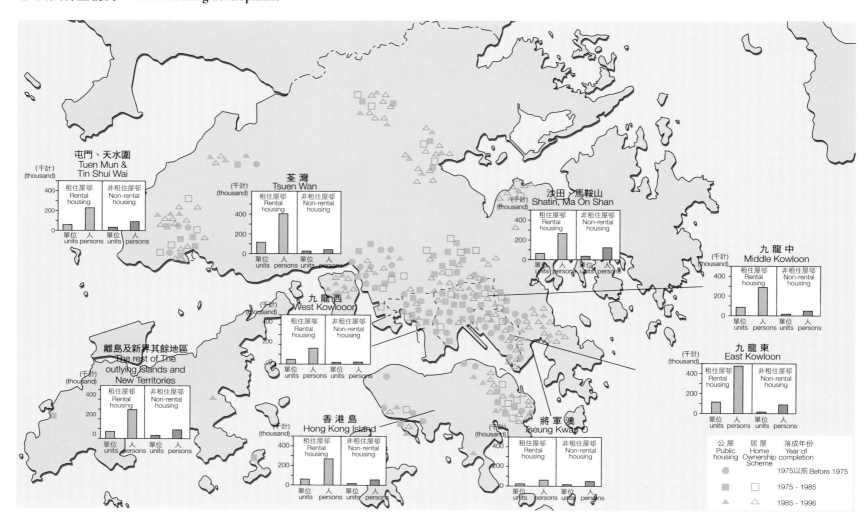

● 1989-2008年公私營房屋供應量　Public and private housing supply, 1989-2008

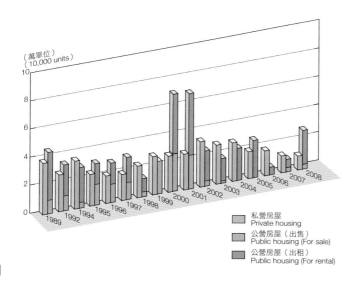

● 1994年公營房屋及居住人口分佈　Distribution of public housing and resident population, 1994

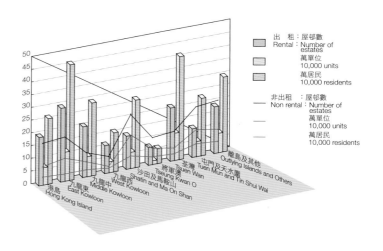

屋，在十年間，讓至少25萬個家庭可以購買現租單位，並公佈長遠房屋政策目標：（一）每年平均建公營房屋5萬單位，私營房屋3.5萬單位，（二）2007年自置居所比例達70%。其後的亞洲金融風暴迫使政府取消此計劃。1970年代前，公共房屋集中在新九龍，其後擴展至香港島。目前公共房屋主要建於新市鎮。公共房屋水平很低，以面積計，一半以上只有40平方米以下，1/3更在30平方米以下。

accommodated about half of the population (3.18 million).

In 1998, the new SAR government began to sell former public rental housing units to their tenants. It planned that by 2008, 250,000 rental units would be sold. In addition, it pledged (1) to construct 50,000 public and 35,000 private housing units annually, and (2) to raise the ownership ratio to 70% by 2007. These plans were abolished after the Asian Financial Crisis. Initially, public housing concentrated in New Kowloon. It later extended to Hong Kong Island. Since late 1980s, they are mainly constructed in the new towns. Public housing units are of low standard. Half of them are smaller than 40m^2 while 1/3 are even less than 30m^2.

● 2008年房屋委員會公共租住房屋分佈　Housing Authority public rental housing distribution in 2008

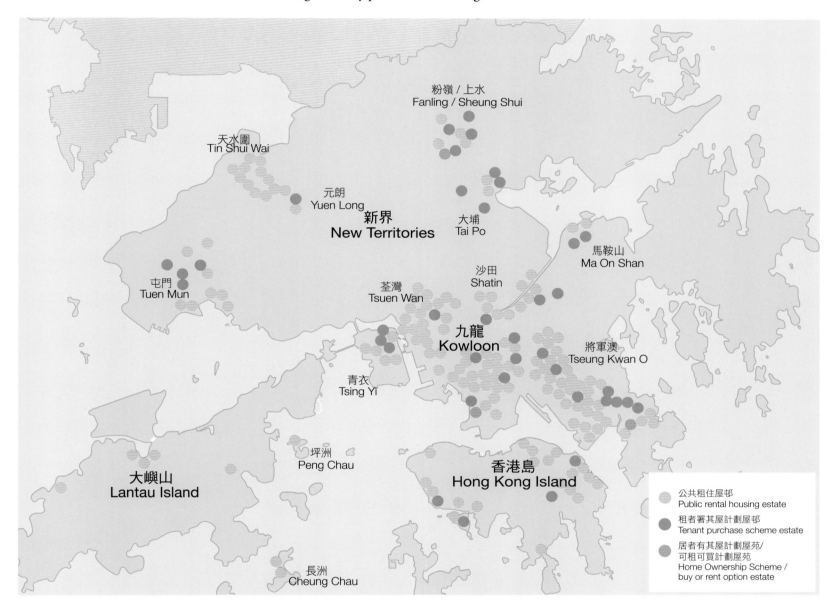

● 1999及2009年居於房委會永久住宅單位的人口分佈　Domestic households in Housing Authority permanent residential flats in 1999 and 2009

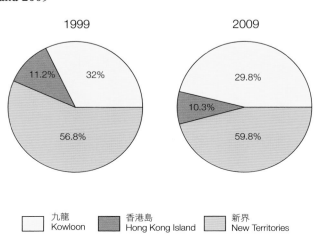

● 1999及2009年按面積（平方米）劃分的房委會公營租住房屋單位　Housing Authority rental flats by floor area (m^2) in 1999 and 2009

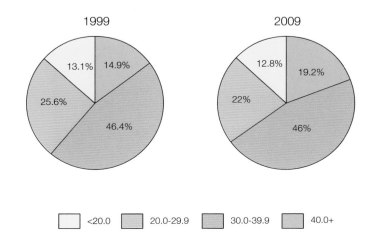

06 大型私人屋邨 Private Housing Estates

大型私人屋邨是有規劃的住宅發展，住宅外，還包括了停車場、購物及服務中心，有些還有中小學、幼稚園、公園、診所、社區設施等。由於市區大塊地皮不多，大型私人屋邨多在新開發地區。九龍最早的屋邨是美孚油庫搬遷後建成的美孚新邨。香港島最早的屋邨是牛奶公司在薄扶林牧場發展的置富花園、鰂魚涌的舊船塢搬遷後建成的太古城。新界以在魚塘區改建的錦繡花園為最早。

1980年代起大型私人屋邨成為私人住宅發展主流。政府出於規劃考慮，也在新發展地區，傾向大型私人屋邨的規劃和賣地辦法。

因為發展規模龐大，私人住宅發展趨向寡頭化。政府也堅持干預地產市場，1987-1997年建成的私人樓宇每年只保持在3萬個單位，但平均每方英尺的售價卻暴漲了8倍。特區成立後，由於房屋供應加大，加上亞洲金融風暴，私人住宅價格大幅回落約45%。自2000年起，特區放棄主導賣地，採用"勾地表"政策和停建"居屋"等，使私人樓宇在2008年供應減至數千單位，樓價回升至1997年的水平。

2008年底，全港有私人住宅單位1,085,922個，32.4%是40平方米以下，48.8%是40-70平方米的小單位。160平方米以上的"超大"單位只有11,276個。私人住宅"超小型化"是香港的特怪現象。

Large-scale private housing estates (PHE) are planned housing development by private developers that include comprehensive services such as schools, clinics, kindergartens, parks, community and shopping centres. Inadequate sites within the urban areas dictate that most PHE are on reclaimed or newly-formed land in the urban fringe and the New Territories. The earliest PHE is Mei Foo San Tsuen in Kowloon, built on a former oil depot. The old dockyard in Quarry Bay was redeveloped into Tai Koo Shing. The earliest PHE in the New Territories–Fairview Park, was built on former fish ponds.

Since the 1980s, PHE have became the main trend in private sector housing development. The government also favoured them through land auctions. PHE therefore lead to oligopolization in the real estate market. In 1987-1997, completed private housing stabilized at around 30,000 units annually, leading to a hike of per-sq ft price by 8-fold. After 1997, increased supply and the Asian Financial Crisis pushed prices down by 45%. Since 2000, a new 'auction list' policy and an abrupt stop of the 'Home Ownership Scheme' resulted in the drop in supply to around 5,000 private units in 2008, and a price rebound per-sq ft back to the 1997 level.

By the end of 2008, there were 1,085,922 private housing units, 32.4% was less than 40m², and 48.8% was 40-70 m² in size. 'Extra-large' units of over 160m² number only 11,276 units. The 'smallness' of Hong Kong housing units is unique.

● 2008年主要私人屋邨位置圖 Location of major private housing estates in 2008

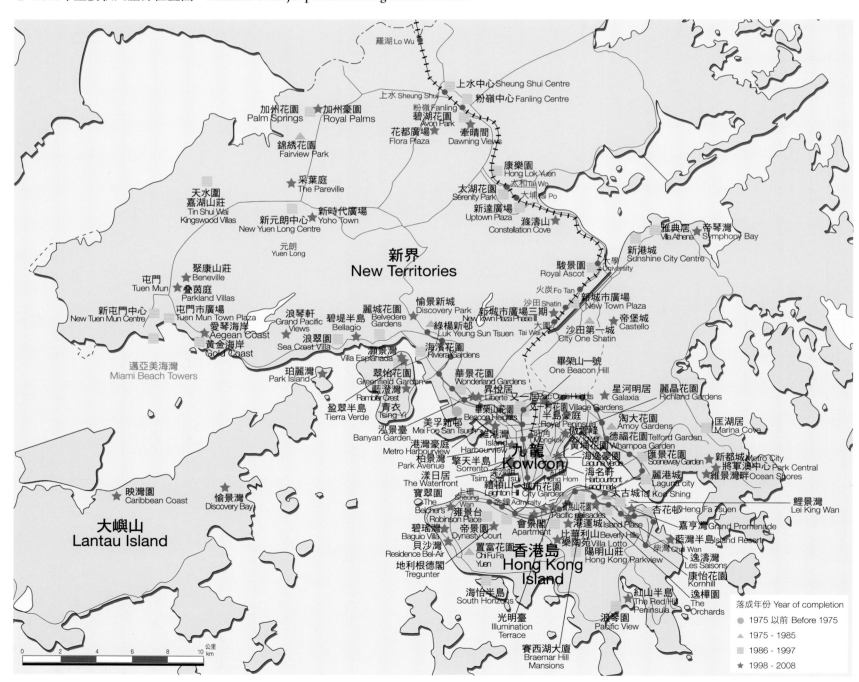

● 1996-1999年私人屋邨及居屋每平方英尺售價　Selling price (per sq. ft.) of private and Home Ownership housing estate flats in 1996-1999

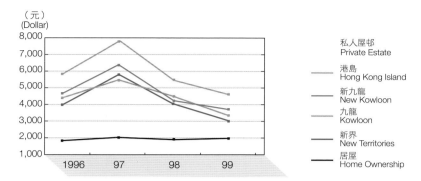

（元）
(Dollar)

私人屋邨
Private Estate

港島
Hong Kong Island

新九龍
New Kowloon

九龍
Kowloon

新界
New Territories

居屋
Home Ownership

● 1976-2008年私人屋邨建成單位　Units of private housing estate built in 1976-2008

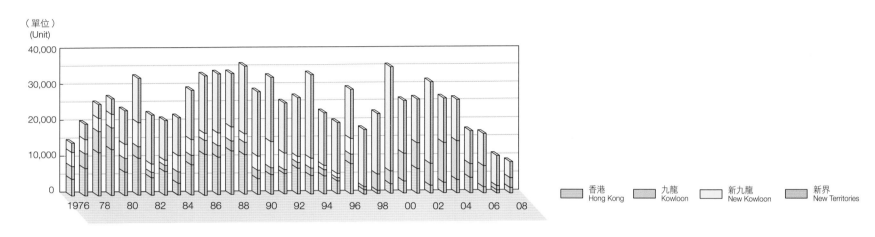

（單位）
(Unit)

香港
Hong Kong

九龍
Kowloon

新九龍
New Kowloon

新界
New Territories

● 1984-2008年小型單位（40-70平方米）每平方米平均售價　Average selling price (per m²) of small units (40-70 m²) in 1984-2008

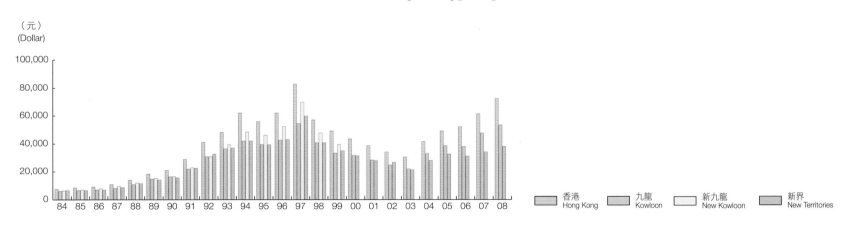

（元）
(Dollar)

香港
Hong Kong

九龍
Kowloon

新九龍
New Kowloon

新界
New Territories

● 1984-2008年大型單位（160平方米以上）每平方米平均售價　Average selling price (per m²) of large units (160 m² or more) in 1984-2008

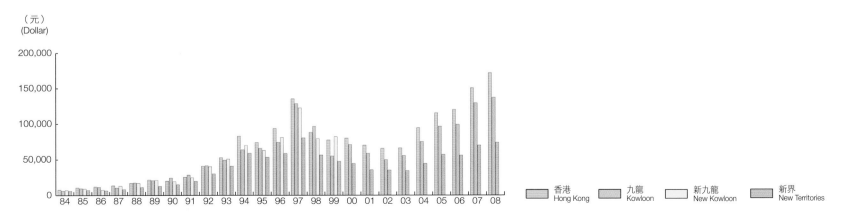

（元）
(Dollar)

香港
Hong Kong

九龍
Kowloon

新九龍
New Kowloon

新界
New Territories

07 供水系統 Water Supply System

香港地勢陡峭，河流少，雖然雨量充沛，卻不能積存足夠淡水。自1841年以來用水便是個大問題，初期只靠打井汲水。

薄扶林水庫於1864年建成。目前共有11個一般水庫，能儲水7,500萬立方米。另外1973年及1978年建成萬宜及船灣海邊淡水湖，總儲量86,696萬立方米，佔全港儲水能力88%。為此，本港1/3面積被劃做集水區。

歷史上的1929年和1963年曾經出現嚴重乾旱，每四天供水四小時，需要以輪船、火車及貨車由東江運來。1965年東江供水工程完成後，問題才基本解決。1964年以前能全日供水的天數在一年中只佔了很少部份。自1984年新的東江供水合約實施後，每日都能24小時供水。東江水佔的比例亦由1964年的57%增至1998年的82.9%。

東江水源距香港83公里，供水工程龐大，是香港城市、經濟發展的重大設施，對社會穩定起很大作用。香港在1970-2000年間人口增加一倍，用水量卻增加九倍。沒有東江水，香港經濟和生活水平必定大受打擊。

Despite abundant precipitation, Hong Kong's hilly geography boasts short and small streams, and inadequate natural storage areas for fresh water. Water supply was dependent on sinking wells and was a perennial problem.

Built in 1864, Pok Fu Lam Reservoir is the earliest reservoir. Today, there are 11 reservoirs with a total capacity of 75 million m^3. Two coastal fresh water reservoirs were constructed in 1973 and 1978 out of shallow bays. They can store 867 million m^3, or 88% of the total capacity of all reservoirs. To collect surface run-off, 1/3 of Hong Kong's area has been legislated as water catchment areas.

In 1929 and 1963, Hong Kong suffered serious draught and tap water supply was limited to four hours in every four days. Ferries, trains and lorries were deployed to ship fresh water from Guangdong. The opening of the East River Water Project ended Hong Kong's chronic water shortage. Before 1964, in any one year, days with 24-hour supply were rare. Since 1984, Hong Kong enjoys 24-hour supply. East River's supply contributed to 57% of local supply in 1964 and it went up to 82.9% in 1998.

● 1990年末預測香港將來的用水供求（百萬立方米）
1990 prediction on water demand and supply (million m^3)

年份 Year	需求量 Demand	東江水 Dongjiang water	本地淡水 Local freshwater	海水* Seawater*	供應源短缺 Shortage	實際使用量 Actual usage
2000	1,249	840	238	171*	0	924
2007	-	715.35	186.65	75*	0	951
2010	1,521	1,100	230	191*	0	-
2013	2,872	1,100	280	243*	1,249	-

* 用於沖廁等
* For flushing, etc.

● 東江—深圳供水示意圖
Dongjiang-Shenzhen water supply system

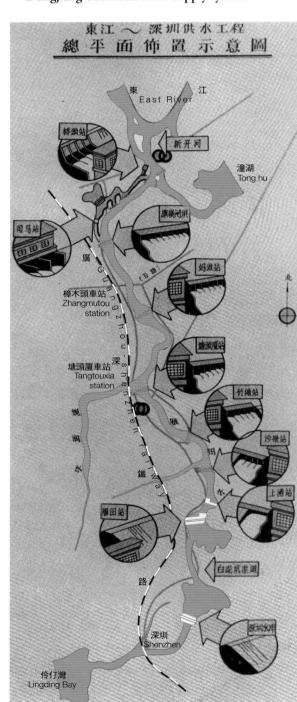

● 1950-1995年全年供水天數 Number of days of water supply in 1950-1995

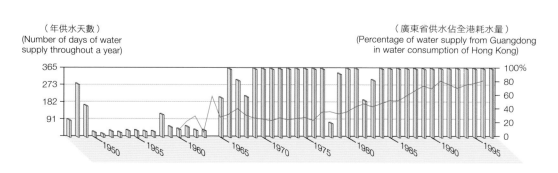

（年供水天數）
(Number of days of water supply throughout a year)

（廣東省供水佔全港耗水量）
(Percentage of water supply from Guangdong in water consumption of Hong Kong)

1960年供水系統　Water supply system in 1960

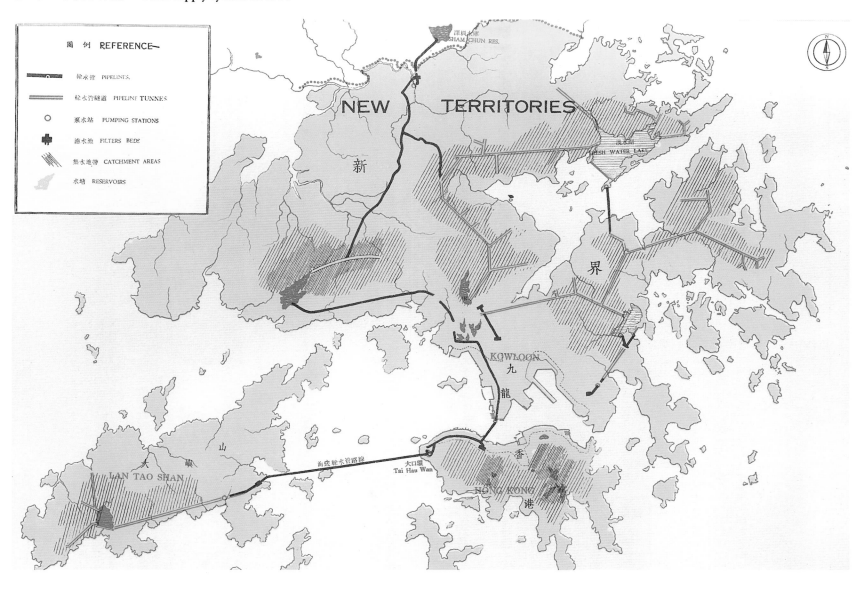

1993年供水系統　Water supply system in 1993

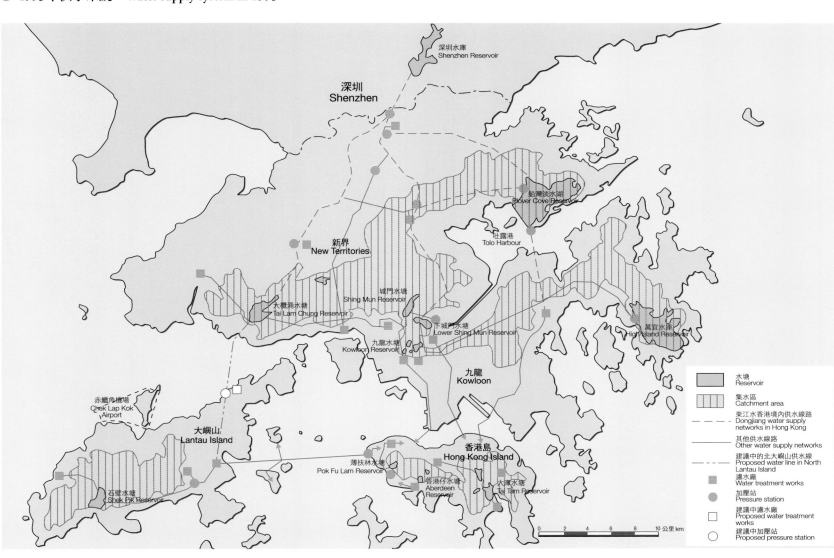

01 新界村鎮與現代交通線 Modern Transport, Towns and Villages in the New Territories

1901–1931年圖中顯示的主要新界村鎮，在《展拓香港界址專條》（1898年）之前已經存在。較大村鎮，與便利的水路和內地（如深圳、南頭）的陸路交通有一定的連繫。

新界現代路網的發展，是為了殖民地管治。最早的現代道路建設是由九龍直達大埔——當時新界的行政中心。1901年由九龍建至沙田，1903-1904年再由沙田建至大埔。其他現代化道路都是在1910年後逐步建成的。當時新界北被視為邊遠之地，其功能是作為英佔的九龍和港島的軍事屏障，因此新界現代公路都是由南至北，而且不與深圳道路連接。西貢陸峭的地形也是該區遲遲未建現代化道路的原因。

Most of the towns and villages in the map existed before the leasing of the New Territories (NT) in 1898. The larger settlements were then closely related to water and land transport that linked with Shenzhen.

The earliest modern road from Kowloon to Tai Po–NT's administrative headquarters, reached Shatin in 1901, and Tai Po in 1904. After 1910, other modern roads were also built. As NT was a military buffer for the ceded territories, all roads ran from the south to north, and did not link with those in Shenzhen.

Completion of the KCR increased the link between eastern NT with Victoria Harbour and enhanced growth along the railway line. Yet, the western and northern parts of Sai Kung were still inadequately served by modern roads.

● 1901-1931年新界主要公路發展
Development of major highways in the New Territories, 1901-1931

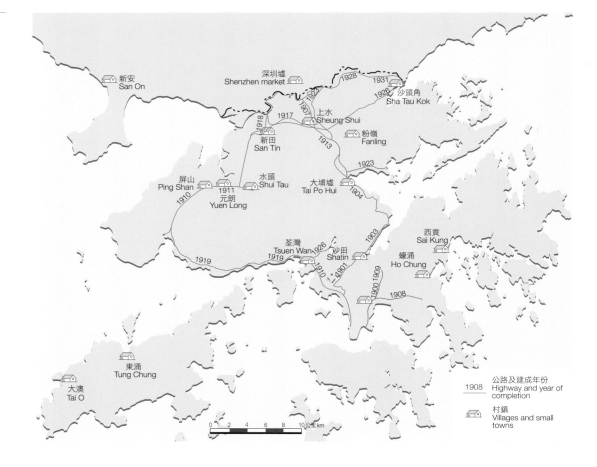

● 1932-1949年新界交通線發展
Traffic route development in the New Territories, 1932-1949

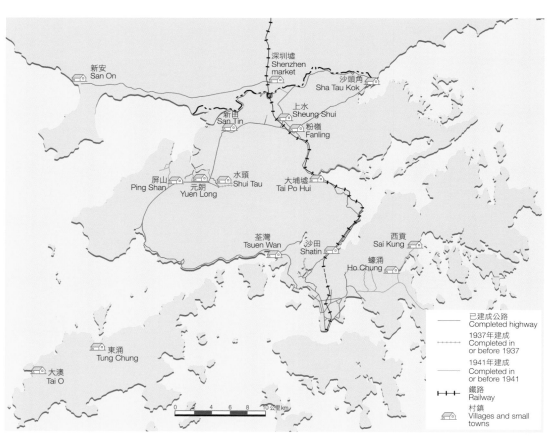

九廣鐵路的建成加強了新界東部和維多利亞港的聯繫，促進了沿線村鎮發展。但西貢西部及北部新建的道路仍很少。

1980年以後，珠三角成為香港的工業基地，大量貨流的南北運輸要求新界路網與珠三角連接。自2000年後，新界由"後方"變成香港與內地連接的前沿，是本地經濟在開發內地因素的重要支柱。回歸後，香港不斷加添與深圳連接的口岸，同時亦逐步與內陸的交通動脈連接。新界的路網發展和地理優勢面臨重大變化。

After 1980, the PRD has became Hong Kong's manufacturing base. Increased north-south traffic demands more transport integration between the two. Since 2000, the former 'buffer' turns into the front interface between Hong Kong and the mainland, a zone that is critical to Hong Kong's future economic viability.

New border crossings and check points have been added since 1997. The New Territories is experiencing a new change in the direction of its traffic pattern with emphasis on linking with the mainland and a change in its locational advantage.

新界和大嶼山主要道路基礎設施計劃　Major road infrastructure proposals for the New Territories and Lantau Island

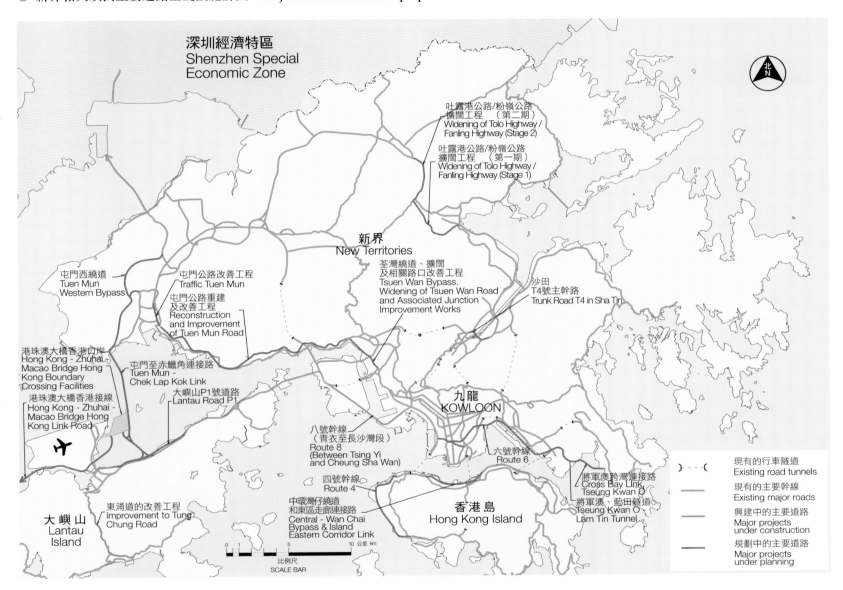

廣深港高速鐵路路線示意圖　Guangzhou-Shenzhen-Hong Kong high-speed train alignment plan

蓮塘/香園圍口岸規劃　Liantang/ Heung Yuen Wai boundary control point place

02 新界各大族姓與圍村 New Territories' Main Clans and Walled Villages

本地的漢代古蹟顯示香港在兩漢時已和中原文化有密切聯繫，但到唐代，除少量屯兵外，新界仍是刀耕火種的"南蠻"之地。北宋開始有較多的中原人南遷，在錦田、新田、上水、粉嶺一帶形成鄧、侯、彭、廖、文五大姓。鄧族在明代伸延至大埔、屏山、廈村一帶。至清初，新界已是個成熟的中國農業社區，平地都納入耕作。元朗舊墟、大埔墟及石湖墟已是重要墟鎮。

清初（1661–1669），朝廷為防備反清活動，強令居民內遷50華里。新安縣有1萬6千人受到影響，部份屬新界人士。解禁之後，只有1,000多人遷回。清政府於是鼓勵廣東、福建及江西居民移民，新界原居民便有了本地和客家之分。

新界傳統聚落多採圍村形式，反映當時治安情況和社會組織。村中民居用有防禦功能的圍牆包起來。圍村受地理和風水的影響，有一定佈

Local archaeological finds reveal a close relationship between Hong Kong and the civilization of Zhongyuan in the Han Dynasty. Yet by Tang Dynasty, except for a small regiment, most of the NT was a land of 'slash and burn'. Since the Northern Song, more immigrants from China's core area arrived. They set up home in Kam Tin, San Tin, Sheung Shui, and Fanling, and were forefathers of the NT's five major clans of Tang, Hou, Pang, Liu and Man. The Tang clan expanded into Tai Po, Ping Shan and Ha Tsuen in the Ming Dynasty. By early Qing, the NT was a mature traditional Chinese agricultural community, and all the flat land was cultivated. Yuen Long Old Market, Tai Po Market and Shek Wu Market were important market towns.

In 1661-1669, the Qing government forced residents there to move inland by 50-li. In San On County (1/2 of it was Hong Kong territory), about 16,000 people, a good proportion being NT residents, moved inland. When the ban was lifted, only about 1,000 returned. The government then encouraged Hakka people

● 1990年代末新界圍村分佈　Distribution of walled villages in the New Territories in late 1990s

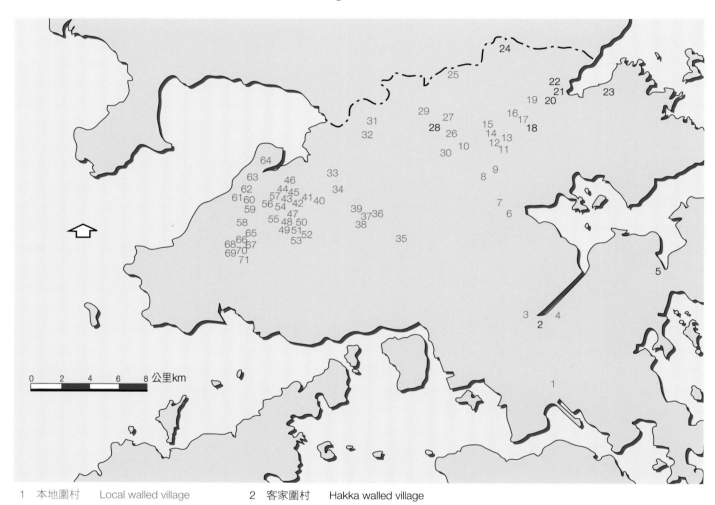

1	本地圍村	Local walled village	
2	客家圍村	Hakka walled village	

● 客家無圍牆圍村（例：三棟屋）
Hakka village without walls (Example: Sam Tung Uk)

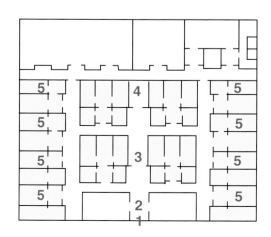

● 客家有圍牆圍村（例：上水客家圍）
Hakka walled village (Example: Sheung Shui Hakka Wai)

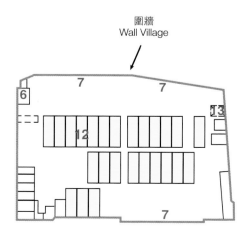

局及朝向，和周圍自然環境和土地利用相配合，成為南中國沿海農村土地利用的特有景觀。

　　圍村主門朝南，祠堂在中軸線北端。圍背多是植有風水樹的山坡。南門外為曬穀、集會及休憩用的地塘，再南是魚塘，之外是連片稻田。

　　現存圍村71條。鄧、彭、侯、文、廖五大姓是這些圍村的主姓。

　　圍村分本地與客家兩類，還有有規律（三棟屋）和無規律（上水客家圍）之分。吉慶圍是有規律本地圍村。城牆建有角樓、槍眼，有護城河，圍內中軸線明顯，祠堂也突出。民居和農具倉庫、畜牲的棚舍有規律地分隔和佈局。

from Guangdong, Jiangxi, and Fujian to settle in the NT. Together with the 'locals' (Punti), they became the main native people before the leasing of the NT.

NT settlements adopted the tradition of walled villages–a reflection of the insecure situation and community organization in 19th-century coastal China. The design and sitting of walled villages follow the principles of fengshui.

The main gate faces south . Its ancestral hall lies in the northern end of the N-S central axis. The village rests on a small knoll of fengshui grove. Outside the main gate is an open space for drying grains and serves as playground. Further out are fish ponds, with paddy fields at further distances.

Seventy-one walled villages exist today. According to their design, two categories can be distinguished: Hakka and Punti. Kat Hing Wai represents a planned Hakka Walled Village. There are corner towers on its wall, with rifle holes, and a moat. The central axis and the orderly separation of residence, storage and livestock sheds are obvious.

● 圍村與主要家族關係　Relationship between walled village and major clans

圍村名 Name of Walled Village	類別 Category	主姓 Major Clans	圍村名 Name of Walled Village	類別 Category	主姓 Major Clans	圍村名 Name of Walled Village	類別 Category	主姓 Major Clans
1. 衙前圍　Nga Tsin Wai	P2	吳 Ng	25. 大湖　Tai Wu	P3	杜 To	49. 山下村　Shan Ha Tsuen	P3	張 Cheung
2. 山下圍　Shan Ha Wai	H1	曾 Tsang	26. 大頭嶺　Tai Tau Leng	P3	鄧 Tang	50. 田寮村　Tin Liu Tsuen	P3	胡 Wu
3. 大圍（沙田）　Tai Wai (Shatin)	P3	韋 Wai	27. 上水圍　Sheung Shui Wai	P1	廖 Liu	51. 木橋頭村　Muk Kiu Tau Tsuen	P3	胡 Wu
4. 田心（沙田）　Tin Sum (Shatin)	P3	韋 Wai	28. 客家圍　Hakka Wai	H2	黃 Wong	52. 水蕉新村　Shui Chiu San Tsuen	P3	楊 Yeung
5. 企嶺下老圍　Kei Ling Ha Lo Wai	H2	何 Ho	29. 老圍（河上鄉）　Lo Wai (Ho Sheung Heung)	P1	侯 Hau	53. 白沙村　Pak Sha Tsuen	P2	/
6. 泮涌　Pan Chung	P3	麥 Mak	30. 丙崗　Ping Kong	P1	侯 Hau	54. 水邊圍　Shui Pin Wai	P3	?
7. 大埔滘新圍　Tai Po Kau San Wai	P2	鄧 Tang	31. 仁壽圍　Yan Sau Wai	P1	文 Man	55. 灰沙圍（屏山）　Fui Sha Wai (Ping Shan)	P2	鄧 Tang
8. 中心圍（泰亨）　Center Wai (Tai Hang)	P1	文 Man	32. 石湖圍　Shek Wu Wai	P1	文 Man	56. 橋頭圍　Kiu Tau Wai	P2	鄧 Tang
9. 灰沙圍（泰亨）　Fui Sha Wai (Thai Pavilion)	P1	文 Man	33. 壆圍　Pok Wai	P3	梁、文 Leung, Man	57. 上璋圍　Sheung Cheung Wai	P2	鄧 Tang
10. 粉嶺正圍　Fanling Ching Wai	P1	彭 Pang	34. 沙埔　Sha Po	P3	伍 Ng	58. 田心（屏山）　Tin Sum (Ping Shan)	P2	陳 Chan
11. 老圍（龍躍頭）　Lo Wai (Lung Yeuk Tau)	P1	鄧 Tang	35. 合山圍　Heshan Wai	P3	郭 Kwok	59. 石塘村　Shek Tong Tsuen	P3	林 Lam
12. 麻笏圍　Li Wat Wai	P1	鄧 Tang	36. 永隆圍　Wing Lung Wai	P1	鄧 Tang	60. 錫降圍　Sik Kong Wai	P1	鄧 Tang
13. 東閣圍　Tung Kok Wai	P1	鄧 Tang	37. 泰康圍　Tai Hong Wai	P1	鄧 Tang	61. 祥降圍　Tseung Kong Wai	P1	鄧 Tang
14. 永寧圍　Wing Ning Wai	P1	鄧 Tang	38. 吉慶圍　Kat Hing Wai	P1	鄧 Tang	62. 新圍（夏村）　San Wai (Ha Tsuen)	P1	鄧 Tang
15. 新圍（龍躍頭）　San Wai (Lung Yeuk Tau)	P1	鄧 Tang	39. 錦慶圍　Kam Hing Wai	P1	鄧 Tang	63. 沙江圍　Sha Kong Wai	P3	莫 Mok
16. 孔嶺　Hung Leng	P3	曾、葉 Tsang, Yip	40. 英龍圍　Ying Lung Wai	P3	鄧 Tang	64. 網井圍　Mong Tseng Wai	P3	鄧 Tang
17. 丹竹坑老圍　Tan Chuk Hang Lo Wai	P1	劉 Lai	41. 大圍（元朗）　Tai Wai (Yuen Long)	P3	黃 Wong	65. 鍾屋村　Chung Uk Tsuen	P3	鍾 Chung
18. 新屋仔　San Uk Tsai	H2	陳 Chan	42. 南邊圍（元朗）　Nam Bin Wai (Yuen Long)	P3	陳、龍 Chan, Lung	66. 順風圍　Sun Fung Wai	P2	梁 Leung
19. 萬屋邊　Man Uk Pin	P3	鍾 Chung	43. 西邊圍　Sai Bin Wai	P3	/	67. 泥圍　Nai Wai	P1	陶 Tao
20. 老圍（上禾坑）　Lo Wai (Sheung Wo Hang)	H2	李 Lee	44. 大橋　Tai Kiu	P3	陳 Chan	68. 青磚圍（屯門）　Tsing Chuen Wai (Tuen Mun)	P1	陶 Tao
21. 下禾坑　Ha Wo Hang	H1	李 Lee	45. 忠心圍（橫洲）　Chung Sam Wai (Wang Chau)	P1	黃 Wong	69. 屯子圍　Tuen Tsz Wai	P3	陶 Tao
22. 麻雀嶺新屋下　Ma Tseuk Leng San Uk Ha	H1	張 Cheung	46. 大井圍　Tai Tseng Wai	P3	梁 Leung	70. 藍地　Lam Tei	P3	陶 Tao
23. 谷埔老圍　Kuk Po Lo Wai	H2	何 Ho	47. 馬田村　Ma Tin Tsuen	P3	黃 Wong	71. 屯門新村　Tuen Mun San Tsuen	P3	陶 Tao
24. 香園圍　Heung Yuen Wai	H1	文 Man	48. 欖口村　Lam Hau Tsuen	P3	張 Cheung			

P1=本地有圍牆圍村　　　　　　P2=本地長形圍村　　　　　　　P3=本地無圍牆圍村　　　　　H1=客家有圍牆圍村　　　　　H2=客家無圍牆圍村
Local (Punti) walled village　　Local (Punti) long walled village　　Local (Punti) walled village without walls　　Hakka walled village　　Hakka walled village without walls

● 本地有圍牆圍村（例：吉慶圍）Local walled village (Example: Kat Hing Wai)

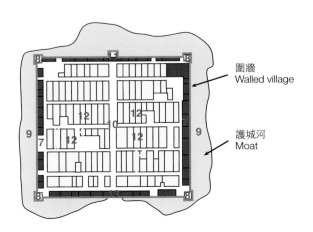

圍牆　Walled village
護城河　Moat

1	進門　Entrance	6	瞭望台　Watch-tower	11	祠堂　Ancestral hall
2	前廳　Front hall	7	獨立城牆　Freestanding wall	12	並排住房　Row houses
3	中堂　Central hall	8	角樓/城樓　Corner tower/ Gate tower	13	門樓　Entrance gate
4	祖堂　Ancestral hall	9	護城河　Moat		
5	橫屋　Horizontal house	10	主街　Main road		

□ 屋　House

■ 農作物倉儲，耕具、飼養棚舍　Storage for farming tools, farming hut

03 新界舊墟鎮：大埔 Old Market Towns: Tai Po

大埔海（吐露港，舊名大步海）自南漢起（963年），歷宋、元、明、清，是個有數千工人的採珠區。在極盛時，與這行業有關的人口近10萬。因此，大埔墟很早便是重要的墟鎮。據史書記載，大埔開墟始於明代（1567-1573年間），是歷史記載的新界最早墟市。海禁解後又於乾隆年間開墟。墟鎮由縣治批准，設有墟長。大埔舊墟一直以太和市為名，在觀音河北，其上有當時新界最大的廣福橋。

1900年英軍展開了連接九龍至大埔墟的道路工程，促進了大埔的發展。新界的管治總部，包括理民府及田土廳都設在大埔墟，新界最早的電話也是在大埔出現的。

From the Southern Han Kingdom to the Qing Dynasty (963-1911), Tolo Harbour was famous for pearl culture. The industry employed about 100,000 people at its peak. Thus Tai Po had been an important market town in history. It was established in Ming Dynasty in about 1567-1573, the earliest recorded market town in the New Territories. It was abandoned when a ban on seatrade and sea travel was enforced. The market reopened in the reign of Qianlong (1736-1795), approved by the county with an officer-in-charge. It was located on the northern shore of Kwun Yam River and was called Tai Wo Market. Road construction to link up Tai Po with Kowloon, which started in 1900, bolstered growth of the town. It was then the headquarters of the New Territories administration, as well as the

● 1902年的大埔　Tai Po in 1902

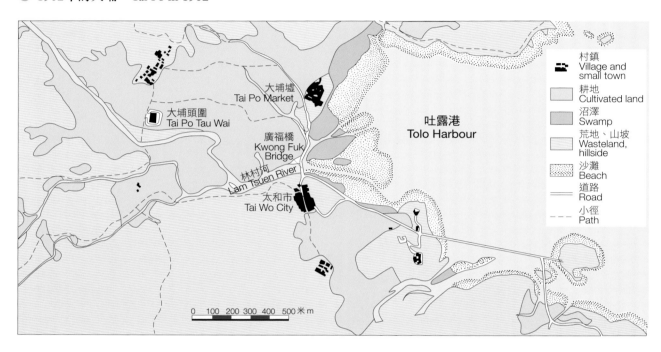

● 1963年的大埔　Tai Po in 1963

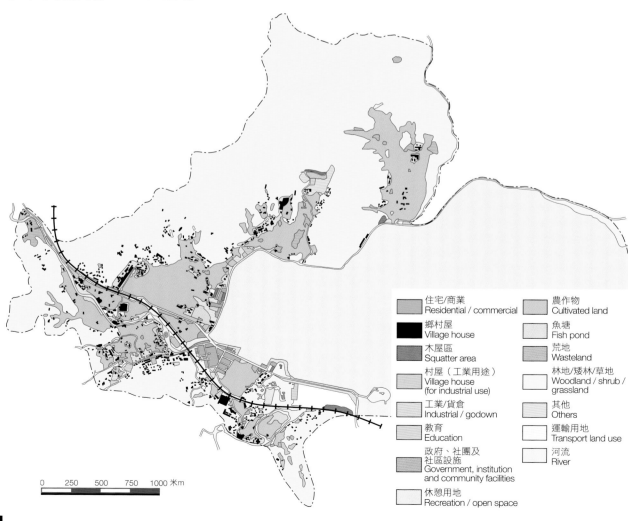

1902年時，公路仍未建成，墟市於1899年已由舊墟遷至文武二帝廟前，即新墟（仍襲舊名太和市）。

1963年大埔仍是個農業區，發展集中在火車站和公路之間的新墟。1981年有三大轉變：（一）在鐵路以東大量填海；（二）設立大埔工業區，及（三）升格為新市鎮（1979年）。大埔新市鎮人口由1968年的4,100人增至1976年的29,000人。1996年大埔區人口近30萬，其中新市鎮人口259,000，已成為香港城區邊沿的臥城。

earliest locale in the NT with telephones.

In 1899, the market moved close to the Wen Wu Temple as shown in the 1902 map. At that time, Tai Po Road had not yet been built.

By 1963, Tai Po was still an agricultural area. Urban development concentrated along the road and around the railway station.

Major changes appeared in the 1981 map, including: (1) large reclamations to the east of the railway, (2) setting up of an industrial estate, and (3) being designated as a 'new town'. Population of the market town grew from 4,100 to 29,000 in 1968-1976. By 1996, the population of Tai Po District was around 300,000, of which 259,000 was in the new town–a well-established dormitory town of Kowloon.

● 1981年的大埔　Tai Po in 1981

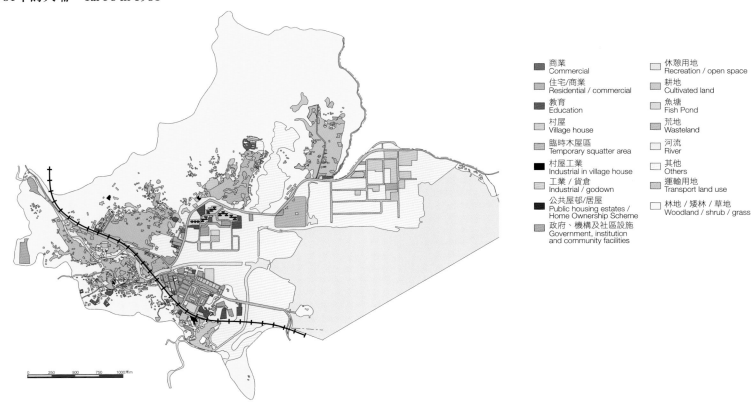

● 2009年的大埔分區計劃大綱圖　Outline Zoning Plan of Tai Po in 2009

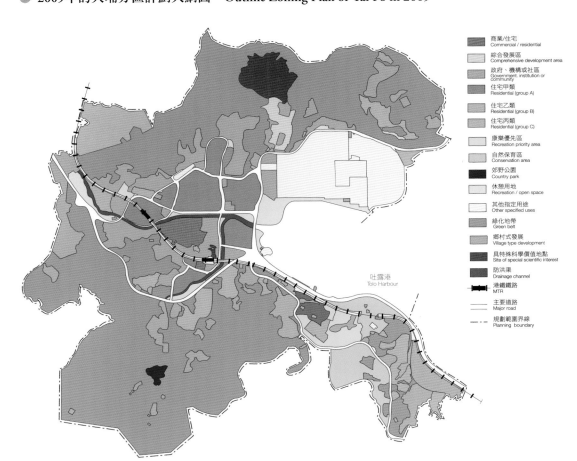

● 1981-2006年按年齡劃分的大埔人口
Tai Po population by age in 1981-2006

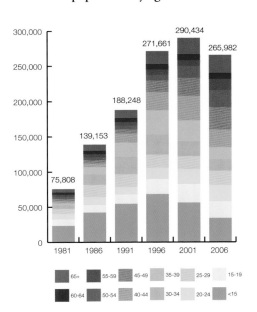

04 新界舊墟鎮：元朗 Old Market Towns: Yuen Long

元（圓）朗在明代嘉靖年間開墟，清代復界後（1669年）遷至舊墟位置。它在明代還只是一條小街，十多間店舖。清代元朗墟有水道和深圳、廣州相連，成為重要的墟鎮。1962年合益街一帶的舊墟仍部份殘存。1911年青山公路延至元朗。公路與東頭村之間形成新墟，其後演變成以同益、中興及洪昌三個街市為中心的 "新商業區"。

1949年後，外來人口增加，商店沿大馬路向西發展。由於元朗戰後農業興旺，元朗墟成為最興旺的墟鎮。1962年，元朗墟共有店舖425家，與農業直接有關的米莊、飼料及肥料、雞鴨、花店、酒莊批發等有131家。服務行業的銀行、酒家、戲院等有159家。

1970年以後，墟鎮功能因為工業化而轉變。不少小型工廠在區內設立。1988年後，工業北移，加上農業衰落，中心地性質的服務及工業功

Yuen Long market town was established in the reign of Jiajing of the Ming Dynasty. When the ban on seatrade and sea travel was lifted in 1669, the market moved to the location of the 'old market'. In the Ming Dynasty, it had a small market of about a dozen shops. In the Qing Dynasty, new water routes that linked it with Shenzhen and Guangzhou bolstered its development. On Hop Yik Street of the 1962 map, remnants of the old market can be traced. However the opening of Castle Peak Road in 1911 led to the formation of a 'new market' near Tung Tau Village forming a new commercial district that included the three markets of Tung Yik, Chung Hing and Hung Cheong.

After 1949, more people moved into Yuen Long and new shops extended westward along the Main Road (Da Ma Lu). Post-war agricultural boom of the district also promoted demand for traditional market town functions. A 1962 survey showed that Yuen Long Market had 425 shops, 131 of which were related

● 1969年元朗墟鎮土地利用　Land use of Yuen Long Market Town in 1969

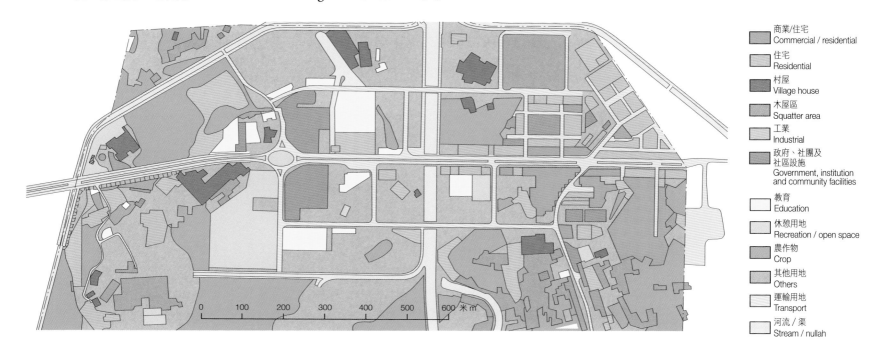

商業/住宅
Commercial / residential

住宅
Residential

村屋
Village house

木屋區
Squatter area

工業
Industrial

政府、社團及
社區設施
Government, institution
and community facilities

教育
Education

休憩用地
Recreation / open space

農作物
Crop

其他用地
Others

運輸用地
Transport

河流 / 渠
Stream / nullah

● 1962年元朗墟　Yuen Long Market Town in 1962

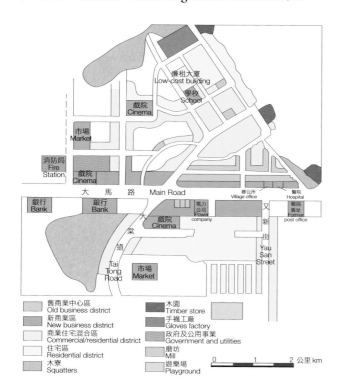

舊商業中心區
Old business district

新商業區
New business district

商業住宅混合區
Commercial/residential district

住宅區
Residential district

木寮
Squatters

木園
Timber store

手襪工廠
Gloves factory

政府及公用事業
Government and utilities

磨坊
Mill

遊樂場
Playground

● 1962年元朗平原土地利用　Land use of Yuen Long Plain in 1962

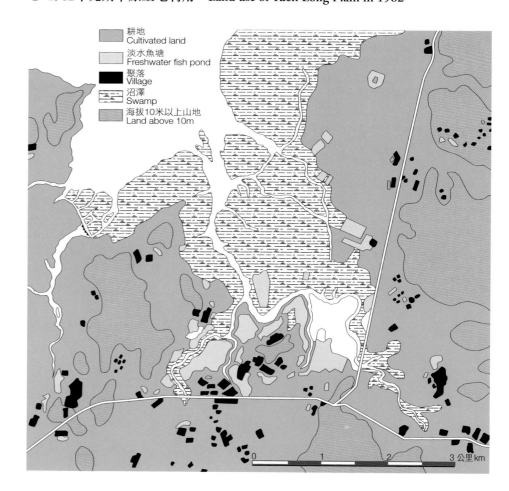

耕地
Cultivated land

淡水魚塘
Freshwater fish pond

聚落
Village

沼澤
Swamp

海拔10米以上山地
Land above 10m

能漸失。元朗已向現代新市鎮發展。1998年底，元朗人口約136,000人，並漸成為疏散九龍舊市區低收入家庭之地。

to rice, animal feeds, fertilizers, poultry and wines. The town also provided central place functions that embraced 159 banking outlets, restaurants and cinemas.

Post-1970 industrialization led to the establishment of many small factories in the town and modified its traditional market town function.

After the 1980s, Yuen Long suffered from a decline in agriculture and local manufacturing. It gradually becomes a dormitory town of low-income people who commute to work in Kowloon. In 1998, it registered a population of 136,000.

● 1988年元朗土地利用　Land use of Yuen Long in 1988

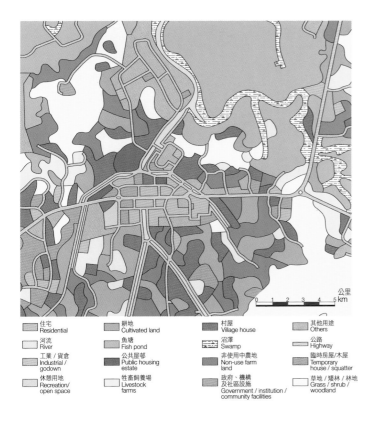

住宅 Residential
河流 River
工業 / 貨食 Industrial / godown
休憩用地 Recreation / open space

耕地 Cultivated land
魚塘 Fish pond
公共屋邨 Public housing estate
牲畜飼養場 Livestock farms

村屋 Village house
沼澤 Swamp
非使用中農地 Non-use farm land
政府、機構 及社區設施 Government / institution / community facilities

其他用途 Others
公路 Highway
臨時房屋/木屋 Temporary house / squatter
草地 / 矮林 / 林地 Grass / shrub / woodland

● 1981-2006年按年齡劃分的元朗人口　Yuen Long population by age in 1981-2006

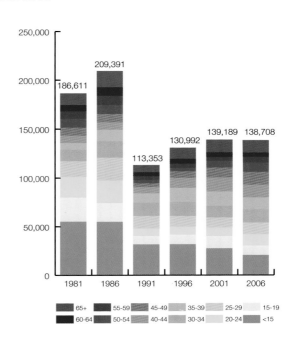

65+　60-64　55-59　50-54　45-49　40-44　35-39　30-34　25-29　20-24　15-19　<15

● 1990年代的元朗墟市鎮發展計劃　Development plan of Yuen Long Market Town in the 1990s

● 2008年元朗墟市鎮分區計劃大綱圖　Outline Zoning Plan of Yuen Long Market Town in 2008

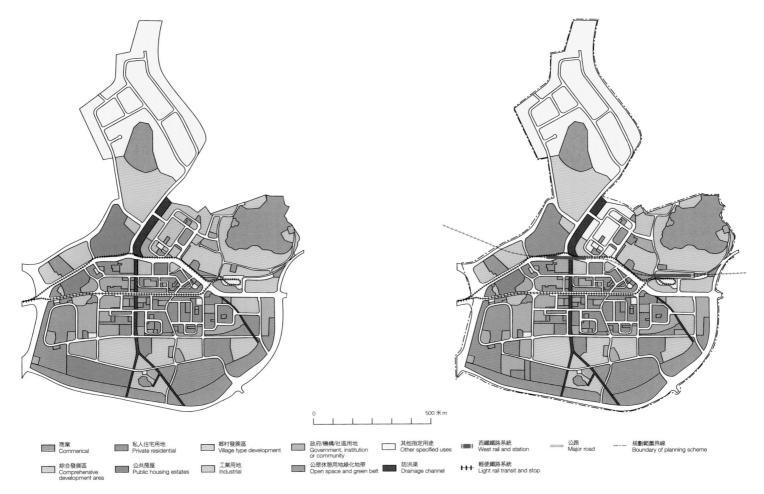

商業 Commerical
綜合發展區 Comprehensive development area

私人住宅用地 Private residential
公共房屋 Public housing estates

鄉村發展區 Village type development
工業用地 Industrial

政府/機構/社區用地 Government, institution or community
公眾休憩用地綠化地帶 Open space and green belt

其他指定用途 Other specified uses
防洪渠 Drainage channel

西鐵鐵路系統 West rail and station
輕便鐵路系統 Light rail transit and stop

公路 Major road

規劃範圍界線 Boundary of planning scheme

05 新界土地利用：1954-1970 New Territories Land Use: 1954-1970

1954年的土地利用圖，是1951年第一次全港土地利用調查的結果。本書並選取了1966、1977、1988和2007年圖，系統地反映新界土地利用的轉變，及其急劇的城市化。

1954年新界平地主要仍然是作農業用途，其中最多必是稻田。至1966年，魚塘開始增多，農業土地利用的格局仍然沒有大變動。

As a result of the 1951 land-use survey, the 1954 map was produced.

The 1966, 1977, 1988 and 2007 maps are chosen to show the change of land use in the New Territories and its rapid urbanization.

In 1954, lowlands of the NT were mainly cultivated, mostly as paddy fields. Although fish ponds became numerous, the pattern of NT agriculture had not changed much in 1966.

● 1954年新界（包括港九）土地利用　Land use of the New Territories (including Hong Kong and Kowloon), 1954

| 已建區 Built-up area | 花園洋樓 Western-style house with garden | 沼澤 Swamp | 耕地 Cultivated land | 風化地 Badland | 草地與矮灌木 Grass and low shrub | 矮林 Shrub | 林地 Woodland |

1966年全港土地利用面積分析　Hong Kong's land use distribution, 1966

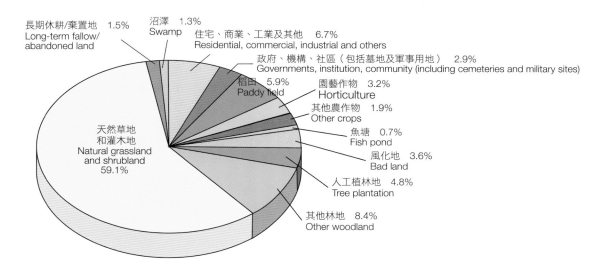

長期休耕/棄置地　1.5%
Long-term fallow/
abandoned land

沼澤　1.3%
Swamp

住宅、商業、工業及其他　6.7%
Residential, commercial, industrial and others

政府、機構、社區（包括墓地及軍事用地）　2.9%
Governments, institution, community (including cemeteries and military sites)

稻田　5.9%
Paddy field

園藝作物　3.2%
Horticulture

其他農作物　1.9%
Other crops

魚塘　0.7%
Fish pond

風化地　3.6%
Bad land

人工植林地　4.8%
Tree plantation

其他林地　8.4%
Other woodland

天然草地
和灌木地
Natural grassland
and shrubland
59.1%

1966年新界（包括港九）土地利用　Land use of New Territories (including Hong Kong and Kowloon) in 1966

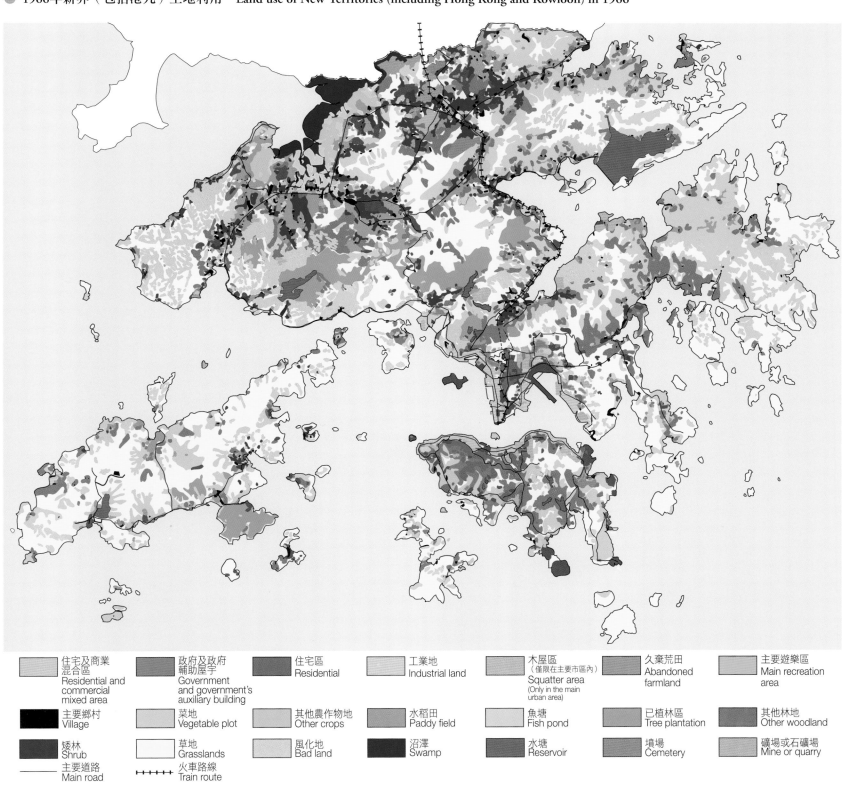

住宅及商業混合區 Residential and commercial mixed area	政府及政府輔助屋宇 Government and government's auxiliary building	住宅區 Residential	工業地 Industrial land	木屋區（僅限在主要市區內）Squatter area (Only in the main urban area)	久棄荒田 Abandoned farmland	主要遊樂區 Main recreation area
主要鄉村 Village	菜地 Vegetable plot	其他農作物地 Other crops	水稻田 Paddy field	魚塘 Fish pond	已植林區 Tree plantation	其他林地 Other woodland
矮林 Shrub	草地 Grasslands	風化地 Bad land	沼澤 Swamp	水塘 Reservoir	墳場 Cemetery	礦場或石礦場 Mine or quarry
主要道路 Main road	火車路線 Train route					

06 新界土地利用：1970-2008 New Territories Land Use: 1970-2008

1988年稻田已經近乎不存在，耕地（主要是菜地）、飼養場和魚塘一起才佔香港總面積的5.5%。城市化是農地流失的重要原因，臨時屋及臨時堆場成為農地的主要用途，後者亦成為環境污染源，破壞郊區景觀。1980年以來，不少坡地被開闢為郊野公園，使本來沒有多大經濟價值的地區，成為最大的市肺。香港是唯一有近四成面積為郊野公園的城市，也是世界之最。

The decline of cultivated land in 1977-1988 was obvious. By 1988, paddy fields had almost disappeared. Cultivated land (mainly for vegetables), poultry and animal farms, and fish ponds, together occupied only 5.5% of Hong Kong's total area. The main cause for agricultural decline is urbanization as most former cultivated land was turned into squatter housing and temporary storages, contributing to pollution and environmental degradation.

Besides, since 1980, most of the slopes on hills were developed into country parks. This has transformed former areas of little economic value into the city's large green 'lung'. Having about 40% of its territory as country parks, Hong Kong is a unique case among big cities of the world.

● 1977年新界（包括港九）土地利用
Land use of New Territories (including Hong Kong and Kowloon) in 1977

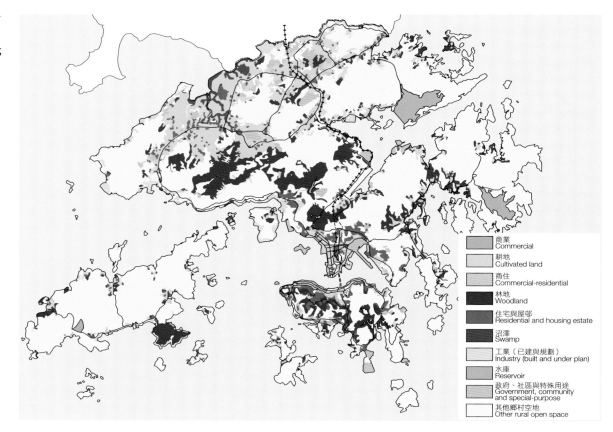

商業 Commercial
耕地 Cultivated land
商住 Commercial-residential
林地 Woodland
住宅與屋邨 Residential and housing estate
沼澤 Swamp
工業（已建與規劃） Industry (built and under plan)
水庫 Reservoir
政府、社區與特殊用途 Government, community and special-purpose
其他鄉村空地 Other rural open space

● 1988年新界（包括港九）土地利用
Land use of the New Territories (including Hong Kong and Kowloon) in 1988

商業 Commercial
公共屋邨 Public housing estate
住宅 Residential
臨時房屋區 Temporary housing areas
政府機構及社區設施 Government, institution, and community facilities
鄉村屋宇/平房區 Village houses / cottage areas
郊野公園 Country park
沼澤 Swamp
水塘/配水庫 Reservoir / service reservoir
礦場/石礦場 Mine / quarry
耕地 Cultivated land
空置發展地/建築進行中 Vacant development land / building in progress

魚塘 Fish pond
休憩用地 Recreation / open space
工業/貨倉 Industrial / godown
墳場/火葬場 Cemeteries / crematoria
臨時及僭建建築物 Temporary and unauthorized building
草地，矮林/林地 Grassland, shrub / woodland
牲畜飼養場 Livestock farm
其他用途 Other uses
非使用中之農地 Non-used agricultural land
主要道路 Main road
地下鐵路 MTR
九廣鐵路 KCR

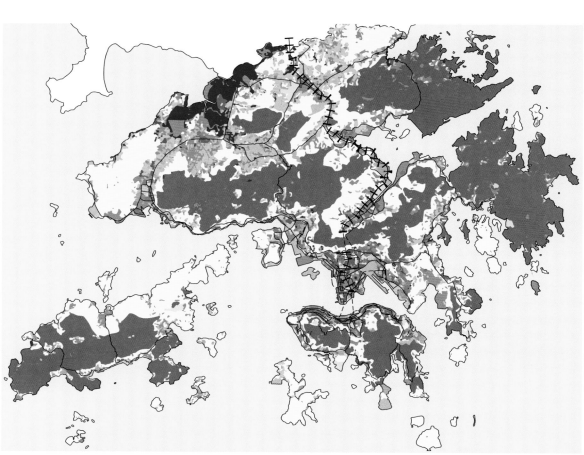

1977年土地利用面積分析　Land use distribution in 1977

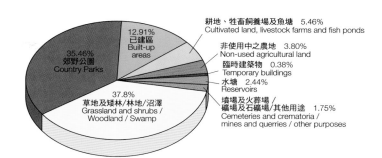

魚塘
Fish pond

荒地
Deserted land

沼澤和紅樹林
Swamp and mangrove

耕地
Cultivated land

已建區
Built-up area

林地
Woodland

天然草地和灌木
Natural grassland and shrubland

1988年土地利用面積分析　Land use distribution in 1988

12.91%
已建區
Built-up areas

35.46%
郊野公園
Country Parks

37.8%
草地及矮林/林地/沼澤
Grassland and shrubs / Woodland / Swamp

耕地、牲畜飼養場及魚塘　5.46%
Cultivated land, livestock farms and fish ponds

非使用中之農地　3.80%
Non-used agricultural land

臨時建築物　0.38%
Temporary buildings

水塘　2.44%
Reservoirs

墳場及火葬場 /
礦場及石礦場 / 其他用途　1.75%
Cemeteries and crematoria /
mines and querries / other purposes

2007年新界土地利用　Land use map of the New Territories in 2007

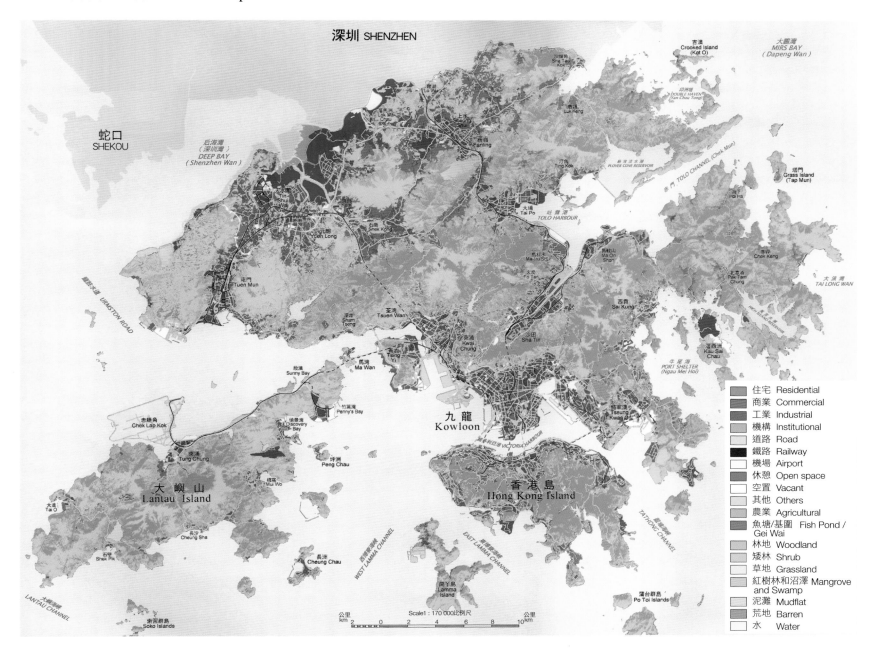

深圳 SHENZHEN

蛇口 SHEKOU

后海灣（深圳灣）DEEP BAY (Shenzhen Wan)

大鵬灣 MIRS BAY (Dapeng Wan)

Crooked Island (Kat O)

DOUBLE HAVEN (Yan Chau Tong)

PLOVER COVE RESERVOIR

TOLO CHANNEL (Chek Mun)

Grass Island (Tap Mun)

URMSTON ROAD

屯門 Tuen Mun

元朗 Yuen Long

大埔 Tai Po

吐露港 TOLO HARBOUR

Chek Keng

大浪灣 TAI LONG WAN

荃灣 Tsuen Wan

沙田 Sha Tin

西貢 Sai Kung

PORT SHELTER (Ngau Mei Hoi)

Kau Sai Chau

九龍 Kowloon

大嶼山 Lantau Island

Chek Lap Kok

東涌 Tung Chung

Discovery Bay

Sunny Bay

Ma Wan

Penny's Bay

Peng Chau

香港島 Hong Kong Island

VICTORIA HARBOUR

TATHONG CHANNEL

WEST LAMMA CHANNEL

EAST LAMMA CHANNEL

長洲 Cheung Chau

南丫島 Lamma Island

蒲台群島 Po Toi Islands

LANTAU CHANNEL

索罟群島 Soko Islands

Scale 1 : 170 000 比例尺

	住宅 Residential
	商業 Commercial
	工業 Industrial
	機構 Institutional
	道路 Road
	鐵路 Railway
	機場 Airport
	休憩 Open space
	空置 Vacant
	其他 Others
	農業 Agricultural
	魚塘/基圍 Fish Pond / Gei Wai
	林地 Woodland
	矮林 Shrub
	草地 Grassland
	紅樹林和沼澤 Mangrove and Swamp
	泥灘 Mudflat
	荒地 Barren
	水 Water

2000年土地利用面積分析　Land use distribution in 2000

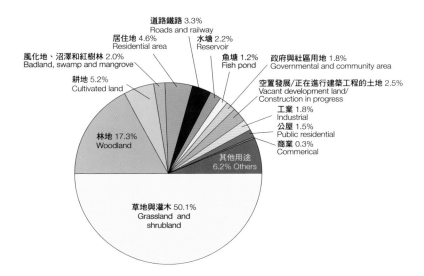

道路鐵路 3.3%
Roads and railway

居住地 4.6%
Residential area

風化地、沼澤和紅樹林 2.0%
Badland, swamp and mangrove

耕地 5.2%
Cultivated land

林地 17.3%
Woodland

草地與灌木 50.1%
Grassland and shrubland

水塘 2.2%
Reservoir

魚塘 1.2%
Fish pond

政府與社區用地 1.8%
Governmental and community area

空置發展/正在進行建築工程的土地 2.5%
Vacant development land/
Construction in progress

工業 1.8%
Industrial

公屋 1.5%
Public residential

商業 0.3%
Comercial

其他用途 6.2% Others

2007年土地利用面積分析　Land use distribution in 2007

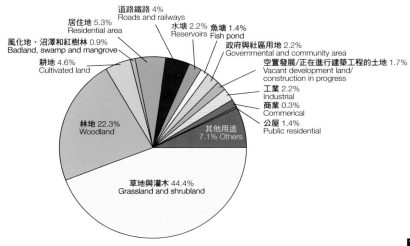

道路鐵路 4%
Roads and railways

居住地 5.3%
Residential area

風化地、沼澤和紅樹林 0.9%
Badland, swamp and mangrove

耕地 4.6%
Cultivated land

林地 22.3%
Woodland

草地與灌木 44.4%
Grassland and shrubland

水塘 2.2%
Reservoirs

魚塘 1.4%
Fish pond

政府與社區用地 2.2%
Governmental and community area

空置發展/正在進行建築工程的土地 1.7%
Vacant development land/
construction in progress

工業 2.2%
Industrial

商業 0.3%
Comerical

公屋 1.4%
Public residential

其他用途 7.1% Others

07 新市鎮 New Towns

香港早期的發展集中在維多利亞港兩岸。1959年政府完成荃灣發展研究報告，響起了新市鎮發展第一炮。但有規劃地作分散式的城市發展卻始於1973年。港督麥理浩為了其十年建屋計劃，推動了新市鎮建設。以後一共發展了三期。第一期包括荃灣、屯門和沙田，規模較大，人口以公共房屋居民為主。第二期是大埔、上水粉嶺和元朗，規模較小，公共房屋和私人樓宇比例均衡。第三期為將軍澳、天水圍和東涌，功能多樣化，公共房屋比例較少，居民以中產階級為主。新市鎮在服務設備上齊全。第一及二期依托工業為主。香港工業自1980年代起走下坡，新市鎮工業減少，居民就業更集中在舊市區，使新市鎮成為臥城，形成嚴重

Post-1841 development clustered around Victoria Harbour in early years. The first attempt on developing new towns was marked by the completion of the Tsuen Wan Development Plan in 1959. However, adoption of a decentralized mode of urban development only started in 1973. To implement his '10-year Housing Target', Governor Mclehose launched a New Towns Development Programme. Three phases of new towns have been constructed since. Phase-one new towns are of larger population which are mainly accommodated in public housing. Phase-two towns are smaller balancing between private and public housing. Phase-three towns are more diverse in function, and are mainly for the middle class. New towns possess comprehensive social, community and healthcare infrastructure. The two

● 1990年代新市鎮分佈　Distribution of new towns in the 1990s

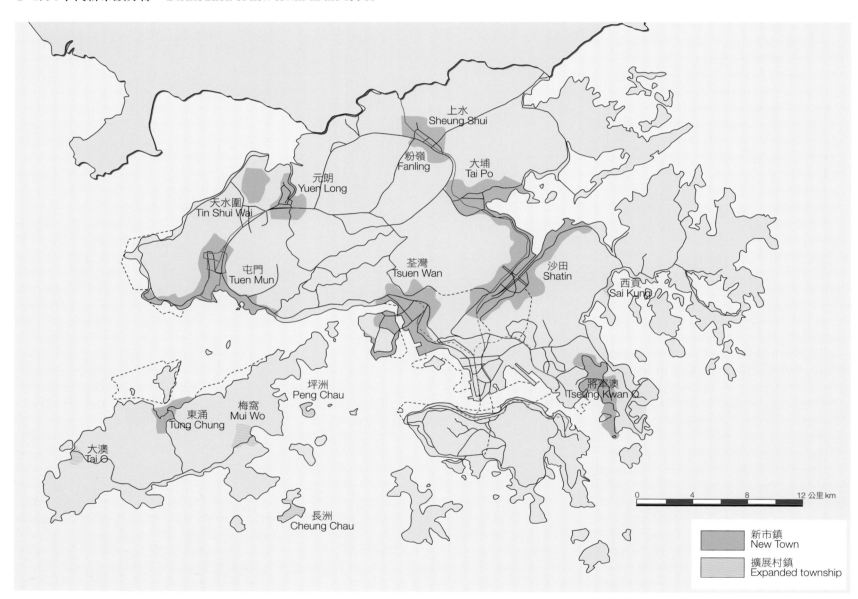

● 新市鎮一般用地規劃　General land use distribution of new towns

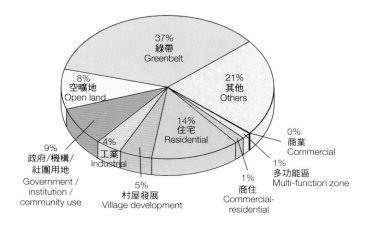

● 新市鎮建設成本構成（按1982年估計）　Composition of cost for constructing new towns (estimates at 1982)

總額504億7千萬港元
Total of 50.47 billion HK$

的上下班交通問題。

　　1971年新市鎮人口只有40萬，佔全港總人口約12%。1996年有人口近260萬，佔總人口42%。1999年底約304萬，佔44%。2008年底約332萬，佔47.5%。

　　新市鎮集中發展，密度高，又大部份依托填海和開山，是有香港地少人多特色的有效率和高密度式的城市發展模式。

early-phase towns are primarily industrial in function. As industries declined in the 1980s, new town residents have to seek employment in the main urban areas. The new towns thus become dormitory towns, with chronic commuting problems.

In 1970, population in the new towns numbered around 400,000–about 12% of the total population. In 1996, it rose to 2,600,000, or 42% of the total. The 1999 population was 3,040,000, or 44% of the total. In 2008, it stood at 3,315,900, or 47.5%.

Hong Kong's new towns have a high population density, and are mostly built on lands relaimed or formed by cutting hillsides. It is characteristic of Hong Kong's tradition of high density and efficient use of space in urban development.

● 1990年已有的新市鎮基本狀況　Basic situation of new towns that existed in 1990

期別 Phase	第一期 1st Phase			第二期 2nd Phase			第三期 3rd Phase		
	荃灣 Tsuen Wan	沙田* Shatin*	屯門 Tuen Mun	大埔 Tai Po	粉嶺/上水 Fanling/ Sheung Shui	元朗 Yuen Long	將軍澳 Tseung Kwan O	天水圍 Tin Shui Wai	東涌 Tung Chung
定名年份 Naming year	1959	1967	1967	1979	1979	1979	1982	1982	1991
與主要市區（九龍）距離（千米） Distance from the main urban area (Kowloon) (,000 m)	5	5	32	19	27	40	5	44	—
總發展面積（公頃） Total development area (ha)	2,360	3,591	1,920	1,270	780	1,170	1,056	500	760
首年人口 Population in 1st year	8,000	24,000	20,000	48,000	44,000	42,000	13,000	3,000	2,000
最終目標人口 Target population	860,000	840,000	627,000	332,000	260,000	280,000	520,000	315,000	220,000
1999年人口 Population in 1999	796,000	630,000	502,000	300,000	230,000	164,000	250,000	150,000	20,000
2008年人口 Population in 2008	805,200	624,500	507,200	267,600	246,000	137,700	353,300	285,400	79,000
設計公/私住宅人口比率 Designed ratio of public/private housing population	70:30	60:40	70:30	47:53	43:57	25:75	—	—	—

* 包括馬鞍山
* Include Ma On Shan

● 2009年擬建新市鎮　New towns proposed in 2009

期別 Phase	古洞北 Kwu Tung North	粉嶺北 Fanling North	坪輋／打鼓嶺 Ping Che /Ta Kwu Ling
預計定名年份 Expected naming year	2019	2019	2019
總發展面積（公頃） Total development area (ha)	450	180	175
2009年人口 Population in 2009 year	3,600	2,400	—
最終目標人口 Final target population	65,000	48,000	17,000
設計公/私住宅人口比率 Ratio of designed public/private housing population	54:46	40:60	—

● 1996年新市鎮的社區設施　Community facilities in new towns, 1996

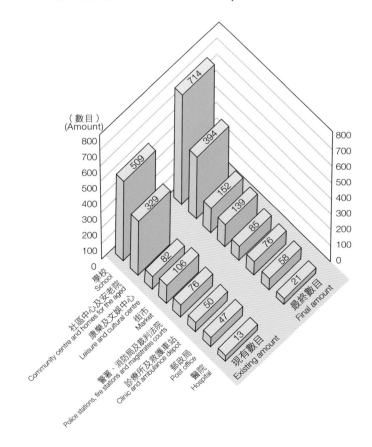

08 沙田新市鎮的演變 Evolution of New Towns: Shatin

沙田為一溺谷海灣，沖積平原闊700米。東南坡背風背陽，井泉較多，村落多分佈於此。1902年大埔公路由九龍貫通沙田，1911年建成九廣鐵路，都是沿西北谷邊。因此，西北坡發展加快，導致沙田墟的興起。

大圍是谷中最大的聚落，在城門河邊，其地位已被沙田墟取代。1949年後，人口遷入增加，西坡地如銅鑼灣、道風山新建園林住宅，大圍也出現大片寮屋。1961年人口增至28,076人。

鐵路也帶來旅遊業，旅遊名勝有西林寺、萬佛寺、紅梅谷等。沙田墟的北面建了跑馬場。1962年沙田仍為重要農業地區。西北部交通便利，是菜地和園藝農場，南部坡地及平地遠離交通線，主要是稻田。1962年沙田規劃為衛星城市，面積7,677畝，其中填海950畝，原有平地410畝，坡地6,317畝，計劃住宅用地2,063畝，商業區151畝，工業區292

Shatin originated from a drowned valley with an alluvial plain of 700 m wide. The sun-ward SE slope is an aquifer. It favours the siting of villages. Tai Po Road reached Shatin in 1902, followed by the opening of the railway station there in 1911. These new communication links opened up the NW slope for development leading to the emergence of the Shatin market to replace Tai Wai on the bank of Shing Mun River as the largest settlement.

Since 1949, population increased due to migration. Garden houses mushroomed in Tung Lo Wan and To Fung Shan on the western slopes, while Tai Wai was swamped by squatter huts. In 1961, its population reached 28,076.

The railway stimulated tourism. Sai Lam Temple, Ten Thousand Buddhas Monastery, and Hung Mui Kuk became tourist attractions. A new race course was constructed at the mouth of the Valley. Yet, Shatin remained agricultural in 1962, with vegetable and horticulture farms close to the roads and railway, and paddy

● 1962年沙田市鎮　Shatin town in 1962

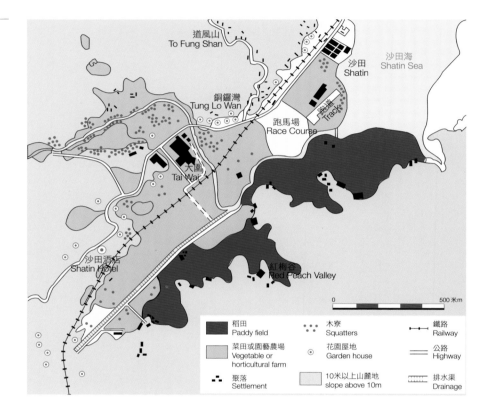

稻田
Paddy field

菜田或園藝農場
Vegetable or horticultural farm

聚落
Settlement

木寮
Squatters

花園屋地
Garden house

10米以上山麓地
slope above 10m

鐵路
Railway

公路
Highway

排水渠
Drainage

0　　　500 米 m

● 1979年沙田新市鎮規劃圖　Planned layout of Shatin New Town in 1979

商業
Commercial

住宅
Residential

工業
Industrial

政府/機構/社區
Government / institution / community

休憩用地
Recreation / open space

耕地
Cultivated land

河流
River

荒地
Abandoned farm land

林地
Woodland

未改良地
Unimproved land

混合用途
Mixed uses

空地
Vacant land

運輸
Transportation

鐵路
Railway

主要道路
Main road

缺，最終人口363,000人。有三片工業區，與後來新市鎮的規劃一致。

　　1971年沙田人口仍只有27,000人；真正的發展要到1973年後；1981年增加至109,472人；1991年達437,395人。之後，又擴展至烏溪沙和馬鞍山。1998年新市鎮總人口60萬人，預計總容納量為84萬人。新市鎮的一條貫通全市的單車徑和沙田馬場，使沙田的綠地增多以及互相通達，較其他新市鎮吸引。

fields in more remote locations.

In 1962, Shatin was planned to become a satellite town, with an area of 7,677 ac, 950 ac to be reclaimed from the sea. There would be 2,063 ac of residential, 292 ac industrial, 151 ac commercial land, and a target population of 363,000.

By 1971, Shatin had a population of only 27,000, less than that of 1961. Its rapid growth began after 1970, when it became a new town. By 1998, it had a population of over 600,000, and a planned population of 840,000, including its extensions in Wu Kai Sha and Ma On Shan. The new town has a bicycle trail, and interlinked green and open space, offering more attraction than other new towns.

● 1993年沙田市鎮　Shatin Town in 1993

● 2007年沙田市鎮分區計劃大綱圖　Outline Zoning Plan of Shatin Town in 2007

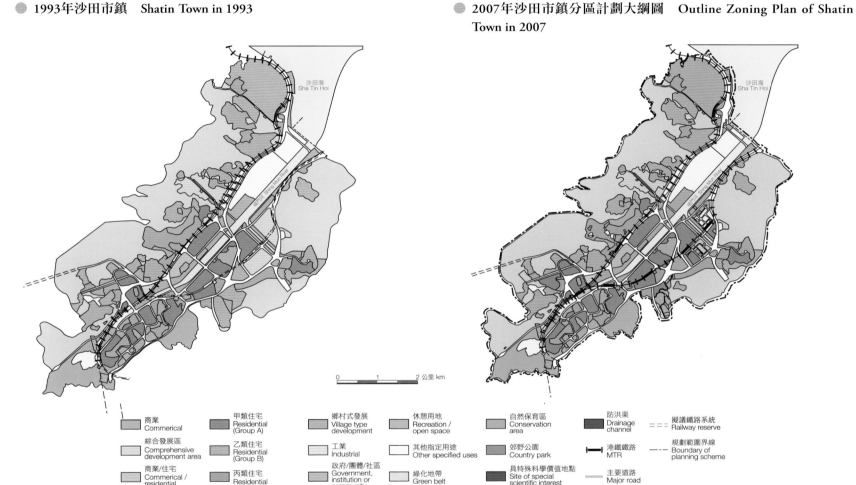

商業 Commerical	甲類住宅 Residential (Group A)
綜合發展區 Comprehensive development area	乙類住宅 Residential (Group B)
商業/住宅 Commerical / residential	丙類住宅 Residential (Group C)

鄉村式發展 Village type development	休憩用地 Recreation / open space
工業 Industrial	其他指定用途 Other specified uses
政府/團體/社區 Government, institution or community	綠化地帶 Green belt

自然保育區 Conservation area	防洪渠 Drainage channel
郊野公園 Country park	港鐵鐵路 MTR
具特殊科學價值地點 Site of special scientific interest	主要道路 Major road

擬議鐵路系統 Railway reserve	
規劃範圍界線 Boundary of planning scheme	

● 2009年馬鞍山分區計劃大綱圖　Outline Zoning Plan of Ma On Shan in 2009

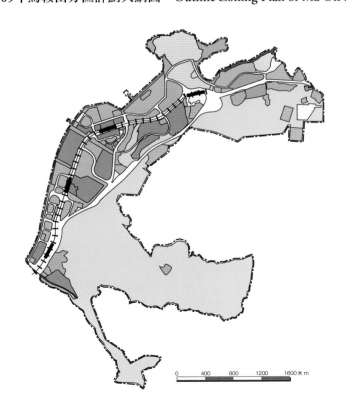

● 1981-2006年按年齡劃分的沙田及馬鞍山人口　Shatin and Ma On Shan population by age in 1981-2006

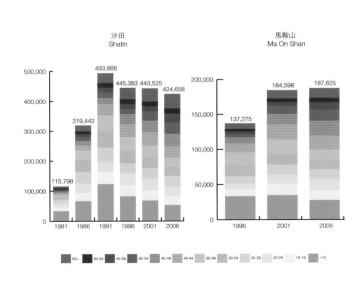

09 屯門新市鎮的演變 Evolution of New Towns: Tuen Mun

屯門古名意為"屯兵之門"，《新唐書》記載："有經略軍，屯門鎮兵。"當時"於山北麓，建立軍寨，並設靖海都巡，同知屯門鎮事"。1899年英國"租借"新界時，最大的聚落'新墟'人口只約250人。舊墟及三聖均是細小的村落。二次大戰前，它主要是漁港和鹽場，清朝曾設鹽官。1904年，除優良港灣和一片鹽田外，只有青山寺、楊小坑、皇家園和規模很小的新墟。屯門是個漁業、產鹽及稻米種植區。在1950年，塘魚也是一大行業。

鹽田已在1963年消失，新墟規模仍小，平地上主要是菜地，但仍有240公頃農田。1973年被規劃為新市鎮後，出現了大規模沿岸填海。1981年，新市鎮海岸線基本形成，屯門公路也經已建成。市內工商業及住宅用地大增，農田減至62公頃。1994年的規劃圖中已沒有農田，工業用途

The name Tuen Mun is derived from Tang classic that recorded the locale as a military base.

When the NT was leased in 1899, San Hui (New market) was the largest settlement there with a population of 250. The 'old market' and Sam Shing were small villages. Until WWII, Tuen Mun remained a fishing port and an area of salt pans, with a salt officer stationing there during the Qing Dynasty.

The 1904 map is marked by a good harbour, large salt pans, Tsing Shan Monastery, and the small New Market. Fishing, salt production and paddy farming were main economic activities.

Salt pans disappeared in the 1963 map. The New Market was still small. On lowlands were vegetable farms. Tuen Mun then still had a cultivated area of 240 ha Large-scale reclamation began in 1973 after its designation as a new town. By

1963年屯門新市鎮規劃 Layout of Tuen Mun New Town in 1963

住宅及商業 Residential and commercial
村屋 Village house
高級花園式住宅 Garden house
職工宿舍 Staff quarters
工業 Industrial
教育 Education
政府、社團及社區設施 Government, civic and community facilities
休憩用地 Recreation / open space
耕地 Cultivated land
魚塘及河流 Fish pond and river
風化地 Badland
林地/矮林 Woodland / shrub
其他 Others

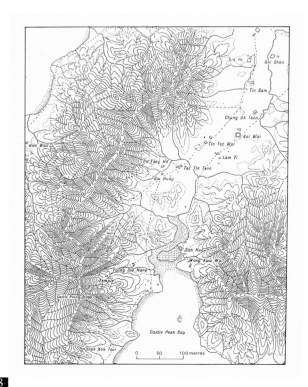

1904年屯門
Tuen Mun in 1904

1950年屯門
Tuen Mun in 1950

聚落 Village
稻田 Paddy
果園 Orchard
沼澤 Swamp
魚塘 Fish pond
道路 Road
林地 Woodland

面積在1963年為4.3公頃，1981年增至23公頃，1994年的規劃為58公頃。1994年舊墟已不是商業中心，新墟起而代之。同年，按規劃的新中心建成為新市鎮的行政、文化及商業活動中心，1996年新市鎮人口43萬（最終人口54萬人，後增至62萬），73%居住公共屋邨。區內有2,200家工廠，僱用4萬工人，成為一個藍領工業城鎮。市中心和中央公園毗連，工業區和住宅區清楚分隔，全市以輕便鐵路為主要交通工具，並與元朗、天水圍連接。1998年底人口已達446,000人。

1981, the present coastline had taken shape. The farm acreage declined to 62 ha. In the 1994 plan, there was no more cultivated land. Industrial land increased from 4.3 ha in 1963 to the planned 58 ha in the new plan. By 1994, the New Market replaced the 'old market' as the commercial zone. The planned core became an administrative, cultural and commercial centre of the new town.

In 1996, the population was 430,000, 73% of which lived in public housing. There were 2,200 factories that employed 40,000 workers. By then, it became a blue-collar industrial town. The industrial and residential uses are clearly separated. There is a central park, and a light rail to provide intra-town transport, as well as to link it with Yuen Long. By the end of 1998, its population reached 446,000.

● 1981年屯門新市鎮規劃圖　Layout of Tuen Mun New Town in 1981

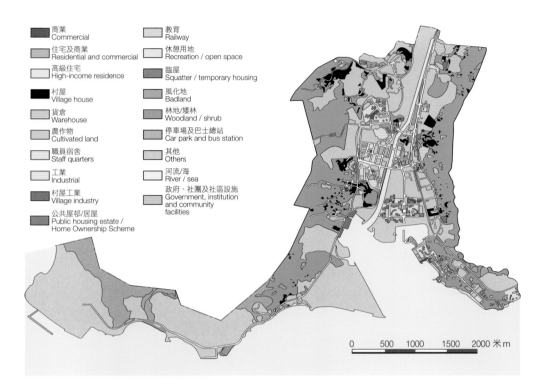

商業　Commercial
住宅及商業　Residential and commercial
高級住宅　High-income residence
村屋　Village house
貨倉　Warehouse
農作物　Cultivated land
職員宿舍　Staff quarters
工業　Industrial
村屋工業　Village industry
公共屋邨/居屋　Public housing estate / Home Ownership Scheme
教育　Railway
休憩用地　Recreation / open space
臨屋　Squatter / temporary housing
風化地　Badland
林地/矮林　Woodland / shrub
停車場及巴士總站　Car park and bus station
其他　Others
河流/海　River / sea
政府、社團及社區設施　Government, institution and community facilities

● 1981-2006年按年齡劃分的屯門人口　Tuen Mun population by age in 1981-2006

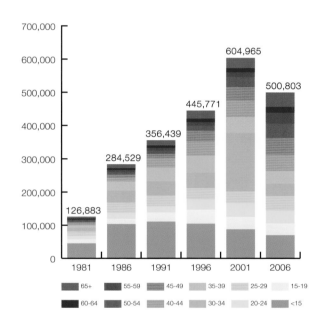

● 1994年屯門新市鎮規劃圖　Layout of Tuen Mun New Town in 1994

● 2009年屯門新市鎮分區計劃大綱圖　Outline Zoning Plan of Tuen Mun New Town in 2009

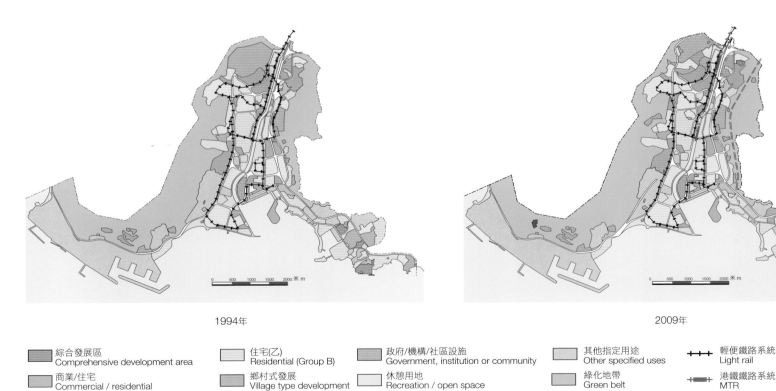

1994年

2009年

綜合發展區　Comprehensive development area
商業/住宅　Commercial / residential
住宅(甲)　Residential (Group A)
住宅(乙)　Residential (Group B)
鄉村式發展　Village type development
工業　Industrial
政府/機構/社區設施　Government, institution or community
休憩用地　Recreation / open space
具特殊科學價值地點　Site of special scientific interest
其他指定用途　Other specified uses
綠化地帶　Green belt
河流/海　River / sea
輕便鐵路系統　Light rail
港鐵鐵路系統　MTR
主要道路　Major road
規劃範圍界線　Boundary of planning scheme

109

01 城市土地利用　Land Use in Main Urban Areas

　　香港舊市區的土地利用在二次大戰後變化明顯。1950年後，轉口經濟轉為出口型工業經濟，對工業用地和住宅的需求擴大。廉價住宅及基本設施，如機場和貨運碼頭，也需擴建。1960-1980年，GDP每年以8%-10%速度增長，工業產值更是在10%以上。

　　1967年已明顯地看到機場的擴充，海港設施大部份已從舊市區移出。已建區擴大。海港填海以供金融及商業之用。舊市區邊沿及香港島的東北岸和西南岸形成了大型的公共屋邨區。

　　1987年填海區進一步擴大，還有工業發展高峰期（1970-1980）所形成的大量工業用地。

Land use in the old city changed drastically after WWII, as the post-war economy moved from dependence on entrepôt trade to export manufacturing. Demand for industrial sites, residential land, airport, and cargo ports increased. The GDP grew at 8%-10% annually during 1960-1980, but the industrial sector grew even faster at a rate of over 10%.

The 1967 map witnessed the expansion of the airport and relocation of shipping and cargo facilities from the old city to Tsuen Wan. Reclamation expanded the built-up area for finance and commercial uses around the harbour. Large-scale public housing dominated the northeast and southwest coast of the Island and the fringe of old Kowloon.

The 1987 map evidenced further reclamation and a large amount of industrial land developed at the peak of industrialization in 1970-1980.

● **1954年城市土地利用　Urban land use in 1954**

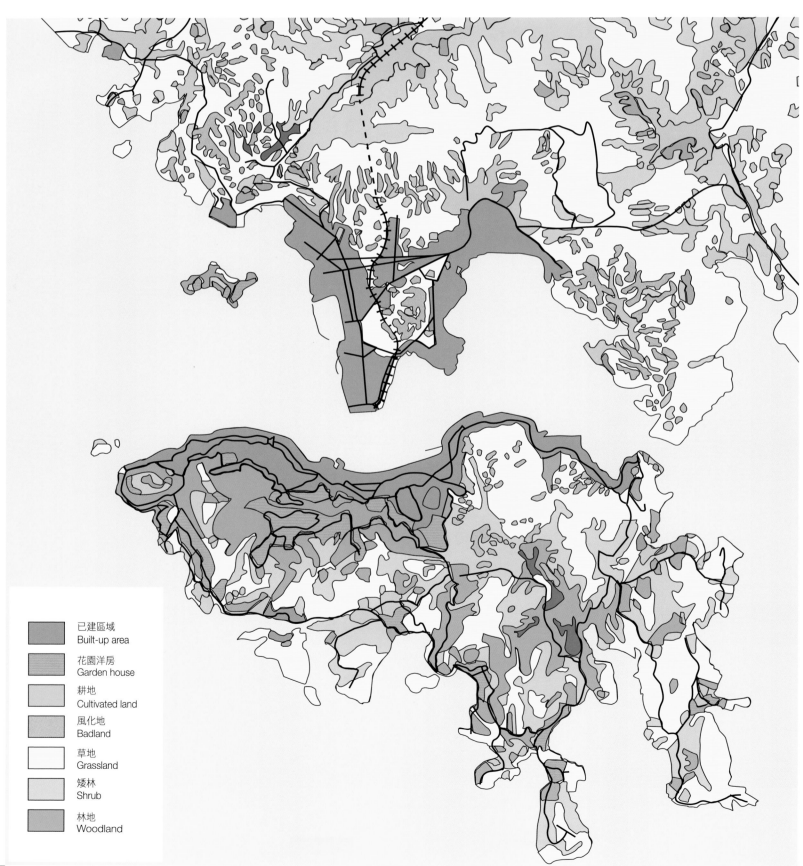

已建區域
Built-up area

花園洋房
Garden house

耕地
Cultivated land

風化地
Badland

草地
Grassland

矮林
Shrub

林地
Woodland

● 1967年城市土地利用　Urban land use in 1967

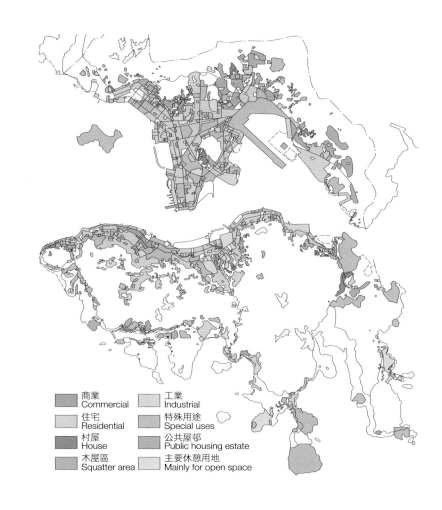

商業 Commercial		工業 Industrial	
住宅 Residential		特殊用途 Special uses	
村屋 House		公共屋邨 Public housing estate	
木屋區 Squatter area		主要休憩用地 Mainly for open space	

● 1987年城市土地利用　Urban land use in 1987

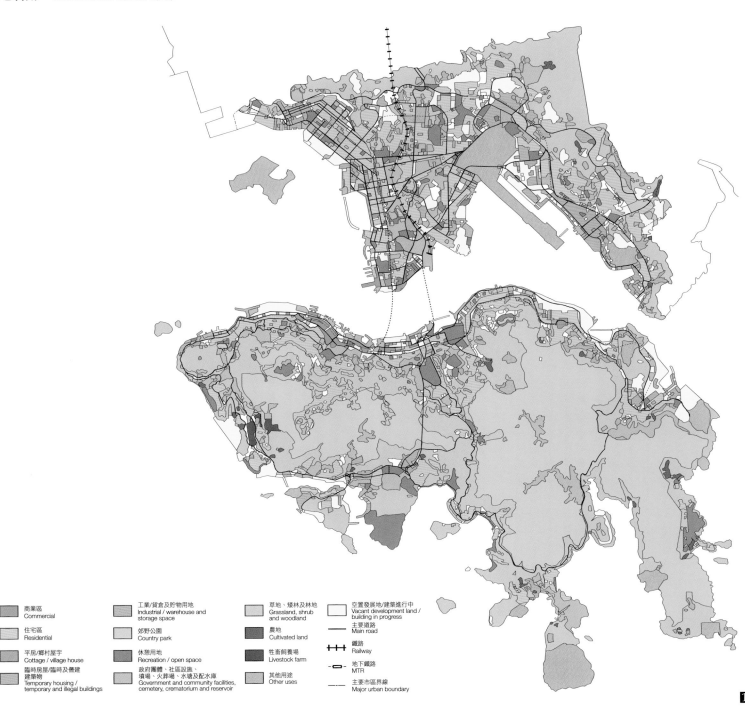

商業區 Commercial	工業/貨倉及貯物用地 Industrial / warehouse and storage space	草地、矮林及林地 Grassland, shrub and woodland	空置發展地/建築進行中 Vacant development land / building in progress
住宅區 Residential	郊野公園 Country park	農地 Cultivated land	主要道路 Main road
平房/鄉村屋宇 Cottage / village house	休憩用地 Recreation / open space	牲畜飼養場 Livestock farm	鐵路 Railway
臨時房屋/臨時及僑建建築物 Temporary housing / temporary and illegal buildings	政府團體、社區設施、墳場、火葬場、水塘及配水庫 Government and community facilities, cemetery, crematorium and reservoir	其他用途 Other uses	地下鐵路 MTR
			主要市區界線 Major urban boundary

111

02 早期海港及交通發展規劃 Early Harbour and Transport Plans

1922年成立了規劃委員會，對港島及九龍進行全面規劃。1922年圖是當時有關海港發展的部份。它建議進行大規模的填海，包括了建立旺角避風塘及中環添馬艦總部，荔枝角及觀塘發展為大型港區，並提出了在九龍加建東西各兩條九廣鐵路支線，以接連主要倉庫碼頭區。

1939年通過了城市規劃條例，並委任城市規劃委員會。1941年圖是成果之一，對九廣鐵路進一步修改，將觀塘新線具體化。建議加添新的海港設施，如設立紅磡灣仔間的汽車渡輪，將土瓜灣發展成為新的避風塘等。

日佔時破壞了1920-1941年規劃資料，劫餘的規劃圖不多。日佔時曾對新界作出總體規劃，建議將吐露港填海，變為大片稻田。

A planning committee was established in 1922 for the planning of Hong Kong Island and Kowloon. The 1922 map shows part of the committee's work. It proposes large-scale reclamation in Mongkok, Central, Kowloon Bay and Kwun Tong. Two railway lines were proposed to link up the warehousing areas.

The first Town Planning Ordinance was enacted and a Planning Board was appointed in 1939. The 1941 map shows further planned modification of the KCR. It also planned to increase harbour facilities, e.g. a typhoon shelter in To Kwa Wan.

Most of the plans in 1920-1941 were lost or damaged during the Japanese occupation. The Japanese also attempted a general plan for Hong Kong during its occupation. One of its ideas was to reclaim Tolo Harbour for paddy growing.

● 1922年城市規劃　Town plan in 1922

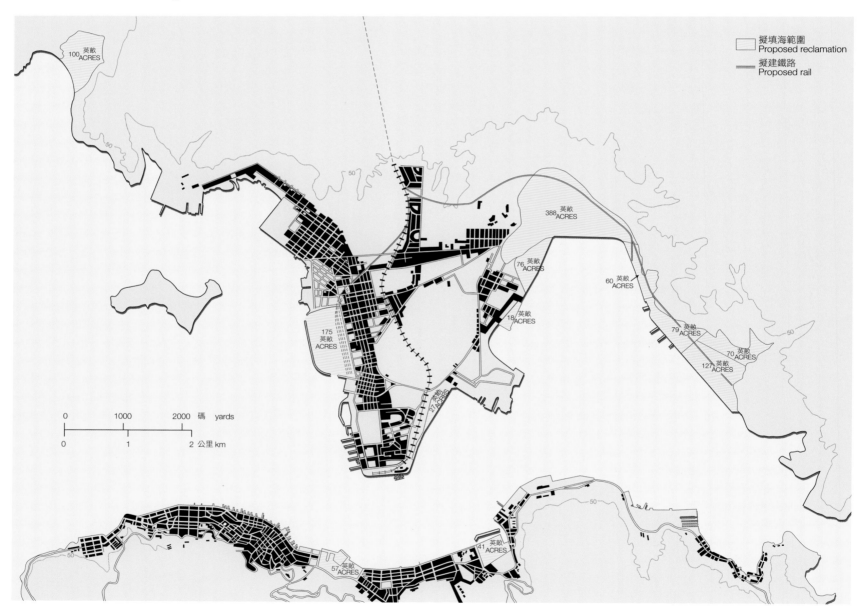

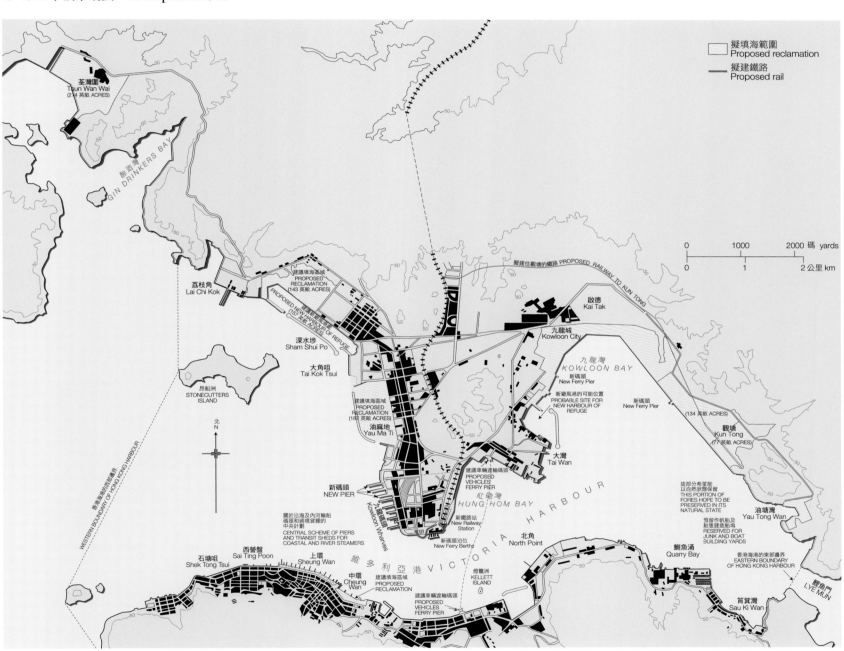

擬填海範圍
Proposed reclamation

擬建鐵路
Proposed rail

荃灣圍
Tsun Wan Wai
(214 英畝 ACRES)

筲箕灣
GIN DRINKERS BAY

擬往往觀塘的鐵路 PROPOSED RAILWAY TO KUN TONG

荔枝角
Lai Chi Kok

建議填海區域
PROPOSED
RECLAMATION
(143 英畝 ACRES)

啟德
Kai Tak

PROPOSED NEW HARBOUR OF REFUGE
(157 英畝 ACRES)

九龍城
Kowloon City

深水埗
Sham Shui Po

九龍灣
KOWLOON BAY

大角咀
Tai Kok Tsui

昂船洲
STONECUTTERS
ISLAND

北
N

新碼頭
New Ferry Pier

新建風港的可能位置
PROBABLE SITE FOR
NEW HARBOUR OF REFUGE

新碼頭
New Ferry Pier

(134 英畝 ACRES)

WESTERN BOUNDARY OF HONG KONG HARBOUR
香港海港的西部邊界

建議填海區域
PROPOSED
RECLAMATION
(180 英畝 ACRES)

油麻地
Yau Ma Ti

觀塘
Kun Tong
(77 英畝 ACRES)

大灣
Tai Wan

新碼頭
NEW PIER

建議車輛渡輪碼頭
PROPOSED
VEHICLES
FERRY PIER

這部分希望置能
以自然狀態保留
THIS PORTION OF
FORES HOPE TO BE
PRESERVED IN ITS
NATURAL STATE

油塘灣
Yau Tong Wan

關於沿海及內河輪船
碼頭和過境貨棚的
中央計劃
CENTRAL SCHEME OF PIERS
AND TRANSIT SHEDS FOR
COASTAL AND RIVER STEAMERS

九龍貨倉
Kowloon Wharves

紅磡灣
HUNG HOM BAY

新鐵路站
New Railway
Station

VICTORIA HARBOUR

香港海港的東部邊界
EASTERN BOUNDARY
OF HONG KONG HARBOUR

留留作帆船及
船隻建造船塢
RESERVED FOR
JUNK AND BOAT
BUILDING YARDS

石塘咀
Shek Tong Tsui

西營盤
Sai Ting Poon

新碼頭泊位
New Ferry Berths

北角
North Point

鯽魚涌
Quarry Bay

上環
Sheung Wan

中環
Cheung
Wan

建議填海區域
PROPOSED
RECLAMATION

維多利亞港 VICTORIA HARBOUR

燈籠洲
KELLETT
ISLAND

鯉魚門
LYE MUN

建議車輛渡輪碼頭
PROPOSED
VEHICLES
FERRY PIER

筲箕灣
Sau Ki Wan

0   1000   2000 碼 yards

0   1   2 公里 km

03 重要規劃圖 Important General Plans

1948年雅伯氏全港規劃大綱

香港政府於1946年要求英國派規劃專家為香港戰後重建作長遠發展規劃。1947年，英國城市規劃之父、大倫敦總體規劃作者雅伯氏抵港，於1948年完成香港規劃史上的第三次重大工作。

雅伯氏重視工業發展。他在東西九龍撥出大部份土地以發展工業，包括將旺角避風塘填為工業用地。除了九鐵觀塘支線外，提議新支線由九龍塘經旺角、避風塘新填地、尖沙咀，以海底隧道方式和中區連接。

在CBD的發展上，他建議自海軍船塢填海，以便向灣仔方向發展。

他並建議北角、柴灣發展為重工業區，和紅磡、馬頭圍並立；又大規模填海，包括紅磡灣、醉酒灣及荃灣；九龍中及九龍北坡地發展為住宅用地以解決戰後人口的增長。

雅伯氏的規劃雖然在1950-1960年代沒有被接受，但與日後的發展方向非常吻合。

1977年的未來大型土地利用發展計劃

此圖反映1970-1990年的主要發展策略。

（一）舊市區內重建、重組及縫合，在達致改善環境的前提下將過

Abercrombie's 1948 Plan

At the request of the Hong Kong government, Abercrombie, 'father of urban planning' and author of the Greater London Plan came in 1947 to draw up Hong Kong's Post-war Development Plan. The Abercrombie Plan is Hong Kong's third major planning exercise.

Abercrombie attached great importance to industrial development, and most of East and West Kowloon was put under industrial use, including reclaiming the Mongkok typhoon shelter as a light industrial area. Besides rail links with the industrial areas, he proposed a cross-harbour rail submarine tunnel. For CBD extension, he proposed reclaiming the naval dockyard and push the development into Wan Chai. North Point and Chai Wan were to become industrial areas as well. Another major idea was to reclaim Gin Drinkers Bay, Hung Hom, and hill-cut in New Kowloon to provide new development sites to solve post-war housing shortage.

Although rejected in 1950-1960, the major trends of development proposed in the Plan were followed in later planning.

1977 Development Plan

The Plan outlines the major strategies in 1970-1990, i.e.

● 雅伯氏1948年規劃圖　Abercrombie's Plan in 1948

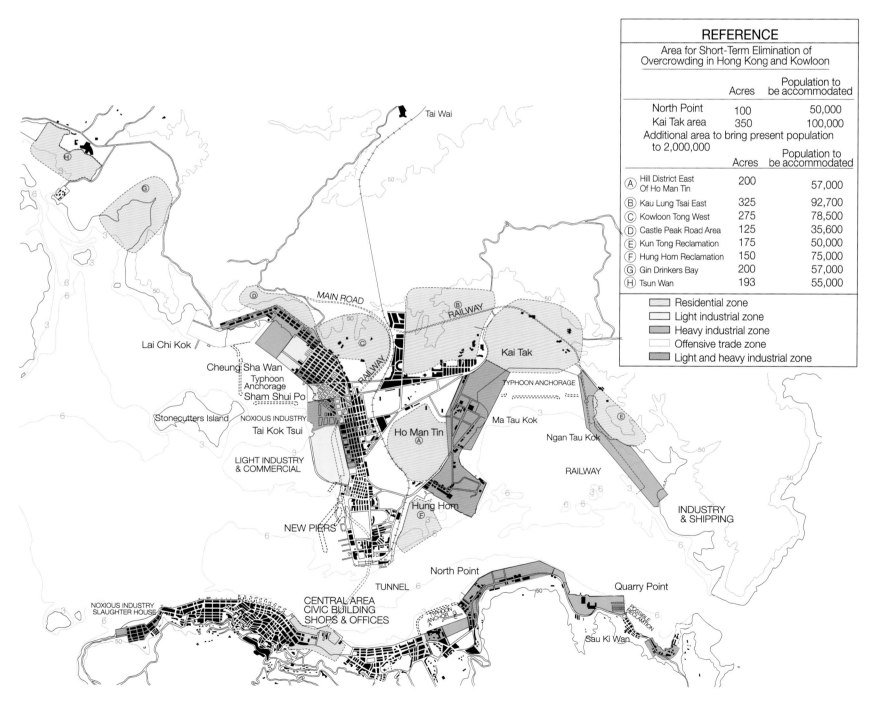

REFERENCE		
Area for Short-Term Elimination of Overcrowding in Hong Kong and Kowloon		
	Acres	Population to be accommodated
North Point	100	50,000
Kai Tak area	350	100,000
Additional area to bring present population to 2,000,000		
	Acres	Population to be accommodated
A Hill District East Of Ho Man Tin	200	57,000
B Kau Lung Tsai East	325	92,700
C Kowloon Tong West	275	78,500
D Castle Peak Road Area	125	35,600
E Kun Tong Reclamation	175	50,000
F Hung Hom Reclamation	150	75,000
G Gin Drinkers Bay	200	57,000
H Tsun Wan	193	55,000

Residential zone
Light industrial zone
Heavy industrial zone
Offensive trade zone
Light and heavy industrial zone

剩的人口外遷。

（二）重點發展八大新市鎮及一些新界村鎮，形成多心式的分散發展。

這個策略在1980年末被新的同心式發展模式，即大都會計劃所取代。

這個規劃是第一次理性地利用全部香港空間，以解決香港的城市用地和環境問題。

1989年機場及海港發展計劃

1989年港英政府公佈所謂"玫瑰園"即新機場與海港發展計劃，其中將新機場以及有關的交通幹線、新城市發展以及填海工程，命名為"十項核心工程"和中方談判。中方最後同意興建。工程在1992年開始，總成本預算減為1,564億元。其中新機場造價707億元，機場鐵路340億元。新機場在1998年7月啟用。

海港的發展沒有按1989年計劃進行。1997年1月決定興建九號貨櫃碼頭，1998年才動工。由於大量貨源來自南中國，而香港的成本高、內部交通網以及環境因素，不能負荷大量貨櫃流，這個行業已向深圳疏散。至2009年仍未決定是否興建大嶼山的碼頭。

(1) decanting population from old urban districts and their redevelopment,

(2) focus on new town development and growth of selected market towns in the NT in a multi-centric pattern of growth,

Though this was the first comprehensive planning to solve Hong Kong's land use and environmental problems, it was superceded by the Metroplan.

PADS (Port and Airport Development Strategy), 1989

In 1989, the government announced PADS, the so-called 'Rose Garden' plan. The plan lumped together 10 projects, focusing on the replacement airport plan at Chek Lap Kok and the new container ports off Southeast Lantau.

PADS soon became a Sino-Anglo dispute issue. After negotiations, China agreed to start work in 1992, with a total cost tag of HK$156.4 billion. The new airport alone costs 70.7 billion. It began operation in July 1998.

However, port development did not follow PADS. Terminal 9 in Tsing Yi only started construction in 1998. As cross-boundary trucking cost is high and the Pearl River Delta ports becoming competitive, there is little demand for new terminal construction.

● 1977年未來大型土地利用建議　Future large-scale land use proposed in 1977

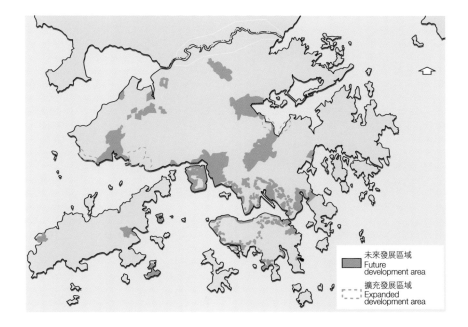

未來發展區域
Future development area

擴充發展區域
Expanded development area

● 1989年機場及海港發展計劃　Port and airport development strategy in 1989

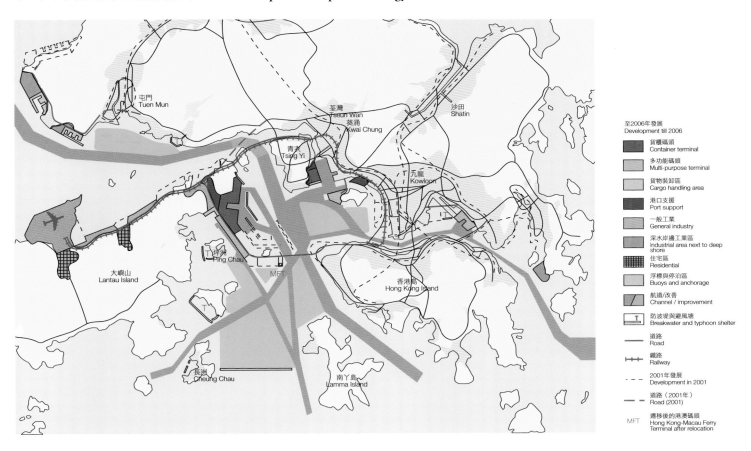

至2006年發展
Development till 2006

貨櫃碼頭
Container terminal

多功能碼頭
Multi-purpose terminal

貨物裝卸區
Cargo handling area

港口支援
Port support

一般工業
General industry

深水岸邊工業區
Industrial area next to deep shore

住宅區
Residential

浮標與停泊區
Buoys and anchorage

航道/改善
Channel / improvement

防波堤與避風塘
Breakwater and typhoon shelter

道路
Road

鐵路
Railway

2001年發展
Development in 2001

道路（2001年）
Road (2001)

遷移後的港澳碼頭
Hong Kong-Macau Ferry Terminal after relocation

04　都會區土地利用遠景計劃　Metroplan: Urban Areas' Long-term Land Use Development

"都會區"指香港島、九龍及荃灣。"都會區"規劃於1990年完成，在1990-1992年間諮詢各界。

計劃對市區重建、土地用途分區以適應工業和經濟轉型以及機場的搬遷，起着促進作用。

但計劃對南中國的發展缺乏考慮，問題很多，主要包括：

（一）規劃的人口及經濟活動過份集中於舊市區。

（二）大量的海港填海收窄維多利亞港，破壞香港珍貴的景觀及影響水流。

（三）沒有從空間規劃配合香港和南中國經濟往來日趨頻密的走勢。

（四）市區交通線重複建設，缺乏經濟效益及可行性。

（五）缺乏考慮新市鎮的持續及較高層次發展。

政府在1999年對都會計劃做第二期檢討。2000年公佈了未來十年（至2011年）土地需求及分佈計劃。預測土地總需求3,872公頃，其中工業用地減少，反映經濟持續轉向商業服務。78%的新增土地將位於新界，新發展策略有利於與中國內地加強合作。

'Metro' refers to Hong Kong Island, Kowloon and Tsuen Wan. The Metroplan was completed in 1990 and public consultation was held during 1990-1992. It stresses urban redevelopment and restructuring urban land use to meet changes in the economy and needs arising from the relocation of the airport. Yet the plan has not considered the rapid changes in South China and shows these main problems:

(1) over-concentration of population and economic activities in old urban districts

(2) large-scale harbour reclamation, damaging Hong Kong's harbour view and disrupting its currents

(3) inadequate response to increasing integration with South China

(4) duplicated urban road construction without concern for economic viability

(5) paying no heed to the role and possible growth of existing new towns

A second review of Metroplan was done in 1999. As a result, an estimated 10-year land demand (2001-2011) was announced. The total demand was 3,872 ha, 78% of it being in the New Territories. Industrial land demand dropped. Both reflected Hong Kong's shift towards the tertiary sector and its closer link with the mainland.

● **2001-2015遠景城市土地利用圖**　Metroplan: long-term urban land use development for 2001-2015

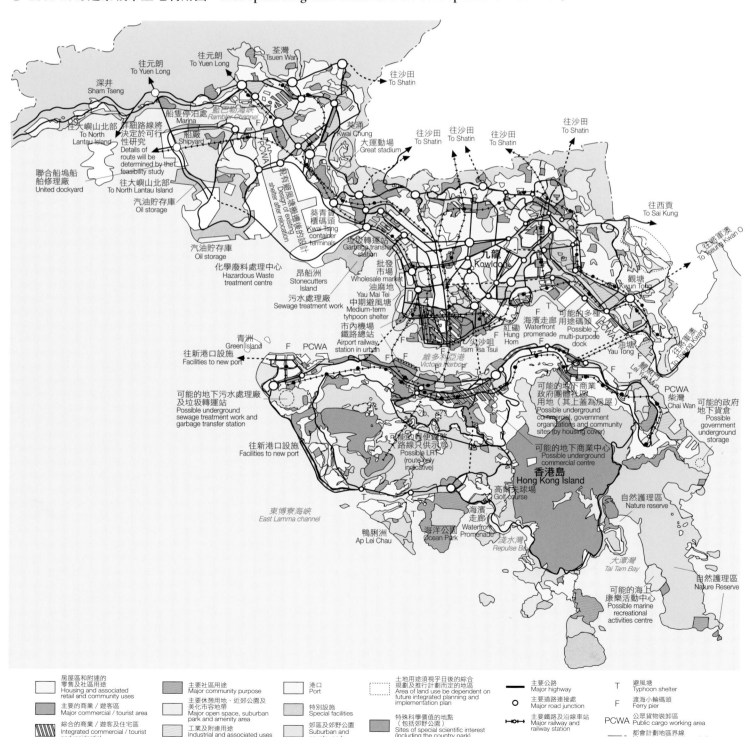

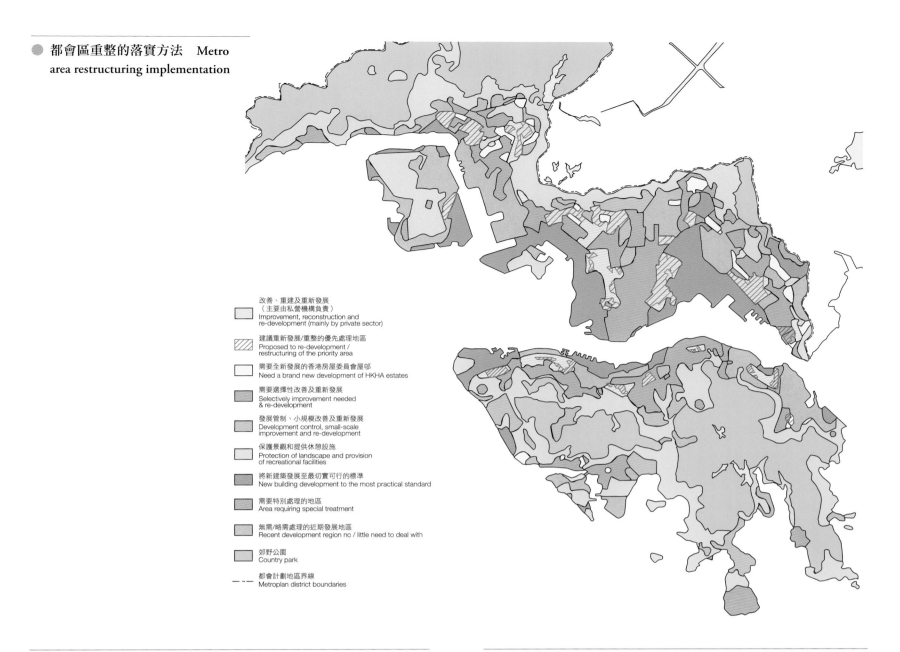

改善、重建及重新發展
（主要由私營機構負責）
Improvement, reconstruction and re-development (mainly by private sector)

建議重新發展/重整的優先處理地區
Proposed to re-development / restructuring of the priority area

需要全新發展的香港房屋委員會屋邨
Need a brand new development of HKHA estates

需要選擇性改善及重新發展
Selectively improvement needed & re-development

發展管制、小規模改善及重新發展
Development control, small-scale improvement and re-development

保護景觀和提供休憩設施
Protection of landscape and provision of recreational facilities

將新建築發展至最切實可行的標準
New building development to the most practical standard

需要特別處理的地區
Area requiring special treatment

無需/略需處理的近期發展地區
Recent development region no / little need to deal with

郊野公園
Country park

都會劃地區界線
Metroplan district boundaries

● 土地用途　Land use

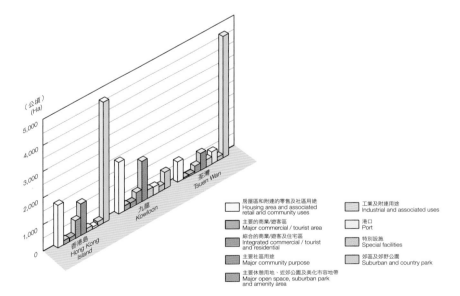

房屋區和附建的零售及社區用途
Housing area and associated retail and community uses

主要的商業/遊客區
Major commercial / tourist area

綜合的商業/遊客及住宅區
Integrated commercial / tourist and residential

主要社區用途
Major community purpose

主要休憩用地、近郊公園及美化市容地帶
Major open space, suburban park and amenity area

工業及附建用途
Industrial and associated uses

港口
Port

特別設施
Special facilities

郊區及郊野公園
Suburban and country park

● 人口及就業人口　Population and employment

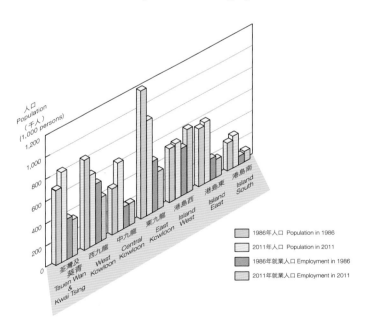

1986年人口　Population in 1986
2011年人口　Population in 2011
1986年就業人口　Employment in 1986
2011年就業人口　Employment in 2011

● 都會區規劃重點假設　Key working assumptions of metroplan

		基準年 Base Year	2010	2020	2030
人口（以百萬計）	Population (million)				
居住	Residential	6.8	7.2	7.8	8.4
工作	Working	3.2	3.6	3.8	3.9
職位（以百萬計）	Employment (million)	3.0	3.5	3.7	4.0
每年本地生產總值增長（%）	Annual GDP growth (%)	—	4.0	3.5	3.0
房屋（以千計）	Housing (thousand)				
單位總數	Total stock	2,394	2,642	2,948	3,319
累計實際需求	Cumulative requirement	—	248	553	924
經濟用地（以百萬平方米計）	Economic landuse (million m²)				
商業中心區甲級辦公室	CBD Grade A offices	4.1	5.1	5.8	6.7
一般商業	General business	33.0	35.5	36.2	38.2
特殊工業	Special industries	4.0	5.5	6.0	6.7

05 2030發展規劃　Hong Kong 2030

特區政府在97回歸後，因與內地關係更緊密和世界經濟發展的新形勢，對香港的未來發展規劃作出了新的考慮，改變了港英時代的傳統：（一）規劃期延長，和（二）重視和內地、特別是和鄰近的珠三角地區的接軌。

2007年完成的"2030研究"首次提出了以"加強與內地的聯繫"，作為主要規劃目標之一。中央與香港在2004年簽定的《更緊密經貿關係的安排》，廣東省2006年完成的《大珠江三角洲城鎮群協調發展規

After 1997, Hong Kong moves closer to the mainland in economic terms, and is confronted with a new global trend. As such, there has been a change in Hong Kong's approach in planning for its future growth, i.e.: (1) it takes on a longer planning horizon, and (2) stresses the link with the mainland, particular the neighbouring Pearl River Delta.

'Hong Kong 2030', released in 2007, is the first major long-term plan that emphasizes strengthening relations with the mainland. In 2004, Beijing and the SAR government signed the 'Closer Economic Partnership Agreement', while two

● 第三階段公眾諮詢發展方案（集中模式）　Development Options for Stage 3 Public Consultation (Consolidation Option)

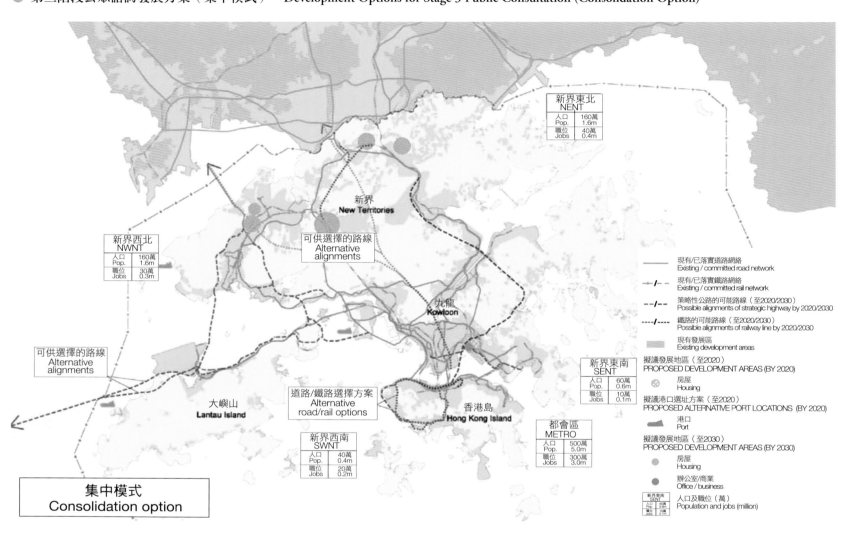

● 建議發展模式　Recommended development pattern

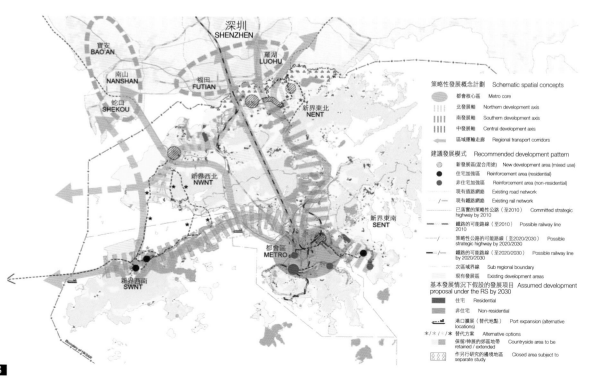

採取的重要假設（百萬人）
Key assumptions adopted (million persons)

	Population 人口	Daytime population 日間人口	Working population 工作人口	Employment 就業
基準年 Base year	6.8	6.8	3.2	3.0
2010	7.2	7.2	3.6	3.5
2020	7.8	7.8	3.8	3.7
2030	8.4	8.4	3.9	4.0

劃》，和2009年初國務院公佈的《大珠三角洲改革與發展綱要》，成為香港未來發展的新動力。

important documents: 'Coordinated Development of the Greater Pearl River Delta Townships' released by Guangdong Province in 2006, and the 'Outline of the Plan for the Reform and Development of the Pearl River Delta (2008-2020)' announced by the State Council in 2009 added further stresses on Hong Kong's closer ties with the mainland and on its important role in the Pearl River Delta. These provide new impetus and direction for Hong Kong's future growth.

● 空間規劃示意圖　Schematic Spatial Plan

● 新發展的大概地點　Broad Locations of New Development Areas

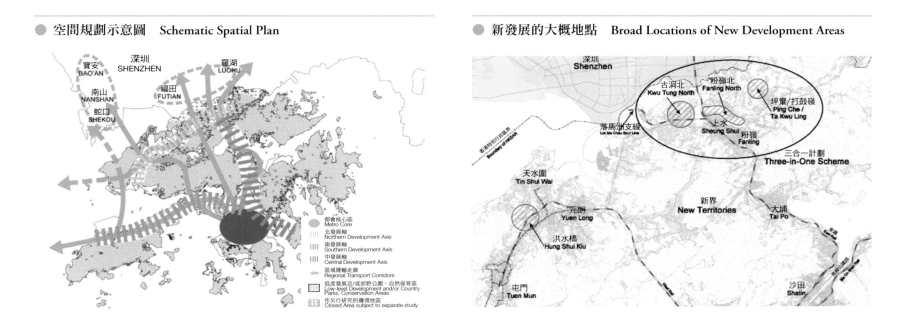

● 珠江三角洲城鎮群協調發展規劃，2004-2020　Coordinated Urban Development Plan for the Pearl River Delta, 2004-2020

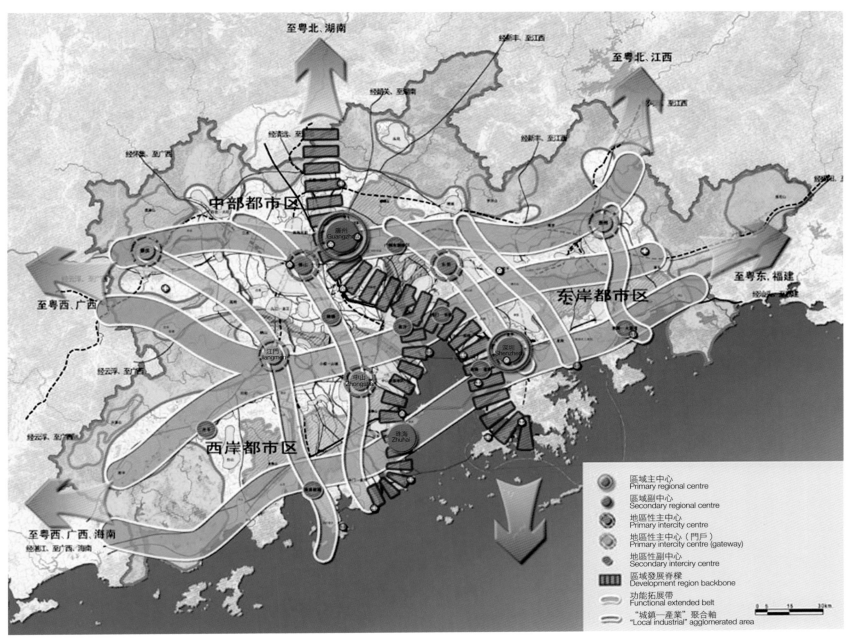

06 西環市區重建計劃 Urban Redevelopment in Western District

由私人進行舊市區重建，會受到土地使用權和發展者的經濟能力及利益考慮的局限，只能進行單幢樓房重建，不能改善以下的一些舊區問題：（一）道路網落後引起交通問題；（二）綠化不足；（三）社區設施不足。只有整區重建才能達致有效的改造，以適合現代的都市生活、經濟和交通的需求。而這種重建只能由公營部門以非牟利性質去落實。

香港最早的市區重建區選在西環。1967年圖是該區重建前的土地利用圖。1993及1999年圖中包括了這個重建區，而重建計劃已大部份完成。路網有明顯的拉直，主路拓寬了，支路減少了，公園、綠地以及社區設施增加了。因此，交通、環境及樓宇素質有明顯的改善。

香港政府自此以後並沒有再積極進行類似計劃。1988年成立土地發展公司，只進行單幢（最多是數條小街巷）重建，規模較小，對地區上的交通、綠化和社區設施沒有很大改進。至1998年只完成了15項小規模重建。中期任務有30項，但同樣是規模較小的。

政府在1999年完成有關立法程序和市區重建策略的研究，並成立了市區重建局，以加快市區重建工作。觀塘舊區重建是該局現時的大型計劃。

There is great limitation for the private sector in undertaking redevelopment of old urban districts. Land rights and lack of financial resources often restrict redevelopment to individual buildings. It helps little in redressing major problems of these old districts: (1) out-dated street/road pattern leading to traffic congestion, (2) inadequate green space and (3) lack of social and amenity facilities. These can only be resolved by wholescale redevelopment of a larger area, and non-profit-making public agents are best to undertake the task.

Hong Kong's earliest large-scale urban redevelopment district lies in Western District. The 1967 map shows the situation before the said redevelopment while the 1993 and 1999 maps chart the results of redevelopment. Main streets have been straightened and widened, while some small side streets disappeared, with an increase in open space, green parks and community facilities. These have led to an improvement in transport and the environment.

However, the scheme has not been extended to other old urban districts. Instead, the government set up an agent: Land Development Corporation in 1988 to undertake redevelopment on a building-by-building approach. By 1995, it had completed 15 small-scale projects, with 30 such at the planning stage.

In 1999, a new legislation was passed for setting up a new agent–Urban Renewal Authority with an aim to undertake larger-scale redevelopment. Kwun Tong old district is its largest scheme at hand.

● 1967年西環市區重建計劃前土地利用狀況　Land use in Western District in 1967 before the urban renewal scheme

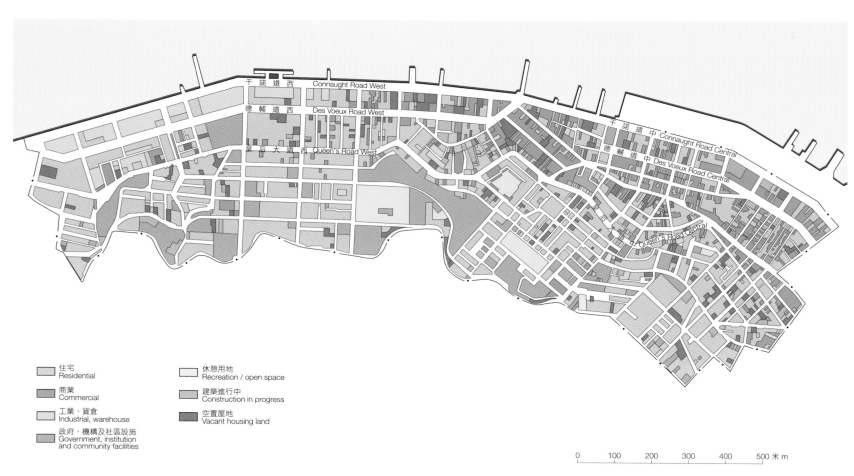

住宅 Residential
商業 Commercial
工業、貨倉 Industrial, warehouse
政府、機構及社區設施 Government, institution and community facilities
休憩用地 Recreation / open space
建築進行中 Construction in progress
空置屋地 Vacant housing land

0　100　200　300　400　500 米 m

1993年西環市區重建計劃土地利用方案　Proposed land use of Western District Urban Renewal Scheme in 1993

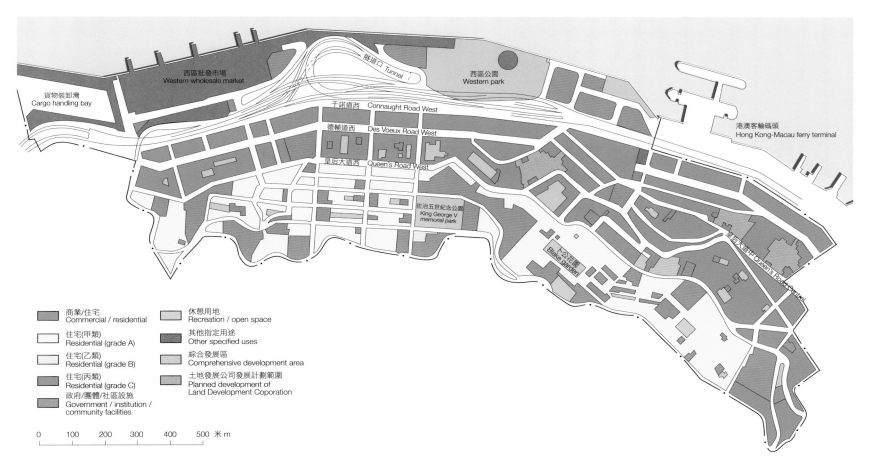

商業/住宅
Commercial / residential

住宅(甲類)
Residential (grade A)

住宅(乙類)
Residential (grade B)

住宅(丙類)
Residential (grade C)

政府/團體/社區設施
Government / institution /
community facilities

休憩用地
Recreation / open space

其他指定用途
Other specified uses

綜合發展區
Comprehensive development area

土地發展公司發展計劃範圍
Planned development of
Land Development Coporation

0　100　200　300　400　500 米 m

1999年西環市區重建計劃後實際土地利用狀況　Actual land use in 1999: after the Urban Renewal Scheme

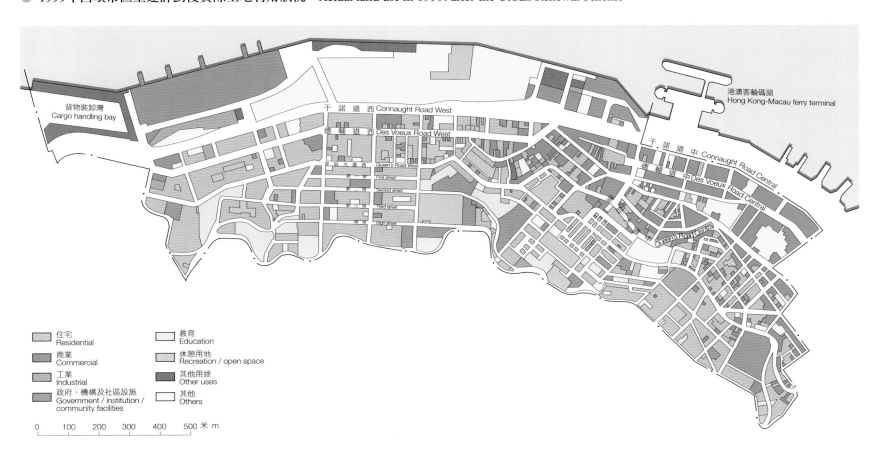

住宅
Residential

商業
Commercial

工業
Industrial

政府、機構及社區設施
Government / institution /
community facilities

教育
Education

休憩用地
Recreation / open space

其他用途
Other uses

其他
Others

0　100　200　300　400　500 米 m

Society and
Community

IV. 社會與社區

01 人口　Population

　　1841年香港島人口7,450人，其中華人約5,600人，漁民2,500人，外國居民1,850人。1858年，人口增至7萬5千人，其中外國居民2,500人。1861年，加上新割佔的九龍半島，人口為119,321人。1866年，蘇彝士運河通航，促進了國際貿易，人口倍增至239,419人，其中外國人近7,000人。

　　1881年起，香港政府每十年進行一次人口普查，1941和1951年除外。

　　1901年的普查首次包括新界，總人口是300,660人。當年的新界人口分佈為荃灣3,272人，元朗23,243人，粉嶺上水13,378人，離島11,808人。

　　1936年人口988,190人。因為日本侵華，人口大增，1941年升至164萬人。日佔時，人口大量回流內地，1945年驟降至65萬人，1947年人口才回升，之後，平均年增長率在2%左右，增長遲緩。

　　In 1841, there were 7,450 persons on the Island, of which 5,600 were Chinese (2,500 fishermen) and 1,850 foreigners. In 1858, the population increased to 75,000 with 2,500 foreigners. In 1861, when Kowloon was added, the population increased further to 119,321. The opening of the Suez Canal in 1866 boosted international trade and Hong Kong's population doubled, reaching 239,419 with about 7,000 foreigners.

　　Since 1881, a government census was held every 10 years, except for 1941 and 1951. The New Territories (NT) was included in the Census in 1901. Hong Kong's population then was 300,660. Among the NT districts, Tsuen Wan had 3,272, Yuen Long, 23,243, Fanling-Sheung Shui, 13,378 and the Outlying Islands, 11,808.

　　In 1936, the population was 988,190. Japan's invasion of China pushed the population to 1,640,000 in 1941. Forced out-migration during the Japanese

● 1931年人口分佈　**Distribution of population in 1931**

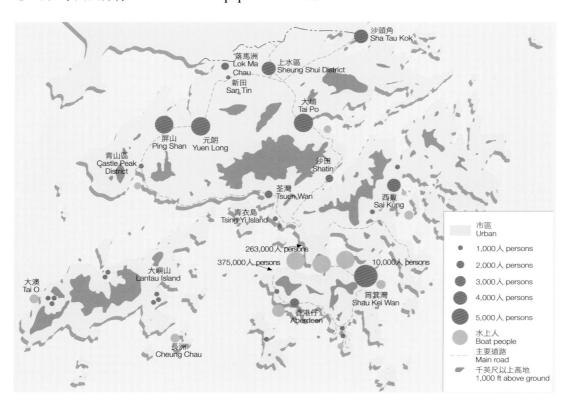

● 1961年人口分佈　**Distribution of population in 1961**

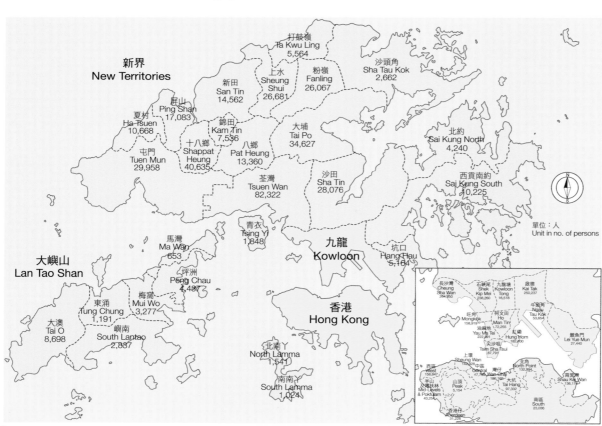

戰前人口一直集中在港島，戰後的首20年則向新九龍分散。1970年代後，更向新界疏散，反映出城市發展的主要趨勢。

occupation reduced the population to 650,000 by 1945. It recuperated to 1.8 million in 1947. Since then, the population has grown at an annual rate of about 2%.

The pre-war population concentrated largely on Hong Kong Island. After the War, it spread to New Kowloon. From 1970 onwards, it leapfrogged into the NT following the development of new towns.

● 1991年人口分佈　Distribution of population in 1991

市區及新市鎮
Urban areas and new towns

郊區
Suburban

1991年人口普查規劃統計界線
Census planning and statistics boundary in 1991

● 各區人口分佈　Distribution of population by district

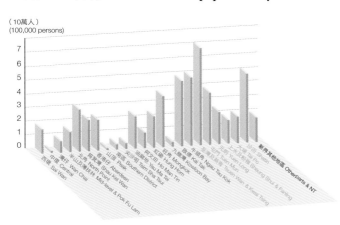

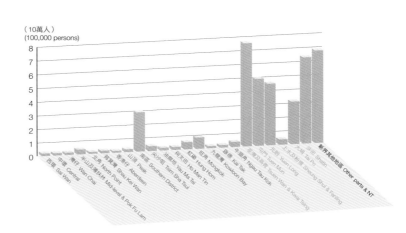

1991
2001

● 2006年各區人口分佈　Distribution of population in 2006

1點代表50人
1 Dot = 50 Persons

● 1841-2008年全港人口　Hong Kong population in 1841-2008

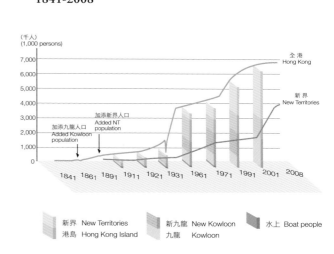

新界 New Territories　　新九龍 New Kowloon　　水上 Boat people
港島 Hong Kong Island　　九龍 Kowloon

125

02 年齡構成與居住密度 Age and Density

年齡構成表現在1911–2006年的七個人口年齡金字塔中。金字塔的形狀變化，反映出影響人口的諸種因素的歷史變化。1911年大量年輕勞動力遷入，形成漸進式的人口結構。高死亡率、大量人口流失及戰後的高生育率分別表現在1961、1971及1981年的人口金字塔中。1991年已變成了低生育以及人口的本地化，反映出經濟的穩定發展。人口素質自1961年以來不斷改進，高中教育人口增加，富裕程度提高，家庭規模縮小。高內遷率也反映出香港城市空間結構不斷擴展和重組。

1997年香港總人口達635萬，密度為世界之冠。1931年時最高密度地區上環也只有每平方公里1,000多人。至1971年不少小區人口密度達每平

The age structure of the population in 1911-2006 is mapped out in seven pyramids. Their changing shapes reflect changing demographic dynamics. The 1911 pyramid points to a typical transient population of young in-migrant labour. High death rate, out-migration and the post-war baby boom combined to shape the pyramids of 1961, 1971 and 1981. By 1991, with a low birth rate and indigenization of the population, a stable and relatively developed economy is reflected.

The quality of population measured by education level, income and household size has improved since 1961. High internal migration rate underlines the city's rapid restructuring into a polycentric urban region.

The population in 1997 reached 6.35 million–the highest population density

● 1971年人口密度 Population density in 1971

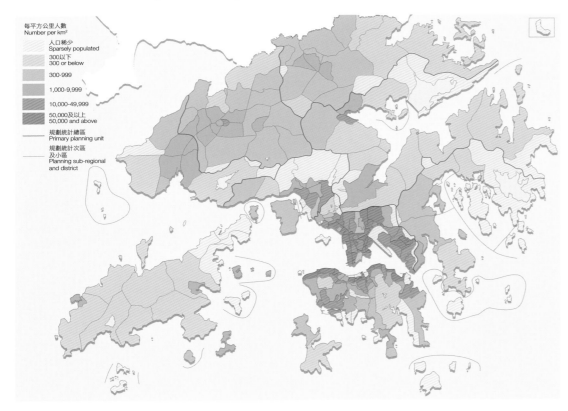

● 1931年人口密度（每英畝人數）
Population density in 1931 (number per acre)

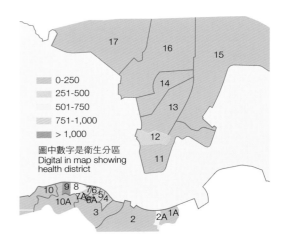

● 1991年人口密度 Population density in 1991

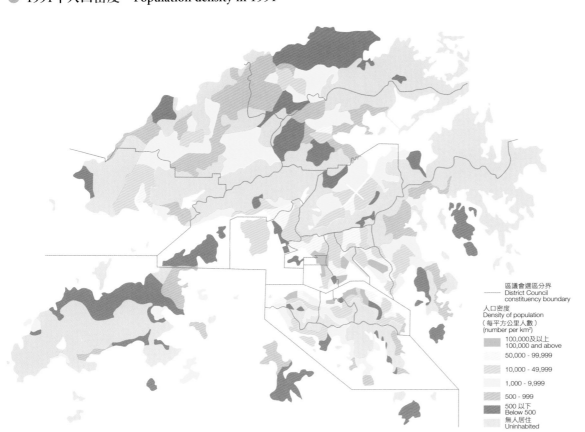

● 1911年及1961年人口年齡金字塔
Age pyramid of 1911 and 1961

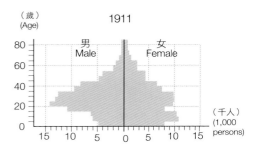

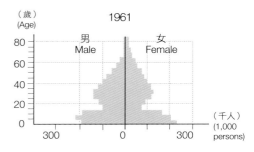

方公里5萬人以上。1991年5萬至10萬人的高密度地帶伸延至所有新市鎮的中心區，新市鎮也呈現高密度形態的城市發展。

in the world.

 In 1931, Sheung Wan had the highest urban density of 1,000 persons per km². By 1971, many districts registered a density of over 50,000 persons per km². In 1991, such high densities were found in many urban districts, including three among the new towns.

2001年人口密度分佈　Population density in 2001

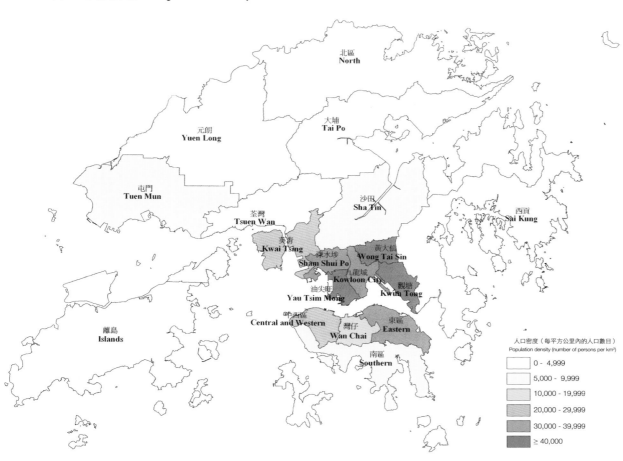

人口密度表（每平方公里人數）　Population density (number of persons per km²)

年份 Year	香港島 Hong Kong Island	九龍 Kowloon	新九龍 New Kowloon	荃灣 Tsuen Wan	其他新界地區 Other parts of NT	全港 Whole Territory
1961	13,303	84,816	27,631	1,266	385	2,916
1971	12,933	78,711	39,489	3,737	482	3,754
1981	15,281	87,022	45,154	8,294	828	4,760
1991	16,561	73,552	65,760	14,144	1,943	5,507
1996	17,377	68,923	45,312	14,703	2,504	6,024
2001	16,775	43,201		4,566	5,925	6,237
2006	15,915	43,033		4,679	6,163	6,352

1971-2006年人口年齡金字塔　Population pyramids of 1971-2006

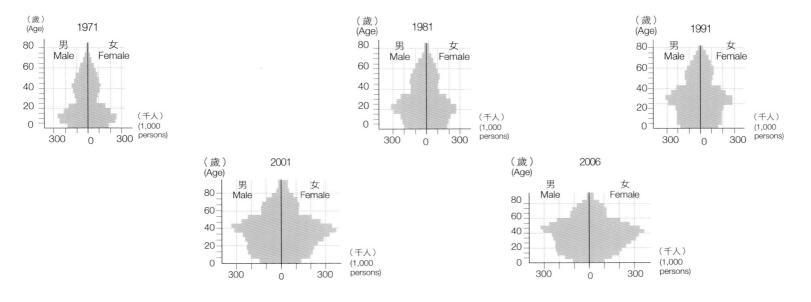

03 國籍分佈　Nationality

圖中1961年和1981年的數字顯示的是不同國籍的人口。在1991年的國籍資料中，不少本地出生的中國人被歸納為英籍，因此我們採用了出生地資料作為國籍反映，因為本地出生的，絕大部份屬中國籍。1997年的《香港年報》稱人口中有95%是中國血統，最多的外籍人士是菲律賓人（128,300），其次是美國人（32,600）、加拿大人（28,200）及英國人（26,700）。印尼、泰國、日本、印度和澳洲等國籍人士差不多都是各約2萬人。它所指的外國籍，大概是非中國血統而持有這些國家護照的人士。2006年的人口中，中國血統的仍佔95%，菲律賓112,453，印尼87,840，白種人36,384，印度20,444，尼泊爾15,953，日本13,189。

The 1961 and 1981 census data was based on nationality, while the 1991 data included some locally-born Chinese as 'British'. In this Atlas, place of birth is used to reflect nationality, as most of the local births are of Chinese descent. In the 1997 Government Yearbook, 95% of the population was of Chinese blood, the largest foreign community was Filipino (128,300), followed by American (32,600), Canadian (28,200), and British (26,700). The size of Indonesians, Thais, Japanese, Indians and Australians were about 20,000 each. The Yearbook defines 'foreigners' as non-Chinese with foreign (including British) passports.

The 1961 population in the New Territories (NT) was largely Chinese. At that time, Sheung Shui, Fanling and Shatin were parts of Tai Po District, and Tuen

● 1961-1991年人口的國籍/出生地分佈　Distribution of nationality / place of birth in 1961-1991

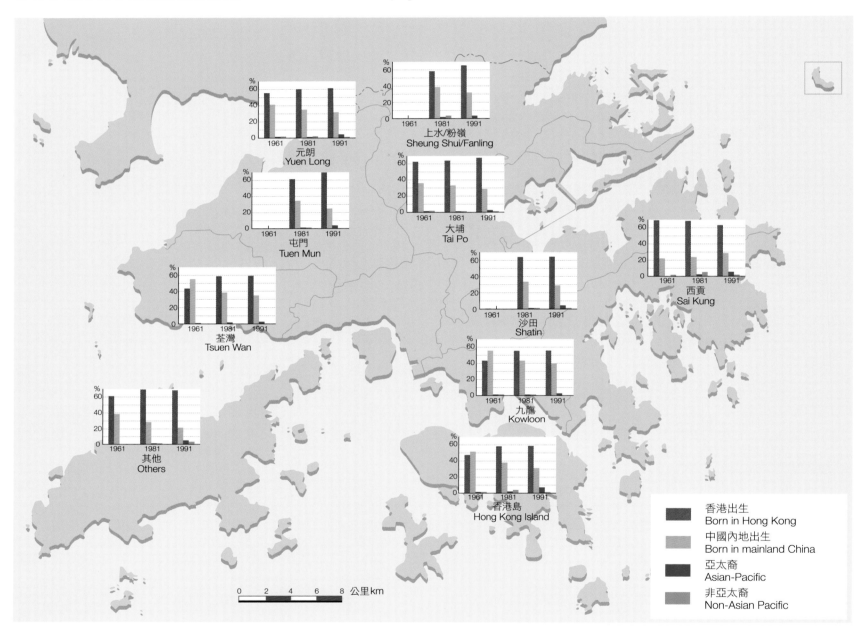

香港出生　Born in Hong Kong
中國內地出生　Born in mainland China
亞太裔　Asian-Pacific
非亞太裔　Non-Asian Pacific

新界人口在1961年時主要是本地出生的中國人。上水、粉嶺及沙田當時併入大埔區；而屯門則併入元朗區。本地出生的市區人口只佔市區人口的四成。自1961年後，本地出生人口比例在各區都有增長。1991年，在非中國籍人士，來自東南亞的外來傭工的比例有明顯增長。

Mun was included into Yuen Long District. The locally-born however, accounted for just 40% of the urban population.

Since 1991, the ratio of locally-born in the population increases steadily. The non-Chinese ratio also rises, fuelled mainly by foreign domestic helpers from South and Southeast Asia.

● 籍貫構成　Composition of nationality

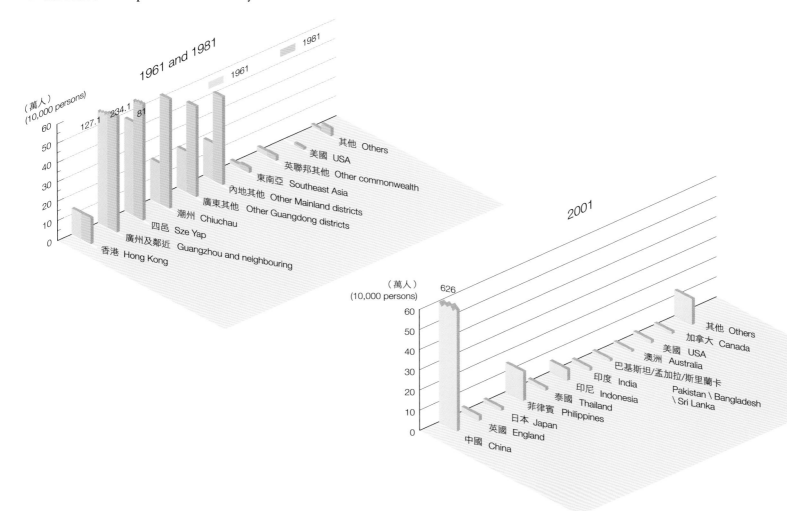

● 語言構成　Composition of languages spoken

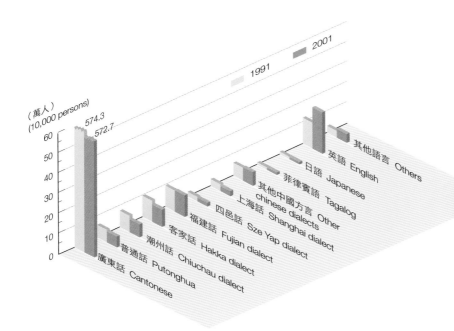

04 中國籍居民的方言構成　Place of Origin and Dialects of Chinese Residents

1961及1981年的人口普查有中國籍居民的籍貫或出生地資料。1991年並沒有這類資料，因而只有用方言資料替代。

報稱廣州及鄰近地區人士者人數最多，四邑（台山、開平、恩平、高鶴）人士也不少。1961年四邑人士主要集中在九龍舊區。在1981年可能由於木屋區清拆而被徙置，改變為較集中在九龍的邊沿新區（如觀塘、慈雲山）及荃灣。潮籍人士較集中在慈雲山、觀塘、荃灣、九龍城及香港島的西環。1991年起，四邑、潮州人士並未能通過語言資料顯示出來。日常使用四邑及潮州語者遠比1961及1981年的少。由於社會轉變，地方標誌減弱，他們不少自視為廣東（或廣府）人。

客家話、福建話也有明顯的地區分佈。福建話主要集中在北角，其次是荃灣及葵青。客家話則集中在新界。

The 1961 and 1981 censuses provide data on place of birth of Chinese citizens, which is absent in the 1991 census. Since there is a close correlation between place of birth and dialects used, dialect data is used to reflect place of birth in 1991.

People from Guangzhou and its neighbourhood form the majority of the local population. Those from Sze Yap (Toishan, Kaiping, Enping, Gaohe) are also many. In 1961, Sze Yap people clustered in the old urban districts in Kowloon. In 1981, possibly due to squatter clearance and internal migration, they concentrated more in New Kowloon's periphery, e.g. Kwun Tong, Tsz Wan Shan, and Tsuen Wan. The Chiuchau were more concentrated in Tsz Wan Shan, Kwun Tong, Tsuen Wan, Kowloon City and Western District.

The 1991 data is unable to indicate the population of the Sze Yap and Chiuchau people. Due to societal changes, they have adopted the predominant Cantonese dialect.

Hakka is deeply rooted in the NT and still shows a clear concentration there, while Fujianese cluster in North Point, with minor concentrations in Tsuen Wan and Kwai Tsing.

● 廣州及鄰近地區人士分佈　Distribution of Guangzhou and neighbouring people

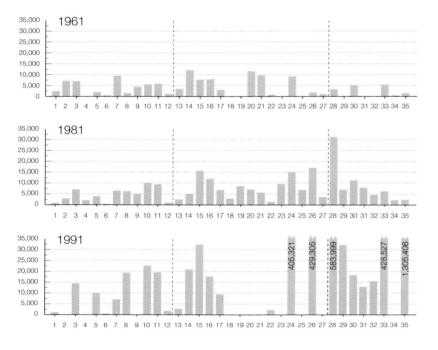

● 潮州人士分佈　Distribution of Chiuchau people

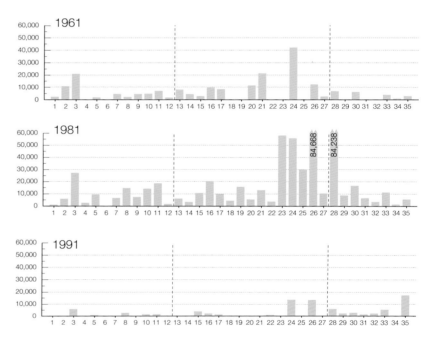

● 四邑人士分佈　Distribution of Sze Yap people

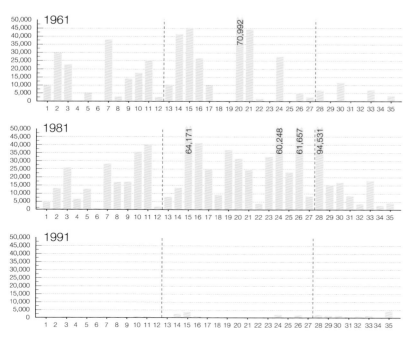

1	中環 Central	11	筲箕灣 Shau Kei Wan	21 石硤尾 Shek Kip Mei	31 上水 / 粉嶺 Sheung Shui / Fanling
2	上環 Sheung Wan	12	南區 Southern District	22 九龍灣 Kowloon Bay	32 大埔 Tai Po
3	西環 Sai Wan	13	尖沙咀 Tsim Sha Tsui	23 九龍城 Kowloon City	33 沙田 Shatin
4	半山 Mid-level	14	油麻地 Yau Ma Tei	24 慈雲山 Tsz Wan Shan	34 西貢 Sai Kung
5	薄扶林 Pok Fu Lam	15	旺角 Mongkok	25 佐敦谷 Jordan Valley	35 離島 Outlying Islands
6	山頂 Peak	16	紅磡 Hung Hom	26 觀塘 Kwun Tong	
7	灣仔 Wan Chai	17	何文田 Ho Man Tin	27 油塘 Yau Tong	
8	香港仔 Aberdeen	18	荔枝角 Lai Chi Kok	28 荃灣 Tsuen Wan	
9	大坑 Tai Hang	19	長沙灣 Cheung Sha Wan	29 屯門 Tuen Mun	
10	北角 North Point	20	深水埗 Sham Shui Po	30 元朗 Yuen Long	

● 1991及2001年客家話及福建話人士分佈　Distribution of Hakka and Fujian dialects in 1991 and 2001

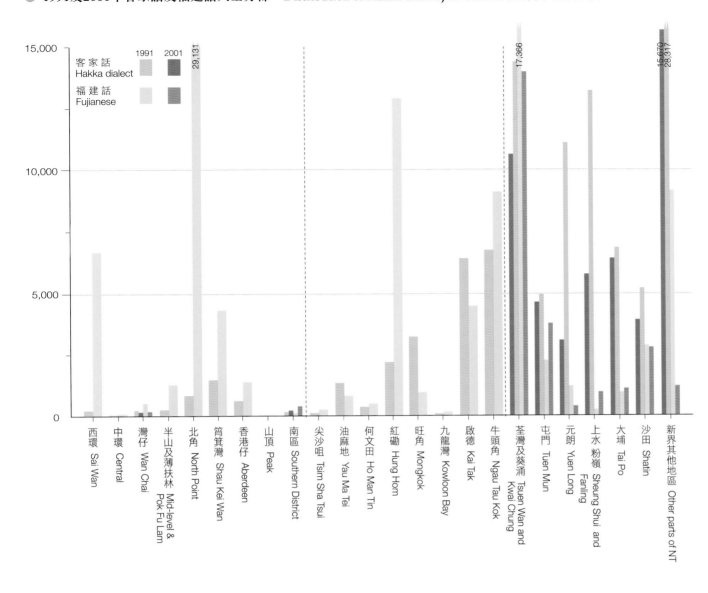

● 1991及2001年普通話及上海話人士分佈　Distribution of Putonghua and Shanghainese in 1991 and 2001

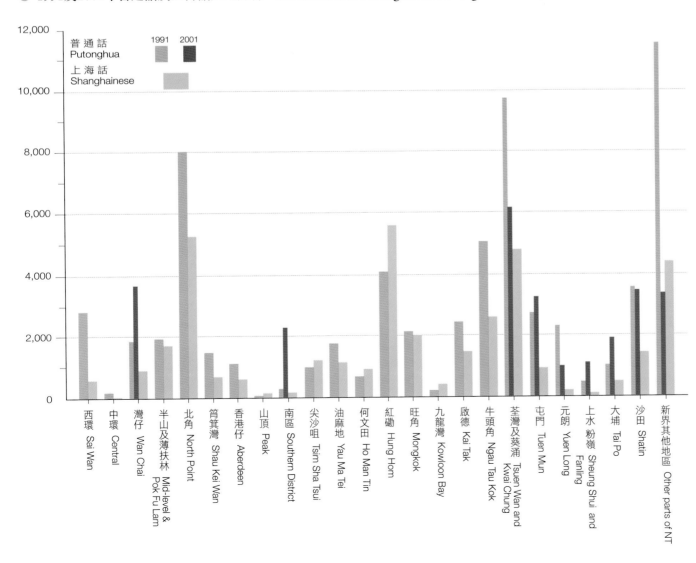

05　外籍居民　Foreign Population

　　1841年時，香港島外籍人士主要是英國人，約有2,500人（相當部份是軍人），佔了總人口的1/3。1841年後，外籍人口一直都在7%以下，二次大戰後更少於4%。

　　1991年的外籍人口，因為是從語言資料估計，包括一些中國籍人士。這18萬的"外籍"人口，約13萬以英語為主要語言，包括了菲律賓傭工。1961年的外籍人士中有六成是英聯邦國籍的，1981年則降至25%。

　　二次大戰前的外籍人士資料較詳細。以1931年為例，約一半是英國人，其他如土生葡萄牙人及印度人所佔比例也較大。但在14,366名英國人中，軍人佔了7,682人，而且全是男性。除了以香港為家的歐亞混血人士、土生葡萄牙人外，其他外國人中的男女比例也不平衡，反映出外國人為了短期的軍事、商業等目的來港，大多數沒有帶家眷。

In 1841, the foreign population (2,500 in total) was mostly British, with about 1/3 being military personnel. Before WWII, the foreign population accounted for about 7% of the population. After the War, it dropped to below 4%.

The 1991 foreign population was estimated by means of their language. It included some Chinese. Of the 180,000 'foreigners', 130,000 spoke English, which included many Filipino domestic helpers. In 1961, 60% of the foreign population were Commonwealth citizens. The ratio dropped to 25% in 1981.

Pre-war data on foreigners shows that in 1931, half were British. Of these, military personnel amounted to 7,682 and were all males. Other sizeable groups included locally-born Portuguese and Indians. Except for a few who treated Hong Kong as their home, there was acute gender imbalance, reflecting their short military or business missions in Hong Kong. As such, most did not bring along their families.

● 1841-2001年外國籍人口數目　**Foreign population in 1841-2001**

年份 Year	外國籍人口 Foreign population	佔總人口百分比 Percentage of total population
1841	2,500	33.5
1850	1,450	3.7
1861	2,942	3.3
1871	8,754	7.0
1881	9,712	6.0
1891	10,446	4.7
1901	9,433	2.4
1911	11,225	2.5
1921	28,322	2.5
1931	28,322	3.4
1961	43,445	1.4
1981	100,128	2.0
1991	185,417	3.3
2001	343,950	5.1

● 1931年的外國籍人口　**Foreign population in 1931**

		男 Male	女 Female	合計 Total
英國	British	11,438	2,928	14,366
其他歐洲人	Other Europeans	1,243	793	2,036
歐亞混血人	Eurasians	389	448	837
土生葡萄牙人	Native-born Portuguese	1,503	1,694	3,197
印度人	Indian	3,989	756	4,745
日本人	Japanese	1,349	856	2,205
其他非中國血統人	Other non-Chinese descent	530	406	936
總數	Total	20,441	7,881	28,322

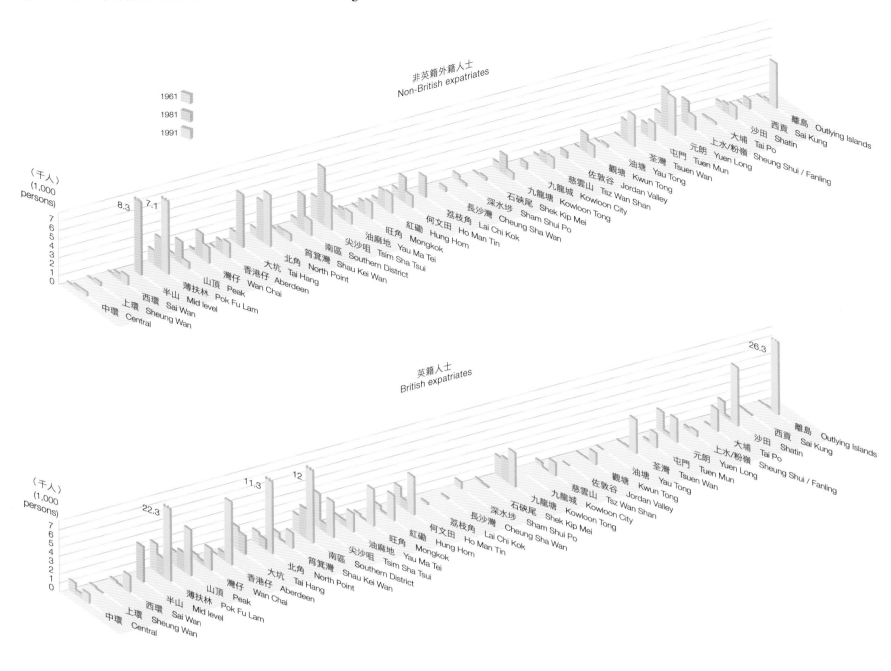

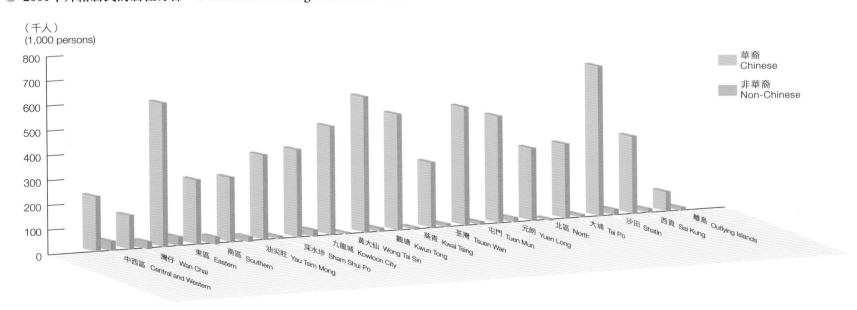

06 各分區的主要方言 Distribution of Chinese Dialects

香港日常用語主要是南中國的方言，說英語的是少數，後者集中在港島半山和山頂。港島南區和大坑，英語也是第二大語言。

1961年，客語是大埔、元朗、粉嶺/上水及荃灣區的第二大方言，在大埔區，每三個居民，便有一個說客語。說客語的人數在1991年大幅度下降，這和大量廣東人士入遷新市鎮有關。

廣東方言中，主要是廣府話。鶴佬（閩南語）是一些舊市區的第二大方言。最混雜的地區是北角區，1991年有英語、鶴佬、普通話和上海話四種日常語。

1996年，95.2%的人口說廣府話，38.1%能說英語，25.3%能說普通

Dialects in South China are the lingua franca, while English is spoken by a small minority that reside on the Peak and Mid-Levels. English is the second common language in Island South and Tai Hang.

In 1961, Hakka was the second most common dialect in the New Territories. One in every three persons in Tai Po spoke Hakka. It dropped sharply in 1991, due to new migrants in the new towns.

Most locals speak Cantonese. Hoklo (Xiamenese) is the second most common dialect in most old urban districts. The dialects/ languages of North Point in 1991 was found to be various, as English, Hoklo, Putonghua and Shanghai dialect were spoken in almost equal numbers.

● 1961年、1991年及2006年市區主要方言 (單位：千人)　Major dialects in urban areas in 1961, 1991 and 2006 (unit: thousand)

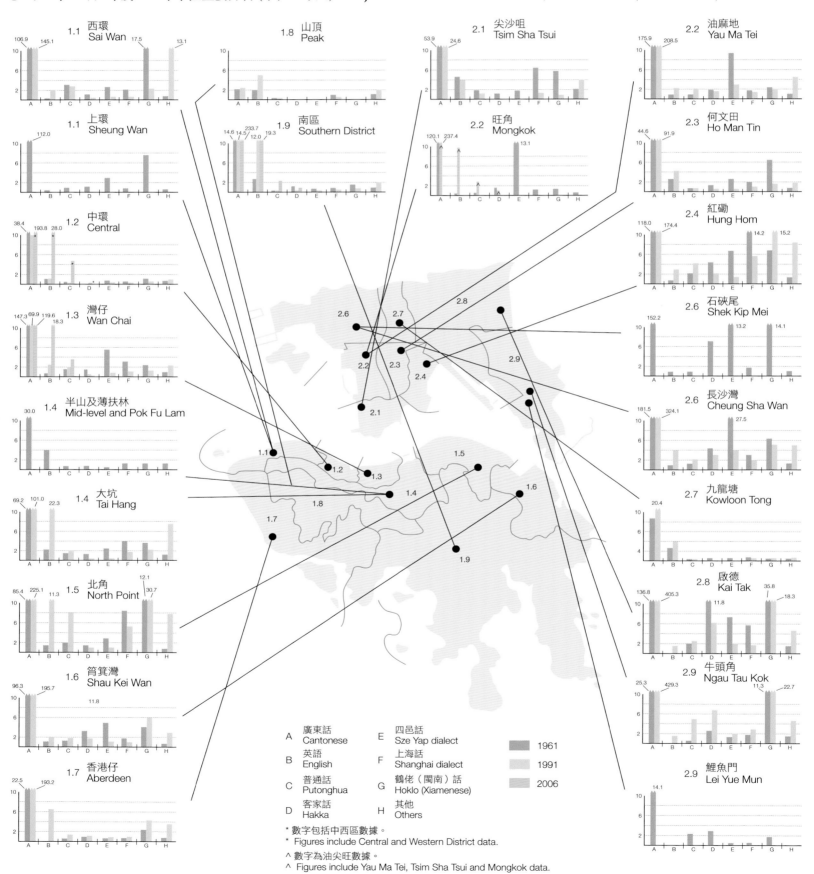

廣東話 Cantonese	E	四邑話 Sze Yap dialect
B 英語 English	F	上海話 Shanghai dialect
C 普通話 Putonghua	G	鶴佬（閩南）話 Hoklo (Xiamenese)
D 客家話 Hakka	H	其他 Others

1961
1991
2006

* 數字包括中西區數據。
* Figures include Central and Western District data.

^ 數字為油尖旺數據。
^ Figures include Yau Ma Tei, Tsim Sha Tsui and Mongkok data.

話：說客語及福建語的減至4.9%和3.9%。語言資料反映香港教育水平及 國際城市地位在提升，也展示和中國內地關係的密切。

In 1996, 95.2% of the population spoke Cantonese, 38.1% could manage English, 25.3% Putonghua. Those the spoke Hakka and Hoklo dropped to 4.9% and 3.9%. Dialects/languages spoken reflect Hong Kong's rising education level, degree of internationalization, and a closer relationship with the mainland.

● 1961年、1991年及2006年新界主要方言（單位：千人） Distribution of major dialects in the New Territories in 1961, 1991 and 2006 (unit: thousand)

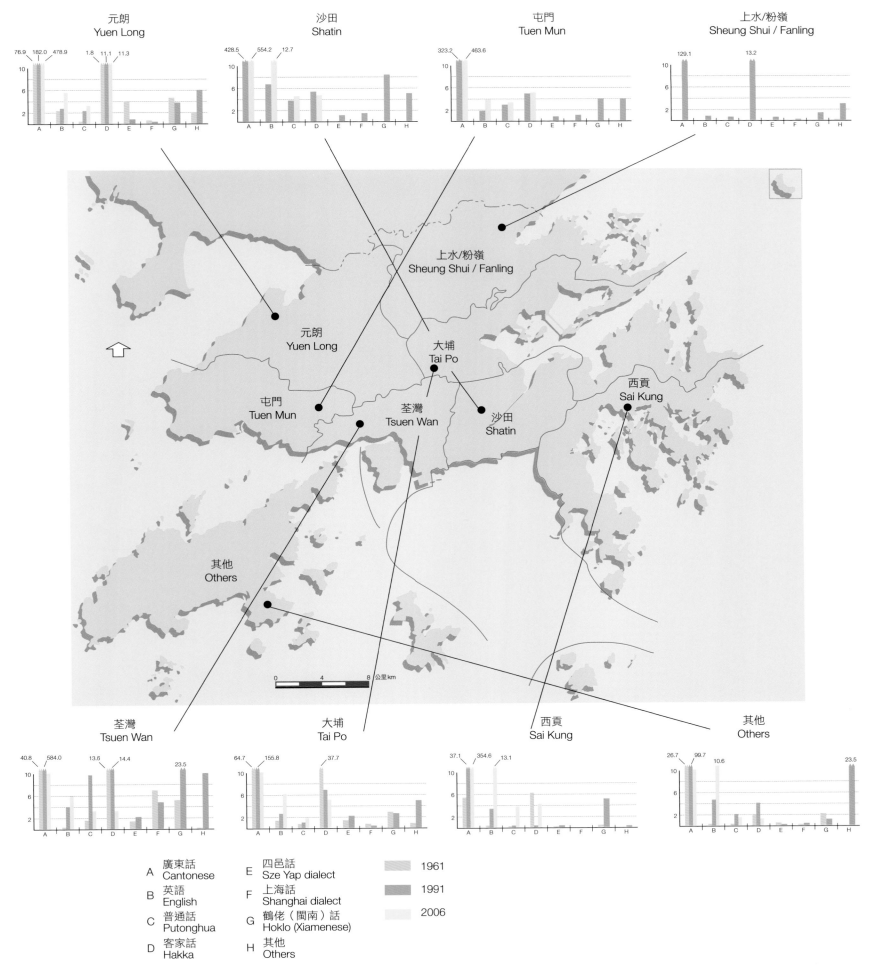

	廣東話 Cantonese		四邑話 Sze Yap dialect			1961
A		E				
B	英語 English	F	上海話 Shanghai dialect			1991
C	普通話 Putonghua	G	鶴佬（閩南）話 Hoklo (Xiamenese)			2006
D	客家話 Hakka	H	其他 Others			

07 就業 Employment

香港的"第一產業"包括農牧業工人、漁民、礦工，但主要是農民。離島區，漁民數目仍不少。"社區服務"主要是社區、社會和個人服務。"商業"包括零售和批發、進出口、飲食、酒店旅遊、財經金融、地產及商業服務。"其他"主要包括公共事業如電燈公司、煤氣公司等。"無資料"指經濟不活躍市民，如老年人、在學人士、小童以及失業人士等。

長沙灣、旺角、紅磡、上環和啟德的居民在1961年的主要職業是製造業。到了1991年，商業幾乎是所有市區的主要職業。

The primary sector includes employment as herdsmen, fishermen, miners, but mainly as famers. In the Outlying Islands, fishmen are still many. 'Community services' include community, social and personal services while 'commerce and business services' include wholesaling, retailing, import-export, restaurants, hotels, tourism, financial services, real estates and business services. 'Others' mainly include utilities, such as electricity company, gas company, etc. 'No data' denotes non-economically active people, e.g. old people, students, children below school age and the unemployed.

In 1961, manufacturing was predominant in Cheung Sha Wan, Mongkok,

● 1961年、1991年、2001年及2006年市區分區就業分佈（單位：萬人）(10,000 persons)　Distribution of employment in urban areas in 1961, 1991, 2001 and 2006

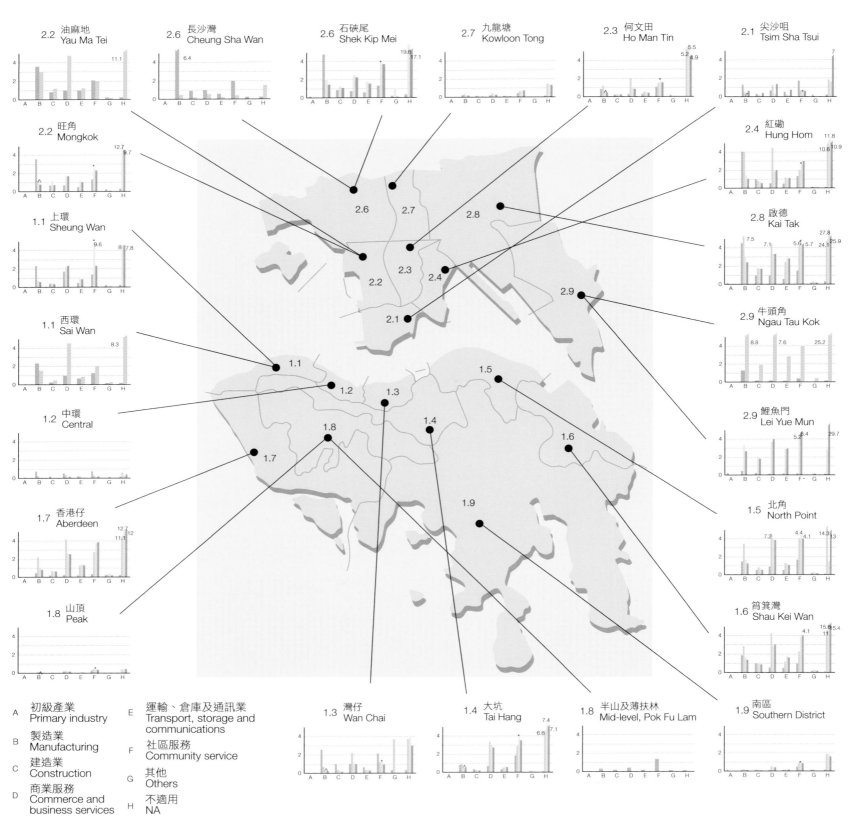

A 初級產業 Primary industry
B 製造業 Manufacturing
C 建造業 Construction
D 商業服務 Commerce and business services
E 運輸、倉庫及通訊業 Transport, storage and communications
F 社區服務 Community service
G 其他 Others
H 不適用 NA

1961　1991　2001　2006

^ 包括建造業就業數字 Includes employment in construction industry
* 包括部份其他就業數字 Includes partly employment in other category
1.1 上環包括西環數據　1.1 Sheung Wan includes data of Sai Wan
1.8 山頂包括半山及薄扶林數據　1.8 Peak includes data of Mid-level & Pok Fu Lam

2.2 旺角包括油麻地數據　2.2 Mongkok includes data of Yau Ma Tei
2.6 石硤尾包括長沙灣數據　2.6 Shek Kip Mei includes data of Cheung Sha Wan
2.9 鯉魚門包括牛頭角數據　2.9 Lei Yue Mun includes data of Ngau Tau Kok

第一產業在1961年是新界各地區的最大就業。1991年，製造業成為屯門和荃灣區的最大就業。沙田和元朗的就業在三大行業中比較平均。

1998年後就業分佈繼續向第三產業發展。

Hung Hom, Sheung Wan and Kai Tak. In 1991, 'commerce' was the main employment in almost all urban districts.

The primary sector predominated in the New Territories in 1961. By 1991, manufacturing replaced it as the main employment in Tuen Mun and Tsuen Wan. Shatin and Tai Po were more balanced in the three sectors.

Post-1998 data indicates the continual trend of tertiarization.

● **1961-2006年新界分區就業分佈（單位：萬人）** Distribution of employment in New Territories in 1961-2006 (10,000 persons)

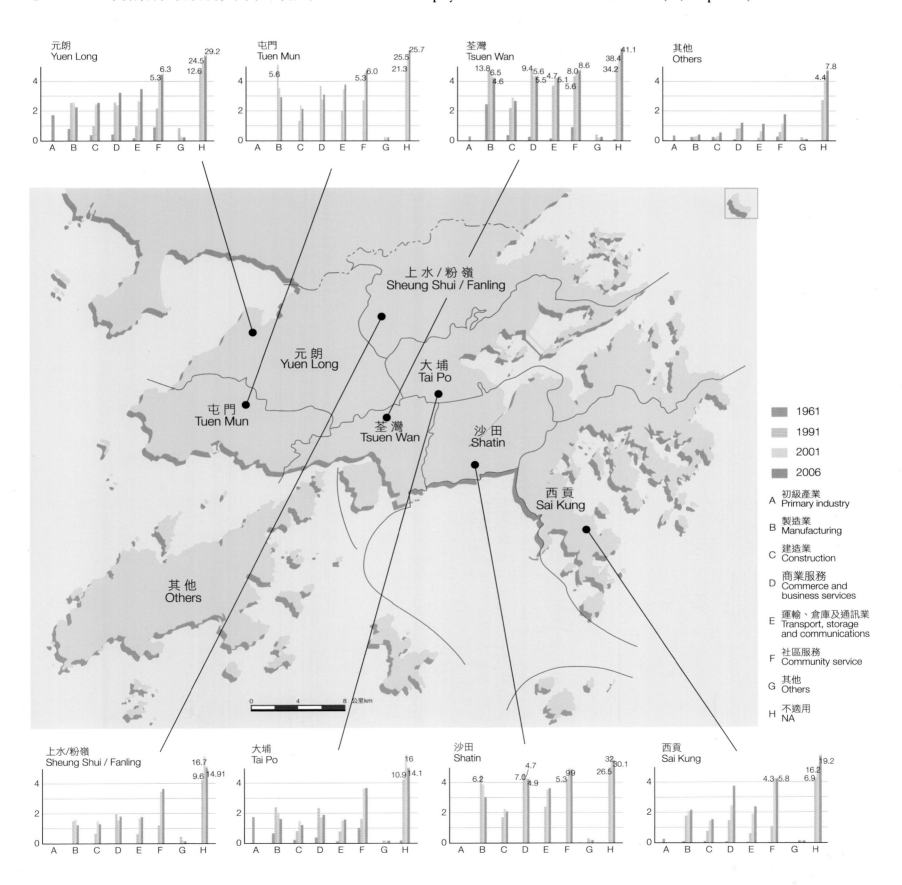

01 教育 Education

香港第一所西式學校是1843年由澳門遷來的馬禮遜紀念學校，而最早的本地的現代學校聖保羅書院於同年在中環鐵崗成立，招收中國學生學習英語及英國學生接受神學教育。聖公會又於1870年加設拔萃男校，並在1899年設立拔萃女校，這是本港現代化教育的主要提供者。

1850-1870年間，政府設教育委員會，1862年委任首名視學官，並成立政府中央書院（後名皇仁書院）。香港開埠至今一直以教會辦學為主，官立學校為輔，也較早地設立了女校及男女校。

15歲以上的中等教育人士的比率由1961年的二成上升至1996年近七成，但在1971年前似乎變化不大，因為1970年初才展開"九年免費教育計劃"。

水上人家的教育水平較低（特別是1961年時），新界農業地區也有超過三成人口沒有受過任何教育。至1961年，一些舊市區的情況好不

The first western school was Morrison Memorial School relocated from Macau in 1843. Yet the earliest modern school, St. Paul's College, was set up in the same year in Central to admit Chinese students for learning English and British students for training as clergy for the Church of England's local diocese. The diocese in 1870 set up the Diocesan Boys School and in 1899, Diocesan Girls School, as major institutes of modern education. In 1850-1870, an Education Committee was set up to oversee education and an Education Inspector was appointed in 1862. In the same year, the first government school–Central College (later Queen's College) was set up. Hong Kong has a long tradition of vesting the responsibility of education to religious organizations, and was Asia's pioneer in modern education for both boys and girls.

In 1961, about 20% of the population of the age of 15 and above had medium-level education. Rapid change has happened since the implementation of the 9-Year free education policy in the early 1970s. By 1996, the above proportion reached

● 1961年及1991年市區各區人口平均教育水平分佈 Distribution of average educational level in urban districts in 1961 and 1991

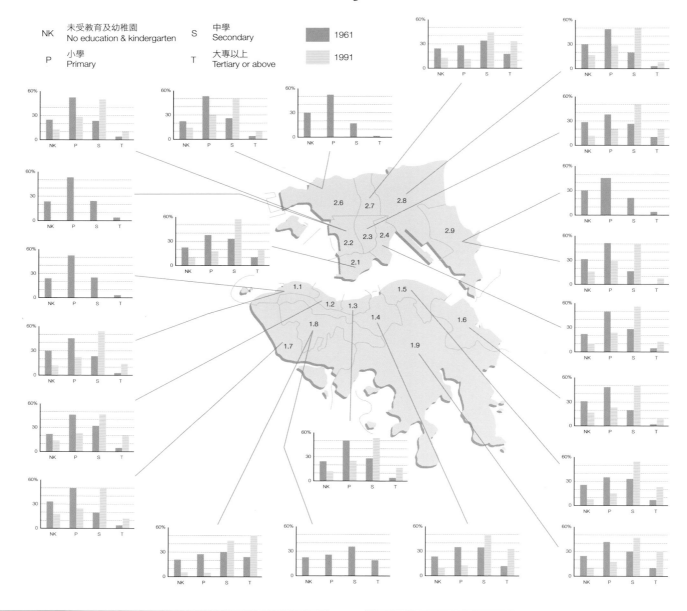

NK 未受教育及幼稚園 No education & kindergarten
P 小學 Primary
S 中學 Secondary
T 大專以上 Tertiary or above
1961
1991

● 1961-1995年政府對各級教育機構的撥款 Government funding for educational institutions, 1961-1995

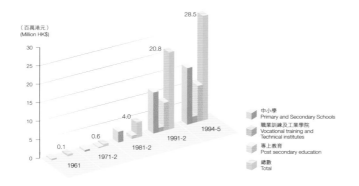

中小學 Primary and Secondary Schools
職業訓練及工業學院 Vocational training and Technical institutes
專上教育 Post secondary education
總數 Total

● 2003-2009年政府對各級教育機構的撥款 Government funding for educational institutions, 2003-2009

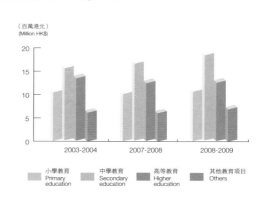

小學教育 Primary education
中學教育 Secondary education
高等教育 Higher education
其他教育項目 Others

了多少。港島半山、大坑、南區和九龍塘，有相當人口受過大專以上教育，它們至今仍是教育水平較高的地區。

1998年香港有約二成人口，即130萬人，是"全職"學生。教育經費佔了該年政府經常性開支的22%及非經常性開支的11%。教育經費，從小學一年級至中學三年級的九年全部費用由政府支付，中四至大學的經費，約83%來自公帑。立法規定適齡兒童一定要入學，否則家長便觸犯法律。大學學位大規模的增多始自1990年，目前大一的招生數和大學入學試的考生數，已接近一比一。本科學位總數與適齡人口的比率約達18%。加上到海外、內地和台灣留學的人數（僅1996年往美、英、加和澳就讀的學生就有14,095人），香港的大學生比例已向發達地區看齊。

70%.

In 1961, the population in the New Territories, especially the marine population, was less educated. Population in the Peak, Mid-levels, Tai Hang, Island South and Kowloon traditionally received a higher level of education.

In 1998, about 20% of local population were full-time students. Education shared 22% and 11% of government's recurrent and non-recurrent expenses. There has been a rapid increase of university admittance since 1990. Hong Kong now ranks close to developed economies in terms of tertiary education provision.

● 1961-1996年受教育人士百分比　Percentage of educated people in 1961-1996

	1961	1971	1981	1991	1996
中學畢業或以上學歷人士 Graduated from high school or above	26.2	23.5	41.2	62.0	67.9
受過正規教育人士 Received formal education	71.6	71.5	77.9	87.2	90.5

● 1866-1906年間學校、學生數目及女生比例　Number of schools, students and percentage of female students, 1866-1906

年份 Year	學校數目 Number of Schools	學生數目 Number of Students	女生數目 Number of female students	女生比例 Ratio of female students
1866	16	1,870	45	7.4
1876	41	2,922	543	18.5
1886	90	5,844	1,683	28.8
1896	120	7,301	2,702	37.0
1906	85	7,642	3,289	43.0

● 1961-1998 年各類學校學生人數　Number of students in all types of schools in 1961-1998

	1961	1971	1981	1991	1998
大專* Tertiary institutions*	15,803	11,799	15,382	74,997	81,415
中學 Secondary school	106,477	295,820	521,581	454,372	455,192
小學 Primary school	484,536	764,313	548,750	517,137	476,682
特殊學校 Special school	691	2,715	12,117	8,224	9,667
總數（百萬）+ Total (million)+	0.607	1.074	1.098	1.055	1.028
全港人口（百萬） Population in Hong Kong (million)	3.226	4.045	5.154	5.822	6.806

+ 不包括幼稚園、成人教育及非日間及兼讀學生
Kindergartens, adult education and evening and part-time students not included
* 包括專科師範及工業學院
Teachers' training college and technical college included

● 1961年及1991年新界各區人口教育水平分佈　Distribution of education level NT in 1961 and 1991

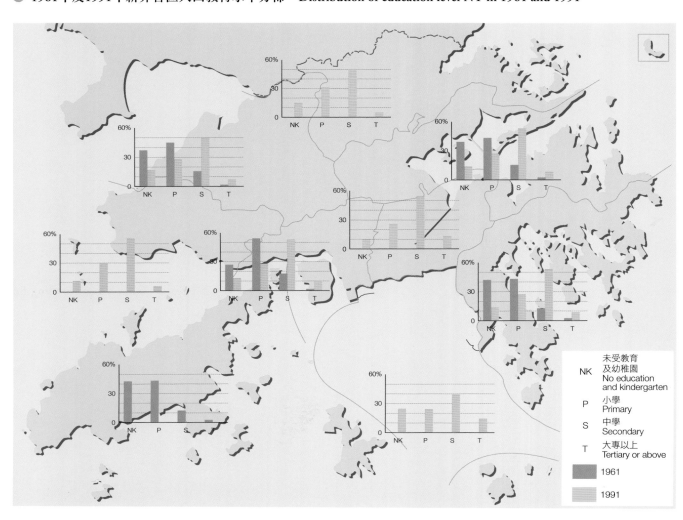

	未受教育及幼稚園 No education and kindergarten
NK	
P	小學 Primary
S	中學 Secondary
T	大專以上 Tertiary or above
■	1961
	1991

02　居住情況　Living Conditions

香港地狹人稠，居住情況素來惡劣。1903年的公共健康與建築條例規定人均居住面積不少於35平方英尺。1948年成立的房屋協會採用了它作為建屋標準。1953年後的徙置區（即以後出現的公屋）的標準是成人為24平方英尺，十歲以下小童減半。早期的徙置大廈因而居住條件惡劣：一個120平方英尺的小室可住上一家六七口，或由兩家人合住；數十家共用一個水龍頭、一個各為120平方英尺的公共廁所及浴室。1968年才將成人居住面積提升至35平方英尺。

當時私人樓宇情況同樣惡劣。1957年的調查顯示，118,000個私人樓宇單位中住了1,265,000人，其中七成的居住單位面積小於120平方英尺。

目前公共出租樓宇的標準已改為：低租金單位每人5.5平方米（約60平方英尺），較高租金單位每人7平方米。

Limited space in Hong Kong resulted in poor living conditions. To maintain basic hygiene and health standards, a 1903 legislation required a minimum per capita living (floor) space of 35ft². The Housing Society (set up in 1948) adopted such a standard in the construction of its housing units. But the Resettlement Programme since 1953 adopted a lower standard of 24ft² per adult and 12ft² per child. Thus in the early resettlement estates, a cubicle of 120ft² could house 6-7 persons or be shared by two small families. About 50 families shared one water tap, a 120ft² public toilet and bathroom. The standard was raised to 35ft² in 1968.

A survey on private housing in 1975 revealed equally poor living conditions. In the 118,000 private housing units lived 1,265,000 persons. 70 % of the units are small cubicles of less than 120 ft².

The current standard for public housing is 60 ft² or 5.5 m² per person. Higher rental estates adopt a 7 m² standard.

● 1986年香港非空置住所的平均居住人數　Average number of occupants in non-vacant homes in 1986

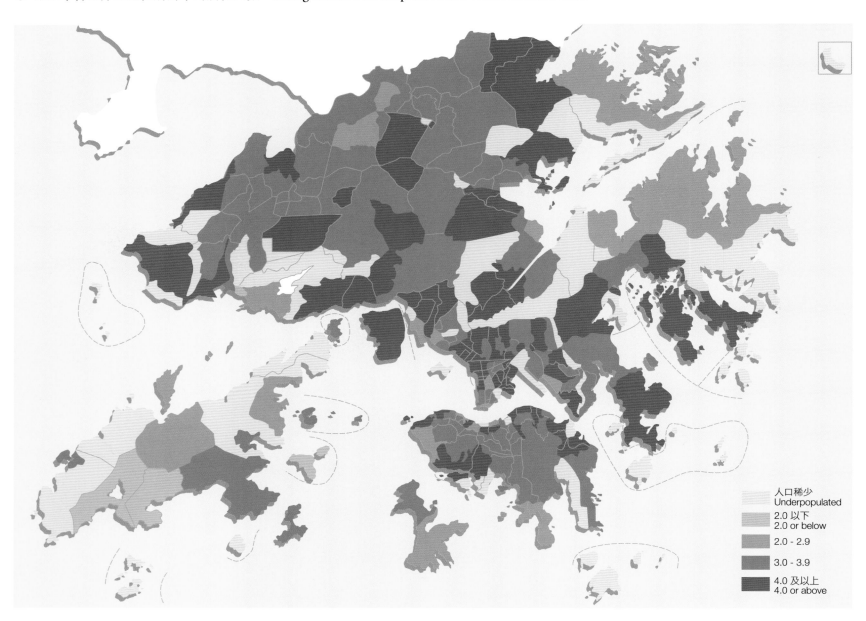

人口稀少
Underpopulated

2.0 以下
2.0 or below

2.0 - 2.9

3.0 - 3.9

4.0 及以上
4.0 or above

● 1996年非空置住所的平均居住人數　Average number of occupants in non-vacant homes in 1996

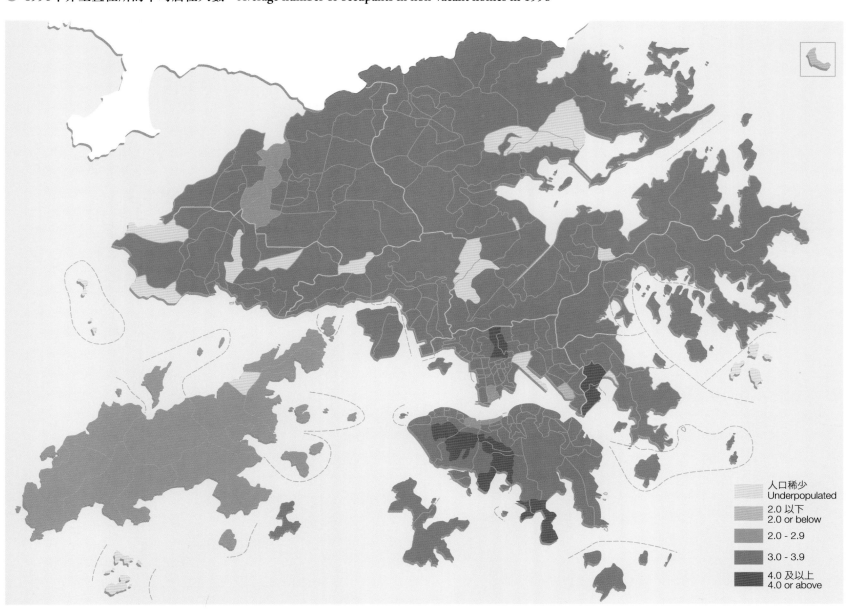

人口稀少
Underpopulated

2.0 以下
2.0 or below

2.0 - 2.9

3.0 - 3.9

4.0 及以上
4.0 or above

03 市區內居住稠密狀況 Sharing in Residential Flats in Urban Districts

在1971年，在市區內一個單位由兩個或以上家庭分住的情況十分普遍，1981-1996年間有明顯的改善。但1996年九龍四個區域的統計顯示，每區仍有1萬至2萬個分住戶。1998年全港分住戶達87,900戶，分住情況達5.51%。

1971年起公共出租樓宇增長遠超過私人住宅。自1980年代中，"居者有其屋"樓宇及房協的出售單位更高速增長。除了九龍塘、半山、山頂和港島南區為高收入和居住環境較好地區外，在市區內的高密度住宅，高、中、低收入人士混雜在同一小區內的情況很普遍。出租公屋住戶的收入受政策影響，收入比較一致。

In 1971, it was common to have two or more families sharing one housing unit. The situation improved in 1981-1996, though in 1996, in four Kowloon districts, there still were 10,000-20,000 families sharing flats in each. In 1998, there were 87,000 families sharing flats, or 5.51% of all families.

Since 1971, public housing construction has far exceeded private housing. From 1980 onwards, public owner-occupier housing increased rapidly.

However, except for Kowloon Tong, Mid-levels, the Peak and Island South whose residents are of high income enjoying a better housing quality, in general, high, middle and low-income family residents are mixed in a small district as a result of high-density residence. Due to the policy on income restriction, public housing estates are more homogeneous in terms of income, i.e. families living there are of low income.

● 1981年市區家庭收入水平分佈 Distribution of household income in urban districts, 1981

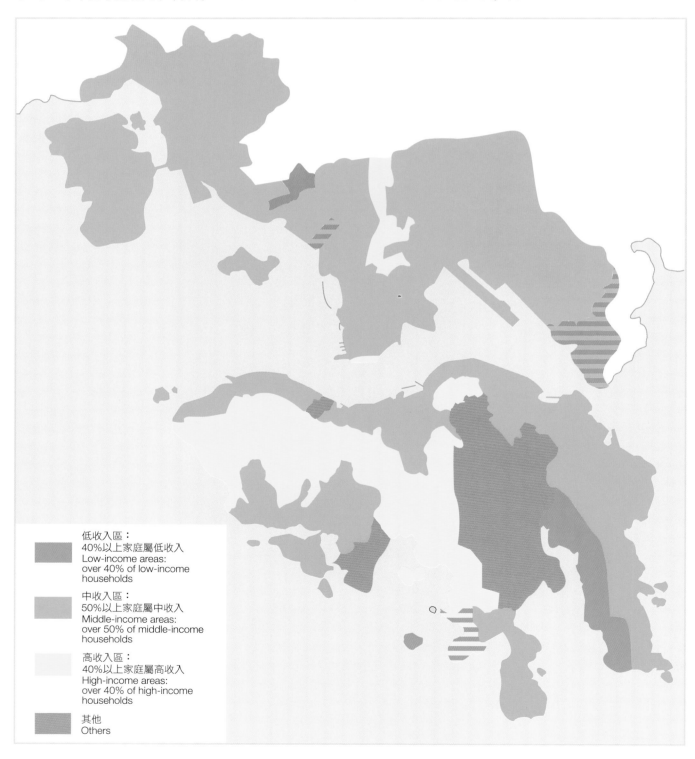

低收入區：
40%以上家庭屬低收入
Low-income areas:
over 40% of low-income
households

中收入區：
50%以上家庭屬中收入
Middle-income areas:
over 50% of middle-income
households

高收入區：
40%以上家庭屬高收入
High-income areas:
over 40% of high-income
households

其他
Others

1971-2006年各類住宅樓宇分住情況　Sharing in sub-types of residential premises, 1971-2006

屋宇單位類型	Households quarter	1971	1981	1991**	1998	2001	2006
私人樓宇	Private housing						
總單位數	Total number of units	434,888	580,004	706,685	870,900	1,025,765	1,109,653
分住比率(%)*	Sub-living ratio(%)*	57.9	43.4	14.9	5.51	—	—
公共出租樓宇	Public rental flats						
總單位數	Total number of units	263,174	413,065	576,313	703,500	627,339	690,788
分住比率(%)	Sub-living ratio(%)	2.4	2.7	1.3	0.13	—	—
居者有其屋樓宇	Home Ownership Scheme flats						
總單位數	Total number of units	—	7,176	115,729	249,200	320,122	362,439
分住比率(%)	Sub-living ratio(%)	—	0.1	—	—	0	—
別墅 / 平房 / 村屋	Villa / bungalow / village houses						
總單位數	Total number of units	66,178	84,103	82,952	150,100	54,550	46,482
分住比率(%)	Sub-living ratio(%)	20.7	20.2	3.3	5.57+	—	—
臨時房屋	Temporary housing						
總單位數	Total number of units	71,636	114,663	65,657	45,700	25,636	17,186
分住比率(%)	Sub-living ratio(%)	12.9	16.4	2.9	5.57+	—	—
全港樓宇	All buildings in Hong Kong						
總單位數	Total number of units	846,670	1,237,643	1,580,072	2,019,400	2,053,412	2,226,548
分住比率(%)	Sub-living ratio(%)	33.2	24.6	7.4	5.51	—	—

* 分住是指兩戶以上同住一單位
** 統計署採用了兩組數字：有兩戶以上同住的單位，
　有分租情況的單位。前一數字遠比後者低，現採用後者
\+ 包括別墅 / 平房 / 村屋及臨時房屋

* Sub-living refers to two or more household sharing a flat
** Census and Statistics Department adopted two sets of figures:
　two or more household sharing units, sub-let unit, the latter is adopted as it is lower
\+ Including villa / bungalow / village house and temporary housing

1981年市區各區自置居所比例　Proportion of self-owned residence in urban districts, 1981

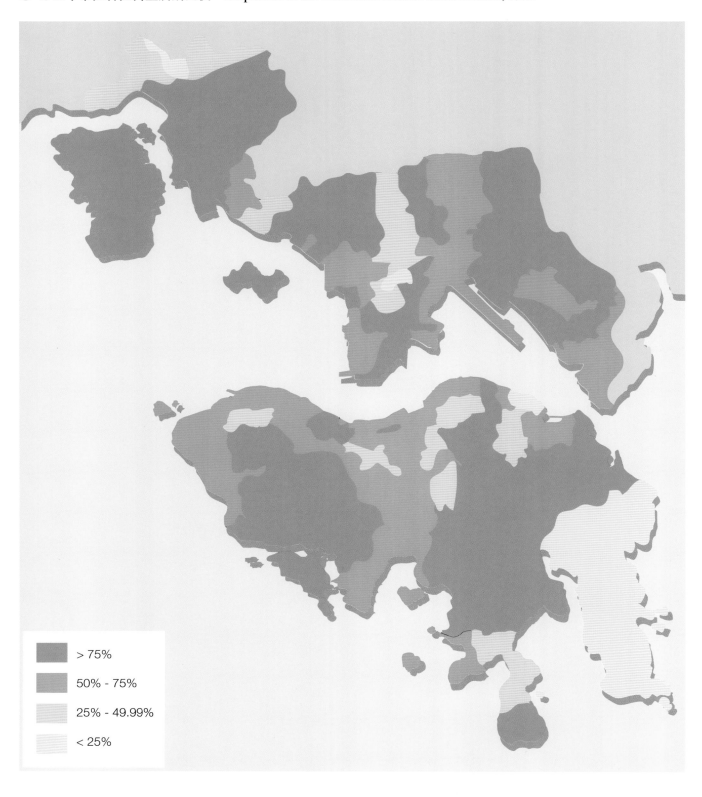

> 75%

50% - 75%

25% - 49.99%

< 25%

04 平均收入 Average Income

香港人口的收入，由1971年的中間戶月入不到1,000元，增至1996年17,500元，增加了17倍。但2006年回落至17,250元，期間每戶人口也由4.78人下降至2006年的3.07人。

1971年各區的收入分佈較向低收入傾斜，水上戶口的收入則比較平均。市區出現雙峰現象。香港島的南區、半山和中環平均收入很高。九龍的九龍塘、尖沙咀、何文田也如是，形成了分佈上的第二峰。

1991年的各區收入分佈較正常，顯示收入的地域分佈和社區趨於均衡。香港島和九龍的雙峰現象仍存在，但第一峰已移至中間位置，說明舊市區人口已中產化，低收入戶口外移及相對地減少。

The median household monthly income increased from less than $1,000 in 1971 to $17,500 in 1996–an increase of 17-fold. In 2006, it dropped back to $17,250. This was accompanied by a drop in average household size of 4.78 persons in 1971 to 3.3 in 1996, and 3.07 in 2006.

The distribution of average income in various districts in 1971 inclined towards the low side while the difference within the marine population is not obvious. The urban districts show double peaks.

From 1991 onwards, the distributions tend to be normal, indicating more spatial balance in income in general. In Kowloon and Hong Kong Island, though double peaks remain, the first peak has migrated to the medium-income position, showing an expanding middle class and a relative decline of low-income households.

● 1971年每戶月平均收入分佈（百分比） Average monthly household income (%) in 1971

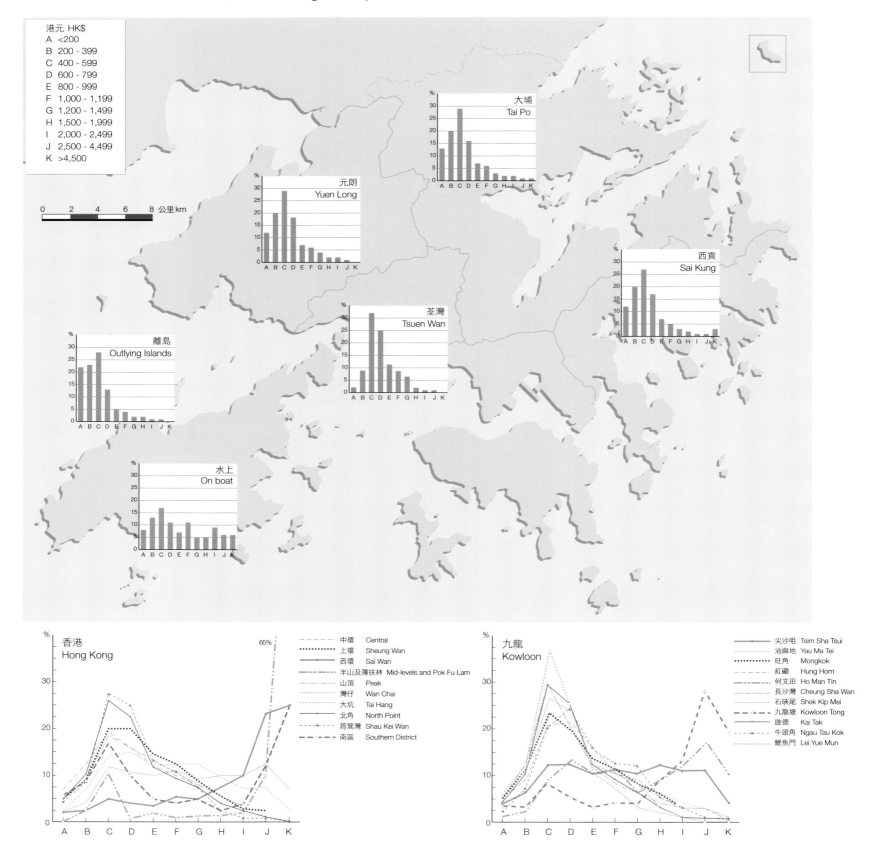

1966-2006年香港每戶月平均收入　Average monthly household income 1966-2006

	1966	1971	1981	1991	1996	2001	2006
平均每戶人數 Average household size	4.78	4.59	4.09	3.49	3.3	3.2	3.0
住公屋戶數（百分比） Public housing household (%)	31.3	31.1	33.6	48.0	49.9	30.0	30.0
每戶每月收入低於2,000元（百分比） Monthly household income less than $2,000 (%)	93.1	92.1	28.5	4.8	3.0	3.2	3.9
中間戶月收入（元） Median monthly household income (HK$)	435	708	2,955	9,964	17,500	18,705	17,260

1991年分區每戶月平均收入分佈（百分比）　Average monthly household income distribution 1991(%)

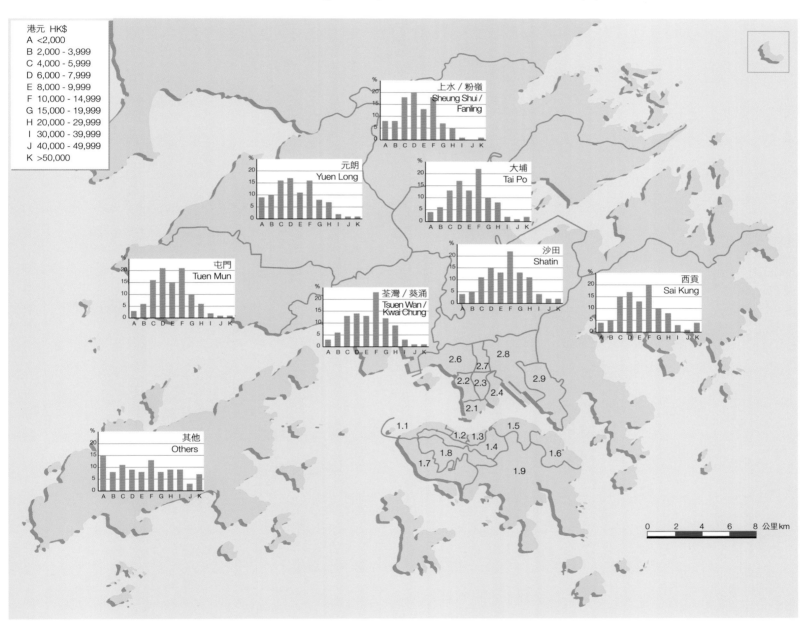

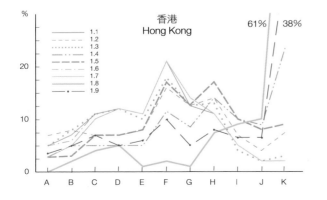

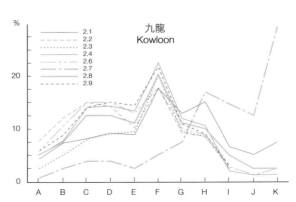

05 境內外的人口遷徙 External and Internal Migration

至1945年，外來遷入是香港人口增長的主因。1946–1951年間，在日佔時期外逃的人口大量回流。1951–1981年，遷入人口只佔總人口增長的一小部份。近年來，遷入人口成為人口增加的主因，其構成也有變化：持中國內地單程通行證者45,986人，其他多以工作簽證來港，來源廣泛，包括中國內地、菲律賓、印尼、泰國等。1996年的淨遷入更達118,500人，其中來自中國內地的61,179人。向外遷出人口在1983–1995年，每年為2–6萬人。回歸後外移人口減少，1997年為30,900人，1998年只有19,300人。

Until 1945, in-migration had been the main source of population increase. During 1946-1951, most local population returned after a brief outward shift forced by the Japanese occupation. In 1951-1981, in-migration contributed only a small part in population growth. Recently, in-migration shot up, bolstered by annual in-migrants on single-trip permits from the mainland. The rest came under temporary work permits, mostly from the Philippines, Indonesia, Thailand and the mainland. In 1996, of 118,500 in-migrants, 61,179 originated from the mainland. Out-migration averaged 20,000-60,000 a year in 1981-1995. In 1997 it dropped to 30,900, and to 19,300 in 1998.

● 1971-2006年人口內部遷移圖　Internal migration in 1971-2006

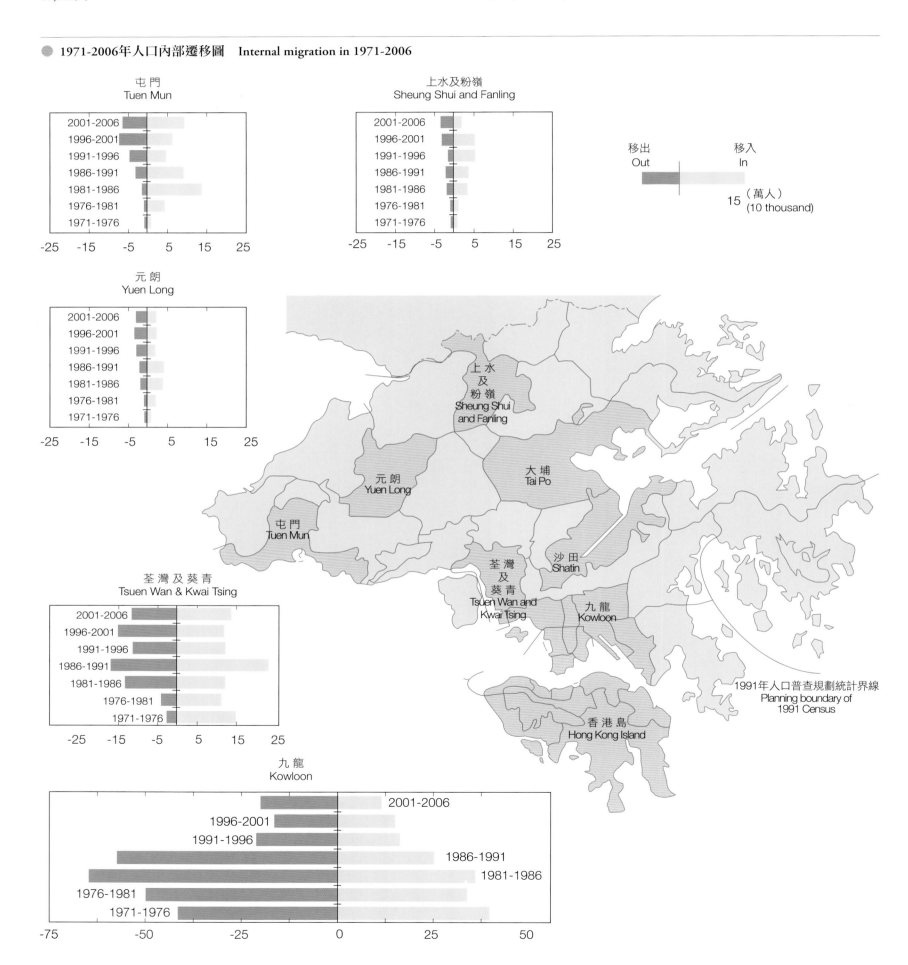

1950年前內部遷移並不顯著，但自1970年代起，市區重建、木屋徙置和新市鎮建設，使人口出現地域上的疏散。沙田、荃灣與葵青的主要人口流入時期是1971–1986年。九龍人口明顯的外移時期為1981–1986年。香港島人口的移入與移出數目平衡，顯示其人口承載力在1971年已達飽和。

Internal migration was not significant before the 1950s. Since 1970, urban redevelopment, squatter clearance and the new towns programme led to internal movements. The growth of Shatin and Tuen Mun new towns peaked in 1971-1986. Kowloon was the main source of the dispersal. By 1971, the population of Hong Kong Island had reached saturation with a balance between in- and out-migrants.

● 1990年代初外部人口遷移　External migrations in early 1990s

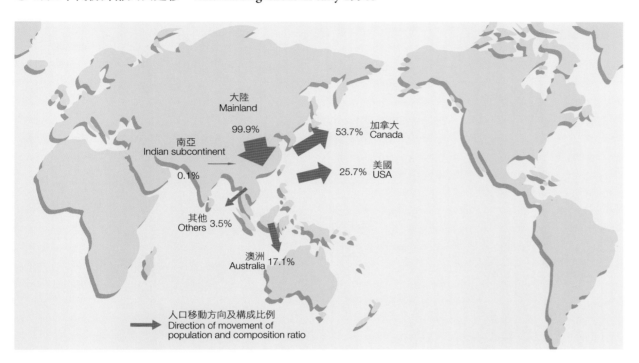

人口移動方向及構成比例
Direction of movement of population and composition ratio

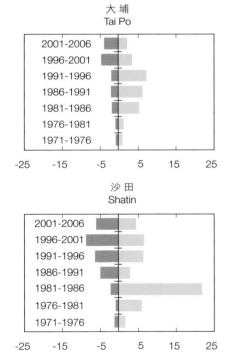

● 戰後人口增長及遷入變化　Changes in population growth and immigration

期間人口增加總數
Total population growth

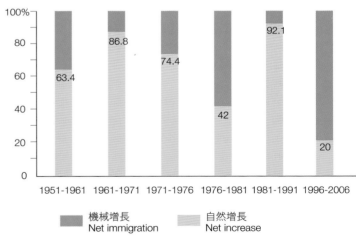

機械增長
Net immigration
自然增長
Net increase

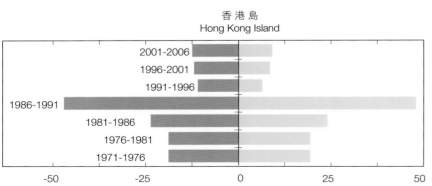

06 城市社會空間 Social Areas

城市裡不同階層和種族往往居住於不同地區，形成不同的社區。美國的社區以種族、經濟及教育水平、人生階段（年齡組）為主要形成因素。殖民地城市裡，種族的分隔是最重要的因素，正如在英佔時期印度的主要城市一樣。

早期的香港也以種族為人口分佈的最重要原因，殖民地政府並且通過有關法例予以促進。1904年的條例，規定香港島海拔788英尺以上為英國人住宅區，華人（除了傭人外）不得留宿。這條例至1946年才取消。當時有一說法：山頂純為英國人區，美國及日本人可住至梅道，堅道為其他歐籍人士，華人則聚居於上環、西環一帶。1920年代初，一些富有的華人及亞洲人，在九龍塘建了一個花園城市式的高級住宅區。堅道後來解禁，但藉口保持住屋外觀的一致性，不容許中式建築。至1960年代，堅道的住宅仍多是港英20世紀初的大圓柱洋房。戰後香港經濟起飛，經濟及教育水平成為社區的主導因素，但山頂和九龍塘兩個高級住宅區，仍印證殖民地的種族主義。

Different social classes and racial groups tend to reside in different parts of a city, forming social areas.

As a colonial city, racial segregation was practised in early Hong Kong same as Indian cities under British rule and was supported by government legislation and policies. A 1904 law zoned all areas above 788ft on Hong Kong Island exclusive for British residence. Chinese (except domestic helpers) were not allowed to stay there over night. The law was only repealed in 1946. During the same period, the Americans and Japanese could only reside in areas up to May Road. Caine Road was resided by other Europeans. Chinese concentrated in Sheung Wan and Western District.

In the early 1920s, some rich Chinese and Indians built a garden city in Kowloon Tong as a counterweight to the Peak. Later, Caine Road was opened to the Chinese, though under the pretext of maintaining the cityscape, no Chinese-style houses were allowed. Until the late 1960s, houses on Caine Road were still mainly of European architecture.

Rapid economic growth in post-War Hong Kong rendered economic status and education as main factors in social area formation, though the Peak and Kowloon Tong remain a testimony of racial segregation in its colonial history.

● 1961年及1971年社會空間圖 Social areas in 1961 and 1971

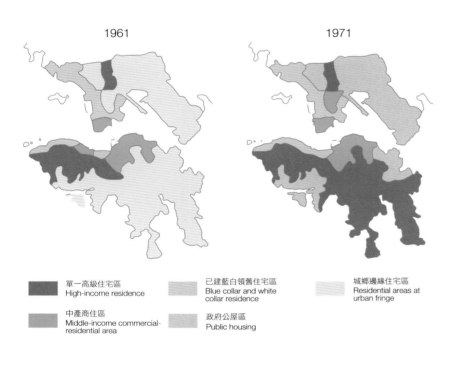

1961　　　1971

- 單一高級住宅區 High-income residence
- 中產商住區 Middle-income commercial-residential area
- 已建藍白領舊住宅區 Blue collar and white collar residence
- 政府公屋區 Public housing
- 城鄉邊緣住宅區 Residential areas at urban fringe

● 1970年代印度城市結構圖，顯示殖民地時代特色 Generalised land use structure of the Indian City of the 1970s showing typical colonial heritage

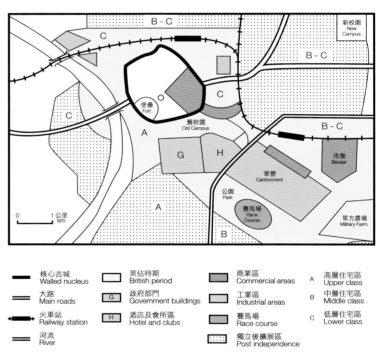

- 核心古城 Walled nucleus
- 大路 Main roads
- 火車站 Railway station
- 河流 River
- 英佔時期 British period
- G 政府部門 Government buildings
- H 酒店及會所區 Hotel and clubs
- 商業區 Commercial areas
- 工業區 Industrial areas
- 賽馬場 Race course
- 獨立後擴展區 Post independence
- A 高層住宅區 Upper class
- B 中層住宅區 Middle class
- C 低層住宅區 Lower class

● 1960年代中香港地區社會空間概念圖 (原作：T.G. McGee) Social areas in Hong Kong in the 1960s (by T. G. McGee)

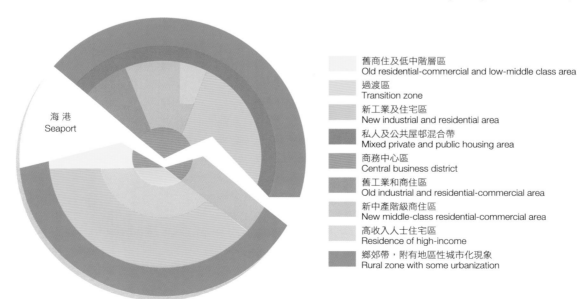

- 舊商住及低中階層區 Old residential-commercial and low-middle class area
- 過渡區 Transition zone
- 新工業及住宅區 New industrial and residential area
- 私人及公共屋邨混合帶 Mixed private and public housing area
- 商務中心區 Central business district
- 舊工業和商住區 Old industrial and residential-commercial area
- 新中產階級商住區 New middle-class residential-commercial area
- 高收入人士住宅區 Residence of high-income
- 鄉郊帶，附有地區性城市化現象 Rural zone with some urbanization

商業區
Commercial

中高至高級住宅區
Upper-middle to high
income residential zone

中上階層高級住宅
與低密度住宅
Upper-middle income and
low density residential zone

中下階層高密度公屋
Lower middle high-density,
public housing

中下階層高密度私人樓宇
Lower middle class high-
density, private housing

低密度高級住宅區
Low-density high income
residential zone

中產高密度住宅
Middle class high-
density residential zone

工業區高密度住宅
Industrial zone with
high-density residence

山坡與已墾海邊高密度住宅
Hillside and high-density
residence on reclaimed land

娛樂公園
Parks

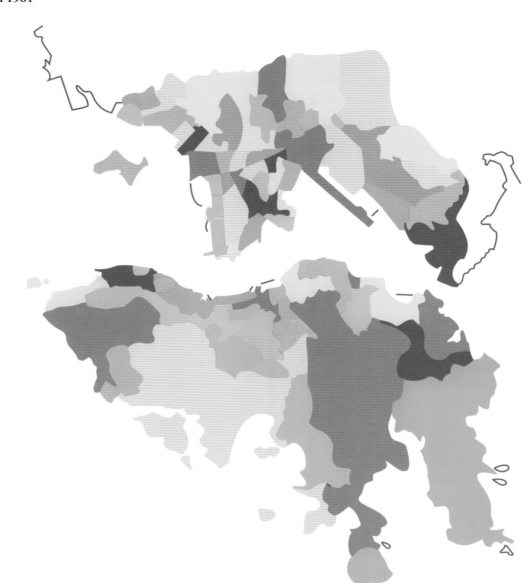

● 1991年社會空間圖　Social areas in 1991

較低層廣東家庭
Low-income Guangdong
families

單親中產家庭
Single-parent middle-
class families

自置居所年輕家庭
Young families under
home ownership scheme

中下階層公屋私屋
Lower-middle class
public/private housing

高收入單身豪庭
High-income singles

單親中產自置居所
Single-parent middle-
class self-owned residence

神職人員私屋
Clergy private house

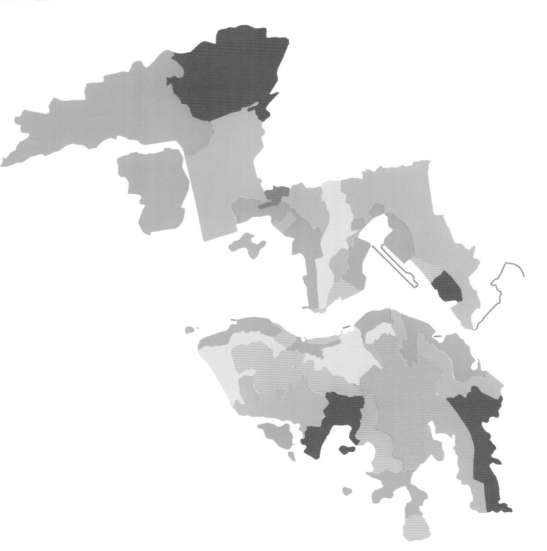

07 醫院、醫療設施及社會福利 Medical, Health Care and Social Welfare

香港早期衛生環境很差。1843年，24%英軍及10%歐籍人口死於熱病。1861年歐美居民的死亡率為6.48%，疫症如霍亂、天花及黑死病很猖獗。黑死病在1894年導致2,552人死亡。政府在1843年成立了公共健康及衛生委員會；1866年任命醫務督察；1881年成立衛生處；1887年成立衛生局，以非官守成員為主。

首間政府醫院建於1891年。華人私辦的東華醫院早於1870年成立；私立的香港華人醫學院成立於1887年，營運期內共收學生102人，其中28人畢業，包括孫文，但得不到英國醫學會承認；1907年重組為新成立的香港大學的一部份。

因為黑死病，政府於1895年清拆上環和西環（太平山）高密度民房，並強迫洗"太平地"。

近年香港急促地走向福利型社會，醫療衛生開支大增。1996年為

Hygiene was bad in Hong Kong's early years. In 1843, 24% of the soldiers and 10% of European residents died of malaria. The death rate of European and American residents was 6.48%. Black death alone killed 2,552 persons in 1894. In 1895, the densely-populated districts of Sheung Wan and Western (Tai Ping Shan) were forcibly cleansed in an attempt to reduce the risk of epidemics.

A Committee of Public Health and Cleanliness was formed in 1843. The first Medical Inspector was appointed in 1866. The Sanitary Department was only set up in 1881. It was turned into the Sanitary Board in 1887, with mostly unofficial members.

The first government civil hospital opened in 1891, later than the private Tung Wah Group of Hospitals that started in 1870. A privately-sponsored Hong Kong College of Medicine for Chinese was formed in 1887. Sun Yat Sen was one of its first batch of 13 students. It was not accredited by the British Medical Council. In two decades, it enrolled only 102 students, of which 28 graduated. In 1907, it became part of The

● 1975-2008年社會福利開支 Expenditure on social welfare 1975-2008

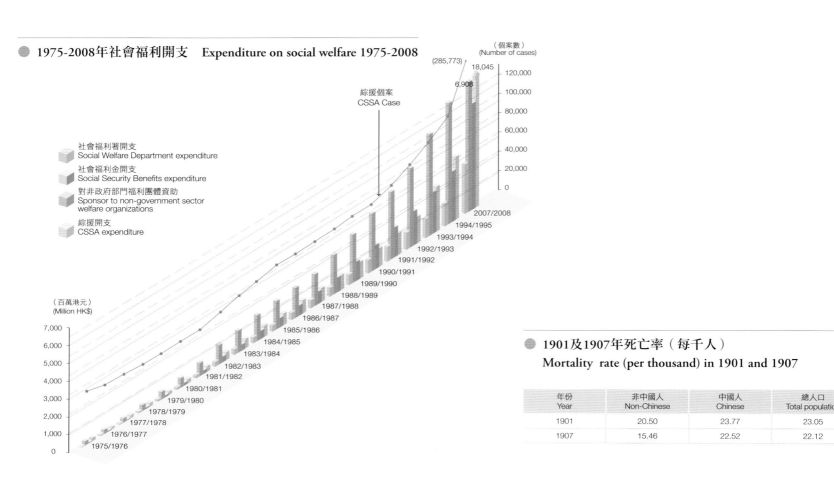

● 1901及1907年死亡率（每千人）
Mortality rate (per thousand) in 1901 and 1907

年份 Year	非中國人 Non-Chinese	中國人 Chinese	總人口 Total population
1901	20.50	23.77	23.05
1907	15.46	22.52	22.12

● 1996年社會服務機構分佈
Distribution of social service agencies, 1996

● 2008年社會服務機構分佈
Distribution of social service agencies in 2008

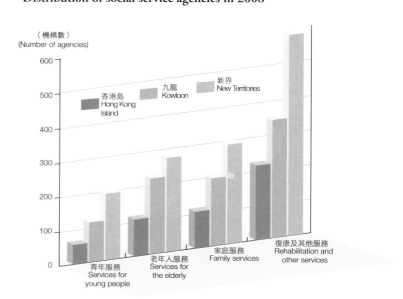

250多億元，佔總財政開支的11.9%。1998年底，有註冊醫生9,527人，護士39,265人，病床32,836張，平均每千人有4.82張，屬發達地區水平。醫院與病床的分佈仍較集中在九龍和香港島。1998年用於社會福利開支佔總開支9.8%。1996年底領取綜合社會保障者有159,100戶，比1995年增24.5%，領取高齡及傷殘津貼者50.3萬人。隨着人口向新界轉移及人口老化，服務老年人的機構增長最快，並且多位於新界地區。

University of Hong Kong.

Recently, Hong Kong's social services provisions increased rapidly. Expenditure on medical and health reached 11.9% of government budget. At the end of 1998, there were 9,527 registered doctors, 39,265 nurses and 32,836 hospital beds, or 4.82 beds per 1,000 residents–a level of that of developed economies. Most hospital facilities are concentrated on Hong Kong Island and Kowloon. Social welfare spending reached 9.8% of government budget in 1998. 159,100 households received Comprehensive Social Security Assistance payments, an increase of 24.5% over that of 1995, with another half a million receiving old age and disability benefits. With an ageing population, institutes for the elderly increases rapidly, and they are mostly located in the New Territories.

● 1974年、1984年、1994年及2008年醫療機構　Medical institutions in 1974, 1984, 1994 and 2008

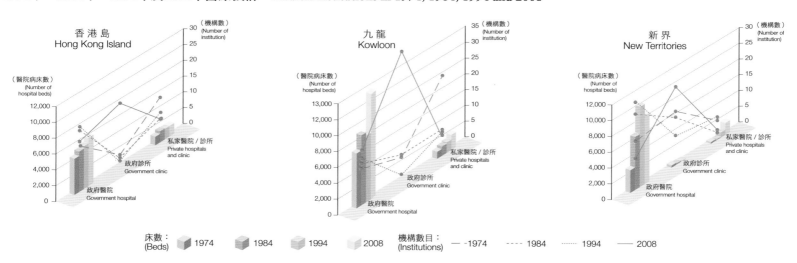

● 2008年醫院分佈　Distribution of hospitals, 2008

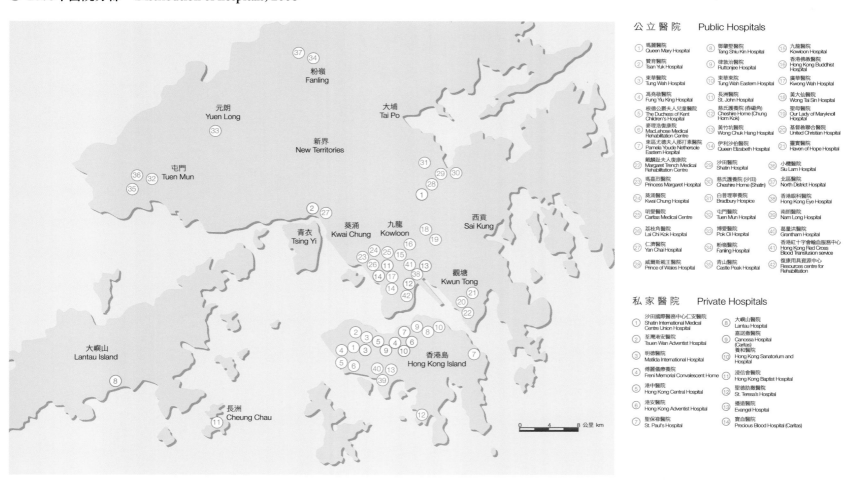

08 新聞出版及廣播 Newspaper and Broadcasting

最早的報紙《廣州郵報》於1834年在廣州面世，1841年遷至香港。該年，政府《憲報》開始每月出版，但一年後交私人承辦。1843年出現了《東半球》及《中國郵報》，同是周刊。1844年通過了出版條例。1881年《香港電訊》創刊。但最早的日報是《中國郵報》及《香港日報》。《中國郵報》其後亦加出華文報紙——《華字日報》。現今最流行的英文日報——《南華早報》創刊於1903年。

電台廣播由私人在1922年發起，政府於1928年接管，台長由郵政專員兼任。1970年成立電視部，後於1950年代的有線麗的呼聲電視及其後

The earliest English newspaper in China–Canton Register was published in 1834 in Guangzhou. It moved to Hong Kong in 1841. In that year, the bi-monthly government Gazette started publication. The operation was subcontracted to a private publisher a year later. The Eastern Globe and China Mail appeared in 1843, both were weekly newspapers. A publishing ordinance was passed in 1844. The Hong Kong Telegraph started in 1881. Yet the earliest daily newspapers were China Mail and Hong Kong Daily. Later, China Mail also published the first Chinese daily–Hua Sze Yat Po. Today's most popular English daily–South China Morning Post, was founded in 1903.

● 1995-2003年新資訊年代的來臨　Coming of new information era in 1995-2003

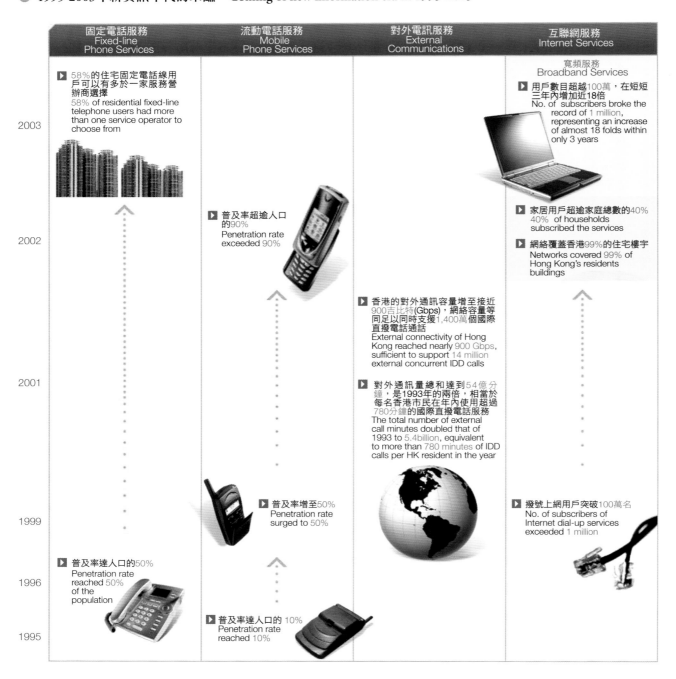

● 2009年的新資訊使用情況　Key telecommunications statistics in 2009

電訊服務 Telecommunication services	數量 Quantity
流動網絡營辦商 Mobile network operators	5
本地有線固定網絡服務營辦商 Wireline-based local fixed telecommunications network services (FTNS) operators	10
本地無線固定網絡服務營辦商 Wireless-based local FTNS operators	1
用作分送本地免費電視節目的固定電訊網絡服務營辦商 FTNS operators for distribution of domestic free TV programme service	2
利用衛星提供服務的對外固定網絡服務營辦商 Satellite-based external FTNS operators	5
利用電纜提供服務的對外固定網絡服務營辦商 Cable-based external FTNS operators	29
對外電訊服務營辦商 External telecommunications services operators	258
住戶固定電話線普及率 Household fixed line penetration rate	101.2%

按人口計算的流動電話服務用戶普及率 Mobile subscriber penetration rate	171.2%
流動電話服務用戶 Mobile subscribers	12,001,128
2.5G及3G流動服務用戶 2.5G and 3G mobile subscribers	4,894,299
互聯網服務 Internet services	數量 Quantity
互聯網服務供應商 Internet service providers	167
已登記的撥號上網用戶帳戶 Registered customer accounts with dial-up access	961,099
已登記的寬頻上網用戶帳戶 Registered customer accounts with broadband access	2,004,074
住戶寬頻普及率 Household broadband penetration rate	79.1%
公共Wi-Fi熱點 Public Wi-Fi access points	8,803

的無綫電視。政府電台於1976年改名為香港電台。

自1980年代起，電視台及電台數目增長迅速，主要是私營的，收視率及收聽率也在增加。報紙數目則由1994年高峯的76份，降至1998年的43份。近年還在減少。周刊和月刊的讀者也在減少。

在2009年，香港已進入資訊社會，流動電話的普及率為171.2%，住戶寬頻普及率達79.1%。

Radio broadcasting that started by amateurs in 1922 became government-sponsored in 1928, with the Postmaster General as its director. Its television section was set up in 1970, later than private stations like Rediffusion and HKTVB. In 1976, the government broadcasting station was renamed Radio Hong Kong.

Since the 1980s, privately-owned radio and TV stations mushroomed, accompanied by a rising number of audience. The number of newspapers reached a peak of 76 in 1994, but thence declined to 43 in 1998. Both weekly and monthly magazines are declining in number and sales volume.

By 2009, Hong Kong became an information society with very high mobile phone and broadband net user rates.

● 報紙與刊物　Newspapers and publications

1997年3月底報紙及期刊數
Number of newspapers and
periodicals by the end of March 1997

報紙
Newspapers
週刊
Weekly publication
週刊及月刊
Weekly and monthly journals
月刊
Monthly publication
不定期刊物
Non-periodical publication
新聞通訊社簡報
Summary from news agencies

2008年報紙及期刊數
Number of newspapers and
periodicals by 2008

報紙
Newspapers
期刊
Journal

報紙及期刊的九歲或以上的讀者數目
Number of readers aged 9 or above of newspapers and periodicals

報紙 Newspapers
周刊 Weekly publication
月刊 Monthly publication

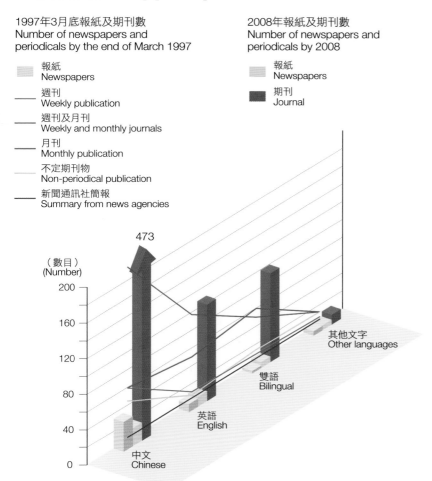

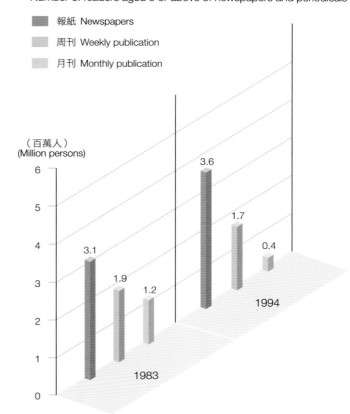

● 廣播與電視　Radio and Television

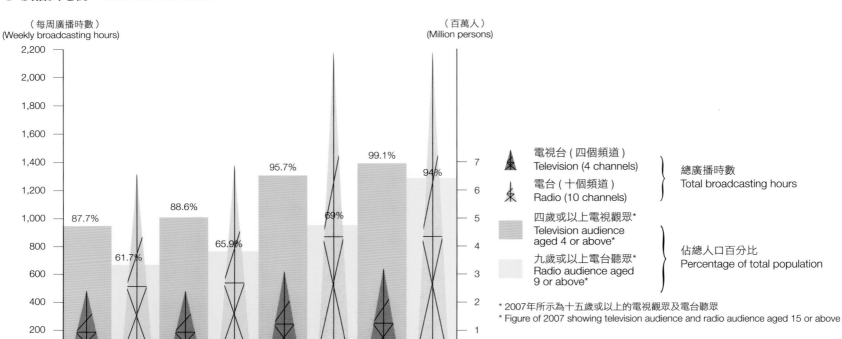

電視台（四個頻道）
Television (4 channels)
電台（十個頻道）
Radio (10 channels)
}
總廣播時數
Total broadcasting hours

四歲或以上電視觀眾*
Television audience
aged 4 or above*
九歲或以上電台聽眾*
Radio audience aged
9 or above*
}
佔總人口百分比
Percentage of total population

* 2007年所示為十五歲或以上的電視觀眾及電台聽眾
* Figure of 2007 showing television audience and radio audience aged 15 or above

09　娛樂文化及康體設施　Art, Entertainment, Culture and Sports Facilities

最早的大型文化娛樂設施是建於1869年的大會堂，擁有一個劇院、兩個表演場、一個音樂室、公眾圖書館、閱覽室和博物館。當時圖書館有書8,000冊。1907年博物館的華人及非華人觀眾每月平均達到29,321及844人。閱覽室平均每月有華人讀者1,412及非華人628人。華人和非華人是受分隔的，如博物館早上開放給華人，下午給非華人。

現今的大會堂是在新址上於1962年建成的。

2008年政府提供的文化娛樂設施包括13個演藝場地、七所大型博物館、兩所文化中心、76間圖書館等。最大的香港文化中心有音樂廳、大

Completed in 1849, the City Hall was the largest cultural and entertainment facilities with a theatre, two performance halls, a music hall, a public library and a museum. It had about 8,000 books. The museum registered in 1907 a monthly Chinese and non-Chinese visitors of 29,312 and 844. Racial segregation was practised with different opening hours for Chinese and non-Chinese. The present City Hall is a facility rebuilt on a new site.

In 2008, government cultural and entertainment facilities included 13 performing venues, 7 museums, 2 cultural centres and 76 libraries. The largest cultural centre has a music hall, a theatre and a multi-functional stage. It registered

● 文娛及藝術場所　Cultural and arts venues

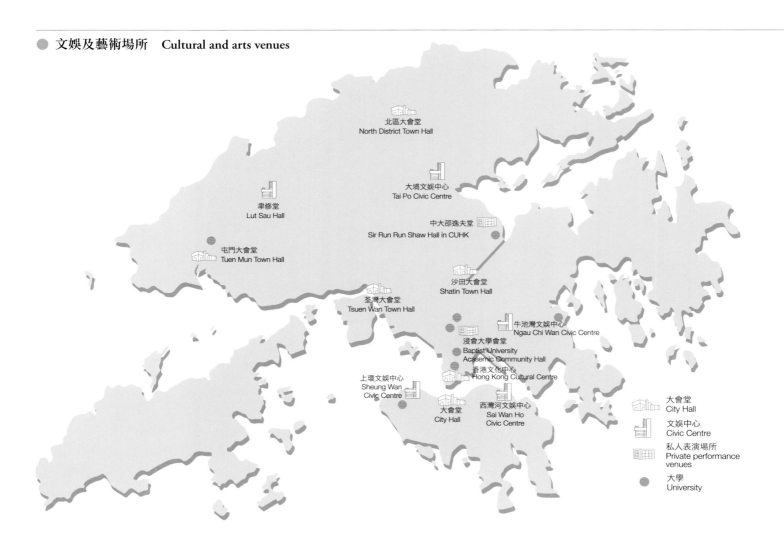

● 室內文化活動參加人數　Number of participants in indoor cultural activities

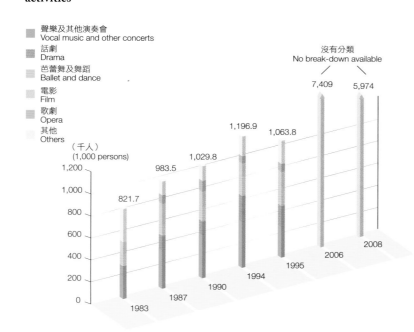

● 公共圖書館增長　Growth of public libraries

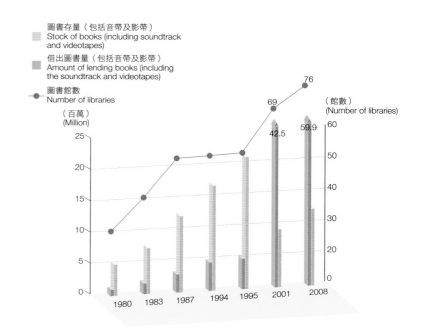

劇院和多功能劇場，當年觀眾849,000人。大會堂有音樂廳及劇院，該年觀眾416,000人。大會堂圖書館（包括地區分館）藏書1,064萬冊，多媒體資料155萬項，登記讀者358萬人。

　　早期的康體活動包括賽馬、各種球類活動和水上活動。設施主要環繞在1884年建成的馬場，主要供公務員、警察和軍隊使用，也包括一些私人球會。中環、深水灣和銅鑼灣也有木球、高球和馬球俱樂部。九龍的康體設施集中在京士柏，由1905年成立的九龍木球會及1900年的部隊俱樂部提供。

　　2008年政府提供服務的刊憲泳灘41個，泳池37個，公園1,450個，其中大型的22個，大球場兩個，最大的可坐4萬人，88個體育館和無數其他球場。這些設施共佔地22平方公里。

849,000 audience in that year while the City Hall registered 416,000. The public libraries have a collection of 10.6 million books, 1.55 million items of multi-media materials, 3.58 million enrolled readers.

Early facilities for entertainment and sports included horse racing, various ball games and water sports. Most facilities hinged on the race course completed in 1884 in Happy Valley. They catered for civil servants, the police and military forces, with some private clubs for the rich and influential. Some other facilities were found in Central and Deep Bay. In Kowloon, they concentrated at King's Park (Ho Man Tin) where the Kowloon Cricket Club was formed in 1905 and a club for the forces in 1900.

In 2008, government facilities included 41 gazetted beaches, 37 swimming pools, 1,450 parks, 2 sports stadiums, 88 indoor sports centres and other sports grounds. These facilities occupied 22 sq. km.

● 室內文化活動出席人數　Attendance of indoor cultural activities

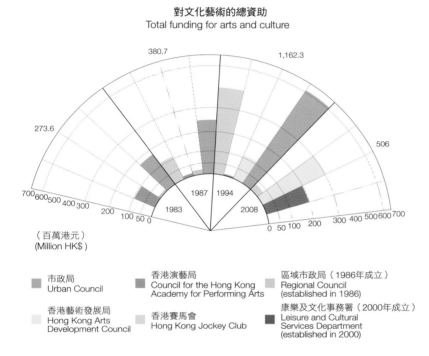

對文化藝術的總資助
Total funding for arts and culture

（百萬港元）
(Million HK$)

市政局
Urban Council

香港演藝局
Council for the Hong Kong
Academy for Performing Arts

區域市政局（1986年成立）
Regional Council
(established in 1986)

香港藝術發展局
Hong Kong Arts
Development Council

香港賽馬會
Hong Kong Jockey Club

康樂及文化事務署（2000年成立）
Leisure and Cultural
Services Department
(established in 2000)

● 博物館訪客人數　Museum visitors

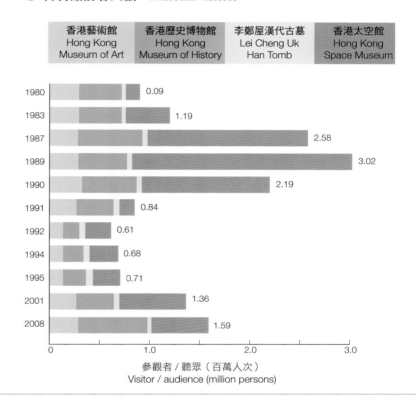

● 主要演藝場所座位數　Seats of major performing arts venues

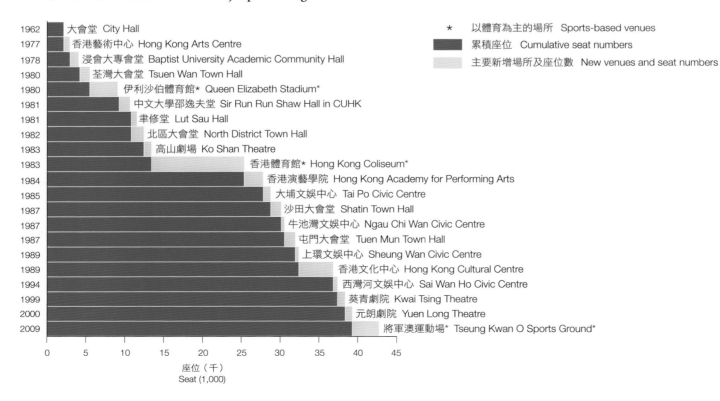

Environment

V. 環境

01　環境污染及市區環境　Environmental Pollution

香港市區狹窄，人口稠密，經濟活動及交通運輸頻繁，如何有效處理廢物及保護環境，實在是個大問題。香港政府對環境的關注，以1989年發表首份環境白皮書為轉捩點。在此之前的1988年，政府投入環保的資源只佔財政支出的0.8%，但到了1995年已達3%。1998年為3.3%。2008年為4.1%。

1998年每天產生19,300噸城市垃圾，建築工程廢物約佔總量的六成以上。住宅廢物則佔近三成。約六成半的垃圾被用作填海，只有一成被回收，3%在焚化爐焚毀。2007年每天的垃圾量減為13,901噸，因為建築廢物量大減。住宅廢物佔了總量的68%。2007年，45%的廢物出口至內地回收。1993-1995年間開設了三個共273公頃的堆填區。1996-2000年恢復了12個堆填區以增加300公頃的堆填面積，使它們可以應付未來20年的需求。不少鄰近大城市經已採用新技術"焚化垃圾發電"來處理大部份城市垃圾。這亦是香港未來的方向。

根據1995年統計，每天約有300萬噸廢水流入鄰近海域。其中住宅污水佔83%，商業污水佔11%，工業污水佔4%。這些污水大部份未經處理。

The smallness and high density of the territory, together with its vibrant economy and busy traffic, make environmental protection and effective disposal and treatment of urban refuse in Hong Kong serious issues. Official concern over the environment started late. The first White Paper on the environment was published in 1989. The year before, government spending in environmental protection was a mere 0.8% of its annual budget. It shot up to 3% in 1995, and reached 3.3% in 1998, 4.1% in 2008.

In 1998, Hong Kong generated 19,300 tonnes of urban solid wastes a day, of which over 60% were construction wastes, and 30% being household refuse. About 60% of the solid wastes is disposed in landfills or for reclamation, 10% recycled while 3% disposed through incineration. In 1993-1995, three landfills were set up, covering an area of 273 ha. A further 12 landfills of a total of 300 ha were added in 1996-2000 for use up to 2030. In 2007 the volume of solid wastes dropped to 13,901 tonnes per day due to shrinkage of the construction industry. Metropolitan wastes then accounted for 68% of the total. About 45% of the wastes were exported to the mainland for recycling. In neighbouring major cities, new incineration technology for disposing most urban wastes and for electricity generation have

● 主要環境污染來源及市區環境狀況　Major pollution source and urban environmental conditions

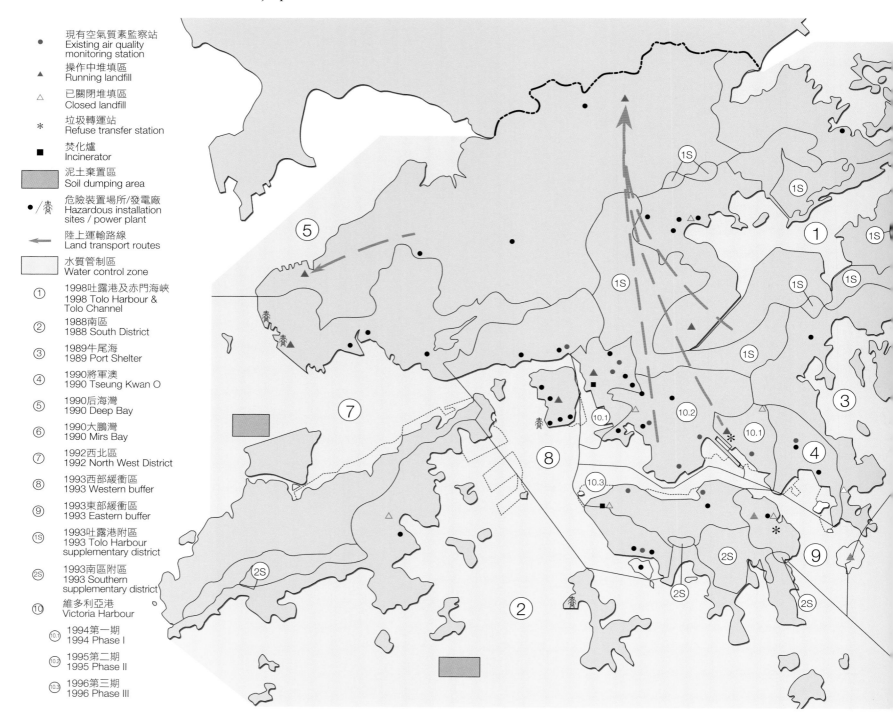

- ● 現有空氣質素監察站　Existing air quality monitoring station
- ▲ 操作中堆填區　Running landfill
- △ 已關閉堆填區　Closed landfill
- ＊ 垃圾轉運站　Refuse transfer station
- ■ 焚化爐　Incinerator
- 泥土棄置區　Soil dumping area
- ●/賣 危險裝置場所/發電廠　Hazardous installation sites / power plant
- ← 陸上運輸路線　Land transport routes
- 水質管制區　Water control zone
- ① 1998吐露港及赤門海峽　1998 Tolo Harbour & Tolo Channel
- ② 1988南區　1988 South District
- ③ 1989牛尾海　1989 Port Shelter
- ④ 1990將軍澳　1990 Tseung Kwan O
- ⑤ 1990后海灣　1990 Deep Bay
- ⑥ 1990大鵬灣　1990 Mirs Bay
- ⑦ 1992西北區　1992 North West District
- ⑧ 1993西部緩衝區　1993 Western buffer
- ⑨ 1993東部緩衝區　1993 Eastern buffer
- ①S 1993吐露港附區　1993 Tolo Harbour supplementary district
- ②S 1993南區附區　1993 Southern supplementary district
- ⑩ 維多利亞港　Victoria Harbour
- ⑩.₁ 1994第一期　1994 Phase I
- ⑩.₂ 1995第二期　1995 Phase II
- ⑩.₃ 1996第三期　1996 Phase III

香港海域的水質，因而正在下降。2001年起政府投入200億元建設排污計劃，將約九成污水收集後進行初級處理，然後再排入外海。

　　稠密的人口和繁忙的工商業活動是香港的主要污染源。汽車、機場、發電廠及焚化爐（今已拆掉），是人口及工商業集中地之外的主要污染源。

been exploited. This will also be Hong Kong's major solution.

　　In 1995, 3 million tonnes of sewage were discharged into the sea daily, 83% was household, 11% commercial, and 4% industrial. Most have not been treated, leading to the degradation of coastal water quality. In 2001, the government invested HK$20 billion in a plan to collect 90% of the sewage and had it treated before discharging into off-shore waters. High population, intensive commercial and industrial activities are main pollution causes. Besides, motor vehicles, the airport, electricity plants and the old incinerators (now dismantaled) are other important sources of pollutants.

● **1988-1995年城市固體垃圾處理 Municipal solid waste handling in 1988-1995**

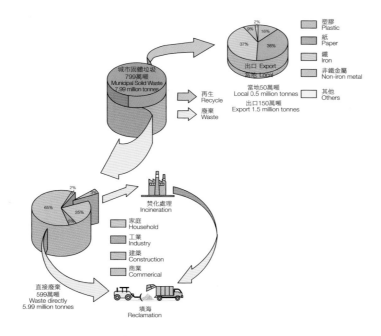

● **2007年城市固體垃圾處理 Municipal solid waste handling in 2007**

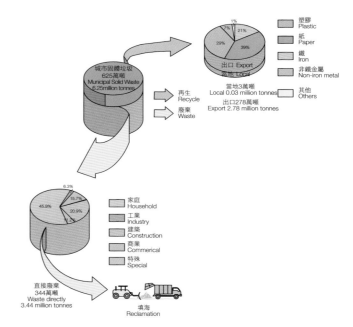

● **1987-1995年政府環境保護資源分配 Government resources devoted to environmental protection work in 1987-1995**

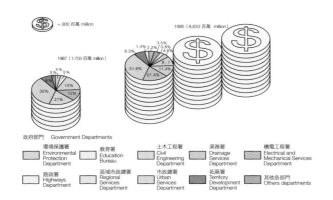

● **2008年政府環境保護資源分配 Government resources devoted to environmental protection work in 2008**

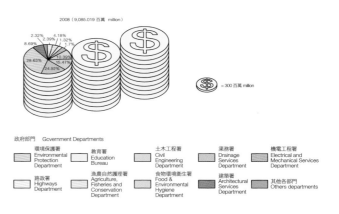

● **1988-2008年海水素質比較 Comparison of water quality in 1988-2008**

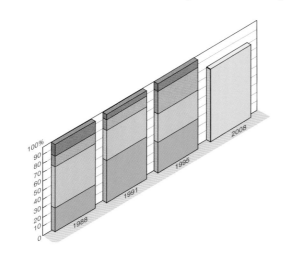

達標 Compliance

優質 Wholesome

可接受 Acceptable

勉強接受 Accepted reluctantly

不可接受 Unacceptable

02 空氣素質 Air Quality

1971年空氣污染的主要構成為：二氧化硫（SO$_2$，44%）、一氧化碳（CO，30%）、氧化氮（NO$_2$，16%）、懸浮粒子（TSP，6%）、碳氫化合物（RSP，4%）。污染來源是發電廠及煤氣廠（44%）、汽車廢氣（31%）、製造業廢氣（9%）和焚化爐（6%）等。

1983年起，政府在市區收集空氣污染資料，並管制電廠、煤氣廠及工廠的排放，二氧化硫（SO$_2$）的污染情況有很大改善。工業區如荃灣、觀塘、紅磡區，改善至為明顯。但汽車廢氣及地盤塵埃仍對一些地區形成超出標準的污染。

1990年，空氣素質最差的仍為荃灣及青衣島的一部份，電廠及工業是主要原因。稠密的舊市區——九龍及香港島北岸，空氣素質也較惡

In 1971, the composition of air pollutants is: SO$_2$, 44%; CO, 30%; NO$_2$, 16%; TSP, 6% and RSP, 4%. Its main sources are electricity and gas plants (44%), vehicle (31%), industrial (9%) and incinerator (6%) emissions.

From 1983 onward, the government has systematically monitored air quality and regulated emissions from electricity, gas and other industrial plants, leading to a decline of SO$_2$ in the air in the industrial areas of Tsuen Wan, Kwun Tong and Hung Hom. Yet vehicle fumes and construction dust still lead to poor air quality in some districts.

In 1990, air quality was worse in Tsuen Wan and Tsing Yi, due to the electricity plant and industries there. Old urban districts like Kowloon and the northern coast of Hong Kong had poor air. The Yuen Long-Tuen Mun corridor was getting worse. These show a close relationship between land use and air quality.

● 1990年空氣污染情況 Air pollution in 1990

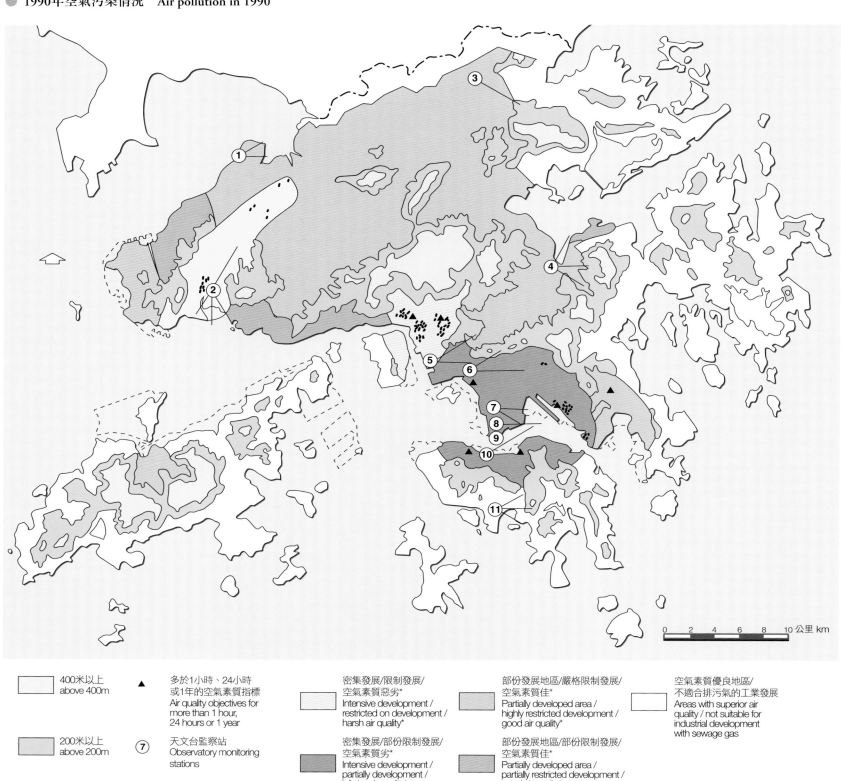

400米以上 above 400m	▲ 多於1小時、24小時或1年的空氣素質指標 Air quality objectives for more than 1 hour, 24 hours or 1 year	密集發展/限制發展/空氣素質惡劣* Intensive development / restricted on development / harsh air quality*	部份發展地區/嚴格限制發展/空氣素質佳* Partially developed area / highly restricted development / good air quality*	空氣素質優良地區/不適合排污氣的工業發展 Areas with superior air quality / not suitable for industrial development with sewage gas
200米以上 above 200m	⑦ 天文台監察站 Observatory monitoring stations	密集發展/部份限制發展/空氣素質劣* Intensive development / partially development / inferior air quality*	部份發展地區/部份限制發展/空氣素質佳* Partially developed area / partially restricted development / good air quality*	
潛在黑點 Potential black spot		已發展地區/部份限制發展/空氣素質差* Developed areas/restricted development / poor air quality*	未發展地區/不受限制/空氣素質佳* Undeveloped area/unrestricted / good air quality*	

*含義是：發展現狀 / 發展規劃 / 空氣素質現狀
*Implications: development status / development plan / air quality status

劣。屯門元朗走廊亦空氣素質較差。顯然，城市土地利用和空氣素質有很密切的關係。

1998年，香港O₃量較芝加哥、費城、巴黎、洛杉磯佳；就SO₂來說，仍較東京、華盛頓、新加坡和紐約為佳；NO₂水平也比波士頓、倫敦、紐約和羅馬好；可吸入的TSP量，不及墨西哥城1/4，也較費城和巴塞隆拿低。

2007年的政府空氣素質報告認為，由於2000年起控制汽車排放，TSP、SO₂、NO₂等逐步改善。但O₃水平卻上升，因為區域性空氣素質下降，影響香港。特區政府正和鄰近政府商討對策。

Compared to some major cities, Hong Kong's air quality in 1998 was not bad: O₃ level was better than that of Philadelphia, Paris, Los Angeles; SO₂ level was better than that of Tokyo, Washington, Singapore and New York; NO₂ level was better than that of Boston, London, New York and Rome; TSP level was only 1/4 of Mexico City, and lower than that of Philadelphia and Barcelona.

In a 2007 report, the government noted improvement in the levels of TSP, SO₂, NO₂, due to controlled emission from vehicles since 2000. However O₃ level has been rising as a result of the deterioration of regional air quality. The government is approaching other governments in the region for a joint solution.

● 1996及2008年全年平均空氣污染濃度及空氣素質標準 **Annual average air pollution concentrations and air quality standards in 1996 and 2008**

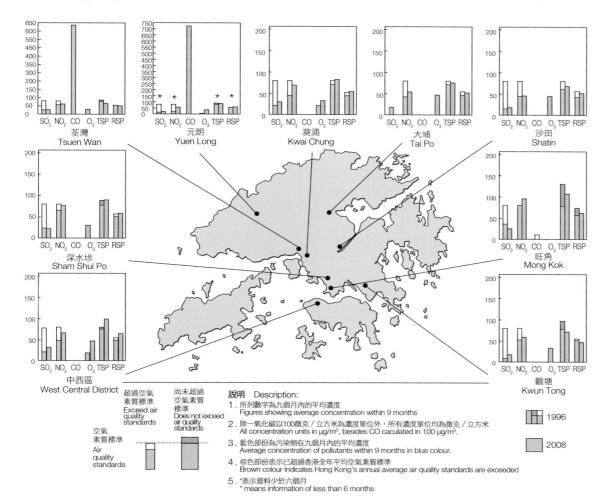

● 1983-1984年及2008年空氣污染水平 **Air pollution levels in 1983-1984 and 2008**

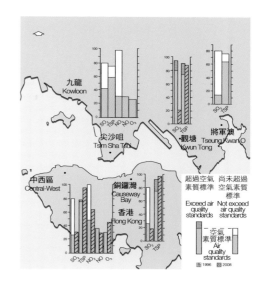

● 2008年二氧化硫污染水平 **Cause of pollution: sulphur dioxide level in 2008**

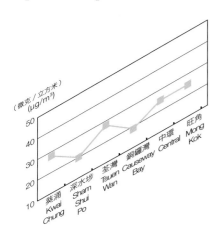

● 1984-1995年二氧化硫污染水平 **Cause of pollution: sulphur dioxide level in 1984-1995**

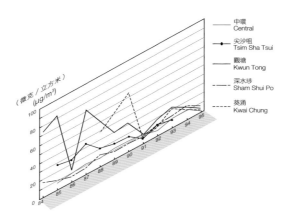

● 1972-1984年二氧化硫污染水平 **Cause of pollution: sulphur dioxide level in 1972-1984**

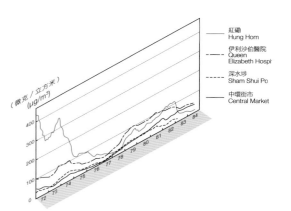

03 機場噪音　Airport Noise Pollution

城市噪音達80分貝便使人厭煩，75分貝以上便不宜學校等設施的建立。城市噪音主要來自交通、工業及建築活動。香港城市噪音水平和倫敦、紐約相近，主要來自汽車。在不少主要道路的交匯點，大部份時間噪音都在80分貝以上。

長久以來最特殊的噪音源是啟德機場。1975年在九龍有50萬以上的人口，每天有約15分鐘以上，要忍受85分貝以上的飛機噪音。按國際標準，等音線（NEF）25以上的地區不宜設立學校，而在啟德附近有100間以上的學校，其中76間的噪音更高達90分貝以上。

新機場對市區的噪音影響比舊機場低很多，政府特設16個飛機噪音監測點，並盡量安排飛機不在凌晨至清晨升降，但一些以前寧靜的地方，如東涌、馬灣、沙田及山頂，噪音卻加大了。

A noise level of over 80 dB will make people feel uncomfortable. A level of over 75 dB is unsuitable for schools. Noise pollution in cities comes mainly from traffic, industries, and construction activities. Noise pollution in Hong Kong is comparable to that in London and New York, and is caused mainly by traffic. Along major road junctions in the daytime, noise level may exceed 80 dB.

However aircraft noise pollution had been a special pollution associated with the old Kai Tak Airport. In 1975, there were over half a million people exposed to over 85 dB for over 15 minutes a day in the airport's vicinity. According to international standard, an NEF of over 25 will not be suitable for schools. Yet around Kai Tak Airport, there were over 100 schools, 76 of them registered over 90 dB at peak fly-over times.

The effect of noise pollution caused by the new Chek Lap Kok Airport on the nearby residences and schools is much reduced. The government has set up 16 monitoring stations and restricted air movements in the sensitive hours of the day (0-7hr). Nevertheless, a few tranquil districts in the past are exposed to increased impact, i.e. Shatin and the Peak, not to mention Tung Chung and Ma Wan.

● 赤鱲角香港國際機場噪音　Noise in Chek Lap Kok Hong Kong International Airport

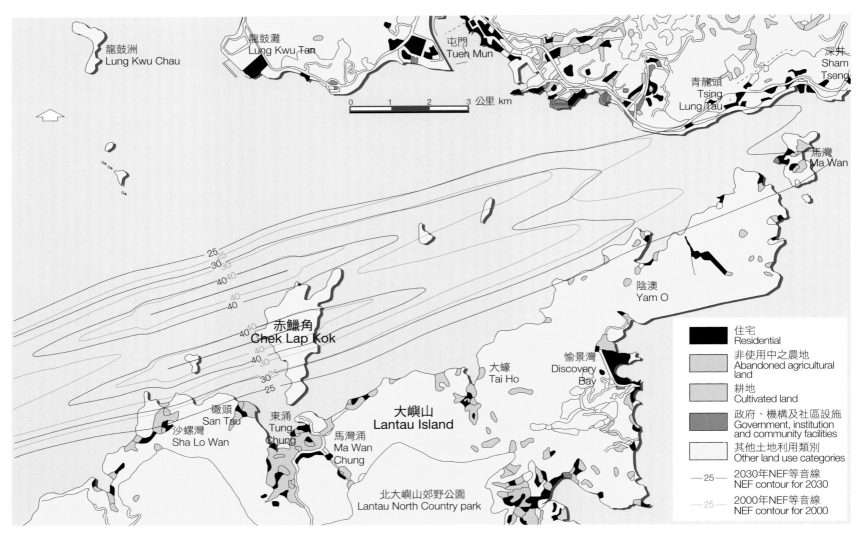

1975年啟德機場噪音　Noise of Kai Tak Airport in 1975

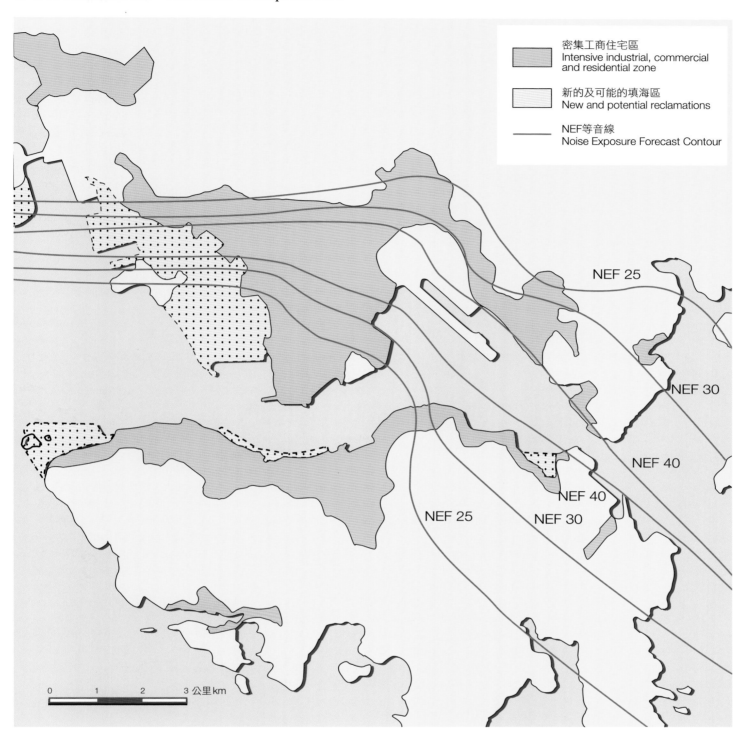

密集工商住宅區
Intensive industrial, commercial and residential zone

新的及可能的填海區
New and potential reclamations

NEF等音線
Noise Exposure Forecast Contour

NEF 25

NEF 30

NEF 40

NEF 40

NEF 25

NEF 30

0　1　2　3 公里 km

飛機噪音分佈　Airplane noise levels in various districts

最高聲浪	Lmax	噪音程度　Distribution of noise levels			
		<65 dB 分貝	65 – 70 dB 分貝	70 – 75 dB 分貝	>75 dB 分貝
沙田	Shatin	0.9873	0.0112	0.001	0.0005
葵涌	Kwai Chung	0.9754	0.015	0.0092	0.0004
汀九	Ting Kau	0.7805	0.1278	0.0881	0.0036
青龍頭	Tsing Lung Tau	0.6881	0.1582	0.1431	0.0106
荃灣西部	Western Tsuen Wan	0.861	0.1062	0.0318	0.001
青衣北	North Tsing Yi	0.9677	0.0161	0.0145	0.0016
北角	North Point	0.9224	0.0512	0.0231	0.0033
中半山	Mid-level	0.9465	0.0446	0.0078	0.001
馬灣	Ma Wan	0.6511	0.2032	0.1188	0.0269
東涌	Tung Chung	0.9393	0.0518	0.0074	0.0016

04 策略性排污系統　Strategic Sewage Treatment

1999年香港每日產生200萬噸污水（2008年290萬噸）。目前全部水域已列入管制區，約6,000個企業被定為排污者，要申請排放牌照，安裝處理系統和接受監督。但是污水只有一成獲得適當處理，四成受到某種程度處理，一半未經處理而排放。

1996年展開基本污水收集系統和污水基本淨化計劃，第一期總建設費200億元，這個計劃目的是將全港污水由管道集中，經簡單處理，然後以長管送至較深海域排放。

政府只承擔計劃的建設成本，系統的運作和保養由商戶和居民分擔。1998年住戶耗水每立方米要繳交1.2元排污費，工商用戶另繳污水附加費。

這個計劃受到質疑。一是污水的處理程度不高，沒有根本解決污染問題；二是將污染引至鄰近地區海域，污染他人；三是以高昂成本由分散地點將污水集中，不如多建分散的處理設施。第一期工程已在2000年完成，第二、三、四期工程，只有第二期甲在2007年批出，其他仍在進行可行性研究中。

In 1999 the daily sewage generated was 2 million tonnes, compared to 2.9 million tonnes in 2008. The waters of Hong Kong are now all controlled areas, and around 6,000 enterprises have been labelled polluting, and have to acquire permits for their discharge. However, at present, only about 10% of the discharge has been properly treated, 40% preliminarily treated, the rest discharged without treatment. The strategic plan for sewage collection and treatment started in 1996. The first phase cost HK$20 billion. The goal is to collect Hong Kong's sewage through underground pipes, have it partially treated, and then led off to the seas by submarine pipes.

The government has to levy a sewage discharge fee to cover the costs of operation and maintenance. In 1998, it amounted to HK$1.2 for 1 m³. of residential water consumption. Commercial and industrial uses paid a higher fee.

There are doubts about the Plan: (1) the level of treatment is low, (2) the sewage is 'dumped' into waters of other jurisdictions, (3) the cost of concentrating the sewage may be higher than treating it in dispersed locations by smaller plants.

Phase one of the Plan was completed in 2000. Contracts for Phase two (A) were signed in 2007. The latter parts of Phase two, and Phase three and four are still being studied.

● 策略性排污系統分期計劃及設施　Stages and facilities for strategic sewage disposal system

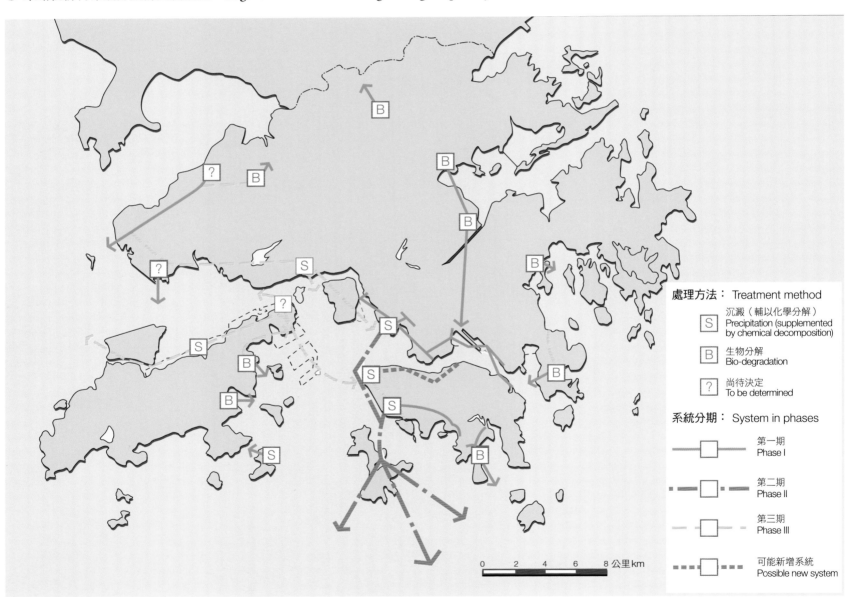

05 新界北區及西北防洪工程　Flood Control in the New Territories

新界北部地勢平坦，易受水浸，加上城市化迅速，自然河道受干擾，逐步形成了五個易受水浸威脅的盆形地區。近年情況更趨惡化，嚴重影響這些地區的魚塘、種菜業以及區內交通。下圖顯示政府自1995年起的五年計劃，目的是改善河道、收集和排泄雨水，解決水浸問題，工程總開支為70億元。

1997年起推行花費87億元的防洪策略，在新界北建741公里的排水渠，其中45公里已建成。還包括27個防洪抽水系統。目前大部份地區載洪及防洪能力已提升至50年一遇的標準。

The flat relief of Northern New Territories makes it susceptible to flooding in days of heavy rain. In addition, rapid urbanization and blockage of stream courses have produced five basin-like flood-prone areas. The situation has worsened since the 1980s, leading to damages to fish ponds, vegetable farming and disruption of local transport.

In 1995, a five-year plan costing HK$7 billion was launched to collect and disburse rainfall as a means to control flooding. In 1997, a land drainage and flood control strategy began. It included the construction of 741 km of drainage channels (45 km completed) and 27 pumping stations, with a capacity to prevent large-scale flooding that may occur once every 50 years.

● 新界北區及西北防洪工程　Flood control in the New Territories

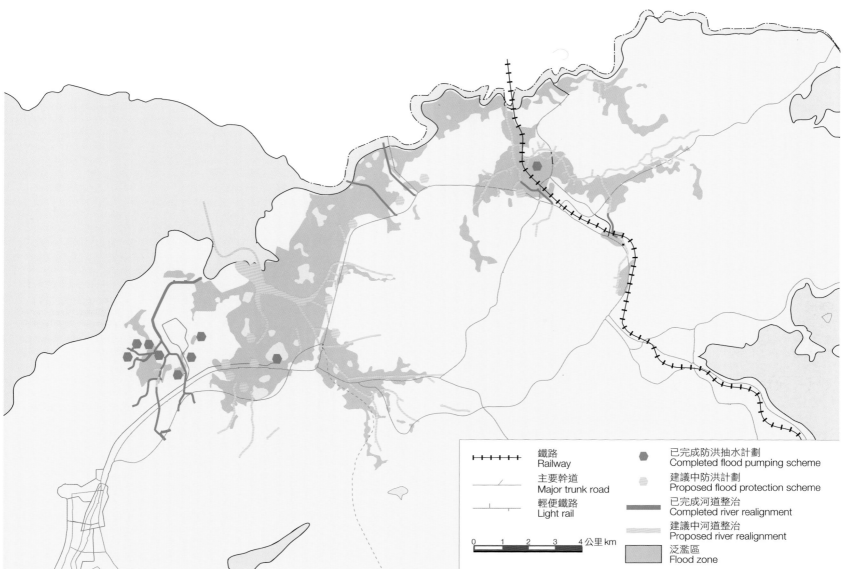

鐵路　Railway
主要幹道　Major trunk road
輕便鐵路　Light rail
0　1　2　3　4公里 km
已完成防洪抽水計劃　Completed flood pumping scheme
建議中防洪計劃　Proposed flood protection scheme
已完成河道整治　Completed river realignment
建議中河道整治　Proposed river realignment
泛濫區　Flood zone

參考文獻　References

書籍　Books

丁新豹、司徒嫣然編，1990，《羅屋民俗館》，香港：市政局。

丁新豹、黃廼錕編，1999，《四環九約》，香港：歷史博物館。

丁新豹、蕭麗娟編，1990，《香港歷史資料文集》，香港：市政局。

丁新豹編，1993，《百年樹人：香港教育發展》，香港：市政局。

王崇熙，1819，《新安縣志》。

王齊樂，1983，《香港中文教育發展史》，香港：波文書局。

王賡武編，1997，《香港史新編》，上、下冊，香港：三聯書店（香港）有限公司。

方國榮、陳迹，1993，《昨日的家園》，香港：三聯書店（香港）有限公司。

中國人民政治協商會議廣東省委員會文史資料研究委員會編，1985，《香港一瞥》，廣東文史資料第四十四輯，廣州：廣東人民出版社。

史深良，1988，《香港政制縱橫談》，香港：三聯書店（香港）有限公司。

布義敦編，1992，《香港文物》，香港：政府印務局。

邢慕寰、金耀基編，1985，《香港之發展經驗》，香港：中文大學出版社。

吳天青，1990，《香港經濟與經濟政策》，香港：中華書局。

吳志華編，1991，《警隊博物館》，香港：皇家香港警務處警隊博物館。

李宏，1988，《香港大事記》，北京：人民日報出版社。

李志剛，1987，《香港基督教會史研究》，香港：道聲出版社。

李後，1997，《回歸的歷程》，香港：三聯書店（香港）有限公司。

李家園，1989，《香港報業雜談》，香港：三聯書店（香港）有限公司。

邱良，1992，《爐峰故事：邱良攝影集》，香港：影藝出版有限公司。

邱東，1992，《新界風物與民情》，香港：三聯書店（香港）有限公司。

何佩然，2008，《建城之道》，香港：香港大學出版社。

余繩武、劉存寬主編，1994，《十九世紀的香港》，香港：麒麟書業有限公司。

余繩武編，1995，《香港歷史問題資料選評：割佔香港島》，香港：三聯書店（香港）有限公司。

林仁超，1970，《天后史蹟》，香港：漢山文化事業。

林友蘭，1985，《香港史話》增訂本，香港：上海印書館。

周永新，1990，《目睹香港四十年》，香港：明報出版社。

金應熙編，1988，《香港史話》，廣州：廣東人民出版社。

明報報業有限公司，《屋苑情報》，1996年2月29日。

科大衛、陸鴻基、吳倫霓霞編，1986，《香港碑銘彙編》，香港：市政局。

香港布政司署房屋科，1997，《長遠房屋策略評議概要》，香港：房屋科。

香港房屋署分區寮屋管制辦事處，《寮屋管制區圖及其人口資料》，香港：分區寮屋管制辦事處，1993-1996。

香港油麻地小輪船有限公司，1996，《渡輪服務與您息息相關》，香港：香港小輪（集團）有限公司。

香港社會福利署，《公共福利金計劃》，香港：社會福利署。

香港政府新聞處，1994，《香港便覽——漁業》，香港：政府印務局。

香港政府新聞處，1994，《香港便覽——弱能人士，復康服務》，香港：政府印務局。

香港政府新聞處，1995，《香港便覽——社會福利》，香港：政府印務局。

香港運輸科，1994，《鐵路發展策略》，香港：運輸科及路政署。

香港博物館編，1982，《香港歷史圖片：博物館藏品精選》，香港：市政局。

徐月清，1999，《原東江縱隊港九獨立大隊》，香港：開益印刷出版有限公司。

通用圖書有限公司，1996，《香港街道大廈詳圖——第三版》，香港：通用圖書有限公司。

通用圖書有限公司，1997，《香港街道駕駛指南》，香港：通用圖書有限公司。

高伯雨，1991，《聽雨樓隨筆》，香港：社會理論出版社。

高添強編，1995，《香港今昔》修訂版，香港：三聯書店（香港）有限公司。

高添強編，2005，《香港今昔》第三版，香港：三聯書店（香港）有限公司。

陳迹，1985，《香港滄桑錄》，香港：三聯書店（香港）有限公司。

陳敬堂、邱小金、陳家亮編，2004，《香港抗戰——東江縱隊港九獨立大隊論文集》，香港：歷史博物館。

陳謙，1987，《香港舊事見聞錄》，香港：中原出版社。

陳鏸勳，1894，《香港雜記》，香港：中華印務總局。

基建研究組織編，1991，《香港替代性機場選點研究摘要》，香港：基建研究。

張炳良，1988，《香港公共行政與政策》，香港：廣角鏡出版社。

梁美儀，1999，《家：香港公屋四十五年》，香港：房屋委員會。

梁蘄善，1962，《香港衛星城市的發展》，《崇基學報》1962年7月第一卷第二期，香港：崇基書院。

馮邦彥，1996，《香港英資財團：1841-1996》，香港：三聯書店（香港）有限公司。

馮邦彥，1998，《香港地產業百年》，香港：三聯書店（香港）有限公司。

馮邦彥，1998，《香港華資財團：1841-1997》，香港：三聯書店（香港）有限公司。

馮邦彥，2002，《香港金融業百年》，香港：三聯書店（香港）有限公司。

程美寶、趙雨樂編，1999，《香港史研究論著選輯》，香港：公開大學出版社。

黃良會、薛鳳旋主編，1990，《香港新機場的挑戰與爭議》，香港：京港學術交流中心。

黃紹倫著、張秀莉譯，2003，《移民企業家：香港的上海工業家》，上海：上海古籍出版社。

彭琪瑞、薛鳳旋、蘇澤霖等編，1986，《香港與澳門》，香港：商務印書館。

靳文謨，1688，《新安縣志》。

萬里機構，1994，《香港全境郊遊圖》，香港：萬里機構出版有限公司。

萬里機構，1996，《香港全境多功能街道圖》，香港：萬里機構出版有限公司。

萬里機構，1996，《香港地鐵及鐵路沿線街道圖》，香港：萬里機構出版有限公司。

楊治明主編，1999，《中國錦繡山河地圖集》，香港：博藝製作有限公司。

董建華，1998，《行政長官一九九八年施政報告》，香港：特別行政區政府。

董建華，1999，《行政長官一九九九年施政報告》，香港：特別行政區政府。

葉靈鳳，1989，《香海浮沉錄》，香港：中華書局。

葉靈鳳，1989，《香島滄桑錄》，香港：中華書局。

葉靈鳳，1989，《香港的失落》，香港：中華書局。

臧示浦、朱崇業、王雲度，1991，《歷代官制、兵制、科舉制表釋》，南京：江蘇古籍出版社。

廖安祥，1989，《梅州大俠香港六十年》，香港：三聯書店（香港）有限公司。

鄭宇碩編，1983，《變遷中的新界》，香港：香港大學出版社。

鄭宇碩編，1986，《變遷中的新界》第二版，香港：香港大學出版社。

鄭宇碩，1989，《過渡期的香港》，香港：三聯書店（香港）有限公司。

鄭寶鴻，2000，《九龍街道百年》，香港：三聯書店（香港）有限公司。

鄭寶鴻，2000，《香港街道百年》，香港：三聯書店（香港）有限公司。

鄭寶鴻，2002，《新界街道百年》，香港：三聯書店（香港）有限公司。

趙雨樂、鍾寶賢編，2001，《香港地區史研究之一：九龍城》，香港：三聯書店（香港）有限公司。

劉存寬編，1995，《香港歷史問題資料選評：租借新界》，香港：三聯書店（香港）有限公司。

劉蜀永編，《香港歷史問題資料選評：割佔九龍》，香港：三聯書店（香港）有限公司。

劉蜀永編著，1997，《香港的歷史與發展》，北京：文化藝術出版社。

劉粵聲，1996，《香港基督教會史》增訂版，香港：浸信教會。

劉潤和，1999，《新界簡史》，香港：三聯書店（香港）有限公司。

劉潤和，2002，《香港市議會史：1883-1999》，香港：香港大學出版社。

魯金，1988，《九龍城寨史話》，香港：三聯書店（香港）有限公司。

蔡榮芳，2001，《香港人之香港史》，香港：牛津大學出版社。

龍炳頤，1992，《香港古今建築》，香港：三聯書店（香港）有限公司。

歷史與文化：香港史研究公開講座，《歷史與文化：香港史研究公開講座文集》，2005，香港：公共圖書館。

盧重興，1999，《香港飛往二十一世紀》，香港：內部報告。

盧瑋鑾編，1983，《香港的憂鬱——文人筆下的香港（1925-1941）》，香港：華風書局。

霍啟昌，1992，《香港與近代中國》，香港：商務印書館。

蕭國健、蕭國鈞，1982，《族譜與香港地方史研究》，香港：顯朝書室。

蕭國健，1986，《清初遷海前後香港之社會》，台灣：商務印書館。

蕭國健，1990，《香港前代社會》，香港：中華書局。

濱下武志，1997，《香港大視野：亞洲網絡中心》，香港：商務印書館。

謝永光，1995，《香港淪陷》，香港：商務印書館。

薛鳳旋、彭雅雋，1982，《屯門——古代海港到將來城市之演變》，香港：香港地理學會、屯門鄉事委員會。

薛鳳旋，1989，《香港工業：政策、企業特點及前景》，香港：香港大學出版社。

薛鳳旋，2000，〈都會經濟區：香港與廣東共同發展的基礎〉，《經濟地理》，總77期，頁37-42。

薩空了，1985，《香港淪陷日記》，北京：讀書、生活、新知三聯書店。

瀨川昌久著、錢杭譯，1999，《族譜：華南漢族的宗族‧風水‧移居》，上海：上海書店。

羅香林，1959，《一八四二年以前之香港及其對外交通》，香港：中國學社。

羅香林，1963，《香港與中西文化交流》，香港：中國學社。

羅香林，1969，《客家史料匯篇》，香港：中國學社。

關禮雄，1993，《日佔時期的香港》，香港：三聯書店（香港）有限公司。

饒玖才，1998，《香港地名探索》，香港：天地圖書。

饒玖才，1999，《香港方物古今》，香港：天地圖書。

饒玖才，2001，《香港舊風物》，香港：天地圖書。

《蘋果日報》，《青衣島伸“八足”結路網》，1997年3月23日。

A record of the actions of the Hong Kong Volunteer Defence Corps in the battle for Hong Kong December 1941. 1953. Hong Kong: Lawspeed.

Abercrombie, Patrick. 1948. *Hong Kong: preliminary planning report.* Hong Kong: Government Printer.

Ashworth, Jennifer M. et.al. 1993. *Hong Kong flora and fauna: computing conservation: Hong Kong ecological database.* Hong Kong: World Wide Fund for Nature Hong Kong.

Baker, Hugh D.R. 1968. *A Chinese lineage village: Sheung Shui.* London: Cass.

Baker, Hugh D.R. 1979. *Ancestral images: a Hong Kong album.* Hong Kong: South China Morning Post.

Baker, Hugh D.R. 1980. *More ancestral images: a second Hong Kong album.* Hong Kong: South China Morning Post.

Banham, Tony. 2003. *Not the slightest chance: the defence of Hong Kong, 1941.* Hong Kong: Hong Kong University Press.

Bard, Solomon. 1988. *Solomon Bard's in search of the past: a guide to the antiquities of Hong Kong.* Hong Kong: Urban Council.

Bard, Solomon. 1993. *Traders of Hong Kong: some foreign merchant houses, 1841-1899.* Hong Kong: Urban Council.

Binnie Maunsell. 1993. *Territorial land drainage and flood control strategy study-phase II (TELADFLOCOSS 2): Executive summary.* Binnie Maunsell Consultants-Drainage Services Department, Hong Kong Government.

Birch, Alan. 1991. *Hong Kong: the colony that never was.* Hong Kong: Guidebook Company.

Birch, Alan, Jao, Y.C., Sinn Elizabeth. (eds.) 1984. *Research materials for Hong Kong studies.* Hong Kong: Centre of Asian Studies, University of Hong Kong.

Blackie, William John. 1955. *Report on agriculture in Hong Kong with policy recommendations.* Hong Kong: Government Press.

Braga, José Maria. 1957. *Hong Kong business symposium: a compilation of authoritative views on the administration, commerce and resources of Britain's Far East outpost.* Hong Kong: South China Morning Post.

Bray, Denis. 2001. *Hong Kong metamorphosis.* Hong Kong: Hong Kong University Press.

Bristow, M. Roger. 1984. *Land-use planning in Hong Kong: history, policies and procedures.* Hong Kong: Oxford University Press.

Bristow, M. Roger. 1989. *Hong Kong's new towns: a selective review.* Hong Kong: Oxford University Press.

Business and Professionals Federation of Hong Kong. 1999. *Hong Kong's Economic Future: working together to create the world city of Asia.* Hong Kong: Business and Professionals Federation of Hong Kong.

Chan Lau, Kit-ching. 1990. *China, Britain and Hong Kong 1895-1945.* Hong Kong: Chinese University Press.

Chan, Wai-kwan. 1991. *The making of Hong Kong society: three studies of class formation in early Hong Kong.* Oxford: Clarendon Press.

Cheng, Irene. 1976. *Clara Ho Tung: a Hong Kong lady, her family and her times.* Hong Kong: Chinese University of Hong Kong.

Cheng, Tong-yung. 1977. *The economy of Hong Kong.* Hong Kong: Far East Publications.

Cheung Cho-lam. et. al. 1990. *Urban redevelopment study in Tai Kok Tsui.* Group workshop report submitted in partial fulfillment of the requirement for degree of Master of Science in Urban Planning. Hong Kong: University of Hong Kong.

Ching, Frank. 1999. *The Li dynasty: Hong Kong aristocrats.* Hong Kong: Oxford University Press.

Chiu, Tze-nang. 1973. *The port of Hong Kong: a survey of its development.* Hong Kong: Hong Kong University Press.

Chiu, Tze-nang. 1983. *A geography of Hong Kong*. T.N. Chiu and C.L. So. ed. Hong Kong: Oxford University Press.

Chiu, Tze-nang. 1986. *A geography of Hong Kong*. T.N. Chiu and C.L. So. 2nd ed. Hong Kong: Oxford University Press.

Choa, Gerald Hugh. 1981. *The life and times of Sir Kai Ho Kai: a prominent figure in nineteenth-century Hong Kong.* Hong Kong: Chinese University Press.

Coates, Austin. 1987. *Myself a mandarin: memoirs of a special magistrate.* Hong Kong: Oxford University Press.

Collies, Maurice. 1946. *Foreign mud: being an account of the Opium Imbroglio at Canton in the 1830's and the Anglo-Chinese War that followed.* London: Faber.

Compiled by E.G. Pryor. 1991. *Hong Kong's port and airport development strategy: a foundation from growth.* Hong Kong: Government Printer.

Compiled by Warner, J. 1981. *Hong Kong illustrated: views and news, 1840-1890.* Hong Kong: John Warner Publications.

Cooper, John. 1970. *Colony in conflict: the Hong Kong disturbances, May 1967-January 1968.* Hong Kong: Swindon Book Company.

Crisswell, Colin N. 1981. *The taipans: Hong Kong's merchant princes.* Hong Kong: Oxford University Press.

Davis, Sydney George. 1949. *Hong Kong in its geographical setting.* London: Collins.

Eitel, Ernest John. 1983. *Europe in China.* Hong Kong: Oxford University Press.

Empson, Hal. 1992. *Mapping Hong Kong: a historical atlas.* Hong Kong: Government Printer.

Endacott, G.B. 1958. *A history of Hong Kong.* London: Oxford University Press.

Endacott, G.B. 1962. *A biographical sketch-book of early Hong Kong.* Singapore: Eastern Universities Press.

Endacott, G.B. 1964. *Government and people in Hong Kong, 1841-1962: a constitutional history.* Hong Kong: Hong Kong University Press.

Endacott, G.B. 1973. *A history of Hong Kong.* Rev. ed. Hong Kong: Oxford University Press.

Endacott, G.B. 1978. *Hong Kong eclipse.* Hong Kong: Oxford University Press.

Endacott, G.B. and Hinton, A. 1968. *Fragrant harbour: a short history of Hong Kong.* 2nd ed. Hong Kong: Oxford University Press.

England, Vaudine. 1998. *The quest of Noel Croucher: Hong Kong's quiet philanthropist.* Hong Kong: Hong Kong University Press.

Fan, Shu-qin. 1972. *Xianggang Jingji.* Singapore: University Education Press. (Chinese text)

Faure David. 1986. *The structure of Chinese rural society: lineage and village in the eastern New Territories, Hong Kong.* Hong Kong: Oxford University Press.

Faure David. 1997. *A Documentary History of Hong Kong: Society.* Hong Kong: Hong Kong University Press.

Faure, David, Hayes, James and Birch, Alan. (eds.) 1984. *From village to city: studies in the traditional roots of Hong Kong society.* Hong Kong: Centre of Asian Studies, University of Hong Kong.

Fok, Kai-cheong. 1990. *Lectures on Hong Kong history: Hong Kong's role in modern Chinese history.* Hong Kong: Commercial Press.

Fullard, Harold. 1978. *Philip/Oxford modern school atlas for Hong Kong.* New ed. London: Philip.

Girard, Greg, Lambot, I. 1993. *City of darkness: life in Kowloon Walled City.* Chiddingford Surrey: Watermark Publications (UK) Ltd.

Grant, Charles J. 1962. *The soils and agriculture of Hong Kong.* Hong Kong: Government Printer.

Grantham, Alexander. 1965. *Via port, from Hong Kong to Hong Kong.* Hong Kong: Hong Kong University Press.

Harland, Kathleen. 1986. *The Royal Navy in Hong Kong since 1841.* Liskeard, Cornwall: Maritime Books.

Hase and Sinn ed. 1995. *Beyond the Metropolis: villages in Hong Kong.* Hong Kong: Joint Publishing (H.K.) Company Ltd.

Hase, P.H. 1999. *In the heart of the metropolis: Yaumatei and its people.* Hong Kong: Joint Publishing (Hong Kong) Company Ltd.

Hayes, James. 1977. *The Hong Kong region, 1850-1911: institutions and leadership in town and countryside.* Hamden: Archon Books.

Hayes, James. 1983. *The rural communities of Hong Kong: studies and themes.* Hong Kong: Oxford University Press.

Hayes, James. 1994. *Tsuen Wan: growth of a "new town" and its people.* USA: Oxford University Press.

Hayes, James. 1996. *Friends and teachers: Hong Kong and its people 1953-87.* Hong Kong: Hong Kong University Press.

Hayes, James. 2001. *South China village culture.* Hong Kong: Oxford University Press.

Ho, Pui Yin. 2001. *Water for a barren rock: 150 years of water supply in Hong Kong.* Hong Kong: Commercial Press.

Hoe, Susanna and Roebuck, Derek. 1999. *The taking of Hong Kong: Charles and Clara Elliot in China waters.* Richmond, Surrey: Curzon Press.

Hong Kong. Hong Kong: Centre of Asian Studies, University of Hong Kong.

Hong Kong: city of vision. 1995. Hong Kong: Hinge Marketing.

Hong Kong Atlas. 1991. Hong Kong: Hai Feng Publishing.

Hong Kong Blue Book. Annual. Various dates. Hong Kong: Government Printer.

Hong Kong Government Administrative and Annual Reports. Various dates. Hong Kong: Government Printer.

Hong Kong trade and shipping returns. Annual. Various dates. Hong Kong: Government Printer.

Hong Kong. Agriculture and Fisheries Department. Various dates. *Annual departmental report.* Hong Kong: Government Printer.

Hong Kong. Census and Statistics Department. 1962. *Report on the 1961 by-*

census. By K.W.A. Barnett. 3 vols. Hong Kong: Government Printer.

Hong Kong. Census and Statistical Planning Office. 1966. *Hong Kong by-census 1966: land and marine training manual.* Hong Kong: Government Printer.

Hong Kong. Census and Statistics Department. 1968. *Report on the 1966 by-census.* By K.W.A. Barnett. 2 vols. Hong Kong: Government Printer.

Hong Kong. Census and Statistics Department. 1969. *Hong Kong statistics 1947-1967.* Hong Kong: Census and Statistics Department.

Hong Kong. Census and Statistics Department. 1972. *1971 Census of manufacturing establishments.* Hong Kong: Census and Statistics Department.

Hong Kong. Census and Statistics Department. 1972. *The 1971 Census: a graphic guide.* Hong Kong: Government Printer.

Hong Kong. Census and Statistics Department. 1973. *Hong Kong population and housing census 1971: technical report.* Hong Kong: Government Printer.

Hong Kong. Census and Statistics Department. 1975. *Hong Kong social and economic trends 1964-1974.* Hong Kong: Government Printer.

Hong Kong. Census and Statistics Department. 1977. *1976 by-census: population by age, by sex, by district, by tertiary planning unit.* Hong Kong: Census and Statistics Department.

Hong Kong. Census and Statistics Department. 1977. *1976 by-census: preliminary report on labour force composition.* Hong Kong: Census and Statistics Department.

Hong Kong. Census and Statistics Department. 1977. *1976 by-census: summary of some results and comparisons.* Hong Kong: Census and Statistics Department.

Hong Kong. Census and Statistics Department. 1978. *1976 by-census: transport characteristics.* Hong Kong: Census and Statistics Department.

Hong Kong. Census and Statistics Department. 1979. *Hong Kong by-census 1976: main report.* 2 vols. Hong Kong: Government Printer.

Hong Kong. Census and Statistics Department. 1979. *Hong Kong by-census 1976, tertiary planning units tabulations, Vol.1: Hong Kong.* Hong Kong: Government Printer.

Hong Kong. Census and Statistics Department. 1979. *Hong Kong by-census 1976, tertiary planning units tabulations, Vol.2: Kowloon and New Kowloon.* Hong Kong: Government Printer.

Hong Kong. Census and Statistics Department. 1979. *Hong Kong by-census 1976, tertiary planning units tabulations, Vol.3: New Territories.* Hong Kong: Government Printer.

Hong Kong. Census and Statistics Department. 1980. *1977 Census of wholesale, retail and import/export trades, restaurants and hotels.* 3 vols. Hong Kong: Census and Statistics Department.

Hong Kong. Census and Statistics Department. 1981. *1981 population census: preliminary report on labour force composition.* Hong Kong: Census and Statistics Department.

Hong Kong. Census and Statistics Department. 1981. *Hong Kong 1981 Census: tertiary planning unit population by age.* Hong Kong: Government Printer.

Hong Kong. Census and Statistics Department. 1982. *Hong Kong 1981 Census: basic tables.* Hong Kong: Census and Statistics Department.

Hong Kong. Census and Statistics Department. 1982. *Hong Kong 1981 Census: graphic guide.* Hong Kong: Government Printer.

Hong Kong. Census and Statistics Department. 1982. *Hong Kong 1981 Census: main report.* 2 vols. Hong Kong: Government Printer.

Hong Kong. Census and Statistics Department. 1982. *Hong Kong 1981 Census: street blocks/village cluster tabulations.* 7 vols. Hong Kong: Government Printer.

Hong Kong. Census and Statistics Department. 1982. *Hong Kong 1981 Census: tertiary planning unit tabulations.* Hong Kong: Government Printer.

Hong Kong. Census and Statistics Department. 1984. *Demographic trends in Hong Kong, 1971-82: an analysis based on vital registration statistics of births marriages, and deaths and on census results.* Hong Kong: Census and Statistics Department.

Hong Kong. Census and Statistics Department. 1986. *Hong Kong 1986 by-census: tertiary planning unit: living quarters, households and population by type of living quarters.* Hong Kong: Census and Statistics Department.

Hong Kong. Census and Statistics Department. 1986. *Hong Kong 1986 by-census: tertiary planning unit: population by age.* Hong Kong: Census and Statistics Department.

Hong Kong. Census and Statistics Department. 1987. *Hong Kong 1986 by-census: social atlas.* Hong Kong: Government Printer.

Hong Kong. Census and Statistics Department. 1987. *Hong Kong 1986 by-census: tertiary planning unit summary tables.* 3 vols. Hong Kong: Government Printer.

Hong Kong. Census and Statistics Department. 1988. *Hong Kong 1986 by-census. Main report.* 2 vols. Hong Kong: Government Printer.

Hong Kong. Census and Statistics Department. 1991. *Hong Kong 1991 population census: tabulations for District Board Districts and Constituency Areas: living quarters, households and population by type of living quarters.* Hong Kong: Census and Statistics Department.

Hong Kong. Census and Statistics Department. 1992. *Hong Kong 1991 population census: basic tables for tertiary planning units: Hong Kong Island.* Hong Kong: Census and Statistics Department.

Hong Kong. Census and Statistics Department. 1992. *Hong Kong 1991 population census: basic tables for tertiary planning units: Kowloon and New Kowloon.* Hong Kong: Census and Statistics Department.

Hong Kong. Census and Statistics Department. 1992. *Hong Kong 1991 population census: basic tables for tertiary planning units: the New Territories.* Hong Kong: Census and Statistics Department .

Hong Kong. Census and Statistics Department. 1992. *Hong Kong 1991 population census: boundary maps complementary to tabulations for tertiary planning units.* Hong Kong: Census and Statistics Department.

Hong Kong. Census and Statistics Department. 1992. *Hong Kong 1991 population census: graphic guide.* Hong Kong: Government Printer.

Hong Kong. Census and Statistics Department. 1992. *Hong Kong 1991 population census: main tables.* Hong Kong: Census and Statistics Department.

Hong Kong. Census and Statistics Department. 1992. *Hong Kong trade statistics classification: S.I.T.C. Rev. 3.* Hong Kong: Government Printer.

Hong Kong. Census and Statistics Department. 1996. *1996 population by-census: summary results.* Hong Kong: Census and Statistics Department.

Hong Kong. Census and Statistics Department. 1996. *1996 Population by-census: tables for tertiary planning units: population by age, and sex.* Hong Kong: Census and Statistics Department.

Hong Kong. Census and Statistics Department. Various dates. *Hong Kong annual digest of statistics.* Hong Kong: Census and Statistics Department.

Hong Kong. Census and Statistics Department. Various dates. *Hong Kong merchandise Trade statistics annual supplement.* Hong Kong: Government Printer.

Hong Kong. Census and Statistics Department. Various dates. *Hong Kong monthly digest of statistics.* Hong Kong: Government Printer.

Hong Kong. Census and Statistics Department. Various dates. *Survey of wholesale, retail and import/export trades, restaurants and hotels.* Annual. Hong Kong: Census and Statistics Department.

Hong Kong. Census and Statistics Department. Building, Construction and Real Estates Statistics Section. 1986. *1986 survey of building, construction and real estates sectors.* Hong Kong: Government Printer.

Hong Kong. Census and Statistics Department. Census Planning Section. 1991. *Hong Kong 1991 population census: summary results.* Hong Kong: Census and Statistics Department.

Hong Kong. Census and Statistics Department. Census Planning Section.

1993. *Hong Kong 1991 population census: main report.* Hong Kong: Census and Statistics Department.

Hong Kong. Census and Statistics Department. Consumer Price Index Section. 1981. *The 1979-1980 consumer price index revision report.* Hong Kong: Census and Statistics Department.

Hong Kong. Census and Statistic Department. Employment Statistics Section. Various dates. *Employment and vacancies statistics (detailed tables). Series A, services sectors.* Hong Kong: Census and Statistics Department.

Hong Kong. Census and Statistics Department. Employment Statistics Section. Various dates. *Employment and vacancies statistics (detailed tables). Series B, wholesale and retail trades, restaurants and hotels.* Annual. Hong Kong: Census and Statistics Department.

Hong Kong. Census and Statistics Department. Employment Statistics Section. Various dates. *Employment and vacancies statistics (detailed tables). Series D, import/export trades.* Annual. Hong Kong: Census and Statistics Department.

Hong Kong. Census and Statistics Department. Employment and Earnings Statistics Section. Various dates. *Employment and vacancies statistics (detailed tables) in manufacturing, mining and quarrying, electricity and gas.* Annual. Hong Kong: Census and Statistics Department.

Hong Kong. Census and Statistics Department. Employment and Earnings Statistics Section. Various dates. *Employment and vacancies statistic (detailed tables) in transport, storage and communication, financing, insurance, real estate and business services, community, social and personal services.* Annual. Hong Kong: Census and Statistics Department.

Hong Kong. Census and Statistics Department. Employment Statistics Section. Various dates. *Employment and vacancies statistics. (detailed tables) in wholesale, retail, import and export trades, restaurants and hotels.* Annual. Hong Kong: Census and Statistics Department.

Hong Kong. Census and Statistics Department. Industrial Production Statistics Section. Various dates. *Survey of industrial production.* Annual. Hong Kong: Census and Statistics Department.

Hong Kong. Census and Statistics Department. Shipping Statistics Section. Various dates. *Hong Kong shipping statistics.* Annual. Hong Kong: Census and Statistics Department.

Hong Kong. Census and Statistics Department. Trade Research Section. Various dates. *Hong Kong external trade: report and tables.* Hong Kong: Census and Statistics Department.

Hong Kong. Census and Statistics Department. Transport and Services Statistics Section. 1990. *Census of storage, communications, financing, insurance and business services.* Hong Kong: Census and Statistics Department.

Hong Kong. Census and Statistics Department. Transport and Services Statistics Section. Various dates. *Survey of storage, communication, financing, insurance and business services.* Annual. Hong Kong: Census and Statistics Department.

Hong Kong. Census and Statistics Department. Wholesale/Retail Trade Statistics Section. Various dates. *Report on survey of wholesale, retail and import and export trades, restaurants and hotels.* Hong Kong: Census and Statistics Department.

Hong Kong. Civil Aviation Department. Various dates. *Annual departmental report.* Hong Kong: Government Printer.

Hong Kong. Civil Aviation Department. Various dates. *Report on Civil Aviation Hong Kong.* Annual. Hong Kong: Civil Aviation Department.

Hong Kong. Crown Lands and Survey Office. Colony Outline Planning Team. 1967. *Land utilization in Hong Kong as at 31st March 1966.* Hong Kong: Government Printer.

Hong Kong. Department of Commerce and Industry. Various dates. *Hong Kong Trade Returns.* Monthly. Hong Kong: Department of Commerce and Industry.

Hong Kong. Department of Health. Various dates. *Annual departmental report by Director of Health for the financial year.* Hong Kong: Department of Health.

Hong Kong. Environmental Protection Department. Various dates. *Environment Hong Kong.* Annual. Hong Kong: Environmental Protection Department.

Hong Kong. Government. 1932. *Historical and Statistical Abstract of the Colony of Hong Kong, 1841-1930.* 3rd Editioned. Hong Kong: Government Printer.

Hong Kong. Government Information Services. 1979. *Rural architecture in Hong Kong.* Hong Kong: Government Information Services.

Hong Kong. Government Information Services. 1989. *Hong Kong heritage.* Hong Kong: Government Information Services.

Hong Kong. Government Information Services. 1994. *Hong Kong the fact, Rehabilitation.* Hong Kong: Government Printer.

Hong Kong. Government Information Services. 1995. *Hong Kong the facts, Social welfare.* Hong Kong: Government Printer.

Hong Kong: Hong Kong Tourist Association. Various dates. *Annual report.* Hong Kong: Hong Kong Tourist Association.

Hong Kong. Hotel, Catering and Tourism Training Board. Various dates. *Manpower survey report on the hotel industry.* Hong Kong: Hotel, Catering and Tourism Training Board.

Hong Kong. Housing Authority. *No. of S.C. surveyed squatter structures and population remaining at April 1996.* Unpublished data.

Hong Kong. Housing Authority. 1994. *Housing in figures.* Hong Kong: Housing Authority.

Hong Kong. Housing Authority. 1994. *Housing stock and location.* Hong Kong: Housing Authority.

Hong Kong. Housing Authority. 1994. *Stock of domestic blocks and flats and estimated population in each HOS court by geographical districts, 1994.*

Hong Kong. Housing Authority. Various dates. *A brief summary in existing squatter areas - position as at 30.9.95.* Unpublished data.

Hong Kong. Housing Authority. Various dates. *Annual departmental report.* Hong Kong: Government Printer.

Hong Kong. Housing Authority. Various dates. *Public housing in Hong Kong.* Hong Kong: Housing Authority.

Hong Kong. Information Services Department. Various dates. *Annual report.* Hong Kong: Government Printer.

Hong Kong Institute of Planners. Planning Development. 1995. *Journal of the Hong Kong Institute of Planners.* Vol. 11, No.2.

Hong Kong. Lands and Work Branch. 1988. *Metroplan: the aims.* Hong Kong: Government Printer.

Hong Kong. Lands and Works Branch. Strategic Planning Units. 1988. *Port and airport development strategy (PADS): background notes.* Hong Kong: Strategic Planning Units.

Hong Kong. Lands Department, Survey Division. Various dates. *Hong Kong official guide map.* Hong Kong: Survey Division, Lands Department.

Hong Kong. Marine Department. Various dates. *Annual departmental report.* Hong Kong: Government Printer.

Hong Kong: Maunsell Consultant Asia Ltd. 1989. *Central and Wanchai Reclamation: Feasibility report.* Final report Vol.3. Hong Kong: Territory Development Department, Urban Area Development office.

Hong Kong. New Airport Projects Co-ordination Office. 1996. *Hong Kong airport core programme—building for the future.* Hong Kong: Government Printer.

Hong Kong. New Territories Development Department. 1979. *Market towns.* Hong Kong: Public Works Department.

Hong Kong. New Territories Development Department. 1984. *Sha Tin.* Hong Kong: New Territories Development Department.

Hong Kong. Planning Department. 1994. *West Kowloon Development statement: consultation digest.* Hong Kong: Planning Department.

Hong Kong. Planning, Environment and Lands Branch. 1995. *The shape of things to come: an overview of the role of harbour reclamations in the future development of Hong Kong.* Hong Kong: Planning, Environment and Lands Branch.

Hong Kong. Planning Department. 1991. *Metroplan: the selected strategy: executive summary.* Hong Kong: Government Printer.

Hong Kong. Planning, Environment and Lands Branch. Strategic Planning Unit. 1989 or 1990. *Metroplan: initial options.* Hong Kong: Government Printer.

Hong Kong. Planning, Environment and Lands Branch. Strategic Planning Unit. 1990. *Metroplan: the foundations and framework.* Hong Kong: Government Printer.

Hong Kong. Planning Department. 1993. *Territorial development strategy review: environmental baseline conditions.* Hong Kong: Planning Department.

Hong Kong. Planning Department. 1993. *Territorial development strategy review: foundation report.* Hong Kong: Planning Department.

Hong Kong. Planning Department. 1995. *A new development framework for Hong Kong: a response to change and challenges.* 4 vols. Hong Kong: Government Printer.

Hong Kong. Productivity Centre. *Directory of Hong Kong industries, 1976-1992.* In collaboration with the Census and Statistics Department. Hong Kong: Hong Kong Productivity Centre.

Hong Kong. Provisional Airport Authority. 1992. *New airport master plan: environmental impact assessment: supplement.* Hong Kong: Provisional Airport Authority.

Hong Kong. Provisional Airport Authority. 1992. *New airport master plan: executive summary.* Hong Kong: Provisional Airport Authority.

Hong Kong. Provisional Authority. 1991. *New airport master plan: environmental impact assessment: final report.* Hong Kong: Provisional Airport Authority.

Hong Kong. Rating and Valuation Department. Various dates. *Property review.* Annual. Hong Kong: Government Printer.

Hong Kong. Royal Hong Kong Regiment. 2004. *Serving Hong Kong: the Hong Kong volunteers.* Hong Kong: Hong Kong Museum of Coastal Defence.

Hong Kong. Royal Observatory. Various dates. *Meteorological results.* Hong Kong: Government Printer.

Hong Kong. Royal Observatory. Various dates. *Monthly weather summary.* Hong Kong: Royal Observatory.

Hong Kong. Royal Observatory. Various dates. *Royal Observatory almanac.* Hong Kong: Royal Observatory.

Hong Kong. Royal Observatory. Various dates. *Surface observation in Hong Kong.* Annual. Hong Kong: Royal Observatory.

Hong Kong. Social Welfare Department. Various dates. *Hong Kong annual departmental report by the Director of Social Welfare for the financial year.* Hong Kong: Government Printer.

Hong Kong. Social Welfare Department. Various dates. *Social Welfare Department in figures.* Hong Kong: Government Printer.

Hong Kong. Territory Development Department. 1993. *Development of urban design parameters for Central and Wanchai Development—Final Report.* Hong Kong: Territorial Development Department.

Hong Kong. Territory Development Department. 1994. *20 Years of New Town development.* Hong Kong: Territory Development Department.

Hong Kong. Territory Development Department. North West New Territories Development Office. 1993. *Tin Shui Wai/Yuen Long development programme.* Hong Kong: Tin Shui Wai/Yuen Long Developmemt Office, Territory Development Department.

Hong Kong. Territory Development Department. Sha Tin Development Office. 1993. *Sha Tin Development Programme.* Hong Kong: Government Printer.

Hong Kong. Territory Development Department. Special Duties Unit. 1993. *Central and Wanchai reclamation development.* Hong Kong: Maunsell Consultants Asia Ltd. and Urbis Travers Morgan Ltd.

Hong Kong. Territory Development Department. Urban Area Development Office. 1989. *Central and Wanchai reclamation feasibility study—Final report—Vol.3: background, analysis and issues.* Hong Kong: Maunsell and Urbis.

Hong Kong. Town Planning Board. Various dates. *Annual report.* Hong Kong: Town Planning Board.

Hurley, R. C. (ed.). 1920. *Handbook of British Crown Colony: Hong Kong.* Hong Kong: Kelly and Walsh.

Irving, R.T.A. and Stimpson, P.G. 1989-1991. *Patterns in geography.* Hong Kong: Jing Kung Educational Press.

Journal of the Hong Kong branch of the royal Asiatic society. 1961-2003. Hong Kong: The Hong Kong Branch of the Royal Asiatic Society.

Jarvie, I.C. (ed.) 1969. *Hong Kong: a society in transition: contributions to the study of Hong Kong society.* London: Routledge and Kegan Paul.

Johnston, J.A. 1974. *Secondary school atlas for Hong Kong.* London: Jacaranda Press.

Keswick, M. 1982. *The thistle and the jade: a celebration of 150 years of Jardine, Matheson and Company.* London: Octopus Books.

Knight, Stanley and Bell, Gordon O. 1988. *Ling Kee new school atlas for Hong Kong.* Hong Kong: Ling Kee Publishing Company.

Lau, S.K. 1982. *Society and politics in Hong Kong.* Hong Kong: Chinese University Press.

Lee, R. (ed.) 1981. *Corruption and its control in Hong Kong: situations up to the late seventies.* Hong Kong: Chinese University Press.

Lethbridge, David. 1984. *The business environment in Hong Kong.* Hong Kong: Oxford University Press.

Lethbridge, Henry J. 1978. *Hong Kong: stability and change: a collection of essays.* Hong Kong: Oxford University Press.

Lethbridge, Henry J. 1985. *Hard graft in Hong Kong: scandal, corruption, the ICAC.* Hong Kong: Oxford University Press.

Li, Shu Fan. 1964. *Hong Kong surgeon.* New York: Dutton.

Liang, Chi-sen. 1966. "Urban land use in Hong Kong and Kowloon Part I: Tsim Sha Tsui District". Reprinted from the *Chung Chi Journal*, Vol. 6, No.1.

Lilius, A. 1991. *I sailed with Chinese pirates.* Hong Kong: Oxford University Press.

Lindsay, Oliver. 1980. *The lasting honour: the fall of Hong Kong, 1941.* London: Sphere Books.

Lindsay, Oliver. 1982. *At the going down of the sun: Hong Kong and South-East Asia, 1941-1945.* London: Sphere Books.

Llewelyn-Davies. 1993. *South East Kowloon development statement: executive summary.* Hong Kong: Planning Department.

Lo, Chor Pang. 1992. *Hong Kong.* London: Belhaven Press.

Lo, Hsiang-lin. et.al. 1963. *Hong Kong and its external communications before 1842: the history of Hong Kong prior to British arrival.* Hong Kong: Institute of Chinese Culture.

Modern certificate atlas for Hong Kong: an integrated approach. 3rd ed. 1985-1989. Hong Kong: Collins - Longman.

Mason, Alexander. 1988. *Views of 18th century China: costumes, history, customs.* London: Studio Editions.

Meacham, W. (ed.) 1978. *Sham Wan, Lamma Island: an archaeological site study.* Hong Kong: Hong Kong Archaeological Society.

Meacham, W. 1980. *Archaeology in Hong Kong.* Hong Kong: Heinemann.

Miners, N. 1987. *Hong Kong under imperial rule: 1912-1941.* Hong Kong:

Oxford University Press.

Miners, N. 1991. *The government and politics of Hong Kong.* Hong Kong: Oxford University Press.

Munn, C. 2001. *Anglo-China: Chinese people and British rule in Hong Kong 1841-1880.* Richmond, Surrey: Curzon.

Ng Lun, Ngai-ha, Alice. 1984. *Interactions of east and west: development of public education in early Hong Kong.* Hong Kong: Chinese University Press.

Ng, Y.L., Peter. 1983. *New peace county: a Chinese gazetteer of the Hong Kong region.* Hong Kong: Hong Kong University Press.

Poynter, Alan. 1981. *Philip/Oxford modern school atlas for Hong Kong.* 2nd ed. London: Philip.

Pryor, E. 1983. *Housing in Hong Kong.* Hong Kong: Oxford University Press.

Rodwell, S. 1991. *Historic Hong Kong: a vistor's guide.* Hong Kong: Odyssey.

Sayer, Geoffrey Robley. 1975. *Hong Kong 1862-1919: years of discretion.* Hong Kong: Hong Kong University Press.

Sayer, Geoffrey Robley. 1980. *Hong Kong 1841-1862: birth, adolescence, and coming of age.* Hong Kong: Hong Kong University Press.

Scott, Foresman. 1989. *World atlas on transparency: world geography.* Hengelo, Netherlands: Transparencies to Educate.

Scott, Ian. 1989. *Political change and the crisis of legitimacy in Hong Kong.* Hong Kong: Oxford University Press.

Selwyn-Clarke, S. 1975. *Footprints: the memoirs of Sir Selwyn Selwyn-Clarke.* Hong Kong: Sino-American Publishing Company.

Shiona, A. 1989. *Thistle and bamboo: the life an times of Sir James Stewart Lockhart.* Hong Kong: Oxford Universiy Press.

Simmons, Jim. and Kamikihara, Shizue. 1995. *The commercial structure of Hong Kong.* Toronto: Ryerson Polytechnic University.

Sinn, Elizabeth. 1989. *Power and charity: the early history of the Tung Wah Hospital, Hong Kong.* Hong Kong: Oxford University Press.

Sinn, Elizabeth. 1990. *Between east and west: aspects of social and political development in Hong Kong.* Hong Kong: Centre of Asian Studies, University of Hong Kong.

Sinn, Elizabeth, Hase, P.H. (eds.) 1995. *Beyond the metropolis: villages in Hong Kong.* Hong Kong: Joint Publishing (H.K.) Company Ltd.

Sit, Fung-shuen, Victor. 1979. "Agriculture in the urban shadow: a review of the postwar experience of Hong Kong". *Pacific Viewpoint*, Vol.20. No.2. pp.189-199.

Sit, Fung-shuen, Victor. ed. 1981. *Urban Hong Kong: collected essays: population, economy, environment, housing, planning, future, etc.* Hong Kong: Summerson.

Sit, Fung-shuen, Victor. 1983. *Made in Hong Kong.* Hong Kong: Summerson Eastern Publishers.

Sit, Fung-shuen, Victor. 1989. "Industrial out-processing: Hong Kong's new relationship with the Pearl River Delta". *Asian Profile*, Vol. 17, No. 1, pp.1-13.

Sit, Fung-shuen, Victor. 1996. "Mega-city, Extended Metropolitan region, desakota, and exo-urbanization: an introduction." *Asian Geographer*. Vol. 15, Nos. 1-2, pp. 1-14.

Sit, Fung-shuen, Victor. 1999. "Hong Kong's transferred industrialisation and Industrial Geography". *Asian Survey*, Vol. 28, No. 9, pp.880-904.

Smith, C.T. 1985. *Chinese Christians: elites, middlemen and the church in Hong Kong.* Hong Kong: Oxford University Press.

Smith, C.T. 1995. *A sense of history: studies in the social and urban history of Hong Kong.* Hong Kong: Hong Kong Educational Publishing Company.

Snow, P. 2003. *The fall of Hong Kong: Britain, China, and the Japanese occupation.* New Haven: Yale University Press.

So, C.L. and Chiu, T.N. (eds) 1983. *A geography of Hong Kong.* Hong Kong:

Oxford University Press.

Stimpson, Philip G. and Iving, R.T.A. 1989-91. *Patterns in geography.* 2nd ed. Hong Kong: Jing Kung Educational Press.

Sweeting, A. 1990 *Education in Hong Kong Pre-1841 to 1941: fact and opinion.* Hong Kong: Hong Kong University Press.

Sweeting, A. 1993. *A phoenix transformed: the reconstruction of education in post-war Hong Kong.* Hong Kong: Oxford University Press.

Szczepanik, Edward F. 1958. *The economic growth of Hong Kong.* London: Oxford University Press.

The Hong Kong guide 1893: with an introduction by H.J. Lethbridge. 1982. Hong Kong: Oxford University Press.

Ticozzi, S. 1997. *Historical documents of the Hong Kong catholic church.* Hong Kong: Hong Kong Catholic Diocesan Archives.

Toussaint, Marcel. 1990. *Hong Kong market atlas.* Hong Kong: Business International Asia/Pacific Ltd.

Tregear, T.R. 1955. *Land utilization in Hong Kong.* Hong Kong: Hong Kong University Press.

Tsai, J.F. 1993. *Hong Kong in Chinese history: community and social unrest in the British colony, 1842-1913.* New York: Columbia University Press.

Tsang, Yui-sang, Steve. 1988. *Democracy shelved: Great Britain, China, and attempts at constitutional reform in Hong Kong, 1945-1952.* Hong Kong: Oxford University Press.

Tsang, Yui-sang, Steve. 1995. *Government and politics: a documentary history of Hong Kong.* Hong Kong: Hong Kong University Press.

Tsang, Yui-sang, Steve. 2004. *A modern history of Hong Kong.* London, New York: I.B. Tauris.

UP's map of the World. 1994. Hong Kong: Universal Publication Ltd.

Watson, R.S. 1985. *Inequality among brothers: class and kinship in south China.* Cambridge: Cambridge University Press.

Watt, J. 1983. *The Han tomb in Lei Cheng Uk.* Hong Kong: Hong Kong Museum of History, Urban Council.

Welsh, Frank. 1993. *A history of Hong Kong.* London: Harper Collins Publisher.

Wesley-Smith, T. 1987. *Unequal treaty 1898-1997.* Hong Kong: Oxford University Press.

Whiteley, John. (Editorial advisor). 1972. *Modern certificate atlas for Hong Kong.* Hong Kong: Collins and Longman.

Wiltshire, T. 1987. *Old Hong Kong.* Hong Kong: Form-Asia.

Wise, M. ed. 1986. *Travellers' tales of the South China coast: Hong Kong, Canton, Macau.* Singapore: Times Book International.

Wong, Heung-wing (ed.). 1970. *Hong Kong certificate atlas.* Hong Kong: Macmillan.

Wong, Heung-wing (ed.). 1975. *Hong Kong certificate atlas.* Rev. ed. Hong Kong: Macmillan.

Wong, Luke, S.K. (ed.). 1978. *Housing in Hong Kong: a multi-disciplinary study.* Hong Kong: Heinemann.

Wright, Arnold (ed.). 1990. *Twentieth Century Impressions of Hong Kong.* Singapore: Graham Brash (1st ed. 1908).

連結　Links

Statistics on Map. http://www.censtatd.gov.hk.

論文　Dissertations

Bau, Wai-ngun. 1971. *Urban development of Tai Po Market－a land use study.* Hong Kong: Department of Geography and Geology, University of Hong

Kong. Thesis (B.A. 138).

Chan, Hung-kwan. 1970. *A study of three major agricultural land uses in Northern Yuen Long.* Hong Kong: Department of Geography and Geology, University of Hong Kong. M.A. Thesis.

Chan, Ka-wing Jack. 1971. *A case study of rural town, Yuen Long.* Hong Kong: Department of Geography and Geology, University of Hong Kong. Thesis (B.A. 139).

Chan, Kwong-kwai Laurence. 1970. *The development of Kwai Chung, with special reference to industry.* Hong Kong: Department of Geography and Geology, University of Hong Kong. Thesis (B.A. 99).

Chan, Wai-chun. 1982. *The development of Tuen Mun from 1963 to 1981: a photographic analysis.* Hong Kong: Department of Geography and Geology, University of Hong Kong. Thesis (B.A. 738).

Chan, Wai-ying. 1977. *The Commercial land use of Wanchai—a reflection of the CBD expansion in Hong Kong.* Hong Kong: Department of Geography and Geology, University of Hong Kong. Thesis (B.A. 392).

Chau, Yat-cheung. 1987. *Development planning for Central and Wanchai reclamation.* Hong Kong: Centre of Urban Studies and Urban Planning, University of Hong Kong. M.Sc. (Urban Planning) Thesis (M. Sc.).

Cheng, Gilletta. 1979. *Commuting patterns of workers in industrial establishments in Kwun Tong.* Hong Kong: Department of Geography and Geology, University of Hong Kong. Thesis (B.A. 532).

Cheng, Yuk-wan. 1982. *Industrial freight transportation in Hong Kong with special reference to Kwun Tong.* Hong Kong: Department of Geography and Geology, University of Hong Kong. Thesis (B.A. 749).

Cheung, Man-hin. 1973. *The changing land use pattern of Shatin.* Hong Kong: Department of Geography and Geology, University of Hong Kong. Thesis (B.A. 238).

Cheung, Shuk-tuen. 1985. *Intra-regional changes in the functional role of the New Territories.* Hong Kong: Department of Geography and Geology, University of Hong Kong. Thesis (B.A. 1000).

Chi, Wai-yin Vivian. 1984. *Dynamism of Hong Kong's CBD—1980 to 1984.* Hong Kong: Department of Geography and Geology, University of Hong Kong. Thesis (B.A. 935).

Choi, Wei-ching. 1974. *Labour as a factor in industrial growth—with reference to light metal products industry.* Hong Kong: Department of Geography and Geology, University of Hong Kong. Thesis (B.A. 270).

Chu, Lap-yan. 1972. *A study of a fringe area of the CBD—the western part of the Central District.* Hong Kong: Department of Geography and Geology, University of Hong Kong. Thesis (B.A. 224).

Chung, Cheuk-ming. 1985. *Industrial landuse in Ha Kwai Chung with analysis on the electronic industry.* Hong Kong: Department of Geography and Geology, University of Hong Kong. Thesis (B.A. 1004).

Drakakis-Smith, David William. 1974. *Housing needs and policies for cities in developing countries, with special reference to Hong Kong.* Hong Kong: Department of Geography and Geology, University of Hong Kong. Thesis (Ph.D.).

Fork, Siu-lam. 1984. *A land use study of Western District waterfront.* Hong Kong: Department of Geography and Geology, University of Hong Kong. Thesis (B.A. 0907).

Fung, Chee-keung, Bosco. 1973. *Commuting patterns of resettled squatters in Hong Kong—a geographical study.* Hong Kong: Department of Geography and Geology, University of Hong Kong. Thesis (M.Phil.).

Ho, Kin-wah. 1975. *Highway development and industrial activities—a study in Tsuen Wan—Kwai Chung area.* Hong Kong: Department of Geography and Geology, University of Hong Kong. Thesis (B.A. 316).

Ho, Kit-chu. 1985. *Urban development in the New Territories since 1949.* Hong Kong: Department of Geography and Geology, University of Hong Kong. Thesis (B.A. 952).

Ho, Mee-fan, Helen. 1968. *A study of the industrial development of Kwun Tong.* Hong Kong: Department of Geography and Geology, University of Hong Kong. Thesis (B.A. 29).

Ho, Moon-fong, Annie. 1972. *The development and recent changes of tourism in Hong Kong.* Hong Kong: Department of Geography and Geology, University of Hong Kong. Thesis (B.A. 197).

Ip, Hing-fong. 1995. *An historical geography of the walled villages of Hong Kong.* Hong Kong: Department of Geography and Geology, University of Hong Kong. Thesis (M.Phil.).

Iu, Oi-chun, Jennifer. 1972. *A topologic-cartographic analysis of roadway network changes in the New Territories, 1898-1971.* Hong Kong: Department of Geography and Geology, University of Hong Kong. Thesis (B.A. 199).

Kwan, Chi-kim, William. 1969. *Industrial development in Kwun Tong.* Hong Kong: Department of Geography and Geology, University of Hong Kong. Thesis (B.A. 48).

Kwan, Sau-kay, Tony. 1983. *Bus responses to rapid railway transit: a case study of KMB and MTR.* Hong Kong: Department of Geography and Geology, University of Hong Kong. Thesis (B.A. 841).

Kwok, Chun-man. 1986. *The evolution of the bus route in the New Territories.* Hong Kong: Department of Geography and Geology, University of Hong Kong. Thesis (B.A. 1036).

Kwong, Chi-kwong. 1981. *Application of aerial photography in urban planning—the case of Sha Tin New Town.* Hong Kong: Department of Geography and Geology, University of Hong Kong. Thesis (B.A. 687).

Lai, Chuen-yan, David. 1964. *Some geographical aspects of industrial development of Hong Kong since 1841.* Hong Kong: Department of Geography and Geology, University of Hong Kong. Thesis (M.A.).

Lam, Mo-shan. 1974. *A study of licensed areas in Hong Kong.* Hong Kong: Department of Geography and Geology, University of Hong Kong. Thesis (B.A. 276).

Lam, Siu-wah. 1981. *Landuse changes in selected areas of New Territories 1962-81—the subdivision of Yuen Long Shap Pat Heung.* Hong Kong: Department of Geography and Geology, University of Hong Kong. Thesis (B.A. 705).

Lam, Wai-shan, Priscilla. 1979. *Public light bus operation in Hong Kong.* Hong Kong: Department of Geography and Geology, University of Hong Kong. Thesis (B.A. 517).

Lam, Ying-kwong. 1982. *Urban redevelopment in Hong Kong—a case study in Sai Ying Pun and Sheung Wan.* Hong Kong: Department of Geography and Geology, University of Hong Kong. Thesis (B.A. 730).

Law, Chi-ngar, Rosalind. 1969. *An industrial survey of Castle Peak.* Hong Kong: Department of Geography and Geology, University of Hong Kong. Thesis (B.A. 81).

Lee, Shuet-kwan, Sylvia. 1968. *Tai Po market, its internal structure and regional influence.* Hong Kong: Department of Geography and Geology, University of Hong Kong. Thesis (B.A. 38).

Leung, Chui-wah. 1981. *Land use change in selected areas of the New Territories, 1962-81—Shui Pin Wai, Yuen Long.* Hong Kong: Department of Geography and Geology, University of Hong Kong. Thesis (B.A. 706).

Leung, Fung-ping, Justine. 1986. *Urban renewal in Hong Kong—a case study in Sheung Wan and Sai Ying Pun.* Hong Kong: Department of Geography and Geology, University of Hong Kong. Thesis (B.A. 1041).

Leung, Kai-fan. 1985. *An assessment of the economic and socio-cultural impact of tourism on Hong Kong.* Hong Kong: Department of Geography and Geology, University of Hong Kong. Thesis (B.A. 1028).

Leung, Pak-chung. 1969. *Industrial survey of Yuen Long Town.* Hong Kong: Department of Geography and Geology, University of Hong Kong. Thesis (B.A. 84).

Leung, Sau-yee, Christina. 1971. *The urban renewal and curio-shops in the Western District.* Hong Kong: Department of Geography and Geology, University of Hong Kong. Thesis (B.A. 180).

Li, Tat-chiu. 1969. *Changes in rural pattern and problems in agriculture resulted from urbanization of towns in the New Territories with Yuen Long and Tsuen Wan.* Hong Kong: Department of Geography and Geology, University of Hong Kong. Thesis (B.A. 852).

Li, Tin-yiu. 1980. *The spatial development of ferry services in Hong Kong, with special reference to the Hong Kong and Yaumati Ferry Co. Ltd.* Hong Kong: Department of Geography and Geology, University of Hong Kong. Thesis (B.A. 569).

Li, Yiu-wai. *Urban renewal and Land Development Corporation.* Hong Kong: Department of Geography and Geology, University of Hong Kong. Thesis (B.A. 1013).

Liu, Mei-fong. 1989. *Hong Kong's CBD towards 1990s.* Hong Kong: Department of Geography and Geology, University of Hong Kong. Thesis (B.A. 1070).

Mak, Lai-wan, Louisa. 1981. *Public transport for the Peak District with special reference to the Peak Tram.* Hong Kong: Department of Geography and Geology, University of Hong Kong. Thesis (B.A. 692).

Mak, Ping-sum. 1977. *The impact of transportation on urban residential property price in Hong Kong.* Hong Kong: Department of Geography and Geology, University of Hong Kong. Thesis (B.A. 421).

Ng, Hon-ying. 1976. *Effects of accessibility on rural life—a study of Ha Pak Wai - Nim Wan area in the New Territories.* Hong Kong: Department of Geography and Geology, University of Hong Kong. Thesis (B.A. 361).

Ng, Sau-fong, Angela. *An industrial survey of the villages north of Castle Peak.* Hong Kong: Department of Geography and Geology, University of Hong Kong. Thesis (B.A. 87).

Poon, Chung-shing. *A case study of factors affecting agricultural land use changes in Castle Peak, 1955-1971.* Hong Kong: Department of Geography and Geology, University of Hong Kong. Thesis (B.A. 157).

Preyor, E.G. 1971. *An assessment of the need and scope for urban renewal in Hong Kong.* Hong Kong: University of Hong Kong. Thesis (Ph.D.).

Pun, Ching-han, Cartinal. 1982. *Tram as a public transport mode—a study of the time and cost elements.* Hong Kong: Department of Geography and Geology, University of Hong Kong. Thesis (B.A. 767).

Pun, Kwok-shing. 1979. *Decentralization versus resource conserving development. A study of their relevance in the formulation of a development policy in Hong Kong.* Hong Kong: Department of Geography and Geology, University of Hong Kong. Thesis (Ph.D.).

Roberts, David-cyffin. 1973. *The Central Business District of Hong Kong: Problems of delimitation within an Asian city.* Hong Kong: Department of Geography and Geology, University of Hong Kong. Thesis (M.Phil.).

Tam, Kar-yan. 1980. *A study of goods transport in Kwai Chung industrial district with special reference to containerization.* Hong Kong: Department of Geography and Geology, University of Hong Kong. Thesis (B.A. 621).

Tang, Siu-yee, William. 1972. *Office development in Wanchai District: a case study of CBD overspill.* Hong Kong: Department of Geography and Geology, University of Hong Kong. Thesis (B.A. 228).

Tsoi, Yuek-lan, Grace. 1976. *The changing agricultural land use in Shatin.* Hong Kong: Department of Geography and Geology, University of Hong Kong. Thesis (B.A. 366).

Tsui, Sui-wah, Anita. 1981. *Spatial and functional changes of the Central Business District since the mid-1970's.* Hong Kong: Department of Geography and Geology, University of Hong Kong. Thesis (B.A. 696).

Wan, Chung-chu. 1968. *The development of civil aviation in Hong Kong.* Hong Kong: Department of Geography and Geology, University of Hong Kong. Thesis (B.A. 16).

Wan, Wai-sai. 2007. *Dynamics of the Central Business District of Hong Kong.* Hong Kong: University of Hong Kong. Dissertation (M.Phil.).

Wong, Hung-fai, Philip. 1971. *A case study on the socio-economic aspects of urban squatters relocation.* Hong Kong: Department of Geography and Geology, University of Hong Kong. Thesis (B.A. 163).

Wong, Man-kong. 1981. *The application of sequential aerial photography in surveying urban squatters, 1956-1980—a case study of Shau Kei Wan.* Hong Kong: Department of Geography and Geology, University of Hong Kong. Thesis (B.A. 674).

Wong, May-yin, Alice. 1983. *A study of solid industrial waste management in Kwun Tong, San Po Kong and Diamond Hill.* Hong Kong: Department of Geography and Geology, University of Hong Kong. Thesis (B.A. 822).

Wong, Siu-kwong, Luke. 1969. *A geographical study of squatter areas in the Victoria-Kowloon areas.* Hong Kong: Department of Geography and Geology, University of Hong Kong. Thesis (M.A.).

Wong, Yin-chuen, Agnes. 1979. *Taxi operation in Hong Kong.* Hong Kong: Department of Geography and Geology, University of Hong Kong. Thesis (B.A. 524).

Wu, Yu-tai. 1979. *A study of bus services in areas of different pop. attributes.* Hong Kong: Department of Geography and Geology, University of Hong Kong. Thesis (B.A. 512).

Yeung, Shiu-kong. 1975. *The development of a new town—Tuen Mun San Hui.* Hong Kong: Department of Geography and Geology, University of Hong Kong. Thesis (B.A. 338).

Yeung, Yee-kam, Anne. 1984. *The observation of non-scheduled public light buses in Hong Kong: with special reference to the impact of Hong Kong.* Hong Kong: Department of Geography and Geology, University of Hong Kong. Thesis (B.A. 930).

Young, Chi-tat. 1985. *Rural villages to urban resettlements: an inquiry into the population dynamics of the Diamond Hill squatters (1949-1988).* Hong Kong: Department of Geography and Geology, University of Hong Kong. Thesis (B.A. 1064).

Yu, Fu-lai. 1982. *Public housing in Hong Kong: an economic evaluation.* Hong Kong: Department of Geography and Geology, University of Hong Kong. Thesis (M.Phil.).

Yuen, Miu-yi, Diana. 1982. *An aerial photographic analysis of the changes in land use in Tai Po District, New Territories, 1963-1981.* Hong Kong: Department of Geography and Geology, University of Hong Kong. Thesis (B.A. 727).

Yung, Choi-kwan, Janice. 1981. *Land use changes in selected areas of New Territories 1962-81—Yuen Long-Pat Heung.* Hong Kong: Department of Geography and Geology, University of Hong Kong. Thesis (B.A. 714).

Zheng, Baohong. 2007. *Early Hong Kong's Kowloon Peninsula.* Chow Mo Oi ed. Hong Kong: University Museum and Art Gallery, University of Hong Kong. English and Chinese edition.

地圖　Maps

Agricultural land use 1964/1965. 1:100,000. Source unknown.

Belchers, E. 1841. *Hong Kong, China.* Surveyed by Captain E. Belchers. 1:63,360. London: Admiralty.

Chen, C.S. 1967. *Distribution of population in Hong Kong, urban and rural for 1961 census.* 1:100,000. Hong Kong: Chinese University Press. Map. Based on 1961 Census.

Chen, C.S. 1967. *Population density in the urban areas of Hong Kong.* Ca 1:31,700. Hong Kong: Chinese University Press. Map. Based on 1961 Census.

Collinson, R.E. 1845. *Hong Kong harbour from a hill above Causeway Bay, 500 ft. high.* Lithographed by Dickinson and Co., London. Panorama.

Collinson, R.E. 1845. *The island of Hong Kong from the summit of the direct road from Kowloon to Mirs Bay, 900 ft. high.* Lithographed by Dickinson and Co., London. Panorama.

Collinson, R.E. 1845. *The ordnance map of Hong Kong.* Surveyed by Leut Collinson R.E. Scale : 4 inches to 1 mile. Map 2 sheets. 123 x 115 cm. Map.

Country and marine parks authority. 2008. *Country parks, special areas, marine parks, marine reserve, sites of special scientific interest, Ramsar site and restricted area.* Hong Kong: Agriculture, Fisheries and Conservation Department. Unpublished map.

Gt. Britain. Directorate of Overseas Survey. 1957. *Hong Kong and the New Territories 1:25,000.* Prepared by D. Survey, War Office and Air Ministry. World Polyconic project; UTM grid. War Office, London. Map 24 sheets. GSGS L8811.

Gt. Britain. Directorate of Overseas Survey. 1968. *Hong Kong 1:10,000.* Directorate of Overseas Survey. Cassini projection. Tolworth: Directorate of Overseas Survey, 1968. Map. D.O.S. 231 Series.

Gt. Britain. Directorate of Overseas Survey. 1968-1971. *Hong Kong 1:10,000.* Directorate of Overseas Survey. Cassini projection. Tolworth: Directorate of Overseas Survey. Map 62 sheets. Series L884 (D.O.S. 231).

Gt. Britain. Ministry of Defense, Military Survey. *Hong Kong 1:25,000.* 1967-1975. Prepared by the British Government's Ministry of Overseas Development. Transverse Mercator Projection. Tolworth: Directorate of Overseas Survey. Map 20 sheets. Series L882. D.O.S. 331.

Gt. Britain. War Office. 1905. *Map of Hong Kong and of the territory leased to Great Britain by China signed at Peking on the 9th of June 1898 1:84,480.* London: War Office. Map.

Gt. Britain. War Office. 1913. *Hong Kong and part of leased territory.* 1:25,344. London: War Office. Map 2 sheets.

Gt. Britain. War Office. 1929-1952. *Hong Kong and the New Territories 1:20,000.* London: War Office. Map 24 sheets: col. GSGS 3868.

Gt. Britain. War Office. 1945. *Hong Kong and the New Territories.* War Office. 2nd ed. 1:80,000. London: War Office. Map: col.

Gt. Britain. War Office. 1946. *Hong Kong and the New Territories.* Published by the War Office, Geographical Section, general Staff. 3rd ed. 1:80,000. London: the War Office. Map. GSGS 3961.

Gt. Britain. War Office. 1949. *Victoria.* Comp. and drawn by the War Office. 4th ed. London: the War Office. Map.

Hill, R.D. 1978. *Walled villages and other pre-colonial settlement features in Hong Kong.* Compiled by R.D. Hill. 1:100,000. Hong Kong: Department of Geography and Geology, University of Hong Kong. Map.

Hong Kong . No dates. Archaeology. 1:80,467. Map.

Hong Kong. Agriculture and Fisheries Department. 1990. *Agricultural land use map for Shatin 1:20,000.* Hong Kong: Agriculture and Fisheries Department. Unpublished map.

Hong Kong. Agriculture and Fisheries Department. 1992. *Fish culture zones map. 1:200,000.* Hong Kong: Agriculture and Fisheries Department. Map.

Hong Kong. Agriculture and Fisheries Department. 1992-1993. *Agricultural land use map for Yuen Long 1:20,000.* Hong Kong: Agriculture and Fisheries Department. Unpublished map.

Hong Kong. Agriculture and Fisheries Department. Various dates. *Agricultural land use map 1:100,000.* Hong Kong: Agriculture and Fisheries Department. Map.

Hong Kong Archaeological Society. 1973. *Archaeology map of Hong Kong.* Hong Kong: Government Printer. Map.

Hong Kong. Boundary and Election Commission. 1993. *1994 district board electoral boundaries for Hong Kong.* Cartographed by Survey and Mapping Office, Lands Department. Various scales. Hong Kong: Boundary and Election Commission.

Hong Kong. Buildings and Lands Department. 1987. *Hong Kong buying from the world January - December 1985.* Cartographed by Survey and Mapping Office. Hong Kong: Survey and Mapping Office. Map. AR/11/BFW.

Hong Kong. Buildings and Lands Department, Survey and Mapping Office. 1988. *Hong Kong building for the future.* Cartographed by Survey and Mapping Office. Hong Kong: Survey and Mapping Office. Map. AR/12/BFF.

Hong Kong. Buildings and Lands Department, Survey and Mapping Office. 1989. *Hong Kong arts and the media.* Cartography by Survey and Mapping Office

Hong Kong: Survey and Mapping Office. Map. AR/13/AM.

Hong Kong. Buildings and Lands Department, Survey and Mapping Office. 1990. *Hong Kong port and airport development strategy.* Cartography by Survey and Mapping Office. Hong Kong: Survey and Mapping Office. Map. AR/14/PADS.

Hong Kong. Buildings and Lands Department, Survey and Mapping Office. 1991. *Environmental protection in Hong Kong.* Cartography by Survey and Mapping Office in Hong Kong: Survey and Mapping Office. Map. AR/15/ED.

Hong Kong. Buildings and Lands Department, Survey and Mapping Office. 1992. *Reclamation and development in Hong Kong.* Cartography by Survey and Mapping Office. 2nd ed. 1:200,000. Hong Kong: Survey and Mapping Office. Map. AR/9/RD.

Hong Kong. Buildings and Lands Department, Town Planning Office. 1987. *Land utilization in Kowloon and Hong Kong. 1:30,000.* Hong Kong: Buildings and Lands Department. Map. Series LUM/U/30.

Hong Kong. Buildings and Lands Department, Town Planning Office. 1988. *Land utilization in Hong Kong. 1:75,000.* Hong Kong: Government Printer. Map. LUM/HK/75.

Hong Kong. Buildings and Lands Department, Survey and Mapping Office. 1992. *Hong Kong population with focus on new town.* Cartography by Survey and Mapping Office. Hong Kong: Survey and Mapping Office. Map. AR/16/P3.

Hong Kong. Census Department. 1960. *Hong Kong Census 1961—Hong Kong, Kowloon, New Kowloon and the New Territories land districts.* Hong Kong: Government Printer. Maps.

Hong Kong. Census Department. 1960. *Hong Kong Census 1961—marine districts.* Hong Kong: Government Printer. Map.

Hong Kong. Crown Lands and Survey Office. 1920. *Map of the Kowloon Peninsula including portion of New Kowloon (New Kowloon) Colony of Hong Kong.* Surveyed by the Crown Lands and Survey Office, Public Works Department. 1: 2,400. Tolworth: Ordinance Survey 1920. Map 6 sheets.

Hong Kong. Crown Lands and Survey Office. 1947. *Kowloon Peninsula, 1947.* 1: 7920. Hong Kong: Crown Lands and Survey Office. Map.

Hong Kong. Government Secretariat. Constitutional Affairs Branch, Registration and Electoral Office. 1990. *District Board—electoral boundaries maps for 1990.* Various scale. Hong Kong: the Office. Maps.

Hong Kong. Hong Kong Tourist Association. 1995. *Hotel guide.* Hong Kong: Hong Kong Tourist Association.

Hong Kong. Lands and Survey Department. 1982. *1982 Hong Kong harbour plan.* Designed and produced for the Director of Marine by Survey Division, Lands Department. 5th ed. 1:38,000. Hong Kong: Lands and Survey Department. Map.

Hong Kong. Lands and Survey Department, Survey and Mapping Office. 1979. *Land utilization in Hong Kong 1:200,000.* Cartography by Lands and Survey Department, Public Works Department. Hong Kong: Government Printer, 1979. Map. AR/1/LU.

Hong Kong. Lands and Survey Department, Survey and Mapping Office. 1982. *Land utilization in Hong Kong 1:200,000.* 2nd. ed. Cartography by Lands and Survey Department, Public Works Department. Hong Kong: Government Printer, 1982. Map. AR/1/LU.

Hong Kong. Lands Department, Survey and Mapping Office. 1994. *Hong Kong official guide map.* 1: 125,000 to 1:10,000. 10th ed. Hong Kong: Lands Department. Map.

Hong Kong. Lands Department, Survey Division. 1984. *Hong Kong Climate.* Cartography by Survey Division Lands Department. Hong Kong: Survey Division, Lands Department. Map. AR/9/RD.

Hong Kong. Lands Department, Survey Division. 1985. *Reclamation and development in Hong Kong.* Cartography by Survey Division. 1:200,000. Hong Kong: Survey Division, Lands Department. Map. AR/9/RD.

Hong Kong. Lands Department, Survey Division. 1986. *Hong Kong communication and trade.* Cartography by Survey Division. Hong Kong: Survey

Division, Lands Department. Map. AR/10/C7.

Hong Kong. Lands Department, Survey Division. 1992. *Hong Kong 1981 census: educational attainment, median household income, occupation and labour force.* Cartography by Survey Division. Various scales. Hong Kong: Survey Division, Lands Department. Map. MM/1/E.

Hong Kong. Lands Department, Survey and Mapping Office. 1994. *Hong Kong's external trade in 1992.* Cartography by Survey and Mapping Office. 2nd. ed. Hong Kong: Government Printer. Map. AR/5/ET.

Hong Kong. Lands Department, Survey and Mapping Office. 1994. *The territory of Hong Kong 1:200,000.* Prepared by Survey and Mapping Office. 18th ed. Hong Kong: Survey and Mapping Office. Map. HM200CL.

Hong Kong. Lands Department, Survey and Mapping Office, 1995. *Hong Kong buying from the world January - December 1994.* 2nd ed. Cartography by Survey and Mapping Office. Hong Kong: Survey and Mapping Office. Map. AR/11/BFW.

Hong Kong. Lands Department, Survey and Mapping Office. 1995. *Reclamation and development in Hong Kong.* Cartography by Survey and Mapping Office. 3rd ed. 1: 200,000. Hong Kong: Survey and Mapping Office. Map. AR/9/RD.

Hong Kong. Lands Department, Survey and Mapping Office. 1996. *District board electoral boundaries for Hong Kong 1996.* Cartography by Survey and Mapping Office. Various scales. Hong Kong: Census and Statistics Department. Maps.

Hong Kong. Lands Department, Survey and Mapping Office. 1996. *Hong Kong in its regional setting.* Cartography by Survey and Mapping Office. Hong Kong: Survey and Mapping Office. Map. AR/18/RS.

Hong Kong. Lands Department, Survey and Mapping Office. 2009. *Orthophoto* Map.

Hong Kong. Lands Department, Survey and Mapping Office. Various dates. *Hong Kong 1:5,000.* Prepared by Survey and Mapping Office. Survey and Mapping Office. Hong Kong: Survey and Mapping Office, various dates. Map 161 sheets. Series HP5C.

Hong Kong. Lands Department. Survey and Mapping Office. Various dates. *Hong Kong street maps.* 1: 10,000. Prepared by Survey and Mapping Office. Hong Kong: Survey and Mapping Office. Map 10 sheets. Series SM10D.

Hong Kong. Lands Department, Survey and Mapping Office. Various dates. *Maps of Hong Kong Countryside Series.* Various scales and sizes. Hong Kong: Lands Department.

Hong Kong. Lands Department. Survey and Mapping Office. Various dates. *Survey plans of Hong Kong and the New Territories 1:1,000.* Prepared by Survey and Mapping Office. Hong Kong: Survey and Mapping Office. Map 2966 sheets HPIC.

Hong Kong. Planning Department. 1969. *Existing land use plan of Yuen Long for 1969.* Surveyed by W.K. Leung and S.T. Cheung. Hong Kong: Planning Department. Maps. Planning unit 5.18 and 5.24.

Hong Kong. Planning Department. 1995. *Existing land use map of Kwun Tong 1995.* Hong Kong: Planning Department. Unpublished planning map TPU No. 295.

Hong Kong. Planning Department. 1995. *Existing land use map of Western District 1995.* Hong Kong: Planning Department. Unpublished map.

Hong Kong. Planning Department. 1995. *Existing Tsuen Wan industrial land use map 1995.* Hong Kong: Planning Department. Unpublished planning map.

Hong Kong. Planning Department. 1995. *Primary and secondary planning unit boundaries—Hong Kong 1996 population by-census.* 1:75,000. Hong Kong: Planning Department. Map.

Hong Kong. Planning Department. 1995. *Tertiary planning units Hong Kong Island, Kowloon and New Territories, 1996 population by-census.* Planning Department. Various scales. Hong Kong: Planning Department. Maps.

Hong Kong. Planning Department. 2007. *Land utilization in Hong Kong.*

1:170,000. Hong Kong: Government Logistics Department. Map. LUM/HK/A3

Hong Kong. Planning Department, Census districts and tertiary planning units. 1991. *Hong Kong, Kowloon, New Kowloon and New Territories—1991 census.* Planning Department and Census and Statistics Department. Various scales. Hong Kong: Planning Department. Maps.

Hong Kong. Planning Department, Town planning ordinance, Hong Kong Town Planning Board. 1993. *Kwai Chung —outline zoning plan.* 1:10,000. Hong Kong: Planning Department. Map. S/KC/9.

Hong Kong. Planning Department, Town planning ordinance, Hong Kong Town Planning Board. 1993. *Sha Tin - outline zoning plan.* 1:10,000. Hong Kong: Planning Department. Map. S/ST/6.

Hong Kong. Planning Department, Town planning ordinance, Hong Kong Town Planning Board. 1993. *Tsuen Wan—outline zoning plan.* 1:10,000. Hong Kong: Planning Department. Map. S/TW/6.

Hong Kong. Planning Department, Town planning ordinance, Hong Kong Town Planning Board. 1994. *Hong Kong planning area no. 4 —Central District— outline zoning plan.* 1:5,000. Hong Kong: Planning Department. Map. S/H4/4.

Hong Kong. Planning Department, Town planning ordinance, Hong Kong Town Planning Board. 1994. *Kowloon planning area no. 14 (part) Kwun Tong (South) —outline zoning plan.* 1:5,000. Hong Kong: Planning Department. Map. SK14S/3.

Hong Kong. Planning Department, Town planning ordinance, Hong Kong Town Planning Board. 1994. *Tsing Yi. —outline zoning plan.* 1:10,000. Hong Kong: Planning Department. Map. S/TY/9.

Hong Kong. Planning Department, Town planning ordinance, Hong Kong Town Planning Board. 1994. *Tuen Mun, —outline zoning plan.* 1:10,000. Hong Kong: Planning Department. Map. S/TM/8.

Hong Kong. Planning Department, Town planning ordinance, Hong Kong Town Planning Board. 1995. *Hong Kong planning area no. 5—Wan Chai—outline zoning plan.* 1:5,000. Hong Kong: Planning Department, 1995. Map. S/H5/9.

Hong Kong. Planning Department, Town planning ordinance, Hong Kong Town Planning Board. 1995. *Yuen Long—outline zoning plan.* 1:5,000. Hong Kong: Planning Department. Map. S/YL/2.

Hong Kong. Planning Department, Town planning ordinance, Hong Kong Town Planning Board. 1996. *Hong Kong planning area no. 3—Sai Ying Pun and Sheung Wan—outline zoning plan.* 1:5000. Hong Kong: Planning Department. Map. S/H3/10.

Hong Kong. Planning Department, Town planning ordinance, Hong Kong Town Planning Board. 2007. *Sha Tin—outline zoning plan.* 1:10,000. Hong Kong: Planning Department. Map. S/ST/23.

Hong Kong. Planning Department, Town planning ordinance, Hong Kong Town Planning Board. 2008. *Tsuen Wan—outline zoning plan.* 1:7,500. Hong Kong: Planning Department. Map. S/TW/26.

Hong Kong. Planning Department, Town planning ordinance, Hong Kong Town Planning Board. 2008. *Yuen Long—outline zoning plan.* 1:5,000. Hong Kong: Planning Department. Map. S/YL/18.

Hong Kong. Planning Department, Town planning ordinance, Hong Kong Town Planning Board. 2009. *Ma On Shan—outline zoning plan.* 1:7,500. Hong Kong: Planning Department. Map. S/MOS/14.

Hong Kong. Planning Department, Town planning ordinance, Hong Kong Town Planning Board. 2009. *South West Kowloon—outline zoning plan.* 1:5,000. Hong Kong: Planning Department. Map. S/K 20/22.

Hong Kong. Planning Department, Town planning ordinance, Hong Kong Town Planning Board. 2009. *Tai Po—outline zoning plan.* 1:10,000. Hong Kong: Planning Department. Map. S/TP/21.

Hong Kong. Planning Department, Town planning ordinance, Hong Kong Town Planning Board. 2009. *Tuen Mun - outline zoning plan.* 1:10,000. Hong Kong: Planning Department. Map. S/TM/25.

Hong Kong. Public Works Department, Crown Lands and Survey Office,

Planning Division. 1968. *Generalised pattern of urban land use: Hong Kong Island —1967/68.* 1:15,840. Hong Kong: Planning Division. Map.

Hong Kong. Public Works Department, Crown Lands and Survey Office, Planning Division. 1968. *Generalised pattern of urban land use: Kowloon and New Territories.* 1:15,840. Hong Kong: Planning Division. Map.

Hong Kong. Public Works Department, Lands, Survey and Town Planning Department. 1981. *District Board electoral boundaries maps for 1981.* Various scales. Hong Kong: Government Printer. Map.

Hong Kong. Public Works Department, Lands and Survey Department. 1981. *Hong Kong's external trade for the period August 1979— July 1980.* Cartography by Lands and Survey Department. Hong Kong: Government Printer. Map. AR/5/ET.

Hong Kong. Public Works Department. Lands, Survey and Town Planning Department. 1982. *Population map Hong Kong.* Cartography by Lands, Survey and Town Planning Department, Public Works Department. Hong Kong: Public Works Department. Map. AR/6/92.

Hong Kong. Public Works Department, Lands and Survey Department. 1978. *Population map of Hong Kong.* Cartography by Lands and Survey Department. Various scales. Hong Kong: Government Printer. Map. AR/2/P.

Hong Kong. Public Works Department, Town Planning Office. 1981. *Census districts and tertiary planning units: Hong Kong Island 1981 census.* 1:15,000. Hong Kong: Public Works Department. Map.

Hong Kong. Public Works Department, Town Planning Office. 1981. *Census districts and tertiary planning units, Kowloon and New Kowloon. 1981 census.* 1:15,000. Hong Kong: Public Works Department. Map.

Hong Kong. Public Works Department, Town Planning Board. 1981. *Census districts and tertiary planning units, New Territories, 1981 census.* 1:50,000. Hong Kong: Public Works Department. Map.

Hong Kong. Survey and Mapping Office. 1993. *Hong Kong in its regional setting.* Survey and Mapping Office, Lands Department. 1:300,000. Hong Kong: Government Printer. Map.

Kowloon Motor Bus Company. Various dates. *KMB route map.* 1:13,000 and smaller. Hong Kong: Kowloon Motor Bus Company. Map.

Law, Wing Cheong (ed.). 1964. *Atlas of Hong Kong.* Hong Kong: Genuine Book Co. (Chinese and English edition)

Leung, W.T. 1972. *Tsuen Wan / Kwai Chung.* 1:5,000. Hong Kong. Unpublished map.

Treaty map of Hong Kong 1860. Scale: 4 inches to 1 mile. Map; 54 x 80 cm.

Tregear, T.R. 1954. *Hong Kong and the New Territories—land utilization survey.* 1: 80,000. Hong Kong: University of Hong Kong.

Tregear, T.R. 1959. *The development of Hong Kong and Kowloon, as told in maps.* T.R. Tregear and L. Berry. Hong Kong: Hong Kong University Press.

University of Hong Kong. Department of Geography and Geology. 1997. *An air photo mosaic of Hong Kong 1995.* Complied by Department of Geography and Geology. Flying height 1:10,000 ft. in Hong Kong. Hong Kong: University of Hong Kong.

Volonteri. 1866. *Map of the San-On-District (Kuangtung Province).*

World Wide Fund for Nature Hong Kong. 1993. *Hong Kong vegetation map 1: 50,000.* Hong Kong: World Wide Fund for Nature Hong Kong. Map 2 sheets.